Music in the
Theatre of
Ben Jonson

MUSIC IN THE THEATRE OF BEN JONSON

by

Mary Chan

CLARENDON PRESS · OXFORD

1980

Oxford University Press, Walton Street, Oxford OX2 6DP

OXFORD LONDON GLASGOW
NEW YORK TORONTO MELBOURNE WELLINGTON
KUALA LUMPUR SINGAPORE JAKARTA HONG KONG TOKYO
DELHI BOMBAY CALCUTTA MADRAS KARACHI
NAIROBI DAR ES SALAAM CAPE TOWN

*Published in the United States
by Oxford University Press,
New York*

© *Mary Chan 1980*

British Library Cataloguing in Publication Data
Chan, Mary
   Music in the theatre of Ben Jonson.
   1. Jonson, Ben—Music
   2. Music and literature
   I. Title
   822'.3   PR2642.M/   79-40835

   ISBN 0-19-812632-8

Filmset in 11/12 *point Baskerville
Printed and Bound in Great Britain
by W & J Mackay Limited, Chatham*

Acknowledgements

Some of the material for this book is based on research work I under-took at the University of Cambridge for the Ph.D degree. I am grateful to the New Zealand University Grants Committee for the award of a Post-graduate Travelling Scholarship in Arts which enabled me to study at Cambridge.

Dr J. E. Stevens, Magdalene College, Cambridge and Dr F. W. Sternfeld, Faculty of Music, Oxford both supervised my degree studies and since have been very generous in offering assistance and advice. I should like to express my warmest thanks to them.

During the course of my study I made use of many library resources and am most grateful for the help I received. In particular, I should like to thank Miss Margaret Crum of the Bodleian Library, Miss Pamela Willetts of the British Library, Department of Western Manuscripts and Mr H. J. R. Wing of Christ Church Library, Oxford. Mr Robert Spencer kindly let me consult the manuscript lute book of Margaret Board and I am also indebted to him for some of the cross-references to other sources of the masque dance music.

I should also like to express sincere gratitude to Professor D. F. McKenzie, Victoria University of Wellington and Dr J. D. Needham, Massey University who read the manuscript at various stages and gave me much helpful criticism.

This book is published with the aid of grants from the British Academy and the University of New South Wales. I should like to record my appreciation to both.

July 1978   MARY CHAN

Contents

List of Plates

List of Musical Examples

Note

REFERENCES TO Jonson's works are to *The Works of Ben Jonson*, edited by C. H. Herford and P. and E. M. Simpson, abbreviated as H & S.

References to the music are given as follows. Arabic numerals refer to bar numbers. References within a bar are given in Roman numerals. These apply to the number of the note, rest, or chord within the bar and have no reference to the time value of the note.

Jonson's masque texts frequently indicate very complex and elaborate orchestration which is not apparent from the simple form in which the dances survive. The extant sources of the masque music are, in most cases, manuscript commonplace books which belonged to private or amateur musicians interested in having a copy of the latest pieces in a form which suited their individual needs. The largest collection of music for the early seventeenth-century masques is British Library manuscript Additional 10444 which belonged to Sir Nicholas Le Strange. The manuscript consists of two part-books (treble and bass) although it is probable that these were originally part of a larger set. In my transcriptions I have preferred to present the arrangements of the music as nearly as possible as they are recorded in their sources.

Introduction

EARLY IN 1629 the King's Men performed Ben Jonson's play, *The New Inn*, at the Blackfriars theatre. The play was also to have been performed at court but the Blackfriars performance was such a dismal failure that it was never revived. Jonson refused to see the failure of the play in the way most critics did: as an indication of his own declining abilities. He blamed the actors and the audience. On the title-page of the octavo edition of 1631 he described the play as 'neuer acted, but most negligently play'd, by some, the Kings Seruants. And more squeamishly beheld, and censured by others, the Kings Subiects.' Criticism of the play's first performance evoked Jonson's anger and scorn in an 'Ode to Himselfe' in which he tells himself to 'leaue the lothed stage, And the more lothsome age' and to have no more to do with an audience made only of 'Braue *plush*, and *veluet*-men'. But since even Jonson's friend and admirer, Thomas Carew, spoke of the play as a falling off 'from the exalted line Toucht by thy Alchymist' (although he made it clear that 'The wiser world doth Greater Thee confess Then all men else, then Thyself only Less'[1]) most critics have been only too ready to seize on Dryden's phrase and label *The New Inn*, with Jonson's other last plays, as a 'dotage'.[2]

The New Inn was not Jonson's last play. It was followed in 1632 by *The Magnetic Lady* and in 1633 by *A Tale of a Tub*—although this latter play is believed by some to be a rewriting and a revival of a play he had written much earlier.[3] Jonson's final play, *The Sad Shepherd*, was incomplete at his death in 1637. *The New Inn* is different from the two plays which immediately followed it, and, indeed, different from all Jonson's earlier plays, in that it has not their sharpness of satire and shows us an altogether more genial side of Jonson. It may have been for this reason—that the play is not in Jonson's usual satirical vein—that the audience found it difficult to understand, and that Jonson felt a need to defend it. Clearly many things in *The New Inn* demand explanation. The implausibility of the plot, which was one aspect contemporary critics ridiculed, and certain undramatic episodes—Lady Frampul's Court of Love is always cited—are two examples.

---

[1] H & S xi, pp. 335–6.
[2] Dryden, 'Of Dramatic Poesy', in *Essays*, Vol. i, p. 81. 'As for Johnson, to whose character I am now arrived, if we look upon him while he was himself (for his last plays were but his dotages), I think him the most learned and judicious writer which any theatre ever had.'
[3] See H & S i, pp. 275–301.

This book has grown out of an attempt to set *The New Inn* (and the incomplete *Sad Shepherd*) in a context different from—although complementary to—that of Jonson's satirical plays in which his contemporary critics appear to have placed it. He was heir to other traditions too, specifically those deriving from the ideals for art and literature of the Renaissance Platonists, and he knew well enough 'how to apt their places'.[4] A different way of looking at *The New Inn* was first suggested to me by my interest in Jonson's use of music and song in his plays and masques and the seeming importance given to Lovel's song in *The New Inn*. The song, Lovel's 'Vision', occurs twice in the play. It is first read to us in Act IV, scene iv and we are told that Lovel's 'boy' is practising singing it. The song is not allowed to be sung, however, until the very end of the play when all misunderstandings and disguises disappear and the characters are leaving the stage. The questions which immediately demanded an answer were first, why is so much made of the song in Act IV and of the fact that it cannot be sung, and second, why does it seem such an appropriate ending to the play?

Such questions may seem peripheral to a modern audience used to regarding music in the theatre as some kind of trimming or sound effect. But a study of the traditions and conventions of Elizabethan and Jacobean theatre music make clear the fact that music was not usually regarded as extraneous. Furthermore, a study of Jonson's own development of the masque form and his adaptation of the masque traditions suggests that he was well acquainted with, and took seriously, philosophical ideas which involved not only music but other arts too. It has been customary in Jonson studies to separate his plays and poems from his masques and to regard the latter as in many respects uncharacteristic of the Jonson who is described as 'classical' or 'witty', the poet concerned with 'deedes, and language, such as men doe vse'.[5] The writing of masques, however, occupied the years in which he was also writing his most popular plays, and for ten years of his life (1616–26) he wrote only masques. It seemed impossible that someone who took his vocation as a poet as seriously as Jonson did could regard his work for the theatre and his work for the court as two completely separate activities and that influences of one on the other would not occur. By concentrating my study initially on Jonson's use of music in the plays and masques such influences became clear; and they were not confined to the occasional use of songs in plays. When Jonson returned to the theatre in 1626 with *The Staple of News* it was not as one making a fresh start in an old medium but as an established playwright continuing the struggle with ideas and values which had preoccupied him in his

---

[4] See 'To Sir Henrie Savile', l. 28. H & S VIII, p. 61.

[5] Prologue to *Every Man in his Humour*, revised version from the 1616 folio.

earlier and popular satirical plays. More specifically, in this last group of plays we find him also building on his experience with the ideals and forms of the masque and re-creating it for the more permanent and more popular medium of the public theatre. The last plays draw not only on the formal characteristics of the masque but on its philosophic–Platonic basis—as an ideal union of all art forms to create an image of perfection.

This is not to suggest that Jonson's chief concerns are more metaphysical than social. His work expresses a view of society which illustrates what L. C. Knights has called 'a lively sense of human limitations'.[6] The plays are mainly satires on, and examinations of, social disorder; and the masques emphasize the positive, human side of what appears as satire in the plays. In this, indeed, their particular strength may lie. Nevertheless, the influence of a more metaphysical mode of thought modifies and supplements a strictly classical approach to man and society in much of Jonson's work, and this influence becomes most apparent through a study of his use of music in the plays and the masques.

Part One of this book begins with an outline of the traditions of music in English drama and concentrates especially on the characteristics of, and influences on, theatre music in the sixteenth century. This first chapter provides an introduction to the separate—although related —traditions which lie behind Jonson's use of song in his plays for children and his plays for the public theatre which is discussed in the chapters which follow. I look first at the plays for the Children of the Chapel in which Jonson exposes the moral degradation and social disintegration of which the abuse of language and eloquence are the main symptoms. In these plays Jonson uses songs to illustrate his main theme and they are mainly satiric of those who affect fashionable, Platonic ideas of setting words to music without recognizing their implications or their proper values. In the middle comedies, particularly those for the public theatre, Jonson develops this simple, parodic use of song into a more complex and dramatically integrated satiric weapon.

The chapters on Jonson's masques in Part Two are introduced by a discussion of the ideas and values which form the basis of the masque ethic as they are expressed in one of the most popularly influential Renaissance books: Hoby's translation of Castiglione's *Il libro del cortegiano*. The function of the music in Jonson's masques cannot be examined separately from its philosophical background and the relationship it holds in this philosophy to other art forms. In a study of the masques we become aware of Jonson working through the problems

[6] Knights, *Drama and Society*, p. 166.

posed by the masque's special form and aims—as part drama, part ritual, part celebration—and returning finally to the theatre as most adequate to express the interests and concerns of a lifetime's work.

Neither of Jonson's two last plays which I consider in Part Three is social satire. *The New Inn* (for *The Sad Shepherd* is unfinished) develops within a dramatic context the aesthetic and conceptual possibilities contained in Jonson's development of the masque form. The final chapter on *The New Inn* and *The Sad Shepherd* is preceded by a consideration of Shakespeare's two last plays: *The Winter's Tale* and *The Tempest*. These two plays were written while the masque could still be regarded as encompassing the ideals of Jacobean society and as being a perfect expression of these ideals. Shakespeare wrote no masques that we know of but his two last plays have borrowed much from the masque, as Jonson was then developing it, to re-create a more permanent expression of the masque's ideals within the truly popular medium of the theatre. The lack of success of Jonson's own attempt to do the same for the popular theatre in *The New Inn* suggests that that play came too late. England of the early 1600s with its hopes for the continuance of political and religious stability in the new king, with the glowing promise of his successor, the talented young Prince Henry, and with its achievements in literature and drama at their peak had, by 1629, degenerated into the precariously poised Caroline court and a politically volatile society, the one attracted and distracted by the showy, the melodramatic, and the superficial, the other suspicious of the very bases of art itself. Jonson no longer had the ear—or the eye—of court or populace. But despite his bitter disappointment and anger at the failure of his audience to understand *The New Inn* Jonson's assurance of the continued importance of his theatre is evident in the way his last play (unfinished at his death in 1637) offers a splendid new form for a society and a prince more than ever in need of the counsels of a true poet.

In this book any contribution I have been able to make beyond a fresh critical reading of Jonson's *œuvre* is specifically musicological. There are hints, however, that other lines of enquiry might lead us to reassess Jonson's relations to the sixteenth-century Platonist tradition. Apart from the significant evidence of the masques themselves Jonson's library contained several books which indicate more than a passing interest in the philosophical traditions,[7] and some of Jonson's closest

---

[7] Herford and Simpson publish two lists of the books in Jonson's library: Vol. i, pp. 250–71, and Vol. xi, pp. 593–603. They are incomplete; Jonson's library was partly destroyed by fire in 1623 and, as he told Drummond, he had 'Sundry tymes . . . devoured his bookes .j. sold ym all for Necessity' (*Conversations*, H & S i, p. 141: xii. 328). Nevertheless Jonson owned several books which display an interest in Renaissance Platonism, among them: Plato's complete works (Paris, 1578); the works of two other *prisci theologi*: *Pythagorae Fragmenta* . . . (Leipzig, 1603) and Hermes Trismegistus, *Opuscula, cum fragmentis* . . . *Item Asclepii Discipuli adiecta* (London, 1611); a

friends, in particular members of the Sidney family and William Camden, were influential in shaping the seventeenth-century manifestations of this Renaissance tradition.[8] It may seem curious, even perverse, to describe a Jonson working not simply throughout his masque career but throughout his whole productive life at least partially within a metaphysical mode. It is a Jonson which popular criticism of his middle comedies at any rate has always ignored.[9] But this is, ineluctably, the experience of the plays, an experience more comprehensive and philosophic than we have been accustomed to see in them because we have divorced his work—and his whole work, not merely one or other aspect of it—too readily from sixteenth-century traditions which Jonson saw as both powerful and profound.

---

fourteenth-century manuscript described as: Salomon, King of Israel, *Opus de arte magica ab Honorio ordinatum*, a work of interest to those who, like Pico, saw an association between Hermetica and Cabbala; Euclid's *Elements of Geometrie*, translated by Henry Billingsley (London, 1576) with John Dee's 'Mathematicall Preface'. Dee's 'Preface' was based on Renaissance versions of Vitruvius' *De architectura*, works which were influential in shaping the Renaissance ideas of art. Jonson owned two important Renaissance editions of Vitruvius' work, that by Daniel Barbaro (Venice, 1567), and that with a commentary by Philander (Lyons, 1586). For the significance of these works in Renaissance philosophy, see Yates, *Theatre*, pp. 20–41; for Dee, see French, *Dee*, pp. 167–77, *et passim*.

[8] Jonson addressed several poems to members of the Sidney family. He could not, of course, have known Sir Philip Sidney whose literary experiments seem to have been influenced by groups like the Italian *Camerata* or the French *Pléiade*—groups concerned with putting into practice Renaissance theories of affective art: see the correspondence between Edmund Spenser and Gabriel Harvey, reprinted in Smith, *Elizabethan Critical Essays*, i, pp. 87–126. William Camden, Jonson's revered master at Westminster School to whom, Jonson said, he owed 'All that I am in arts, all that I know' (*Epigrammes*, no. XIV) was a friend of John Dee and encouraged by him in his great antiquarian work, *Britannia*: see French, *Dee*, pp. 199, 204–5.

[9] The view that *The Alchemist* is a satire on John Dee and the Renaissance Platonist alchemical tradition as he developed it in early seventeenth-century England has long been held up as evidence that Jonson despised all alchemists. Such an assumption is naïve. The suggestion was first made by Margaret of Newcastle in *The Description of a New World, called the Blazing World* (1666 and 1668): see H & S x. p. 47. This appeared only a few years after the publication by Meric Casaubon in 1659 of Dee's so-called 'Spiritual Diaries'. Casaubon's Preface, which made Dee out to be a fraudulent and scurrilous magician, was personally motivated (see French, *Dee*, pp. 11–13; Yates, *Rosicrucian Enlightenment*, p. 188); nevertheless it became part of a general campaign to dishonour Dee and initiated a view which has prevailed until recently. The imputation of satire on Dee in *The Alchemist* belongs in this historical context. It was perpetuated by Gifford and revived recently by Furio Jesi, 'John Dee e il suo sapere', *Comunita*, no. 166 (1972), p. 272 and Frances Yates, *Shakespeare's Last Plays*, pp. 109–21.

PART ONE

I

Music in the theatre

THE MUSICAL conventions and traditions inherited by the Elizabethan theatre are as old as drama itself. The most direct influences are from medieval drama and the Tudor Interlude, although we cannot ignore the significance of pageants, Lord Mayors' Shows, or the contemporary Italian and French theatre. Just as the Elizabethans inherited from the middle ages the musical philosophy of world harmony and Boethius' categories of music, so too they inherited the medieval use of music in drama to symbolize God and Heaven, and supernatural events in men's lives.[1] This function for music developed in several ways in Elizabethan and Jacobean drama. One of the most significant influences in the development of the symbolic use of instrumental music in drama comes from the Elizabethan translations and imitations of Seneca, popular with playwrights from the universities or the inns of court from the mid-sixteenth century. The convention of interspersing action with song in comedies, particularly common in the Tudor interludes, was of course made use of in Elizabethan comedy as well. The comedies written for children often used music in this way, possibly because the children were in any case trained in singing. It was also customary for the children to give musical performances, often quite unrelated to the plays, when they acted at the Blackfriars theatre.

Children's plays, then, gave wide scope for musical performances, songs, and interludes, mainly because of the richer musical resources of the children's companies. But in plays for the public theatres too, songs and instrumental music were frequently employed. Certainly, there was always a place for what might be called 'representational' music: music for battles, banquets, coronations. The difference in quantity of

---

[1] Boethius in his *De institutione musica* divided music into three parts: *musica mundana*, the music of the spheres; *musica humana*, the 'music' of man's body, spirit, and soul and of human affairs such as the ordering of societies and states; and *musica instrumentalis*, actual music of voices or instruments. Renaissance philosophers inherited, through medieval philosophy, the ancient theory—which derives ultimately from the Pythagoreans and Plato's *Timaeus*—of the harmonic proportions on which the universe is constructed and which are reflected in man, the 'microcosm'. For details of this philosophy of world harmony, for discussions of ideas of music in Elizabethan England, and for stories of the marvellous effects of music in ancient times—stories deriving largely from Plato and Plutarch—see: Hollander, *Untuning of the Sky*; Kerman, *Elizabethan Madrigal*; Mellers, *Harmonious Meeting*; Pattison, *Music and Poetry*; Pietzsch, *Die Klassifikation*; Spitzer, 'World Harmony'; Sternfeld, *Music in Shakespearean Tragedy*; Walker, *Spiritual and Demonic Magic*. For a discussion of popular ideas about music celebrated in poetry of the *laus musicae* topos see Hutton, 'Some English Poems in Praise of Music'.

music required in plays for adults performing in the public theatres and those for either children or adults performing in the 'private' theatres, at court or at the inns of court, may have been largely due to the fact that the public theatres depended on daylight, and the time a performance took was thus an important consideration. But the differences also lead us to an examination of other things: the employment of musicians, the location of musicians in the theatre, the kinds of instruments required, and, most importantly, what music or song was performed in any particular instance. Although this last question is often difficult to answer it remains important in any attempt to assess the significance for the play as a whole of any music that is called for. Is it merely an interlude, has it some conventional or symbolic meaning, or is the playwright reshaping a convention to make a particular point of his own?

One fact becomes clear from a survey of the traditions and conventions of the Elizabethan use of music in the theatre: music was not used almost continuously, in the way it is in many modern films, for instance, to create a background, a 'mood', or an 'atmosphere' for the audience. Music was used in small episodes only, and where it seems to have been used to express a 'mood' its function is usually also related to an earlier, conventional use of music in drama and can be traced back to the medieval, ethical notion of world harmony.

We shall begin by considering the conventions which grew up for the use of music in the Elizabethan Senecan drama, as these conventions have far-reaching influences on the use of music in both public-theatre plays and plays for the court or private theatres.

I

In an article on music in Elizabethan 'Senecan' tragedies, F. W. Sternfeld has traced the development of lyric verse forms from Seneca's original Greek models, through Seneca's own plays, through Elizabethan translations of Seneca, and finally to imitations of various Senecan 'devices' in plays which are not direct translations from the Roman drama.[2] One important feature of this sequence was a shift from choral passages, in lyric verse, probably intended to be sung in the Greek drama, to choruses in the English developments whose verse form is not distinct from the exalted rhetorical style, often in the 'fourteener' line, of the whole play. The rhetorical nature of 'Englished' Seneca would have tended to confirm the Elizabethan opinion that the genre of high tragedy excluded the performance of song.

[2] Sternfeld, 'La Musique dans les tragédies élisabéthaines inspirées de Sénèque'.

It did not, however, exclude the performance of instrumental music. The first Senecan tragedy in English was Norton and Sackville's *Gorboduc*, performed at the Inner Temple in 1561. It was also the first English tragedy to introduce dumb-show.[3] The dumb-show in this, as in later Senecan plays, was accompanied by music; and although the dumb-show here does not replace the Chorus, which speaks at the end of each act, it may derive from the Chorus in Greek drama. I suggest this because the dumb-show does not merely reproduce in mime the main action of what is to follow, but enacts its moral significance. In two later plays—*Jocasta* (1566) and *The Misfortunes of Arthur* (1587)—the dumb-shows have the same function. On the other hand, Dr Sternfeld has suggested that in the use of dumb-show to precede each act of *Gorboduc* Norton and Sackville may have been influenced by the contemporary Italian dramatic practice of using *intermedii* and perhaps by the English custom of dumb-shows in masques and street festivals.[4] But whatever its immediate inspiration the device became associated almost exclusively with Senecan drama. The dumb-shows in *Gorboduc* were a great success and were imitated in several similar kinds of plays performed at the inns of court in succeeding years. Although not more than a handful of extant plays use dumb-show before each act, the device became widely used within Senecan plays, from *The Spanish Tragedy* to *Hamlet* and plays by Tourneur.

The descriptions of the dumb-shows in *Gorboduc* and *Jocasta* are particularly interesting in that they mention the instruments which accompanied the mimed action and suggest a kind of symbolism which attached to different instruments or instrumental tone qualities. These symbolic qualities seem to have been fairly generally accepted if one can judge by reference to instrumental music in stage directions throughout the period. The mime itself and the symbolic qualities of the instruments that accompanied it were considered most important: never, or only very rarely, is the actual music, or even the kind of music played, mentioned specifically.

The first dumb-show in *Gorboduc* is accompanied by 'the Musicke of Violenze' and the action 'signified, that a state knit in vnitie doth continue strong against all force. But being diuided, is easily destroyed.' The music of stringed instruments usually symbolizes the harmony of the universe. In the second dumb-show the cornets signify the presence of royalty, in the third, the flutes signify a funeral, in the fourth, oboes (hautboys) accompany supernatural spirits from hell and presage murder, and in the fifth, drums and flutes signify battle. In the

---

[3] For a discussion of the history and development of the dumb-show see Mehl, *Elizabethan Dumb Show*.

[4] Sternfeld, 'La Musique', p. 147.

case of the cornets for the second dumb-show and the drums and flutes for the fifth, the music may be said to be 'representational' rather than symbolic: it reproduces what would be normal practice in real life. The use of violins, flutes, and hautboys, on the other hand, is symbolic; and these instruments are used with similar meanings again and again in later plays. For instance in Shakespeare's *Macbeth* the music of hautboys which announces the arrival of Duncan at Macbeth's castle (i. vi) is important and noticeable to the audience in that it is not the cornets or trumpets which would usually accompany royalty. The music of hautboys provides a suggestion of treachery and a sinister quality which undercuts with very sharp irony Duncan's opening speech:

> This castle hath a pleasant seat; the air
> Nimbly and sweetly recommends itself
> Unto our gentle senses.[5]

Similarly, the following scene (i. vii) begins with evidence of preparations for a banquet to welcome Duncan, but once again the pretence of Macbeth's hospitality is shown up by the fact that the music for this banquet is performed on hautboys. The festive preparations, and the sinister music which accompanies them, prepare us for the conflict in Macbeth's own mind, shown in the speech which opens the scene. Finally, the 'Show of eight Kings, *and BANQUO last; the last king with a glass in his hand*' which appears to Macbeth at the witches' command (iv. i. 112), and which is a direct descendant of the Senecan dumb-show, is accompanied by hautboys. Although in the quarto texts of *Hamlet* the dumb-show which precedes *The Mousetrap* is heralded by trumpets, the first folio has the direction: '*Hoboyes play. The dumbe shew enters.*' Another, often quoted, use of hautboys to presage evil is in *Antony and Cleopatra* (iv. iii) where the soldiers hear '*Music of the Hautboys . . . under the stage*' and understand that it foretells that 'the god Hercules, whom Antony lov'd/Now leaves him' (iv. iii. 16–17).

From our point of view the importance of formal dumb-show in the early Senecan tragedies lies in two aspects of the device which were developed in later plays. These are, first, the symbolic qualities attached to the sound of different instruments and thus the association of music with some clear moral point; and second, the use of music in drama to accompany stylized action without words. Adaptions of the dumb-show occur in later plays, sometimes in conjunction with that other very popular Senecan device, the banquet, as a cover for carrying out the revenge itself. One example is the banquet in Tourneur's *The Revenger's Tragedy* (1607), iii. v. 200 ff., where music playing covers up

---

[5] Dr Sternfeld discusses the music in *Macbeth* in some detail in 'La Musique'. See especially p. 149.

the cries of the murdered; another is the masque towards the end of the same play (v. iii. 56) where murder is carried out under the disguise of music and dance. Earlier, *The Spanish Tragedy* (c.1587) had ended with a rather similar method of revenge; and such a device is reflected in Hamlet's dumb-show and play to 'catch the conscience of the king'. In Marston's *The Malcontent* (1604) dancing and music take place during the conversation that informs the audience that the duke has been murdered (iv. ii) and thus conceal this information from the characters on-stage. All these are, of course, similar to the use Shakespeare makes of the banquet in the early scenes of *Macbeth* which we have already considered.

Symbolic qualities for music in plays which owe something to the Senecan tradition but qualities not necessarily associated with festivities or banquets are indicated by the 'vilest out of tune Musicke' which comes from Malevole's chamber at the beginning of *The Malcontent*, and by the 'sour sweet music' which is played to Richard in prison in Shakespeare's *Richard II* (v. v). The music in this latter example is played on a stringed instrument and thus points up (as does Richard's soliloquy on hearing the music) the disorder and lack of harmony in Richard's own mind and kingdom. Whether the music to be played is actually 'sour' with 'no proportion kept', the music of a 'disordered string', or whether it is only Richard's state of mind which 'hath no music in [itself]' and therefore thinks the music is out of tune, the main point is the same. If the music is not 'disordered' it makes its point in a rather sharper way by contrasting with, rather than simply reflecting, Richard's own tragedy.

The formal dumb-show became less common towards the end of the century but did not die out altogether. Marston used the device in *Antonio's Revenge* (1600) to precede Acts III and V. This play is of further interest in that at the end of Act I and the beginning of Act II Marston has adapted and drawn together the conventions of chorus and dumb-show, and music as traditionally associated with both these, in a way which appears to be new. Pandulpho has just discovered his son murdered and he shocks his nephew, Alberto, by being unable to do anything but laugh. Alberto, in amazement, says:

> Why laugh you uncle? Thats my cuz, your son,
> Whose brest hangs cased in his cluttered gore.

And Pandulpho replies:

> True man, true: why, wherfore should I weepe?
> Come sit, kinde Nephew: come on: thou and I
> Will talke as *Chorus* to this tragedie.

> Intreat the musick straine their instruments,
> With a slight touch, whilst we—Say on faire cuz.
>
> *Alberto*   He was the very hope of Italy,
>   [*Musick sounds softly.*
> The blooming honour of your dropping age.
>
> *Pandulpho*   True cuz, true. They say that men of hope are crusht:
> Good are supprest by base desertlesse clods,
> That stifle gasping vertue . . .

After some thirty or so lines of moralizing in this strain while the music plays, Pandulpho concludes the scene, having bid 'good morrow' to his son's corpse, thus:

> Sound lowder musick: let my breath exact,
> You strike sad Tones unto this dismall act.

The 'lowder musick' that Pandulpho calls for is, presumably, played on the cornets which, we are told, heralded Act I I and played during what is a kind of dumb-show. Antonio's father, Andrugio, has also been murdered, and in this dumb-show his coffin, followed by his mourners, is brought on-stage. Piero, the Duke and murderer, follows the group and after the mourners have left the stage he stays behind and speaks. In the respect that one of the actors in the dumb-show steps forward and takes part in the following scene this dumb-show is different from dumb-shows in earlier plays and indeed from the other two in this play (at Acts I I I and V); it is different too in that it concentrates on simple actions rather than moralizing. Although this dumb-show appears to follow directly from Pandulpho's final speeches of Act I and may have been intended to suggest a formal relationship with the use of the Chorus in Greek tragedy, the sequence seems designed mainly to create a mannered and virtuoso effect from an old convention rather than to use the adaptation of chorus and dumb-show for any special dramatic point.

Pandulpho's calling for music to conclude the act, to comment on its 'dismall' events, and at the same time to usher in the action of the second act, may borrow something from another convention, a convention particularly common in the private theatres, and one which may, itself, have developed from the Senecan interact dumb-shows. This is the custom of playing music between the acts of plays. Until the King's Men took over the Blackfriars theatre in 1608 the performances in the so-called 'private' or indoor theatres (theatres which were private only in the sense that they charged far higher prices than the public theatres) were given exclusively by children's companies. These were formed largely from the choir-schools—of St Paul's Cathedral, the Chapel Royal, and the Chapel at Windsor. Because the boys were primarily musicians plays written especially for them always contained a good deal of music and it seems that their musical 'concerts' were as popular as the plays themselves.[6] The play most often cited in discussions of the use of interact music in children's plays is Marston's *Sophonisba* (1605), performed by the Children of the Queen's Revels at the Blackfriars.[7] The play gives detailed descriptions of the instruments used in the interact music and one is tempted to see the music as providing some kind of commentary on the action about to take place by applying the conventional symbolic meanings of the instruments. Certainly, the cornets which played between Acts I and II were appropriate in that Massinissa is about to go off to battle; and perhaps the 'Organs Violls and Voices' which were heard before Act IV and the 'Base Lute and a Treble Violl' which played before Act V pointed up the contrast between the seeming peace and harmony at the beginning of each of these acts and the revelation of deceit which follows almost immediately. But we are probably pressing the convention too far in looking for special significance in the interact music, particularly when we have no idea of the kind of music played nor how long it lasted in each case. The custom of interact music seems at first to have been confined to the private theatres. In the Induction to the version of *The Malcontent* which was performed by the King's Men at the Globe we are told that some additions have been made to the play, 'Sooth not greatly needefull, only as your sallet to your greate feast, to entertaine a little more time, and to abridge the not received custome of musicke in our Theater'.[8]

II

I have said that the children's plays contained a large amount of both instrumental music and song; and in many cases, particularly in the comedies, the music is more or less an interlude with very little relation to the action of the play. One kind of song which seems to have been associated solely with children's plays of the 1560s and 1570s is the

---

[6] See Wallace, *Children of the Chapel at Blackfriars*, pp. 106–7. For discussion of children's plays and acting companies see Hillebrand, *Child Actors* and Harbage, *Shakespeare and the Rival Traditions*, but note the *caveat* about Harbage by Gurr in *Shakespearean Stage*, p. 172, note 11 to Chapter I.

[7] See the note that Marston appended to the printed version of the play: 'After all, let me intreat my Reader not to taxe me, for the fashion of the Entrances and Musique of this Tragidy, for know it is printed onely as it was presented by youths, & after the fashion of the private stage.'

[8] The Induction and the additions are attributed to John Webster. Lawrence, 'Music and Song in the Elizabethan Theatre', in *The Elizabethan Playhouse*, 1st ser., pp. 78–9, draws attention to this Induction in his discussion of the interact music for *The Malcontent*. See also Ingram, 'Use of Music in the Plays of Marston'. Hosley, 'Was there a music-room . . .?', p. 119, suggests there is further evidence for the difference in practice between the two kinds of theatres in a stage direction for Shakespeare's *A Midsummer Night's Dream*. The folio of 1623 has a stage direction, lacking in the quarto of 1600, at the end of Act III for the four lovers to '*sleepe all the Act*'. Hosley believes this means they are to sleep on-stage during an interval for music between Acts III and IV.

lament, a form which certainly derives from the rhetorical laments popular in the contemporary Senecan drama of the inns of court.

The earliest of these musical laments, and the only one which can be assigned to an extant play, is 'Awake ye woeful wights' from Richard Edwards's *Damon and Pithias*, performed at court in 1564 by the Children of the Chapel. Richard Edwards was Master of the Children of the Chapel from 1561 until his death in 1566 and was a composer as well as a playwright. It is probable that he composed music for all the songs in *Damon and Pithias* although only that for the first song, the lament, survives. A setting occurs in British Library MS Add. 15117, f. 3 in an arrangement for voice and lute accompaniment;[9] and although the stage directions for the performance of the song in *Damon and Pithias* indicate that 'Here Pithias singes, and the Regalles play' it is almost certainly an arrangement of the song in MS Add. 15117 which is required here.[10]

The lament was a rhetorical form very popular in the Elizabethan imitations of Senecan drama, and because of the formally rhetorical nature of Senecan plays and the importance given to the study of classical rhetoric in the mid-sixteenth century it is not surprising that the performance of 'set' speeches and of drama imitating the style of classical rhetoric should form part of the boys' educational programme.[11] Although *Damon and Pithias* as a whole can hardly be called Senecan, the function of the lament, 'Awake ye woeful wights', clearly is in the Senecan tradition. Like the laments in Senecan plays, the lament in *Damon and Pithias* is not strictly dramatic; not, that is, as a soliloquy might be, an expression of a personal and inward debate. It is static, a highly formalized expression of emotion, and the setting of the text in the British Library manuscript complements the impersonal quality of the words. The vocal line does not 'express' the words in more than a very general sense, and the accompaniment weaves about this voice part. The lack of expressiveness is accentuated by the fact that the cadential points seldom coincide with the verbal punctuation. So although the vocal line provides a vehicle for clear declamation of the words—in the sense that there is, on the whole, only one note to each

[9] See my discussion, Joiner, 'B.M. MS Add. 15117', pp. 55–6, 67–8, 95–6.

[10] The 'regalles', or portative organ, is a small keyboard instrument played with one hand while the other works the bellows. The song was very popular. 'The tune of Damon and Pithias', together with the vocal line of the version in B.L. MS Add. 15117, occurs on a broadside ballad dated 1568: M. Osb[orne], 'A Newe Ballade of a Louer Extollinge his ladye'. The tune is named for singing several other ballads. See Ward, 'Music for *A Handefull of Pleasant Delites*', p. 167; Simpson, *British Broadside Ballad*, pp. 157–9. There is, however, a slight possibility that the lament may itself derive from a ballad and not vice versa. See Simpson, op. cit., p. 159, and my discussion, Joiner, 'A Song in *Damon and Pithias*', pp. 99–100.

[11] See Clemen, *English Tragedy Before Shakespeare*, Chapter II. Clemen discusses the lament in Chapter XV.

EXAMPLE 1. 'Awake ye wofull weights'

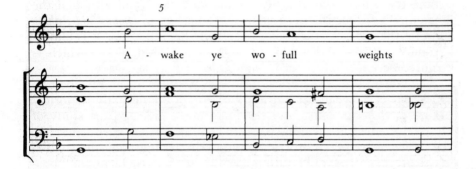

A - wake ye wo - full weights

that long hathe wept in woe

re - signe to me your plaints and

teares   my hap - les _____ happ to

showe   my wo no tonge can

tell   ne pen cann ___ well dis -

- crye   O what a deathe is

The losse of worldlye welthe, mans wisedom canne restore,
And physicke hath provided eake, a salve for everye sore.

B.L. MS Add.15117, f. 3.

syllable— the setting as a whole exists as a form separable, though not separate, from the words.

The reason why Edwards set Pithias' lament to music rather than have him simply declaim it is not immediately obvious. Edwards may simply have thought that a boy's voice was not strong enough to support the highly rhetorical style of a formal lament and thus may have made a virtue of the fact that the children performing the play were trained musicians, better able to sing than to declaim. Or he may have been influenced by Continental ideas of the classical relationship of words and music which were being developed in both France and Italy under the inspiration of Florentine neo-Platonism. If this latter were the case, Edwards was probably aiming at a kind of heightened eloquence in the setting of the lament to music. However, influence of French and Italian experiments with an ideal relationship of words and music is not generally evident in English song as early as 1564 and it seems unlikely that Edwards was inspired by contemporary Continental theory in setting the song.

The lament in *Damon and Pithias* seems to have been immediately popular, for there exists from the 1560s and 1570s a large number of laments of a similar kind, most of them suggestive of a dramatic context although none of their plays now survives. The extant laments exist in the form of consort songs; that is, songs for solo voice, either treble, 'mean', or alto, with accompaniment in three or four parts for a consort of viols.[12] Although the stage directions for 'Awake ye woeful wights' do not indicate a consort of viols and the extant accompaniment is for lute, its form— with the imitative style of accompaniment— is suggestive of the consort song, and indeed the work may have been performed with a consort accompaniment in other productions of the play. Pithias' lament is characteristic of other extant laments which, in fact, develop certain of its motifs. One of these motifs is a deliberate indecision between the major and minor third and what later becomes a formula— based on the minor third interval and the cadential figure as at bars 36–8 of 'Awake ye woeful wights'— for expression of a final 'I die' or 'Oh pity' phrase, often repeated *ad nauseam*.[13] The formulaic quality which finally attached to both musical and poetic aspects of the laments (although many of those extant are far more than a mere succession of formulae) is clear in the parodying of some of these in a general way in Pyramus' final speech in Bottom's play in *A Midsummer Night's Dream* (v. i. 296). The formula appears to have been also adapted to a Petrarchan 'complaint' in a song which may well be a version of a

[12] For a full discussion see Brett, 'The English Consort Song'.

[13] For examples see Brett, *Consort Songs*, pp. 1–32; Warlock, *Elizabethan Songs*. For a discussion of these songs in the drama see Arkwright, 'Elizabethan Choirboy Plays'.

consort song from an early seventeenth-century play: 'Sweet wanton wag'.[14]

The origins of the consort song are obscure. As a form of setting songs in children's plays it was popular right up until the dissolution of the children's companies in 1608.[15] But consort songs unrelated to plays, composed for private performance, were also popular in the last decades of the sixteenth century. The consort song probably developed in a court context, perhaps mainly within the courtly drama of the mid-sixteenth century;[16] and the form differs from the pre-Reformation secular songs, whose melody is usually in the tenor part, in that its melody is in one of the upper parts.[17] In the development and

EXAMPLE 2(a). 'Sweett wantton wagg'

Sweett want - ton wagg whose chaire of ___ state   is   mount-ed

is [mount-ed   is mount-ed]   in   my   mis - tries__

---

[14] From Christ Church, Oxford, MS Mus. 439, p. 66.

[15] Brett, *Consort Songs*, Introduction. Brett's edition contains several post-1600 consort songs. Some of these are probably from children's plays.

[16] Brett, *Consort Songs*, Introduction, p. xv.

[17] Brett, 'Songs of William Byrd', p. 41. For a full discussion of pre-Reformation songs see J. Stevens, *Music and Poetry*, especially Chapters 6 and 7.

Christ Church MS Mus. 439, p.66.
cf. the endings of 'Pandolpho' and 'A doleful deadly pang'.

popularization of this form in the 1580s and 1590s (William Byrd is the most important composer of consort songs in this period) we see what can be regarded as a peculiarly English tradition. It holds its own against the rise in popularity of the madrigal at the end of the sixteenth century, although many of Byrd's songs are printed with words for each part, perhaps in recognition of the new interest in madrigals.

The popularity of consort songs in children's plays provides the clearest indication of the usual function for songs in these plays: that is,

EXAMPLE 2(b). Ending of 'Pandolpho'

Ed. P. Brett, *Consort Songs*, p. 12.

as an interlude in the acting and as an entertainment for the audience.
Evidently a consort of viols to accompany a song would be rather
clumsy to integrate within the dramatic action of a play. For example,
the song in Middleton's *A Trick to Catch the Old One*, performed in 1605
by Paul's Boys—'My master is so wise' (v. v. 1)—has no specific
significance as part of the dramatic action. Audrey sits singing to
Dampit as she spins, and almost any song would be suitable in this
context. The setting of the song which is extant in Ravenscroft's *Melis-*
mata (1611) for treble voice and a consort of viols may well have been
performed in Middleton's play.[18] The fact that the song was provided
as much to amuse the audience before the scene began as for any
dramatic purpose is clear if one attempts to explain the presence of an
accompanying consort of viols in a bedchamber. A consort song with an
even more clearly interlude function is 'What meat eats the Spaniard'
from another play by Middleton, *Blurt Master Constable* (1601), 1. ii. 209.
A setting of the song is preserved in British Library MSS Add.
17786–17791.[19] This song is sung between Acts I and I I and although
it makes some reference to the play it has virtually no integral dramatic
function. The setting, a dialogue-song with consort accompaniment, is
sophisticated and provides a kind of interact musical comedy in little by
turning the almost nonsense words into a flippant and clever musical

[18] *Melismata*, Sig. D.3ᵛ–D.4. The song-text in the play begins at line 3: 'Let the usurer cram
him . . .'.

[19] The song is no. 28 in this collection. See also the discussion and transcription by Sabol, 'Two
Songs with Accompaniment', p. 155.

EXAMPLE 2(c). Ending of 'A doleful deadly pang'

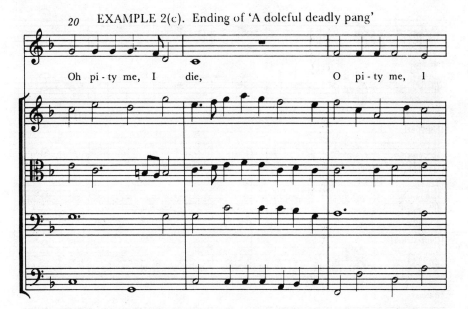

Oh pi - ty me, I die, O pi - ty me, I

die, I die, I die, I die, I die, I die, I die.

Ed. P. Brett, *Consort Songs*, p. 19.

EXAMPLE 3. 'What meat eats the Spaniard'

[Sextus]

[Medius]   [Doyt]

                                              [What meat eats the

[Superius]

[Tenor]

[Contratenor]

[Bassus]

[Pilcher]   10

Drie   Pil - chers Pil-chers Pil - chers drie   Pil-chers and poore John

                                              [Dandypratt]

Span- iard]   [A -

15

my flesh is falne and

-las, thou 'art, art al - most marr'd.]

20

gone falne & gone

[Would'st thou not would'st thou not

O how my teeth my

leap   would'st thou not leap, not leap at a piece of meat]

teeth   O how my teeth doe wat-er   I could eate   for the heavens   my

flesh is al -most gone   with eat-inge pilchers[pilchers pilchers] and __ poore

John with eatinge pilchers pilchers pilchers and   poore   John.

Cf. the edition by A.J. Sabol, *Studies in the Renaissance*, V (1958), pp. 155-7.The song occurs in BL MSS Add. 17786-91, no. 28. Words are given for the Sextus only. Sabol has added words from the text to the Medius part.

parody, a satire of fashionable madrigalian devices of setting words to music.

The use of songs in children's plays purely for the amusement of the audience and to break up the speaking parts is common in plays right back to *Damon and Pithias*. The song 'at the shaving of the Collier' in the comic scene with Grim the collier in that play is an example.[20] The rather complex issue of the songs in Lyly's plays, written for Paul's Boys, suggests that more or fewer songs may have been inserted in various performances of the plays and that the songs themselves may have varied too. The large number of song texts in the 1632 edition of the plays probably does not indicate the songs required for every performance.[21]

Much of the vocal music in children's plays, particularly in the comedies, might best be described as music for a sophisticated audience, wanting to hear the latest and most fashionable music but wanting at the same time primarily to be entertained. The four publications of music by Thomas Ravenscroft—*Pammelia* (1609), *Deuteromelia* (1609), *Melismata* (1611), and *A Briefe Discourse* (1614)—all of which have been shown to contain songs from choirboy plays, illustrate the kind of music the audience liked to hear.[22] The songs in Ravenscroft's collections have simple texts and the settings are homophonic part-songs, canons, rounds, or simple balletts with 'fa-la' or nonsense refrains. The songs might be described as 'popular' but, unlike ballads for instance, their popularity includes a self-conscious sophistication.[23] Often the songs were social or political satires, and this is also characteristic of some of the plays themselves, which appeal to a sophisticated audience.[24]

III

A custom which was more popular in the public theatre than in private-theatre or court performances was that of finishing a performance with a jig after the play. The stage jig was popular from the era of

[20] Malone Society Reprint, l. 1677.

[21] The plays were first published with song-texts by Blount in his edition of 1632 and the authenticity of these song-texts has been questioned. Hunter, *John Lyly*, pp. 367–72, sums up the evidence and concludes that Blount probably had access to the music library of Paul's Boys whence he derived his song-texts. See also the following contributions to the discussion of Lyly's songs: Best, 'A Note on the Songs in Lyly's Plays'; Dodds, 'Songs in Lyly's Plays'; Greg, 'The Authorship of the Songs in Lyly's Plays'; Lawrence, 'The Problem of Lyly's Songs'; Moore, 'The Songs in Lyly's Plays'.

[22] See: Lawrence, 'Thomas Ravenscroft's Theatrical Associations'; Sabol, 'Ravenscroft's *Melismata* and the Children of Paul's'; 'Two Songs with Accompaniment'; Chan, '*Cynthia's Revels* and Music for a Choir School'.

[23] I have shown elsewhere that songs characteristic of choirboy plays occur in the manuscript in Christ Church Library, MS Mus. 439: see my article cited in note 22 above.

[24] Harbage, *Shakespeare and the Rival Traditions*, pp. 78–9.

Richard Tarlton (d. 1588)—the comedian in the Queen's Company and famous in the 1570s and 1580s—until the turn of the century. The jigs were brief farcical dramas, mainly sung and accompanied by dancing. They never formed the main entertainment but were performed simply as an after-piece. The jigs have their origins in the singing, dancing, and ballad-making of seasonal festivities; but in the theatre the jig became a formal dramatic genre, involving sometimes one actor, sometimes several.[25]

While the jig remained informal entertainment its musical accompaniment, if any, was probably very simple, as in the ballads from which it was often derived. When the jig became more formal and part of a theatrical entertainment, it seems to have been quite an elaborate affair. It has been suggested by Sidney Beck that the stage jigs in the Elizabethan theatre were commonly accompanied by the ensemble known as the broken consort which consisted of six instruments—the treble viol, flute, bass viol, lute, cittern, and pandora.[26] Mr Beck believes that the practice of accompanying the jigs with music grew out of the tradition of accompanying the dumb-shows in the university and court drama with music. However the custom arose, the existence of many ballad tunes, including pieces with titles such as 'Tarlton's Jigg', 'A Northern Jigge', 'Kemp's Jigge', in the extant repertoire of the broken consort provides evidence for Mr Beck's hypothesis. He imagines the Elizabethan jig to have been a performance of this kind:

Though the antics and merry-making of the clown held the attention of the spectators, it would seem almost inevitable that his colleagues, providing the instrumental accompaniment, should enter into the spirit of the entertainment by engaging in some musical improvisation, especially since the constant repetition of a single tune was a challenging limitation in the early days of the jigg.[27]

Mr Beck bases his hypothesis on the fact that the settings of jig tunes in the repertoire of the broken consort consist of virtuoso variations on a basic and very simple theme.

Although there is very little evidence in the plays themselves, or in stage directions, it is possible that the broken consort was heard fairly frequently in the theatre, especially in the public theatre, and in music other than that required simply for jigs; and it may later have become the standard 'band'.[28] Mr Beck makes the point that at least for

---

[25] For a full discussion see Baskervill, *Elizabethan Jig*, in particular Chapters I and III.

[26] See the Introduction to Beck's edition of Morley's *Consort Lessons* (1599), pp. 7–8.

[27] Beck (ed.), Introduction, p. 8.

[28] J. Stevens, 'Music of the Elizabethan Stage', p. 24, quotes the following passage from Dekker's *Old Fortunatus* which suggests that the broken consort was used in the theatre for music other than that required by the jigs: '*Musicke still: Enter Shaddow* . . . Musicke? O delicate warble [flute or recorder] . . . O delicious strings [viols and lute]: these heavenly wyre-drawers [cittern and pandora].'

performances in the public theatres, which were open-air, it would be necessary to provide a combination of musical instruments with a good carrying quality, such as the broken consort. Furthermore, the very instruments which make up the broken consort are mentioned among lists of possessions of actors and acting companies;[29] and the Dutch collection of Adriaen Valerius—*Nederlandtsch'e Gedenck-Clanck* (1626) —contains among its seventy-nine pieces seventeen English airs, believed to have been made popular by travelling English acting troupes, and 'provides parts for the lute, cittern, and bass viol to accompany the songs'.[30]

On the whole, however, it is unlikely that many of the acting companies had a permanent band of musicians, at least in the late sixteenth century. If music was required in a play the most obvious musicians to call on would be either the City Waits, a band of musicians whose main job was to play for civic occasions, or the King's Musick, the royal musicians.[31] Certainly there is evidence that the waits performed in the playhouses—evidence provided by complaints by the city aldermen that the waits could not perform at a civic function because they were 'then employed at playhouses'.[32]

The broken consort seems to have been quite a common and popular combination of instruments in the performances given by waits by the end of the sixteenth century. Morley's *First Book of Consort Lessons*, a collection of twenty-five pieces by several composers, arranged for broken consort and published in 1599,[33] was dedicated to the 'Lord Mayor of the Citty of London and to the Right Worshipfvl the Aldermen of the same', making it clear that, while the collection would appeal to private and amateur groups, ideally the City Waits should be the performers.[34] Because Morley dedicated his collection to the waits of London, because it is known that the waits sometimes played in the public theatres, and because of the kind of music which Morley's collection contains, Mr Beck suggests that there was a close association between the development of the broken consort and its use in the theatre. Much of the repertoire of the broken consort—in Morley's

---

[29] Beck (ed.), Introduction, p. 13.

[30] Beck (ed.), Introduction, p. 9 and footnote 28.

[31] For a full discussion of the origins of bands of city waits see Woodfill, *Musicians in English Society*.

[32] Quoted in Woodfill, *Musicians in English Society*, p. 30. In a dialogue between the Citizen and the Prologue in Beaumont and Fletcher's *The Knight of the Burning Pestle*, Induction, the Citizen asks, 'What stately music have you?' and then gives the Prologue two shillings with the remark: 'let's have the waits of Southwark; they are as rare fellows as any are in England. . . .' The passage is also quoted and discussed by J. Stevens, 'Music of the Elizabethan Theatre', p. 25.

[33] See the edition by Beck. My discussion of the work's significance for the Elizabethan and Jacobean theatre largely follows Beck's Introduction.

[34] Thomas Morley, *The First Book of Consort Lessons* (London, 1599), Sig. A.2. Beck reproduces the title-page in facsimile, p. ix, and discusses this on pp. 3 ff.

collection, in a later publication by Rosseter,[35] and in manuscript sources[36]—consists of arrangements of simple ballad and popular tunes. Indeed, this combination of instruments is not suitable for the performance of polyphonic music, such as the fantasia which depends on the perfect balancing of all the parts. In arrangements of music for the broken consort the bowed instruments (and the flute), which are principally melodic, carry the 'tune', while the plucked, wire-strung instruments emphasize the rhythmic basis of the melody and the lute provides virtuoso variations of the melody in the repeated sections. The broken consort is most suitable for the performance of dance music and popular song.

Before about 1600 plays for the public theatres do not require much instrumental music—apart, that is, from what might be used to accompany a final jig. Furthermore, when instrumental music was required obviously the full broken consort would not necessarily perform it. What Mr Beck's hypothesis about the close relation between the broken consort and the theatre and his study of the repertoire do suggest is the kind of music which would be likely to have been played, the tunes the audience might have expected to hear. If the taste of the Citizen and his wife in Beaumont and Fletcher's *The Knight of the Burning Pestle* is an accurate indication of that of most audiences in the public theatre then Mr Beck's suggestion that popular and ballad tunes would have been most commonly heard is plausible. In the Interlude between Acts I and II the tune played is the famous 'Lachrimae'. The Citizen wants to hear 'Baloo' instead. Arrangements of both these occur in Morley's *Consort Lessons* (nos. 7 and 18). It seems unlikely that instrumental music was composed especially for any single incident in a play, and if we accept Mr Beck's hypothesis we can assume that popular tunes were widely used. So, for example, when in Marlowe's *Dr Faustus* 'Music sounds and Helen passeth ouer the stage'; or in *Antony and Cleopatra* 'music of the hautboys is [heard] under the stage'; or in *King Lear* (IV. vii. 25) music plays for Lear's recovery, the music might have been 'Lachrimae Pavin', or 'Can she excuse', or 'In Nomine Pavin', all of which were also published in broken consort arrangements by Morley; although in these particular instances a full consort arrangement is not required.

Songs are, of course, common in adult plays: many actors were also singers and songs were sometimes included for a particular actor.[37] But

---

[35] Rosseter, *Lessons for Consort* (London, 1609).

[36] See the incomplete set of part-books in the Cambridge University Library: Dd. 3. 18 (lute); Dd. 5. 20 (bass viol); Dd. 5. 21 (recorder); Dd. 14. 24 (cittern). The recorder book includes some parts for 'treble violan'. See also my discussion, Joiner, 'B.M. MS Add. 15117'.

[37] See, for example, the discussion in Sternfeld, *Music in Shakespearean Tragedy*, pp. 98 ff. of the songs written for Robert Armin. There is a more general discussion of Armin in Bradbrook,

on the whole we do not find in these plays anything to match the
elaborate musical performances of the boy actors; and songs in adult
plays often have a more integral relation to the play itself and do not
have so markedly the function of interlude performances that many
children's songs have. This may be partly due to the fact that, in the
public theatres at any rate which depended on daylight, the performance of a play had to be over before the sun went down. Furthermore,
the private theatres were, like the banqueting halls, acoustically
superior to the public theatres. The lavish use of music is characteristic
of most indoor productions, whether by adult companies or by boys.
Shakespeare's *Twelfth Night*, believed to have been performed either at
court or at the Middle Temple by the Lord Chamberlain's Men in 1601
or 1602, requires far more music than most of his other plays.[38] When
the King's Men took over the Blackfriars theatre in 1608 their plays too
required more music.

IV

In the foregoing discussion we have been mainly concerned with the
kinds of music an audience might have heard and we have seen in
passing some of the instrumental resources owned or required by
actors. We must now consider the location of the musicians in the
theatre and how far this affected the function of music in the plays.

We have seen that music was very common in the plays performed
by children in the private theatres; and the Blackfriars theatre, at any
rate, had a music room, a curtained space above the stage in the
tiring-house façade where the musicians could be located throughout
the performance of the play if necessary. The curtain could conceal the
musicians from the audience if the music was from 'within': or it could
be drawn back, perhaps for the performance of interact music. Where
music was included as part of the action on-stage, the music room
would not, of course, be required. Because there was no custom of
interact music in the public theatres, at least before 1604,[39] it is probable that there was no special music room as there was in the Blackfriars.[40] Richard Hosley has examined plays performed at the first
Globe theatre between 1599 and 1608 (the date at which the King's

---

Shakespeare the Craftsman, Chapter IV. Hotson, *First Night*, p. 142, suggests that 'Come away, death'
(*Twelfth Night*, IV. iv) was written for Robert Hales.

[38] See Hotson, *First Night*, who argues for a court performance in 1601, and Akrigg's refutation of
this hypothesis in '*Twelfth Night* at the Middle Temple'. Akrigg dates the first performance as
1602.

[39] See above, p. 15, the passage from Webster's Induction to the Globe performance of *The
Malcontent*, and Hosley, 'Was there a music-room . . .?' pp. 116–17.

[40] Hosley, 'Was there a music-room . . .?'.

Men who played at the Globe took over the Blackfriars theatre) and has discovered no stage directions or requirements for music which could not have been fulfilled by placing the musicians either on-stage, within the tiring-house itself at stage level, or, on the rare occasions when music from above was required, by placing the musicians on the balcony in the tiring-house façade.[41] When the King's Men took over the Blackfriars theatre in 1608 they probably took over some of its customs as well, perhaps even that of performing interact music. But where plays might be performed at both the Globe and Blackfriars, or at either, it would have been simple enough to adapt one of the Lords' rooms in the Globe (or any of the other public theatres) and fit it with curtains so that music could be performed 'above' and concealed. If Shakespeare's *The Tempest* was, in fact, performed at both theatres, an arrangement of this kind would have been made for Ariel's music.

The function of the music room itself, the source for the music, within the dramatic illusion of the play sometimes has a special significance. In a situation like Audrey's singing to Dampit in Middleton's *A Trick to Catch the Old One* (v. v. 1), described above (p. 24), the location of the musicians is quite straightforward. Even if the song was accompanied by a consort of viols from the music room rather than from the stage, the audience's attention would have been focused primarily on the singer and the words and they would have accepted without question an anonymous or invisible accompaniment. But there is another, affective, function for dramatic music which Marston was the first to develop. While this probably derives from the classical ideas of music's affective powers which were revived by the Florentine *Camerata* and which led to experiments in opera,[42] the technical possibility in the private theatres of concealing the musicians above the stage may have contributed to its popularity and widespread use because a sense of mystery and the supernatural could be thus attached to it. The earliest instance of affective music occurs in Marston's *Antonio and Mellida*, Part I, Act IV, performed by Paul's Boys in 1599. In this instance the musicians are not concealed, although it is the music which is important and not the identity of the musicians. In Part II of the same play (*Antonio's Revenge*) Marston develops this use of music by concealing the musicians within the music room.

In *Antonio and Mellida*, Part I, Act IV, Antonio calls for a song to be sung, one which will match and express his grief. No particular song is

[41] See Hosley, op. cit.; Lawrence, 'Music and Song in the Elizabethan Theatre', in *The Elizabethan Playhouse*, 1st ser., pp. 90–6; Yates, *Theatre of the World*. Yates assigns the music room to the central balcony above the acting area. For a discussion of the music room in the Blackfriars theatre see Smith, *Shakespeare's Blackfriars Playhouse*, pp. 408–11.

[42] See pp. 40f.

requested and the stage directions are simply 'CANTANT'. Antonio asks for the song in this way:

> I pree thee sing, but sirra (marke you me)
> Let each note breath the heart of passion,
> The sad extracture of extreamest griefe.
> Make me a straine; speake, groning like a bell,
> That towles departing soules.
> Breath me a point that may inforce me weepe,
> To wring my hands, to breake my cursed breast,
> Rave, and exclaime, lie groveling on the earth
> Straight start up frantick, crying, *Mellida*.
> Sing but, *Antonio* hath lost *Mellida*,
> And thou shalt see mee (like a man possest)
> Howle out such passion, that even this brinish marsh
> Will squease out teares, from out his spungy cheekes,
> The rocks even groane, and— . . .

CANTANT

At first glance Antonio's song appears to be similar to the lament Pithias (in *Damon and Pithias*) sings to express his grief, and no doubt Antonio's song develops the convention of the formal lament in a virtuoso and extravagant way. But in their contexts the songs have quite different effects. In *Damon and Pithias*, we saw, the song (as lament) was part of a larger, patterned context. The music was part of a formal convention and to that degree Pithias' lament formalized and depersonalized passion. This song in *Antonio and Mellida*, on the other hand, does not underline a non-realistic mode for the play. It seems rather an attempt to heighten the play's realism by concentrating our attention on Antonio's grief. This is one of the earliest examples in the theatre of 'atmosphere' or 'mood' music.

We might point up the distinctive nature of Marston's use of music by comparing it with Shakespeare's music in *Twelfth Night* which helps to characterize the Duke Orsino: in particular, we might look at the music with which the play opens, and Feste's 'command' performance of 'Come away death' (II. iv. 50). The difference lies in the fact that Orsino's longing for music as 'the food of love' and his desire for 'that old and antique song we heard last night' (II. iv. 3) illustrate an aspect of what is shown elsewhere in the play to be his sentimentality and his lack of self-awareness.[43] The difference in Shakespeare's use of music here from Marston's in Act IV of *Antonio and Mellida* is that in *Twelfth Night* the music is a form of self-indulgence, it is to affect Orsino rather than the audience (who may remain critical of him) and is thus con-

---

[43] For a full discussion of the music in *Twelfth Night* see Hollander, *Untuning of the Sky*, pp. 153–61.

tained within the play; whereas in *Antonio and Mellida* the song is clearly
to affect the audience as much as Antonio, to draw the audience into
uncritical sympathy with Antonio, in a way which, unlike the effect of
Pithias' lament, breaks down the 'play' qualities of the play.

The singers of Antonio's song in *Antonio and Mellida* are on-stage, and
although they are anonymous they are contained within the dramatic
illusion as Antonio's servants. But in the case of music with a similar
function performed anonymously off-stage, the role of the musicians
themselves and the illusion of the music room have changed. We have
already considered the passage from Part II of *Antonio and Mellida*
(*Antonio's Revenge*), Act I, where Pandulpho has discovered his son
murdered and Alberto is appalled at his inability to grieve (pp. 13–14). I
suggested that this is probably an adaptation and conflation of the
Roman and Greek Chorus conventions. As Alberto and Pandulpho
continue their discussion of Felice's virtues and his past life while
'Musick sounds softly', it seems that the identity of the theatre musicians who play until the end of the scene, and who are presumably
invisible to the audience, would become merged in what might now be
regarded as a 'supernatural' source for music. The music is also quite
obviously expressive of Pandulpho's grief. This use of purely expressive
music to provide a vaguely supernatural context, music which, unlike
the supernatural music in 'th'air or th'earth', or the music which
accompanies dumb-show, has no specific moral significance, is
exploited later by Fletcher. One of Fletcher's most extended examples
is the musical sequence in Act IV, scene i of *The Mad Lover*, performed
by the King's Men at the Blackfriars theatre in 1616.[44]

By the way in which 'expressive' music directly addresses the audience, these examples of Marston's use of music, and later uses of theatre
music which may have developed from these, are related to operatic
techniques and assumptions. By contrast, the older, more traditional,
perhaps more conservative use of music which may have been retained
longer in the public theatres draws the musical performance into the
dramatic illusion: that is, the play creates an illusory world on-stage
which is complete in itself. Purely affective music, of the kind we have
looked at in Marston's two plays, places emphasis on the play as
performance, as show, with the consequence that it stresses a distinction between the play and its audience.[45] On the other hand, where the
music is assimilated into the dramatic illusion, the presence of an

[44] The music for this scene has been transcribed by Cutts, *La Musique*, pp. 58–66. Cutts's work
contains transcriptions of all the extant music for Fletcher's plays. See also Cutts's discussion of
this in 'Music and *The Mad Lover*'.
[45] Cf. Mellers, *Harmonious Meeting*, pp. 108–9, which discusses the virtuoso or 'show' element in
the Caroline lyric.

audience is not directly acknowledged and, paradoxically, this means that the audience is required to be less, not more, passive than the audience of, for instance, *Antonio's Revenge*. The audience becomes subtly included: it is asked to share in an ethical world which the play as a whole, and in all its aspects, creates, and there is no longer any question of its being appropriately affected by individual characters or scenes. This subtle inclusion of the audience is often evident in the respect that the music may well be 'tunes' that the audience will readily recognize.

V

Of the songs in early children's plays, the laments were composed by the Master of the children's company by which the play was presented, composers such as Richard Edwards, Richard Farrant, Nathaniel Giles, Robert Parsons. Where settings of songs for later plays, both for children and for adults, exist, the composer is not usually identified. Instrumental music was most likely to be an adaptation of music already in existence, either a dance or a popular tune. In most cases, where the author of the play was not himself a musician (as were some of the authors of the early plays for children) we do not even know what musicians the playwright would have been acquainted with, what musical interest and knowledge he had, or how he chose a composer to set one of his songs.

In the case of Ben Jonson we are more fortunate. We know something of the musicians who set his lyrics, particularly those musicians who collaborated with him in his masques. Of these, the most important are Alfonso Ferrabosco the younger, Robert Johnson, and Nicholas Lanier. We know that Ferrabosco also wrote the music for Volpone's song to Celia in *Volpone* (III. vii)[46] and Robert Johnson possibly wrote the music for Wittipol's song in *The Devil is an Ass* (II. vi). Because the songs are mainly solo songs with lute or viol accompaniment it is important to see these within the development of the English lute-song tradition.

The lute ayre, or solo song with lute accompaniment, a form which flourished in England in the early years of the seventeenth century, has its roots in a native tradition but was influenced too by various Continental song forms and ideas.[47] John Dowland's *First Book of Ayres*, published in 1597, was the first of a long series of publications of songs

---

[46] David Fuller, 'Ben Jonson's Plays and their Contemporary Music', believes that if Volpone's song to Celia was sung in production it was not sung to Ferrabosco's music. There seems to me no very good reason for denying Ferrabosco's setting to Volpone.

[47] For a full and very clear discussion of the development of the English lute ayre see Poulton, *Dowland*, pp. 181–213.

for solo voice and lute, or lute and bass viol. Not only by the fact that his ayres were the first to be published, but in many other respects, Dowland leads the 'school' of lute-song writers. Many of Dowland's songs, especially in his first and second collections, give alternative arrangements for singing in four parts, although in most cases the upper part is clearly predominant and the words do not always fit the other parts very well. It is sometimes suggested that in providing alternative four-part versions Dowland and the other composers who arranged songs in this way were influenced by the French *air de cour*. But the polyphonic part-song had traditions in England and it is difficult to be certain about specific Continental influence. It has also been suggested that Dowland's frequent use of dance forms in his early collections of songs derives from his association with French musicians. But again, the setting of words to pre-existing dance tunes was common in England; and even if Dowland's dance ayres are his own and not arrangements of existing tunes, there is ample precedent in England throughout the sixteenth century and earlier for the combination of song and dance. The use of dance forms in the setting of lute ayres was followed also by other composers of lute songs: Thomas Campion (1567–1620) and Robert Jones (dates unknown) in particular. In the later works of Campion the basic dance forms are still used but are often rhythmically altered or distorted for special effect. The influence on Dowland's early work of late sixteenth-century Continental ideas of setting words to music, both French and Italian, is not particularly marked, although his feeling for verbal rhythms and simple word treatment may show influence of the French air. On the other hand one should not ignore, either, the influence of the Geneva Psalter on the simple setting of words to music.[48]

Several lute-song writers were more clearly influenced by Continental theories of setting words to music than Dowland was—at least in his early work. Two important composers whose work shows a consciousness of 'new' ideas are Campion and Ferrabosco II, both of whom also composed music for masques. (Campion wrote both the script and some of the music for his masques.)

Continental theories of setting words to music in the late sixteenth century were influenced by Ficino's experiments in the late fifteenth century with words and music. These experiments were revived nearly one hundred years later by French poets and musicians attempting to rediscover the miraculous powers of music described by classical writers. The men most influential in this were Pierre de Ronsard, Joachim du Bellay, and Pontus de Tyard, who came together with others in Paris as an informal group known as the *Pléiade*. In 1570, two members

[48] See the discussion by J. Stevens, *Music and Poetry*, referred to in note 17.

of this group, Jean Antoine de Baïf and Joachim Thibaut de Courville, formed another, more formal group, the *Académie de poésie et de musique*, which was given royal charter. The aim of the founders was to adapt classical prosody to French verse which could then be set quantitatively to music. The members developed a new style of song, a kind of chant, known as *musique mesurée à l'antique*. It was believed to come close to the classical music which, according to accounts by classical writers, had had great power over the listener. Although not in itself musically interesting, the 'measured music' had a far-reaching effect on the practice of contemporary musicians.[49]

At about the same time that academies were flourishing in France, Count Giovanni de' Bardi established a group with similar aims in Florence. The group was known as the *Camerata*. Bardi gathered together the most famous musicians in the city including Vincenzo Galilei, a theoretician as well as composer and lutenist, and Giulio Caccini, a composer and singer. The *Camerata* was interested not simply in recreating the ancient 'effects' of music but in imitating ancient Greek tragedy, which they believed to have been sung. The group's knowledge of the principles of the Greek musical system was advanced by the work of the historian and philologist, Girolamo Mei, who, though not himself a musician and not interested in musical reforms, put his discoveries at the disposal of the *Camerata*. Mei believed that the effects described by ancient writers could have been created only by the fact that they used a single musical line, that Greek music, both choral and solo, was monodic.[50] Members of the *Camerata* consequently developed a monodic style of singing which they believed came close to the Greek style; and their experiments with a musical drama, sung throughout, led to the creation of opera. The emphasis of the *Camerata* in giving rules for setting words to music was on the clear declamation of the words, and on not attempting to represent in music the meaning of individual words in a text. The practice of 'word painting' was common in madrigal settings in particular and was encouraged by Zarlino's instructions in Part IV, Chapter 32 of his *Institutioni armoniche* (Venice, 1573). Thomas Morley, giving advice on setting words to music in his *A Plain and Easy Introduction* (London, 1597), follows Zarlino's instructions fairly closely.[51] The 'rules' for setting were often carried to absurd extremes and it is these kinds of settings that the *Camerata* attacked. Galilei, for instance, described the pitfalls of exaggerated 'word painting' in his *Dialogo della musica antica e*

---

[49] See Yates, *French Academies*. The impetus behind the formation of the academies was neo-Platonist rather than humanist.
[50] See Poulton, *Dowland*, p. 199.
[51] See Morley, ed. Harman and Dart, pp. 290–2.

della moderna (1581). He speaks of some of the absurdities of this kind of setting in the following passage.

At another time they will say that they are imitating the words when among the conceptions of these there are any meaning 'to flee' or 'to fly'; these they will declaim with the greatest rapidity and the least grace imaginable. In connection with words meaning 'to disappear', 'to swoon', 'to die', or actually 'to be extinct' they have made the parts break off so abruptly, that instead of inducing the passion corresponding to any of these, they have aroused laughter and at other times contempt in the listeners, who felt that they were being ridiculed. Then with words meaning 'alone', 'two', or 'together' they have caused one lone part, or two, or all the parts together to sing with unheard-of elegance. Others, in the singing of this particular line from one of the sestinas of Petrarch:

And with the lame ox he will be pursuing Laura,

have declaimed it to staggering, wavering, syncopated notes as though they had the hiccups. And when, as sometimes happens, the conceptions they have had in hand made mention of the rolling of the drum, or of the sound of the trumpet or any other such instrument, they have sought to represent its sound in their music, without minding at all that they were pronouncing these words in some unheard-of manner.[52]

In England there were no formal groups similar to Baïf's *Académie* or Bardi's *Camerata*, although Sir Philip Sidney and a group of friends seem to have been interested in quantitative metres as most appropriate for musical setting.[53] William Byrd's experiment in quantitative setting in his song 'Constant Penelope' may have been inspired by this group.[54] Campion also experimented with quantitative setting in 'Come let us sound', published in Rosseter's *Ayres* (1601), no. XXI. Campion expressed his ideas about the relation of words and music in several places, but notably in the Preface to Part I of Rosseter's *Ayres* for which he wrote both the words and the music. Campion's comments on setting words to music are similar to those of Galilei which made clear that the *Camerata* did not wish to encourage the extremes of some madrigal composers. Campion says:

But there are some, who to appeare the more deepe, and singular in their iudgement, will admit no Musicke but that which is long, intricate, bated with fuge, chaind with

[52] Trans. Strunk, *Source Readings*, pp. 316–17. Strunk translates a large portion of Galilei's *Dialogo*. For an example of Morley's advice to composers (following Zarlino) see below, Chapter II, pp. 58–61.

[53] Sidney's discussion of the merits of rhyme and quantity takes place in a dialogue between Lalus and Dicus in the cancelled passage from the *Arcadia* which is found in Queen's College Library, Oxford, MS R. 38/301. The passage is printed in full in Zandvoort, *Sidney's Arcadia*, pp. 11–12. The conclusions of this debate are summarized in Sidney's *Apologie* (ed. Smith), I, pp. 204–5.

[54] See *Psalmes, Sonets and songs of sadness and pietie* . . . (London, 1588), no. XXIII.

sincopation, and where the nature of euerie word is precisely exprest in the Note, like the old exploided action in Comedies, when if they did pronounce Memeni, *they would point to the hinder part of their heads, if* Video, *put their finger in their eye. But such childish obseruing of words is altogether ridiculous, and we ought to maintaine as well in Notes, as in action a manly cariage, gracing no word, but that which is eminent, and emphaticall.*

Most of Campion's songs are strophic and many of those in Rosseter's *Ayres* in particular are based on dance patterns. Thus Campion marries both the old traditions of setting with the new. The first English composer to write in a style which often comes close to the declamatory style advocated by the *Camerata* is Alfonso Ferrabosco the younger (1575–1628).

Ferrabosco's father, also called Alfonso, was an Italian who lived in England for the greater part of his life. He was employed at the court of Queen Elizabeth. His son, who was born in England and spent most of his life there, was also employed by the Queen from 1592; and when James came to the throne he was appointed one of the King's Musicians for the Violin, a post which he held until his death. In 1604 he was appointed music-master to Prince Henry, and then to Prince Charles after the death of Henry in 1612. After the accession of Charles I he retained his posts at court and was also made Composer of Music in Ordinary and Composer of the King's Music.

Ferrabosco was most famous in his lifetime for his compositions for, and performance on, the lyra viol.[55] In 1609 he published a collection of lyra viol music, in tablature—*Lessons for 1, 2, and 3 Viols*—which he dedicated to the Earl of Southampton. But he is perhaps best remembered for his songs, in particular those which he set for Jonson's early masques. Settings of songs by Ferrabosco are extant for the following masques by Jonson: *Blackness* (1605), *Beauty* (1608), *The Haddington Masque* (1608), *Queens* (1609), *Oberon* (1611), and *Love Freed from Ignorance and Folly* (1611); and it is known that he also set the songs for *Hymenaei* (1606).[56] All the extant songs for the masques, except those for *Oberon* and *Love Freed*, were printed in Ferrabosco's *Ayres* (1609), his only other published collection, for which Jonson wrote a commendatory verse.[57] Settings for the two masques of 1611 occur in a manuscript in St. Michael's College, Tenbury, MS 1018.[58] Although after 1611 Ferrabosco collaborated only rarely with Jonson, until 1611 he appears to have been the only composer of songs for Jonson's masques.

All the songs in the *Ayres*, including those from Jonson's masques and

[55] The lyra viol is a bass member of the viol family which has the ability to play chords.

[56] A passage after line 678 (H & S vii, p. 232) in the quarto was cancelled in the folios. See below, Chapter VI, note 16, p. 272.

[57] This was also reprinted in *Epigrammes*, no. CXXX. No. CXXXI is also in commendation of Ferrabosco.

[58] These songs are reproduced and discussed in Chapter VI.

'Come my Celia' (no. VI) from Jonson's *Volpone*, are in a style which while not strictly declamatory at least follows the shape of the poetic line very closely in accentuation and phrasing and does not, on the whole, create a melodic shape which would have any point apart from the words—as the dance ayres of Dowland and of Campion, for instance, do. While some of the songs are strophic, in most cases only the first stanza fits the vocal line well. The accompaniments—for lute supported by a bass viol—are, unlike Dowland's lute accompaniments, very simple, chordal and non-contrapuntal, so that the vocal line is alone important rather than being the most important part of a complex polyphonic whole. The accompaniment supports the vocal line harmonically and sometimes, as in 'Come my Celia', provides a kind of rhythmic counterpointing. In both the simplicity of the accompaniment and the partially declamatory vocal line Ferrabosco's settings come closer than earlier English lute ayres to those recommended by Baïf's *Académie* and the *Camerata*. They are in a style which, from the *Camerata*'s point of view, was particularly suited to 'affecting' the listener, to projecting the eloquence of the words.

Robert Johnson (? *c.*1583–1633) was appointed a King's Musician for the Lute in 1604 and one of Prince Henry's musicians in 1611. From accounts for payments for masques we know that he was involved in several of Jonson's masques and some of the surviving dance music for these has been tentatively ascribed to him.[59] He also appears to have been closely associated with the King's Men from about 1610, for he set several extant songs for plays by Fletcher; and music by him for Shakespeare's *The Tempest*, possibly that used in the early performances, survives in John Wilson's *Cheerful Ayres* (1659). Only one song by him for a masque by Ben Jonson survives: 'From the famous peak of Darby' (*The Gypsies Metamorphosed*, 1621), although this is in a late publication, *The Musicall Companion* (London, 1672). It is possible that Johnson composed the music for the one song in Jonson's play *The Devil is an Ass* (1616).[60] The style of Johnson's song settings is somewhat similar to Ferrabosco's: a tuneful declamatory style supported by a simple harmonic accompaniment.

The third composer to collaborate in Jonson's masques was Nicholas Lanier (1588–1666), a singer, composer, and painter, one of Prince Henry's musicians, and from 1626 Master of the King's Musick. As far as we know he first collaborated with Jonson in *Lovers Made Men* (1617), a masque not presented at court but commissioned by Lord Haye and presented at his house. Although the quarto of 1617 does not mention Lanier's part in the masque, in the 1640 folio edition the

[59] See Cutts, 'Jacobean Masque and Stage Music' and 'Robert Johnson'.
[60] See below, Chapter III.

opening stage direction was amplified with the comment:

And the whole Maske was sung (after the Italian manner) Stylo recitativo, *by Master* Nicholas Lanier; *who ordered and made both the Scene, and the Musicke.*[61]

None of Lanier's music for the masque exists so it is difficult to know precisely what was meant by 'stylo recitativo', particularly since a true recitative style was not common in England until later than 1617. It has been suggested that the remark added to the folio text was made in retrospect, and that the music was more likely to have been declamatory ayre.[62] The extant masque songs by Lanier (the earliest is 'Bring away this sacred tree' from Campion's *Somerset Masque*, 1614) reflect an interest in a declamatory singing style.[63]

The settings which survive for songs in Jonson's masques and plays by these three composers, like the anonymous settings for the early plays, show an interest not so much in the style of the early lute song, a basically native English style, but mainly in the new Continental ideas of setting, ideas which stem from a philosophical interest in the legendary effects of ancient music. The music is addressed to an audience, it has an ethical purpose, and is thus unlike the early lute song which is primarily for private recreation—although this too had a 'moral' function of bringing the performer in harmony with the cosmic music and dance. The new music is particularly suited to the ethical aims of the Jonsonian masque as a whole, aims which appear to be carried over into the last plays. In the early plays Jonson uses the new music mainly for satire.

---

[61] H & S vii, p. 454, ll. 26–8. See also below, Chapter VI.

[62] See Emslie, 'Three Early Settings of Jonson'; 'Nicholas Lanier's Innovations in English Song'.

[63] The music was printed with the quarto edition of the masque.

2

Ben Jonson: Cynthia's Revels, Poetaster, Epicoene

THE EARLIEST references we have to Jonson's theatrical career are those in Henslowe's Diary, dated 1597,[1] where we learn that he was employed as a playwright. It has been suggested that he joined Henslowe's company earlier, as a journeyman actor, when Henslowe bought the Paris Garden in 1595, and that before he secured a much-coveted position in the London theatre Jonson spent some time as a strolling player. Dekker's play *Satiromastix* (1602), which satirizes Jonson under the character of Horace, is thought to allude to this when Tucca says to Horace: 'Thou hast forgot how thou amble⟨d⟩st (in a leather pilch) by a play-wagon in the high way . . .'[2] Whatever Jonson's beginnings, his early career must have been difficult and precarious. Having thrown in his trade of bricklaying (his stepfather's trade), to which he was apprenticed on leaving Westminster School, and having sought for excitement in the war in Flanders, Jonson returned to England penniless. Further, sometime between 1592 and 1595 he had married.[3] Jonson's keen and sharp-tongued observations of men and manners clearly indicate not simply an energetic and outspoken nature attracted towards the trenchant wit of the classical writers but also an often bitter first-hand experience.

None of Jonson's early plays for Henslowe survives, nor did Jonson himself consider them worth preserving in his 1616 folio edition of the plays.[4] His earliest surviving play is *The Case is Altered* (1597–8), although details of the first performances are unknown. The earliest text surviving is a quarto of 1609 whose title-page describes the play: 'As it hath been sundry times Acted by the Children of the Black-friers'. As Herford and Simpson point out, the company did not take this title until about 1606. (The company was first formed in 1600 as 'The Children of Queen Elizabeth's Chapel' and after 1603 was known as 'The Children of her Majesty's Revels'.[5]) We know more of the stage history of Jonson's next play, *Every Man in his Humour*, which was

---

[1] See *Diary*, ed. Foakes and Rickert, pp. 52 and 73.
[2] *Satiromastix*, Sig. G.4; quoted in H & S I, p. 13.
[3] See H & S I, p. 8; also footnote 1, p. 6.
[4] See H & S I, p. 21.
[5] H & S IX, p. 166. For a discussion of the 1609 quarto and facsimiles of the two title-pages see H & S III, pp. 94–102. See also Harbage and Schoenbaum, *Annals*, pp. 64–5.

performed in 1598 at the Curtain theatre by the Lord Chamberlain's Company.[6]. The play seems to have been an immediate success, and Jonson followed it the next year with *Every Man out of his Humour*.[7]

The two Humour plays do not make any significant use of the musical traditions of the theatre. This is, perhaps, to be expected in the early work of a playwright. *The Case is Altered* uses more songs, but these are probably later additions for the performances by the Children of Blackfriars mentioned on the quarto title-page. Not until Jonson's next two plays, in 1600 and 1601—*Cynthia's Revels* and *Poetaster*—both for the Children of the Chapel, do we see him exploiting the traditions of children's theatre music and making music and song an integral part of the play's meaning. Both plays are satires on bad poetry and bad poets; and in using songs as part of the satire Jonson draws on recent, Continental, ideas about the relationship of words to music. The earlier play, *Cynthia's Revels*, also uses music in a non-satiric way. In this chapter I discuss both plays; and finally, I turn to *Epicoene*, Jonson's last play for the Children of the Chapel and written eight years after *Poetaster*, in 1609, when Jonson had already written *Volpone* and several masques for the court. In the use of music in this later play he solved some of the technical problems which *Cynthia's Revels* created: *Epicoene* brings Jonson's achievement in children's drama to its highest point. But the lessons Jonson learnt for *Epicoene* he learnt in the court masque on the one hand and the public theatre on the other; and it is in these two fields that his best work was accomplished.

This chapter makes few points that are new. Here, I rather seek to draw together various aspects of Jonson's use of music within the early plays in order that we may understand the ground plan on which Jonson's later use of music and his ideas of the relationship of words and music were built.

I

In 1599 John Marston (1576–1634), a younger contemporary and admirer of Jonson, revised the old play *Histriomastix* and remodelled the pedant in the play, Chrisoganus, into a parody of Jonson's manners and speech. The portrait was intended to flatter Jonson but unfortunately it was not received as flattery. Jonson retaliated by making Clove in *Every Man out of his Humour* imitate some of the more extravagant characteristics of Marston's own language. Obviously offended that his compliment had been so ill-received Marston took revenge in *Jack*

---

[6] The earliest text of this play is a quarto of 1601. This is the 'Italian' version of the play. When the play was printed in the 1616 folio Jonson revised the text and anglicized the characters' names.

[7] This was the first play Jonson published. It survives in a quarto of 1600, and was reprinted in the 1616 folio.

Drum's Entertainment (1600). The quarrel was brought to a head in two plays Jonson wrote for the Children of the Chapel. He satirized Marston as Hedon in *Cynthia's Revels* and as Crispinus in *Poetaster*.[8] Both plays are satires on manners and speech and centre on the larger theme of the importance of language to the health of society.

The first of these plays, *Cynthia's Revels*, was not however designed entirely as a satire on bad poets. It was probably intended as a Twelfth Night play for the Christmas festivities at court in 1600–1, and may even have vied for favour with Shakespeare's *Twelfth Night*.[9] *Cynthia's Revels* is an elaborate compliment to Queen Elizabeth who, according to the common Elizabethan convention, is allegorized as Cynthia. Cynthia's court, the model of morals, manners, and eloquence, is infected by a group of would-be courtiers and would-be poets—of which Hedon is one—and the action of the play is concerned with purging the court of these. Jonson sees these would-be courtiers as suffering from 'self-love': the vice of ignorant pride which was one of the most common for mockery in Saturnalian revels.[10] The play begins with a scene enacting the myth of Echo and Narcissus and demonstrating the significance of the play's theme of self-love. According to mythology, Echo was so enamoured of Narcissus that she pined until she became only an echo, for Narcissus, infatuated with himself, would take no notice of her. Narcissus was changed into a daffodil, yellow in colour (the traditional colour of self-love), which 'Hangs the repentant head, back from the streame/As if it wish'd, would I had neuer look'd/In such a flattering mirrour' (i. ii. 27–9).

Cynthia's Revels has been considered awkward and unsuccessful.[11] It has been suggested that the play 'resembles the fully developed masque' in its 'heavily mythological and allegorical superstructure, and its idealized resolution', and that the contrast between the realistic and the allegorical elements in the play resembles the subsequent contrast of antimasque and masque.[12] Certainly Jonson tries out in this play the possibilities of including myth within drama; although myth and allegory are more properly and more fully developed in his masques. In *Cynthia's Revels* Cynthia as a mythical and symbolic figure embodies all the ideals of human aspiration, especially in literature and morals; she

[8] H & S I, pp. 25 ff.; Small, *Stage-Quarrel*.

[9] Hotson, *First Night*, p. 17.

[10] Hotson, *First Night*, pp. 98–9. In Shakespeare's *Twelfth Night* Malvolio is the character infected with self-love.

[11] Thayer, *Ben Jonson*, considers it an experimental play and suggests that 'perhaps the experiment has not succeeded fully' (p. 34). Hotson, *First Night*, pp. 95–8, sees the play as too sharp and critical to be successful as the twelfth-night entertainment he believes it was written to provide. Ingram, 'Dramatic Use of Music in English Drama', p. 107, sees the second scene as quite separate from the rest of the play in both style and meaning.

[12] Thayer, *Ben Jonson*, p. 37.

is an emblem of the play's values, and her court is the touchstone of manners and morals, of eloquence and wisdom. The play shows us the meaning of these ideals through satire on their antitheses, illustrating the effects on literature and on morals of the courtly abuse of language and eloquence.

In *Cynthia's Revels* Jonson uses song as part of both the mythic and the satirical forms of expression. The use of music in the mythic scenes invokes the philosophical traditions of music as an image of the universal harmony, of a state beyond the temporal dimension of man's actions. The satirical scenes use music as parody. In each case Jonson makes use of the Renaissance Platonist view of music as a symbol of the highest form of wisdom and particularly, when joined with poetry, as having power to lead man to an understanding of the moral basis of the universal plan and to moral action within the microcosm of society.

The first two scenes of the play present us with the two different modes of the play's action and illustrate the relation between them. In this way our response to the satire which forms the centre of the play is given clear direction. Mercury as god of eloquence presides over the whole action. In the first scene Mercury and Cupid, as anthropomorphic figures, meet and discuss Cupid's plan to mingle, as a page, with Cynthia's courtiers in the forthcoming revels[13] and to take revenge on them for 'their so long and ouer-nice proscription of my *deitie*, from their court' (I. i. 111–12).[14] We find later that the reasons for the exclusion of Cupid are twofold. Cynthia, of course, as 'Queen and huntress, chaste and fair', as the 'Virgin Queen', has nothing to do with Cupid; but the 'false' courtiers in her court have excluded him for far less exalted reasons. Simply, they are overcome with *self*-love. Mercury, seeing the possibilities for some amusement, says that he too will disguise himself as a page and join Cupid as soon as he has fulfilled his mission from Jove, which is to allow Echo to

> take a corporall figure, and ascend,
> Enricht with vocall, and articulate power;
>
> (I. ii. 10–11)

and 'to speake [her] sorrowes' by the fountain where her 'loue did pine'.

The second scene of the play, with Echo and Mercury, contains within its emblematic character a synthesis of the play which follows,

---

[13] The reason for Cynthia's revels is told to us by Cupid: 'The Huntresse, and Queene of these groues, DIANA (in regard of some black and enuious slanders hourely breath'd against her, for her diuine iustice on ACTAEON, as shee pretends) hath here in the vale of *Gargaphy*, proclaim'd a solemne reuells, which (her god-head put off) shee will descend to grace, with the full and royall expence of one of her cleerest moones' (I. i. 91–7). Talbert, 'Classical Mythology', p. 193, refers to the generally recognized view that Actaeon represents Essex.

[14] Scene i is based on Lucian's *Dialogues of the Gods*: cf. H & S IX, pp. 492–3. See also Talbert, 'Classical Mythology'.

and in this it may be seen as remoulding the function of dumb-show. The story of Narcissus's self-love provides the lesson on which the rest of the play is based. The song, which Echo sings (ll. 65–75) as the culmination of her long lament distilling the grief and anguish inflicted by the vice of self-love, may be seen as drawing together the two most significant uses of music in the early Senecan and children's drama: that of the dumb-show and the musical lament. Here the music draws attention to the extra-personal qualities of the scene—in a manner similar to the symbolic use of music in dumb-show and to the settings of the musical laments in early children's plays. The song broadens the feeling of personal grief and personal loss, and becomes an image of the universal misery of self-love. So Mercury asks all Nature to join in Echo's song of mourning:

> Begin, and (more to grace thy cunning voice)
> The humorous aire shall mixe her solemne tunes,
> With thy sad words: strike musicque from the spheares,
> And with your golden raptures swell our eares.
>
> (I. ii. 61–4)

The song follows:

> *Slow, slow, fresh fount, keepe time with my salt teares;*
> *Yet slower, yet, ô faintly gentle springs:*
> *List to the heauy part the musique beares,*
> 　　*'Woe weepes out her diuision, when shee sings.*
> 　　　*Droupe hearbs, and flowres;*
> 　　　*Fall griefe in showres;*
> 　　　*'Our beauties are not ours:*
> 　　　　*O, I could still*
> *(Like melting snow vpon some craggie hill,)*
> 　　　*drop, drop, drop, drop,*
> *Since natures pride is, now, a wither'd daffodill.*
>
> (I. ii. 65–75)

Echo's grief has become an image for the opposite of the timeless Truth, the wholeness of vision, which Cynthia's court is and towards a rediscovery of which the play is directed. We are transported here to the realm of absolute grief and chaos which turns even the music of the spheres to a lament. As a summary of the whole scene, as a projection of the universal moral disorder of self-love and not of a personal anguish, the song is not to be merely expressive: the accompaniment 'from the spheares' (presumably the musicians are to be concealed in the music room above the stage) emphasizes these moral qualities and would not be regarded simply as fantastic or supernatural. A comparison with the function of the song in Marston's *Antonio and Mellida* (Act IV) which

EXAMPLE 4. 'Slow, slow, fresh fount'

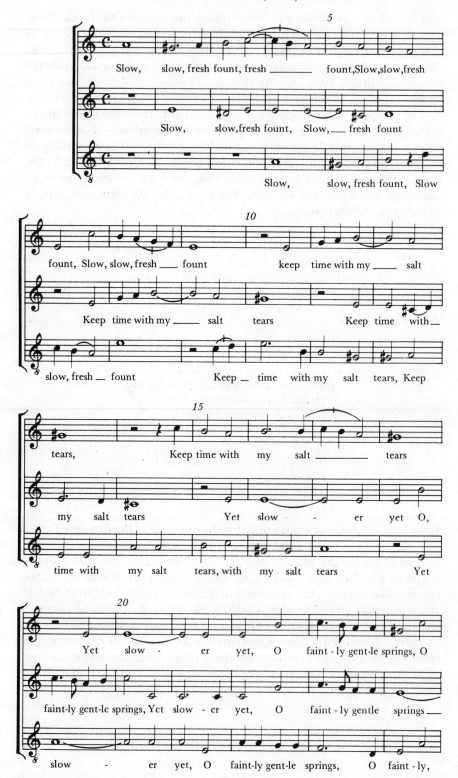

was discussed in Chapter I makes clear in its context the importance of the impersonal qualities of Echo's lament.[15]

There is an extant setting of Echo's lament, by Henry Youll, published in his *Canzonets to Three Voices* (1608). Because this setting is for three voices it is not usually regarded as belonging to a performance of *Cynthia's Revels*; and, indeed, it is common to find songs from plays in arrangements which can have no place in an actual performance of the play. The fact that nothing at all is known about Youll himself makes one even less confident in assigning this setting to Jonson's play. However, it is possible that Youll's setting was originally a solo song for treble, and that the two lower voice parts were added later, for publication, adapted from an instrumental accompaniment. If the upper part only is regarded as a voice part with accompanying instrumental parts weaving and circling about it, the song gains more clear formal definition, for it appears that the music is structurally controlled by the verbal phrases as set in the upper voice part. Anticipations of 'points' by the second and third parts, as in Youll's setting, are common in instrumental accompaniment to solo songs and not only in part-songs. Consort songs provide examples of this. As a solo song the music points up the elegiac mood of Jonson's words and at the same time maintains the musical rather than the verbal form as dominant, in a manner similar to the setting of Pithias' lament in *Damon and Pithias*; a similar relation of words and music is found in the dance ayres of Dowland and Campion.

After Echo's song the scene dissolves and shifts with kaleidoscopic effect resolving itself in the sharper lines of satire. This is clear in the double vision we have of Echo herself. Mercury asks: 'Now, ha' you done?' (I. ii. 76); and Echo, requesting a little longer to retain her voice, now curses Cynthia:

> Here yong ACTAEON fell, pursu'de, and torne
> By CYNTHIA's wrath (more eager, then his hounds)
> And here, (ay me, the place is fatall) see
> The weeping NIOBE, translated hither
> From *Phrygian* mountaines: and by PHŒBE rear'd
> As the proud trophæe of her sharpe reuenge.
>
>   (I. ii. 82–7)

Mercury now reproves Echo's speech as mere idle chattering:

>   Stint thy babling tongue;
> Fond ECCHO, thou prophan'st the grace is done thee:
> So idle worldings (meerely made of voice)
> Censure the powers aboue them.
>
>   (I. ii. 92–5)

---

[15] See above, pp. 35–8.

Jonson draws together in the Echo scene two distinct versions of her story.[16] The first, of Echo as Truth, is clear in her long lament where she says she

> would haue dropt away her selfe in teares,
> Till shee had all turn'd water, that in her,
> (As in a truer glasse)

(I. ii. 32–4)

Narcissus might have seen his own beauty. In this she symbolizes the antithesis of self-love. But as her lament is finished her censure becomes mere idle words, and in 'profaning' the gift of speech she becomes—like the foolish courtiers we are to see in the scene which follows immediately—merely an echo again. Jonson's deliberate conflation of two sources for the story lays emphasis on the fact that the scene is an emblem of the play's meaning. Furthermore, Mercury's final reproof of Echo and Echo's consequent transformation back into a mere echo both lead us forward to the next scene where we meet the first of the 'false' courtiers, Amorphus, and also point up the enclosed and idealistic mode of the lament and the song.

It is this idealistic quality which is presented in the world of Cynthia herself when she appears in Act V; here we realize that she and her world are the ideal which Echo's eloquence has already shown us. The song which introduces v. vi, 'Qveene, and Huntresse' (and for which no music now exists), celebrates the arrival of Cynthia and establishes her non-realistic, idealistic significance.

> Qveene, *and* Huntresse, *chaste, and faire,*
> *Now the* Sunne *is laid to sleepe,*
> *Seated, in thy siluer chaire,*
> *State in wonted manner keepe:*
> HESPERVS *intreats thy light*
> *Goddesse, excellently bright.*
> *Earth, let not thy enuious shade*
> *Dare it selfe to interpose;*
> CYNTHIAS *shining orbe was made*
> *Heauen to cleere, when day did close:*
> *Blesse vs then with wished sight.*
> *Goddesse, excellently bright.*
> *Lay thy bow of pearle apart,*
> *And thy cristall-shining quiuer;*
> *Giue vnto the flying hart*
> *Space to breathe, how short soeuer:*
> *Thou that mak'st a day of night,*
> *Goddesse, excellently bright.*

(V. vi. 1–18)

[16] See Talbert, 'Classical Mythology', pp. 194–8.

The song itself, in its stanzaic form and in its use of a refrain which emphasizes the static, cyclic quality of the poem, is pre-eminently poetry for music. Its patterning of language directs attention to its celebratory and formal, rather than narrative, qualities and in this imitates, and would be complemented by, a dance form and dance music in the style of Dowland's early ayres, for instance. The song which opens v. vi distils the essential significance of the long speeches which follow it and enlarge upon the terms of its celebration.

Between the first and the last acts we are among the would-be courtiers. The play's central scenes are developed as satire on the debasement of morals and manners expressed as a debasement of eloquence. The scene which has immediate satiric point by contrast with Echo's scene (i. ii) is iv. iii in which Hedon and Amorphus each performs his own song. Here Jonson parodies 'fashionable' ideas of the affective relation of words and music, ideas which were taken to absurd extremes in many madrigals, for instance. In this, he shows his own position to be similar to that of the critics in the *Camerata*.[17] The parody is heightened by the fact that the would-be courtiers who perform and discuss the music consider their activities to be in line with the highest philosophical and aesthetic principles. In this scene, the courtiers arrive to meet the ladies of the court who are 'priuately brought in by MORIA' (ii. iv. 109); and together they wait for their pages to bring them water from the newly discovered 'fountain of self-love', Echo's fountain. Cupid has told Mercury that 'Madam MORIA [is] guardian of the *Nymphs'*, that she is 'one that is not now to be perswaded of her wit, shee will thinke her selfe wise against all the iudgements that come. A lady made all of voice, and aire, talkes any thing of any thing. Shee is like one of your ignorant *Poetasters* of the time, who when they haue got acquainted with a strange word, neuer rest till they haue wroong it in, though it loosen the whole fabricke of their sense' (ii. iv. 11–18). Madam Moria reminds us, indeed, of that mother of all Folly Erasmus has shown us; and like Erasmus's Folly this Moria too has her 'women and handmaides'.[18] It is little wonder that they are bored with their own company while they wait for the water of self-love. Erasmus's Folly told us:

[17] See the reference above, pp. 40–1, to Galilei's strictures.

[18] Erasmus, *Folie*, trans. Chaloner (E E T S), p. 13: '[T]his mayde truely, whom ye maie beholde with browes vpcast, lokyng euer as if she wondered at somethyng, is called **Selfloue**. This next hir that fareth as if she flired vpon you, and clappeth hir handes together, is **Adulacion**. This slouggerd, and drowsie head, is named **Obliuion**. This, than, that leaneth on hir elbowes, claspyng hir handes togethers, is called **Lythernes**. This besides hir with the Rose garlande on hir head, and all to perfumed with sweete sauours, is cleped **Voluptuousnes**. This with the rollyng and vnstedfaste eies, is **Madnes**. This other with the slicke skinne, and fayre fedde bodie, is called **Delicacie**.'

take awaie this saulce of **Selflikyng**, which is euin the verie relesse of mans life
and doynges, and by and by ye shal see the **Oratour** cold in his mattier, the
Musicien mislyked with all his discant, the **Plaier** hissed out of the place, the
Poete and his muses laught to skorne . . . [For s]o behouable is it (loe) that
euery man dooe clappe hym selfe on the backe, and with some flattrie be
commendable to hym selfe, ere he can be commended of others.[19]

When the Nymphs and courtiers first meet they devise games to pass
the time. These are word games and acting games modelled on the
pastimes of courts like that of Duke Guidubaldo, described in that most
famous handbook of courtly behaviour, Castiglione's *Il libro del cortegiano*:[20] Moria's nymphs and their lovers have clearly learnt the 'rules'
of courtly manners. Among the entertainments Hedon and Amorphus
are requested to sing to the company. In accordance with the 'rules'
their songs are, of course, to be love songs; for, we are told, the perfect
courtier will inspire love through his music.[21] Hedon's song which is
performed first is called 'The Kisse'.

> *O, That ioy so soone should waste!*
>   *or so sweet a blisse*
>   *as a kisse,*
> *Might not for euer last!*
> *So sugred, so melting, so soft, so delicious,*
>   *The dew that lyes on roses,*
> *When the morne her selfe discloses,*
>   *is not so precious.*
> *O, rather then I would it smother,*
> *Were I to taste such another;*
>   *It should bee my wishing*
>   *That I might dye, kissing.*

(IV. III. 242–53)

Hedon's song-text has the most 'fashionable' of sources in popular
Platonism.[22] That the source is important is clear in that Amorphus's
song about a glove which follows Hedon's song cannot possibly be
sung until he has told a long story about the circumstance of its composition. Amorphus's sources are as impeccable as Hedon's: his story
and his song have been inspired by an episode in Sidney's *Arcadia*.[23]

[19] Erasmus, *Folie*, trans. Chaloner, pp. 29–30.
[20] See below, Chapter I V.
[21] Castiglione, *Il libro del cortegiano*, trans. Hoby, ed. Raleigh, II, p. 119.
[22] In Book I V of *The Courier* Bembo has this to say on the subject: 'although the mouthe be a
percell of the bodye, yet is it an issue for the wordes, that be the enterpreters of the soule, and for
the inwarde breth, which is also called the soule: . . . Whereupon a kisse may be said to be rather a
coopling together of the soule, then of the bodye, bicause it hath such force in her, that it draweth
her unto it, and (as it were) seperateth her from the bodye' (ed. Raleigh, IV, pp. 355–6).
[23] Old version, Book I I I. *The Prose Works of Sir Philip Sidney*, ed. A. Feuillerat, 4 vols.
(Cambridge, 1912), Vol. III, pp. 159–60. The passage is quoted in H & S IX, p. 515.

Furthermore, the songs are accompanied on the fashionable lyra viol, an instrument which had renewed popularity in court circles around 1600 when Daniel Farrant introduced a new form of the instrument to court.[24] When Philautia wishes Hedon to sing she says:

for loue's sake let's haue some musike, till they come. *Ambition*, reach the *lyra*, I pray you—

(IV. iii. 230–1)

and Amorphus comments on the instrument just before he sings:

. . . I composde this *ode*, and set it to my most affected instrument, the *lyra*.

(IV. iii. 303–4)

No setting of Amorphus's song is extant; but there is a contemporary anonymous setting of Hedon's song which was almost certainly written for performance in the play. This occurs in a manuscript in Christ Church, Oxford, Mus. 439, pp. 38–9.[25] The 'philosophy' Hedon's song expresses is a mockery of all that is valuable in the Renaissance Platonist tradition in its exaltation not of the union of two spirits but of the 'baser' senses of taste and touch. This is expressed in poetry which is merely a string of conventional clichés: the 'dew that lies on roses', the rhyme of 'bliss' and 'kiss'. The setting is in the freely declamatory style, for solo voice, advocated by the *Camerata*. But Hedon has also tried to follow the principle of 'expressing' the words in the music, a principle especially recommended by Zarlino in his *Institutioni harmoniche* (1573) and, following Zarlino, by Morley in his *Plain and Easy Introduction* (1597); and in his 'word painting' Hedon has committed the very 'faults' members of the *Camerata* ridiculed. Morley gives this advice for 'expressive' setting:

You must then when you would express any word signifying hardness, cruelty, bitterness, and other such like make the harmony like unto it, that is somewhat harsh and hard, but yet so that it offend not. Likewise when any of your words shall express complaint, dolour, repentance, sighs, tears, and such like let your harmony be sad and doleful. So that if you would have your music signify hardness, cruelty, or other such affects you must cause the parts proceed in their motions without the half note, that is, you must cause them proceed by

[24] See Galpin, *Old English Instruments*, pp. 68–9. The new form of the instrument had sympathetic metal strings beneath the finger-board. We are told that Ficino accompanied his hymns to the sun on an instrument which he called his *lyra* and often his *lyra orphica*: see the discussion by Walker, 'Le Chant orphique'. The relation of the name lyra viol with Ficino's instrument (and the ancient Greek lyra) probably represents a philosophical tradition. See also my discussion, Chan '*Cynthia's Revels*', p. 140.

[25] See also Sabol, 'Newly Discovered Contemporary Song Setting'; Sabol, 'Two Unpublished Stage Songs'; Chan, '*Cynthia's Revels*'. This last discussion considers the song in the context of the whole manuscript. There is also a later setting of 'The Kisse' in the Henry Lawes manuscript in the British Library, catalogued as Loan MS 35 and now renumbered as Add. MS 53723, f.5. This setting was possibly made for a revival of the play although none is recorded beyond one of 1601.

EXAMPLE 5. 'O the joyes that soone should wast'

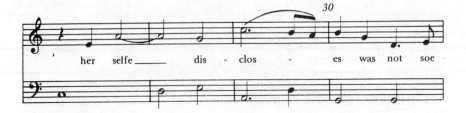

her selfe _____ dis - clos - es was not soe

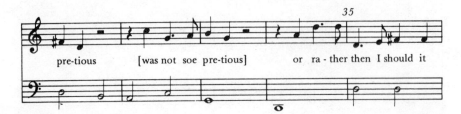

pre-tious [was not soe pre-tious] or ra - ther then I should it

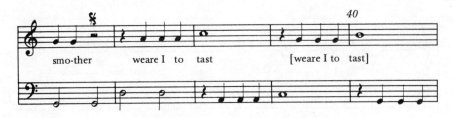

smo-ther weare I to tast [weare I to tast]

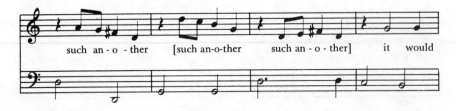

such an - o - ther [such an-o-ther such an - o - ther] it would

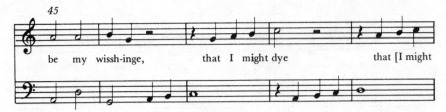

be my wissh-inge, that I might dye that [I might

dye] _____ kiss-inge. [kiss-inge.]

Christ Church MS Mus. 439, pp. 38-9.

[dal segno]

whole notes, sharp thirds, sharp sixths, and such like (when I speak of sharp or flat thirds and sixths you must understand that they ought to be so to the bass); you may also use cadences bound with the fourth or seventh which, being in long notes, will exasperate the harmony. But when you would express a lamentable passion then must you use motions proceeding by half notes, flat thirds, and flat sixths, which of their nature are sweet, specially being taken in the true tune and natural air with discretion and judgement. . . .

We must also have a care so to apply the notes to the words as in singing there be no barbarism committed; that is that we cause no syllable which is by nature short be expressed by many notes or one long note, nor no long syllables be expressed with a short note.[26]

Hedon has taken the 'rules' for setting too literally; and this, coupled with the fact that the words contain very little 'wisdom' worth expressing in any case, creates a setting which is little more than a string of musical clichés, of affective devices. Examples of such devices are the drawn-out ending to the first phrase (bars 12–15), the sequences on 'as a kisse' (bars 7–10) and 'soe soft soe delitious' (bars 18–21), or the minor third on 'soe soft' (bars 18–20). Hedon is particularly proud of the long 'die' note which he discusses with Amorphus after performing the song. The essentially trite nature of the musical setting becomes parodic when its string of affectives devices supports the equally trivial text.

Amorphus's analysis of his song, 'The Glove', shows that he too is aware of the rules for good setting.[27] But it is also clear that Amorphus, like Hedon, is interested merely in following rules.

In children's plays it was common for interlude songs, sometimes songs in some way commenting on the action of the play, to be sung by minor characters between scenes or acts.[28] Jonson uses this convention in *Cynthia's Revels* as part of his criticism of the foolish courtiers in the song which Asotus's page, Prosaites (the beggar), sings (II. v. 1 ff.) as he and the other two pages, Cos (whetstone) and Gelaia (laughter), go off to fetch the water from the Fountain of Self-love.

> *Come follow me, my wagges, and say as I say.*
> *There's no riches but in ragges; hey day, hey day.*
> *You that professe this arte, come away, come away.*
> *And helpe to beare a part. Hey day; hey day, &c.*

(II. v. 1–4)

The quarto text of the play, which almost certainly represents that which was used in the first performance, gives a very much longer version of the song than does the folio text.[29] It may be that this was a

---

[26] Morley, *A Plain and Easy Introduction*, ed. Harman and Dart, pp. 290 and 291.
[27] Amorphus too appears to have read Morley.
[28] See above, pp. 23–30.
[29] H & S IV, p. 80.

popular song and Jonson thought it was therefore not necessary to print the words in full in the folio text. But it seems more plausible that the song is Jonson's own, for it may be seen as deliberately burlesquing the tradition of interact comic song by minor characters. The performance by the pages takes us behind the false and glittering mask which is the world of the foolish courtiers, their masters. In its imitation of cant song, Prosaites' song can only highlight the emptiness of the more superficially polished manners and utterances of the courtiers. Such a point could be effectively made by printing simply the first stanza of the song, as in the folio text.

The link between the false and true courts is Crites. From the beginning we see that the 'false' courtiers regard him as a melancholy and sour man. Hedon says this of him:

I protest, if I had no musique in me, no courtship, that I were not a reueller and could dance, or had not those excellent qualities that giue a man life, and perfection, but a meere poore scholer as he is, I thinke I should make some desperate way with my selfe . . .

(IV. v. 54–8)

At several points in the action Crites comes forward and moralizes on the follies of the false courtiers: his speeches are sharp and epigrammatic criticism, spurning their distrust of him. His role does not touch theirs until Mercury, the god of eloquence (now disguised as Hedon's page), draws him into his plot to expose the false courtiers by outwitting them at their own game of 'court compliment' (v. i).

At this point Crites realizes his responsiblity, as a poet and a scholar, to educate the courtiers. He had at first taken part with Mercury in their game in order simply to expose their falsity. He must now take his art further and make them conform 'To *God's* high figures'; for Crites realizes that, in exposing them, the courtiers—particularly Amorphus and Anaides—believe he is behaving as a madman and are only the more convinced of the harmlessness of their own activities. Mercury's plan has been simply

to make them know
How farre beneath the dignitie of man
Their serious, and most practis'd actions are;

(v. i. 20–2)

but Crites points out that

the huge estate
Phansie, and forme, and sensuall pride haue gotten,
Will make them blush for anger, not for shame;
And turne shewne nakednesse, to impudence.

(v. iv. 625–8)

So Crites, with the help of Arete and the inspiration of Mercury, plans a masque in honour of Cynthia in which these courtiers will take part. Arete says that the presence of Cynthia

> Will keepe them within ring; especially
> When they are not presented as themselues,
> But masqu'd like others.
>
> (v. v. 26–8)

It is, finally, through art that the two aspects of Cynthia's court are brought together and united. The false courtiers are brought to understand their folly not through satire but through taking part in the masque by which they can understand the meaning of Cynthia's court and its true values. Arete's claims for the value of the masque are very close to the claims Jonson later made for his own masques.

After the recantation (the Palinode), the play ends with a song probably sung by all the courtiers:[30]

> *Now each one drie his weeping eyes,*
> *And to the well of knowledge haste;*
> *Where purged of your maladies,*
> *You may of sweeter waters taste;*
> *And, with refined voice, report*
> *The grace of* CYNTHIA, *and her court.*
>
> (Palinode, 35–40)

Songs at the ends of children's plays were common and often served a function similar to that of an epilogue. The song at the end of *Cynthia's Revels* seems deliberately to refer not only to the characters in the play but also outwards to the audience in the theatre; for the play was to be acted at court before Queen Elizabeth and the ending of the play thus delicately compliments the Queen by making clear that she and Cynthia are identified. The song expresses the reconciliation of the true and false aspects of Cynthia's court, a reconciliation brought about by the virtue of Cynthia herself. Furthermore, the song in itself re-creates the essence of Cynthia's court; in that as an image of the ideal of art and virtue the court is also an imitation of the order expressed and symbolized by music.

II

Poetaster, written and performed the following year (1601), continued Jonson's quarrel with Marston. Like *Cynthia's Revels* this play is about the moral significance of bad poetry, although in *Poetaster* Jonson

---

[30] Gifford's edition gives the song to Mercury and Crites.

extended his comments to the relationship of poets to the state rather than restricting himself, as he had done in *Cynthia's Revels*, to the court. The play is set in Augustan Rome: the ideal statesman is illustrated in the person of Caesar Augustus while Horace and Virgil represent the ideal poets.

A consideration of Jonson's use of song in *Poetaster* involves us far less than did *Cynthia's Revels* in an examination of the structure of the play; for the whole play uses no mode other than satire and the songs are rather isolated set pieces serving mainly to sharpen the satire of the scenes in which they occur. Despite the play's title, Crispinus the poetaster is by no means a central figure in the play; although as would-be poet and song-writer he sings at least part of every song except that with which the play ends. This discussion concentrates attention on Jonson's satire of Marston.

I look first at the only song in the play for which a contemporary setting exists: 'If I freely may discouer'.

> *If I freely may discouer,*
> *What would please me in my louer:*
> *I would haue her faire, and wittie,*
> *Sauoring more of court, then cittie;*
> *A little proud, but full of pittie:*
> *Light, and humorous in her toying.*
> *Oft building hopes, and soone destroying,*
> *Long, but sweet in the enioying,*
> *Neither too easie, nor too hard:*
> *All extremes I would haue bard.*[31]

(II. ii. 163–72)

The song is 'one of [Hermogenes'] owne compositions' although Crispinus sings the first stanza and Hermogenes the second, for Crispinus has nothing of his own in spite of all his angling to be entreated to sing. The 'occasion' is a gathering of the 'nobles' who have been invited to the house of the citizen, Albius, to meet Cytheris, Crispinus's cousin, and at which Ovid and his friends discuss their poetry. As was the case with Hedon's and Amorphus's songs, the context of Crispinus's song suggests that he too sets store by following 'rules' for setting words to music, although he, like Hedon, appears oblivious of the conflict between followers of Zarlino and followers of Galilei.

The setting of 'If I freely may discouer' in British Library MS Add. 24665, ff. 59ᵛ–60, seems to belong to an early performance of the play because it makes clear the fashionable quality of Crispinus's song in its

---

[31] There is another stanza to this song, I. ii. 179–88. This is not given with the musical setting, and the 'affection' in the setting corresponds to the words of stanza one only.

EXAMPLE 6. 'Yf I freely may discouer'

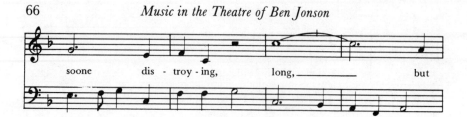

soone   dis - troy - ing,   long, _____   but

30

sweet   in   her   en - ioy - ing,

35

nei - ther   too   ea - sy,   nor   too   hard,   but

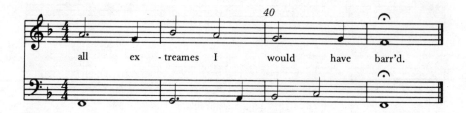

40

all   ex - treames   I   would   have   barr'd.

B.L. MS Add. 24665, ff. 59v-60.

Notes.

3	Bass II	:	MS = F
18	Treble I	:	MS = minim rest
27	Bass I	:	MS = E
28-9			Editorial tie
33	Bass I	:	MS = ♩
	Treble	:	MS gives only 2 minim rests before the triple-time bar.
36	Bass	:	There appears to be a bar missing. If we accept the two minim rests in the treble (32 and 33) and make the triple-time section begin one bar earlier, reading ♩ ♩ ♩ (33 bass) as ♩. ♩ the missing bar is accounted for - numerically. It makes unsatisfactory harmony, however.

context and emphasizes the satiric purpose of the words.[32] Like Hedon's song the music attempts to express the words both in rhythm and sense; but because the sense of the words is trivial the setting too sounds banal and its close following of the words becomes parodic. Crispinus uses a *tripla* section at bars 19–22 and in the final line (bars 34–7) to support the sense of 'humorous' (although in the manuscript version this is given as 'amorous') and 'neither too easy', he uses long notes to express 'full' (bar 16) and 'long' (bars 28–9), and he sets 'oft building hopes' (bars 24–5) to an ascending passage while 'and soon destroying' is set to a descending figure ending with a drop of a perfect fourth on 'destroying.' Clear declamation of the words is carried to extremes by the very four-square, tedious emphasis given to the opening lines.

The British Library manuscript version gives a bass viol accompaniment, and if Crispinus sang his song accompanied this would probably have been the instrument he used. In Act IV, scene iii when Crispinus again asks to be entreated to sing he approaches the subject by pretending to have just noticed that there is a viol in the room which he assumes is 'my cousin CYTHERIS violl' (IV. iii. 52–3). The song which Crispinus sings at this point, and which turns out to be mostly cribbed from Horace himself, is obviously accompanied on the viol.[33] Just as Hedon followed the Continental fashion in accompanying himself on the lyra viol so too Crispinus's song requires a simple bass viol accompaniment which harmonically supports the melodic line rather than a more elaborate or polyphonic accompaniment such as could be provided by a lute.

The satire on Crispinus is a minor part of the main action which centres on the poetry and ideals of the younger Ovid. Crispinus illustrates the more foolish and ridiculous aspects of Ovid's cultivation of poetry and of his extravagant and exaggerated expression of his love for Julia, as, for example, in his long soliloquy in I. ii. 229–56 or his conversation with Tibullus, I. iii. 20–58. The turning-point of the play is Act IV scene v in which the literary circle meets for a banquet disguised as gods and goddesses. The revelry has degenerated into tipsy quarrelling when Augustus bursts in and banishes the would-be

---

[32] Although there is a later setting of the song by Henry Lawes in B.L. M S Add. 53723, f. 7 (see note on the cataloguing of this manuscript, note 25 above) and in New York Public Library, Drexel M S 4257 (John Gamble's Commonplace Book), no. 25, this setting would not belong to an early seventeenth-century performance of the play, but may have been used for a revival, although none is recorded. Lawes's setting seems to take Jonson's words too seriously. The claim that the setting in B.L. M S Add. 24665 was used in the play, on the other hand, may be supported by the fact that this manuscript contains several other songs which can be identified with plays. See Chan, '*Cynthia's Revels*', p. 150, footnote 32; p. 158, footnote 56; and p. 161, footnote 63.

[33] There is no music extant for this song.

poets from the court. Although later his anger is balanced and modified by the more moderate judgement of Horace that this is 'innocent mirth,/And harmelesse pleasures, bred, of noble wit' and thus no direct menace to the state, the degeneracy of the feast from the ideal banquet and masque it was to have been is shown to us very clearly; and it is clear also in the song. As in *Cynthia's Revels* while the courtiers waited for the water from the Fountain of Self-love they were entertained by songs to relieve their boredom, so in this scene in *Poetaster* Albius, Crispinus, and Hermogenes sing. The songs exhort their friends to more mirth and feasting and to awake from their drowsiness. Hermogenes the musician, here ironically masked as Mercury the god of eloquence, and Crispinus masked as Momus the critic, express the disorder of the whole scene in this song. It is towards the rectifying of this disorder that the ending of the play is directed.

[*Crispinus:*]
> *Wake, our mirth begins to die:*
> *Quicken it with tunes, and wine:*
> *Raise your notes, you're out: fie, fie,*
> *This drouzinesse, is an ill signe.*
> *We banish him the queere of Gods,*
> *That droops agen:*
> *Then all are men,*
> *For here's not one, but nods.* [34]

HERM.   *Then, in a free and lofty straine,*
        Our broken tunes we thus repaire;
CRIS.   *And we answere them againe,*
        Running diuision on the panting aire;
AMBO.   *To celebrate this feast of* sense,
        As free from scandall, as offence.
HERM.   *Heare is* beautie, *for the eye;*
CRIS.   *For the eare, sweet* melodie;
HERM.   Ambrosiack odours, *for the smell;*
CRIS.   *Delicious* nectar, *for the taste;*
AMBO.   *For the touch, a* ladies waste;
        Which doth all the rest excell!

                        (VI. v. 176–83, 188–99)

Like *Cynthia's Revels*, this play too ends with a song, probably sung by all the characters on-stage:

> *Blush, folly, blush: here's none that feares*
> *The wagging of an asses eares,*
> *Although a wooluish case he weares.*

---

[34] Gifford's edition gives this song to Albius.

> *Detraction is but basenesse varlet;*
> *And apes are apes, though cloth'd in scarlet.*
> (v. iii, 626–30)[35]

However, unlike the song at the end of *Cynthia's Revels*, 'Blush, folly blush' simply moralizes on folly and goes no further than providing a conventional ending to the play.

In his use of music in *Poetaster* Jonson has retreated from the ambitious and rather complex experiments with different modes which he used in *Cynthia's Revels*. In *Poetaster* the songs are used mainly as incidental and supporting satire, and the scenes in which they occur are not central in the play. Maybe Jonson realized that within the confines of 'comicall satyre' the songs in the mythical scenes of *Cynthia's Revels* would, in performance, appear to have little more than an illustrative function; perhaps the mixing of modes was not in itself completely successful. On the other hand the larger scope of *Poetaster*'s social satire obviously demanded a style different from that of *Cynthia's Revels*. The songs in *Poetaster*, then, have a simple and purely parodic function as satires on folly and immorality.

III

Jonson's final play for the Children of the Chapel (or the Children of her Majesty's Revels as they were now called) was *Epicoene* (1609). Although in this play Jonson moved away from the more esoteric realm of court satire which we saw in *Cynthia's Revels* and from the classical setting of *Poetaster*, nevertheless, like those two, *Epicoene* is about abuses of language and speech as symptoms of an immoral society. But *Epicoene* takes us directly into Jonson's London.

The pernicious and extensive nature of the society's lack of decorum in manners and language is pointed up in the contrast Jonson creates between the first act of the play which takes place in Clerimont's house and the subsequent acts which take place at Morose's and Mistress Otter's houses. The first act also contains the only song in the play (I. i),[36] and its function in the first scene may have been developed from the function of Echo's song in the second scene of *Cynthia's Revels*, which provided a touchstone of values, an exposition against which the rest of the play was measured. However, in *Cynthia's Revels* the contrast between the mythic and the satiric scenes was absolute; and although Jonson attempted to bring allegory and realism together through the figure of Crites, the final lesson of the play was more explicitly didactic

---

[35] There is no music extant for this song.

[36] One could, perhaps, count Sir Jack Daw's *'madrigall* of modestie' (II. iii. 25 f.) and his verses (II. iii. 123 f.) written for Epicoene but there is no indication that these were to be sung in a performance of the play.

than allegory alone might have been. In *Epicoene*, the relationship between the first scene and those following it is rather more complex.

The scene opens in Clerimont's house. Clerimont's page is about to perform a song Clerimont has composed when they are interrupted by Truewit who rebukes Clerimont for idly wasting his time 'betweene his mistris abroad, and his engle at home, high fare, soft lodging, fine clothes, and his fiddle' (I. i. 24–6). Already we hear expressed—in Truewit's comment on Clerimont's manner of existence—a hint of the confusion of sexual decorum we see later in the play, and we have heard it expressed too in the conversation between Clerimont and his page before Truewit's arrival. The page has told of his reception by Clerimont's mistress, Lady Haughty, like this;

The gentlewomen play with me, and throw me o' the bed; and carry me in to my lady; and shee kisses me with her oil'd face; and puts a perruke o' my head; and askes me an' I will weare her gowne; and I say, no: and then she hits me a blow o' the eare, and calls me innocent, and lets me goe.

(I. i. 13–18)

However, Clerimont appears to believe himself isolated from London gossip and affairs: he tells Truewit he 'came but from court, yesterday' (I. i. 72). He has not heard of the new college which, Truewit now tells him, is presided over by Clerimont's mistress, the Lady Haughty. On hearing this Clerimont believes that the unnaturalness of the college simply confirms the validity of his instinctive dislike of his mistress's elaborate dressing and make-up. It is on this very subject that he has composed his song which the Page will now sing for Truewit.

> *Still to be neat, still to be drest,*
> *As, you were going to a feast;*
> *Still to be pou'drd, still perfum'd:*
> *Lady, it is to be presum'd,*
> *Though arts hid causes are not found,*
> *All is not sweet, all is not sound.*
>
> *Giue me a looke, giue me a face,*
> *That makes simplicitie a grace;*
> *Robes loosely flowing, haire as free:*
> *Such sweet neglect more taketh me,*
> *Then all th'adulteries of art.*
> *They strike mine eyes, but not my heart.*

(I. i. 91–102)

Two seventeenth-century settings of the song exist; both are almost certainly later than 1609, the date of the play's first performance. One setting occurs in New York Public Library, Drexel MS 4257, no. 179 and in Drexel MS 4041, no. 64; the other is in John Playford's *Select*

Ayres and Dialogues (1669), Sig. M.2 (p. 51), entitled 'On a Proud Lady'. The setting in the two Drexel manuscripts may have been used in the revival of the play in 1636 by the King's Men; and although Playford's version is probably an anthology piece it is possible that it is the setting used in one or more of the revivals of the play in the early 1660s.[37] The song may quite early have been regarded as an anthology piece, for its function in the first scene appears to be somewhat of a 'set piece'—from the point of view both of Clerimont himself and of the subsequent action of the play. For however fine Clerimont's aesthetic values may appear from his song, we have seen in the conversation immediately preceding it (I. i. 85–9) that his real dislike of Lady Haughty's elaborate dress preparations lies in the fact that they cause him to be kept waiting at her door! The song, both in its statement and in the circumstances of its composition, reflects an ideal of courtly behaviour with which Clerimont clearly wishes to be associated. The words themselves are part of the very popular Renaissance debate of art versus nature: in the first stanza Clerimont describes the 'unsoundness' of over-elaboration, and in stanza two suggests instead the value, not of complete artlessness, but of art emulating nature, art concealing art.[38] As a set piece the song is a commentary on artistic value which may be expanded to include aspects of other social values criticized within the scenes that follow. In this respect its function is rather similar to that of the second, mythic scene of *Cynthia's Revels*. The difference, however, is important. Attention is drawn to the song by the fact that near the very beginning of the scene the boy is about to sing it when he is interrupted by Truewit's entry; and by the time the boy is requested to sing again we have already listened to the conversation between Truewit and Clerimont about the song's subject, Lady Haughty, and her membership of the college. After the song and Truewit's ardent support of 'painting' and dressing the conversation shifts to Morose and then, with Dauphine's entrance, to a discussion of Epicoene herself. Thus, the conversation surrounding the actual performance of the song hedges and qualifies the simplicity of its values—as it qualifies the seeming simplicity of Clerimont's own attitude. Through the play we see these qualifications worked out and exemplified as Clerimont himself becomes involved in Dauphine's plot, and is forced to prove his allegiance to these values—something which was not tested in the solitude of his room. Later in the play we see Clerimont falling in with Truewit's admiration of 'a good dressing' (IV. i. 32–4). To this extent

---

[37] Lefkowitz, *William Lawes*, p. 159, ascribes the Playford version to William Lawes. William Lawes was composing for the King's Men in the 1630s so this could well have been written for a revival then. See Cutts, 'B.M. M S Add. 31432'.

[38] For a full discussion see Thayer, *Ben Jonson*, pp. 71–2.

the song remains precept only. It stands on its own, as an ideal never achieved.

Unlike the other two children's plays, and in contrast to the custom in children's comedies, this play does not end with a song. Although the trick against Morose is worked out and concluded fortunately, the rest of the immoral society remains: in particular the college. So the values of Clerimont's song for the whole play are not illustrated in a simple didactic resolution. Rather, the acknowledgement of the song's values for the play lies with the audience—in their laughter.

IV

Jonson's three plays for children examine the relation of language to social order and decorum, and in this they expand the satire of many of the epigrams which criticize foppery, plagiarism, affectation of fine clothes, cowardice, all of which in *Epicoene* are shown to be not only unnatural, and therefore laughable, but to cause social degradation and chaos. Because Jonson's chief concern in these plays is with various kinds of language, in the plays' use of song he draws on current philosophical ideas about music as an aspect of affective rhetoric, as an 'ornament' of eloquent discourse, and as reflecting in men's affairs the order of divine harmony which music was believed to imitate. Hedon's, Amorphus's, and Crispinus's abuse of this kind of eloquence exemplifies their stupidity and inanity and the inanity of the society which applauds them. The other side of this coin, the ideal, is reflected in the music of Cynthia's court, a music which expresses perfect order and supreme eloquence. Clerimont's song, which remains free from the action of the play while at the same time being included within its dramatic meaning, makes a more subtle point than the simple evocation of a 'philosophy' of music, which is, perhaps, as far as Jonson goes in the two earlier children's plays. This may be largely attributed to the fact that *Epicoene* is a more tightly constructed play than *Cynthia's Revels*.

In the next chapter I consider the use of song in two plays for the wider audience of the public theatre, especially in *Volpone* (1605) written four years before *Epicoene*. This play demonstrates a similar conviction about language and society and in it Jonson again makes use of ideas of words and music as illustrating an aesthetic and moral ideal. Jonson's statement of his principles about the poet's relation to society in the Dedication of *Volpone* is a statement of the principles we see informing *Cynthia's Revels*, *Poetaster*, and *Epicoene* as well. But the vigour of Volpone takes these ideas far beyond what is, even in *Epicoene*, a lesson rather too neatly set out.

3

Volpone *and* The Devil is an Ass

JONSON'S DEDICATION of *Volpone* to 'the two famous Universities' contains perhaps his most often cited statements about poetry. Certainly, the substance of many passages in the Dedication which refer to the social function of poetry occurs in some form in the Prologues to his other plays, and is applicable not only to *Volpone*. Crites, for instance, in *Cynthia's Revels*, and Horace, in *Poetaster*, have both demonstrated Jonson's claim that 'if men will impartially, and not à-squint, looke toward the offices, and function of a Poet, they will easily conclude to themselues, the impossibility of any mans being the good Poet, without first being a good man'.[1] But the comedies Jonson wrote for the public theatre, between 1605 and 1616, reach beyond the fairly simple didactic statements of the early children's plays. This chapter will consider some aspects of the first and last plays in this group—*Volpone* and *The Devil is an Ass*—because in these two plays Jonson has used song, and the Renaissance ideals of the relationship of poetry to music, in a manner which appears to be a development of his parodic use of song in *Cynthia's Revels* and *Poetaster*. The songs in *Volpone*, for instance, are an important part of a comic portrayal of immorality and greed. But they seem better integrated within the play and are not used to discredit the characters in the simple way Hedon's and Crispinus's were. Furthermore, although Volpone's famous song to Celia (III. vii. 165) as an anthology piece appears to conform to some of the Renaissance ideals of love-song, it is not a direct expression of a possible ideal—such as Clerimont's song in *Epicoene* represents. In this chapter I shall discuss *Volpone* first, and in some detail, because Jonson's use of song here is more complex and interesting and because this play in any case is more richly allusive than the later *The Devil is an Ass*.

I

There are four songs in *Volpone*. The first occurs in I. ii. 66–81 and is the song which Nano and Castrone sing in praise of the fool, Androgyno, to conclude the Interlude Mosca has arranged for Volpone's entertainment. There are two songs, the first performed by Nano and the second by Nano and Mosca, in the scene where Volpone, disguised as a mountebank, entertains the crowd beneath the window of Corvino's

---

[1] *Volpone*, Dedication, ll. 20–3.

house: II. ii. 120–32, 191–203. The fourth song, and the only one for which music survives, is the song Volpone sings to woo Corvino's wife Celia: III. vii. 165–83 and 236–9. Because we have a setting of this last song, one which would almost certainly have been used in the first performances of the play, the discussion of Volpone's song to Celia can be fuller than that of the other three. It will be considered in relation both to the other songs in the play and to the play itself.

The main theme of the play, like that of the earlier plays for children, centres on the relationships between language and social morality and decorum. But in *Volpone* the comedy is much sharper and more bitter than in the earlier plays. Volpone is an actor—in the methods he uses both to deceive the birds of prey and to attract the attention of Corvino's wife, Celia. Through Volpone's various kinds of role-playing—and also through the roles Mosca, his servant, plays—and by the relationship of action and speech, Jonson illustrates his theme of the decadence of language and decorum in contemporary society. But the values which Jonson expresses in the Dedication of the play are shown not as simple ones (as they appeared in the earlier plays); rather they are shown to us through a continually shifting interplay between role and identity, and it is in this that the comedy also lies. For the adoption of roles within the play is not only deliberate, but, more disastrously for Volpone, becomes also unconscious. The audience is made to laugh first of all *with* Volpone, at his tricking of the birds of prey: not until later in the play do we find we are also laughing *at* a mimicry of ourselves. The most obvious instance of this interplay between role and identity, and that which carries the main action of the play, is the comic relationship between Volpone playing the fox who feigns dead and our view of Volpone, the fox. On the one hand, by drawing on popular folklore and bestiaries which describe the cunning of the fox and treat him as anthropomorphic, Jonson is able to maintain our laughter and sympathy with Volpone. On the other hand, by inverting the popular stories where a fox behaves like a man, and making a man behave like a fox, he is at the same time forcing us to make moral judgements.

In particular, there are two main sources in folklore and beast-fable which Jonson appears to have used in *Volpone*. Both would have been thoroughly familiar to his audience at the Globe in 1605, part of traditional inherited lore. The first of these sources is the bestiaries, medieval natural-history books which described both observable and fabulous characteristics of the behaviour of certain animals and drew from these a moralistic comment pointing a parallel between animal and human nature. A recent translation of a medieval bestiary gives this entry under 'fox' (*volpis*):

[The fox] is a fraudulent and ingenious animal. When he is hungry and nothing turns up for him to devour, he rolls himself in red mud so that he looks as if he were stained with blood. Then he throws himself on the ground and holds his breath, so that he positively does not seem to breathe. The birds, seeing that he is not breathing, and that he looks as if he were covered with blood with his tongue hanging out, think he is dead and come down to sit on him. Well, thus he grabs them and gobbles them up.

The Devil has the nature of this same.

With all those who are living according to the flesh he feigns himself to be dead until he gets them in his gullet and punishes them. But for spiritual men of faith he is truly dead and reduced to nothing.[2]

In the bestiary, the fable is a moral *exemplum*: the identification of the fox with the Devil in the final paragraph is precisely the point of the whole tale. The cunning of the fox is wicked and immoral because he is really the Devil. So, we might say, at the end of Jonson's play, the fox is punished as though he were the devil of the bestiary story. The play, however, is not so simple as the beast-fable, nor can the ending be seen in the simple black and white of the bestiary story. This is at any rate partly due to the fact that Jonson draws on another very popular source for fox stories: *Reynard the Fox*.[3]

From his first appearance in the twelfth-century animal epic by Pierre de St Cloud (*c.*1175) Reynard the fox had a long and complicated history in Europe throughout the middle ages, for the original epic ended in such a way that it could be continued and imitated very easily. The fox appears briefly in England in a short poem, nearly one hundred years later than the original epic, *Of the Vox and the Wolf* (*c.*1250). He does not reappear in English literature until about 1390 when we find him in Chaucer's 'Nun's Priest's Tale' in the *Canterbury Tales*, under the name of Daun Russell. In 1481, almost one hundred years later again, William Caxton translated and published *The History of Reynard the Fox*, a translation from a Dutch edition, printed in Gouda, which was itself a translation of a Flemish version of the story.

Because Reynard appears only sporadically and comparatively late

[2] White, *The Book of Beasts*, pp. 53–4. This is a translation of a manuscript prose bestiary copied in the twelfth century and now in the University Library, Cambridge, self-mark II. 4. 26. See also McCulloch, *Medieval Latin and French Bestiaries*, pp. 119–20. The association of fox and Devil is biblical: Christ refers to Herod as a fox in Luke 13: 32. The first part of the quotation which describes the behaviour of real foxes is discussed by Knoll, *Jonson's Plays*, pp. 83–7. The story also occurs in a more 'scientific' natural-history book which Jonson owned: Conrad Gesner, *Historia animalium* (1557). This work is mentioned by Knoll and discussed in detail by Schève, 'Jonson's *Volpone*'. Jonson's audience would have also been familiar with Spenser's 'Mother Hubbard's Tale'.

[3] Knoll, *Jonson's Plays*, also refers to the stories of Reynard but he does not suggest any specific connections between Volpone and Reynard. He points out (p. 88) that in Caxton's translation there is a story which shows Reynard behaving like the bestiary fox who feigns dead. The story is on p. 109 of Sands's edition.

in English literature he escapes the moralizing—much of it super-ficial—that surrounded the French stories of Reynard throughout the middle ages. These, like the bestiaries, identified the fox as the Devil. Reynard was well known in England, however, throughout the middle ages and this was why Chaucer's story was so popular although it was much later than the original epic. Reynard would probably have been known from oral tradition, although the influence of this is difficult to assess. But perhaps the most obvious source of knowledge is to be found in the numerous carvings in medieval churches throughout England of the exploits of Reynard.[4] His appearance in church probably stems from the French use of the story as a moral *exemplum*; but because his adventures were described only in pictures, with no text to draw a moral, Reynard remained in the English tradition, as in the early versions, a kind of villain-hero, and did not necessarily become identified with the Devil. Furthermore, in Flemish versions of the Reynard stories, perpetuated in English versions by Caxton's transla-tion, the court of Noble the Lion, King of the Beasts, to which Reynard is brought several times to answer for his misdeeds, is an easily corrupt-ible one. This makes Reynard's escape the more acceptable.

Jonson's audience at the Globe, watching *Volpone*, would recognize in the play some of the characteristics of the Reynard stories. For instance, one of the most popular of these stories tells of Reynard's seduction of Hersent, the wife of Isengrin, the wolf. Jonson uses this, ironically, in the attempted 'seduction' of Volpone by Lady Politique Would-bee, to whom Volpone refers as 'my shee-wolfe' (v. ii. 66). Reynard lives in a castle called Maupertuis ('evil hole') which has many secret exits so when he is inside he is safe from harm. Similarly, Volpone's house is a kind of 'safe' territory in which his duping of the birds of prey in order to gain their wealth appears comic rather than immoral. Disaster comes for Volpone only when he finally leaves his house to taunt the birds of prey in the streets of Venice. The court which judges Volpone, like that which judges Reynard, is manifestly corrupt and corruptible. Finally, both Reynard and Volpone have a charac-teristic in common which is essential to their trickery; both enjoy acting parts and are, on the whole successful. Volpone says to Mosca,

> Yet, I glory
> More in the cunning purchase of my wealth,
> Then in the glad possession.
>
> (i. i. 30–2)

At the same time as they hint at the more sinister implications of Volpone's desire for gold, the opening scenes of the play exhibit this

[4] See Varty, *Reynard the Fox*, for a full discussion, illustrations, and a list of sources.

delight in acting in the way Volpone tricks the birds of prey. Even in the
opening scene of the play, Volpone's 'morning hymn' to his gold, we are
aware of both aspects of Volpone. As William Empson has pointed out,
the speech acts rather as satire intended by Volpone than satire of
Volpone.[5] This means that our initial response is one of humour at
Volpone's extravagant language rather than revulsion at the inversion
of Christian values. We are amused rather than shocked at Volpone's
praise of riches as 'the dumbe god, that giu'st all men tongues'. If we
consider Volpone's opening speech beside the speech of Marlowe's
miser, Barabas, at the opening of *The Jew of Malta* the source of our
amusement at Volpone becomes clearer. Jonson may even have
intended to evoke Barabas's speech in his audience's mind so that the
parodic qualities of Volpone's speech might be more obvious.[6] The
difference between the two lies in the extravagance and exuberance of
Volpone's praise of his gold, an exuberance which is continued
throughout the scene in the way Mosca and Volpone egg one another
on. The extravagance suspends for the moment our response to the
moral implications of the scene and in this way Jonson leads us,
deliberately, into sharing Volpone's delight at his tricking the birds of
prey.

But Mosca's role is neither entirely passive nor entirely as subser-
vient as Volpone appears to believe. In the second scene of the play,
Nano, Androgyno, and Castrone perform Mosca's Interlude for Volpone's entertainment. The Interlude promotes the suspension of our
judgement and the confusion of values which the opening scene created
by diverting our attention from the main promises of action suggested
by that scene. But the Interlude, in which Nano describes the doctrine
of metempsychosis, is more than merely a reflection of the chaotic
'values' of Volpone's household, it does more than simply show us the
debasement of Volpone's values— by showing us that the soul of Apollo
now resides in the hermaphrodite Androgyno, Volpone's household
fool.[7] Furthermore, its emphasis on the importance of the fool, his

[5] Empson, 'Volpone', p. 653.

[6] Although the differences between the the two opening speeches are important the implications
of the Machiavel which Barabas is in Marlowe's play are carried over, satirically, to Volpone. If
we do not immediately call to mind Machiavelli's own remark that the statesman must be a
combination of fox and lion, we later meet the caricature of the Would-be Machiavel, Sir Politique
Would-bee, who claims to learn from 'NIC: MACHIAVEL, and monsieur BODINE' (IV. i. 26). See
also Barish, 'Double Plot'. For the meanings of the word 'politic' in sixteenth-century England, see
Praz, *Machiavelli and the Elizabethans*, pp. 10–15, and p. 26 for a discussion of Jonson's Sir Politique
Would-bee. Not until later in the play do we see the relation between Sir Politique Would-bee and
Volpone himself. The setting of *Volpone* in Venice would have supported, in the popular imagina-
tion, any sinister implications of Volpone as Machiavel: see Levin, 'Jonson's Metempsychosis', p.
235.

[7] Thayer, *Ben Jonson*, pp. 50–66 describes how the 'golden age' of Apollo has now become the
'golden age' of Volpone.

ability to speak 'truth, free from slaughter' (I. ii. 75) because of his
freedom from social bonds and values, does not merely reflect Volpone's special position with regard to the legacy hunters. Because the
Interlude is Mosca's 'inuention' it also speaks for Mosca himself and
hints that Mosca's position with regard to Volpone in some respects
mirrors that of Volpone with the birds of prey.[8] This more sinister
undertone—sinister because Mosca does not appear to take himself
quite so seriously as Volpone—is brought to the surface later in the
play where we see Mosca more clearly revealed in his soliloquy in
praise of parasites. Here Mosca muses that

> All the wise world is little else, in nature,
> But Parasites, or Sub-parasites,

and sees himself not as a common parasite but

> your fine, elegant rascall, that can rise,
> And stoope (almost together) like an arrow;
> Shoot through the aire, as nimbly as a starre;
> Turne short, as doth a swallow; and be here,
> And there, and here, and yonder, all at once;
> Present to any humour, all occasion;
> And change a visor, swifter, then a thought!
>
> (III. i. 23–9)

The Interlude does not simply reinforce but complicates the view we
have had of Volpone in Act I, scene i.[9] Mosca too has a part to play.
And we cannot fail to notice that although the Fox is only feigning dead
he has already attracted the flesh-fly. Only after these two scenes do we
see the way Volpone and Mosca behave towards the birds of prey as
they gather one by one.

After Corvino, the last of the legacy hunters, has left, Mosca tells
Volpone about Corvino's beautiful wife, Celia, who is kept locked up by
her jealous husband and guarded by paid spies. Volpone immediately
falls for Mosca's description. And it is his desire to add her to his horde

---

[8] But the song which ends the interlude closely follows passages from Erasmus's *Praise of Folly*.
See H & S IX, p. 693. This must qualify it—for the audience—as praise of either Volpone or
Mosca.

[9] Mosca's Interlude is discussed in some detail by Levin, 'Jonson's Metempsychosis'. Levin
points out the source of the Interlude, Lucian's *The Dream*, to which Nano refers in l. 24 when he
mentions the cobbler's cock. In Lucian's story the poor cobbler is dreaming that great wealth is
about to be bestowed on him when he is awakened by his cock crowing. His annoyance at being
woken gives way to astonishment when the cock begins to speak to him, describing how he has
inherited the soul of Pythagoras. The story of the cobbler's cock is paralleled in *Volpone* by
Volpone's deception of the birds of prey, but it is also paralleled, ironically, in what happens to
Volpone himself. The cock and the fool are traditionally associated: see Willeford, *The Fool and his
Sceptre*, Chapter I. From the time that Volpone's own household fool, Androgyno, is set free to
roam abroad in the streets, Volpone's downfall is imminent.

which complicates his plots and finally brings about his downfall. Mosca describes Celia like this:

> O, sir, the wonder,
> The blazing starre of *Italie!* a wench
> O' the first yeere! a beautie, ripe, as haruest!
> Whose skin is whiter then a swan, all ouer!
> Then siluer, snow, or lillies! a soft lip,
> Would tempt you to eternitie of kissing!
> And flesh, that melteth, in the touch, to bloud!
> Bright as your gold! and louely, as your gold!
>
> (i. v. 107–14)

The rhetoric of Volpone's 'hymn' to his gold with which the first act opened, and that of Mosca's praise of Celia which almost concludes the act are dangerously similar. Was Volpone's 'hymn' after all so clearly conscious satire, so clearly disinterested, that he seems now unaware that Mosca parodies him? Or is it simply that Mosca has unconsciously picked up Volpone's idiom? Volpone's desire to excel all men in cleverness, which is central to his adoption of roles, is equalled only by his desire to excel them in possessions. In this he takes himself too seriously and makes himself vulnerable to Mosca's suggestion. Volpone absolutely must see Celia, even if only in disguise and through a window. The first act, as a whole, provides us with an indication of the play's mode and direction.

II

After Act I we are not immediately shown Volpone's next move: we are shown instead a completely different situation and a completely different set of characters. Our response to the ridiculous conversation which takes place in Act II, scene i between Peregrine and Sir Politique Would-bee parallels our equivocal response to the action of Act I.

As his name suggests, Sir Politique Would-bee tries to emulate the 'politic' Machiavel.[10] But the name by which he is most often addressed in the play, Sir Pol, reminds us that he too belongs within the beast fable: he is part of this world of animal-men. He is the parrot, the mimic, the 'would-be' politic.[11] It has been suggested that Sir Pol is a comic distortion of Volpone himself;[12] and, indeed, the whole of the sub-plot is a burlesque of Volpone's own plots. Sir Pol is both the guller and the gull, in that he invents plots and then spends his time escaping from them. He has characteristics of both Volpone and the birds of prey. Furthermore, Sir Pol is an outsider in Venetian society: he is an

[10] See note 6.
[11] See Barish, 'Double Plot' for a full discussion.
[12] See Barish, 'Double Plot'.

Englishman travelling in Italy, and thus the sub-plot connects the main action with Jonson's own country and brings its point closer to Jonson's audience. Peregrine has been described as performing in a minor way Jonson's own role of comic poet. But this is complicated by the fact that Peregrine's final tricking of Sir Pol is motivated at least partly by revenge for a plot which Peregrine simply imagined was Sir Pol's.[13] Nevertheless, Peregrine may remind us of the pilgrim falcon, a bird 'sacred to APOLLO' as Jonson describes it in Epigramme 85, who 'doth instruct men by her gallant flight . . . to strike ignorance . . . [and] make the foole [her] quarrie'.[14] The sub-plot echoes, on a level of almost pure farce, some of the complications and implications of the main plot.

The only scene in which Peregrine and Sir Pol appear as part of the main plot is the scene in which Volpone disguises himself as a mountebank and sets up his platform in the piazza under Celia's window (II. ii). Peregrine and Sir Pol form part of his audience. Peregrine's scorn of mountebanks as impostors, on the one hand, and Sir Pol's admiration, on the other, provide ironic commentary on Volpone's whole act. Sir Pol describes mountebanks as

> the onely-knowing men of *Europe!*
> Great generall schollers, excellent phisicians,
> Most admir'd states-men, profest fauorites,
> And cabinet-counsellors, to the greatest princes!
> The onely languag'd-men, of all the world!
>
> (II. ii. 9–13)

while Peregrine regards mountebanks as

> most lewd imposters;
> Made all of termes, and shreds; no lesse belyers
> Of great-mens fauors, then their owne vile med'cines.
>
> (II. ii. 14–16)

This scene is important not only as Volpone's first attempt to gain Celia's attention and thus as initiating the central part of the plot, but also, and more specifically from the point of view of our interest in Jonson's use of song, as complementary to the scene in which Volpone tries to seduce Celia in his own house (III. vii). In both scenes songs are integral to the action and define more clearly our attitude to Volpone himself.

In order to attract Celia's attention Volpone takes on another role. He disguises himself as Scoto of Mantua, a famous contemporary mountebank and entertainer, and sets up his wares for sale under

---

[13] IV. iii. 19–24.
[14] *Epigrammes*, no. LXXXV, ll. 5–10.

Celia's window.[15] His long discourse about the effects of his 'oil' which will make those who drink it *'euer faire and yong/Stout of teeth and strong of tongue'* and able to *'liue free from all diseases'* (II. ii. 194–5, 200) comes very close to contemporary accounts of the patter of actual mountebanks. Finally, Volpone says he will, as a special favour, sell his oil this once at cut-price, and he asks his audience to *'tosse'* [their] *handkerchiefes, chearefully, chearefully'* (II. ii. 215) as a sign of their acceptance of his offer. Peregrine, who has been watching Volpone's performance with Sir Pol, thinks Sir Pol has been completely taken in by Volpone's patter and will be the first to throw his handkerchief. But even the gullible Sir Pol is outdone by Celia who, from her window overlooking the *piazza*, throws down her handkerchief. The irony of the situation for Celia and Volpone is pointed up by Peregrine's amused and detached comment when Volpone makes his request of the audience. Peregrine says:

> Will you be that heroique sparke, sir POL?
> O, see! the windore has preuented you.
>
> (II. ii. 220–1)

The point of the scene becomes clear when we understand why Jonson has Volpone disguise himself as a mountebank in order to attract Celia's attention. The mountebanks were not simply out-door salesmen of quack medicines; and the scene does not rest solely on the irony of the situation of Volpone who once feigned diseases to gain riches now attempting to sell cures for diseases to gain Celia. The fame of the mountebanks rested on their ability as entertainers of the crowds. While the main purpose of their entertainments was, of course, to induce the crowd to buy their wares, their performances were often quite elaborate, sometimes including stock characters and scenes from the *commedia dell'arte* repertoire.[16] That Volpone regards his act as Scoto

---

[15] See H & S IX, pp. 702–4 for a discussion of mountebanks and note to II. ii. 22 for Scoto.

[16] See Nicoll, *Masks, Mimes and Miracles*, pp. 223–4; and Nicoll, *Harlequin*, p. 26: '. . . many of those who earned their livings by assuming commedia dell'arte roles were little more than charlatans' accomplices.' See also H & S IX, pp. 702–3, note to II. ii.

In disguising himself as a mountebank, a seller of quack medicines, Volpone is also imitating the hero of one of the most popular Renaissance comedies. Machiavelli's *Mandragola* provides a striking parallel to the central plot of *Volpone*, Volpone's wooing of Celia. (See also the discussion by Daniel Boughner, in *The Devil's Disciple*.) The hero of *Mandragola*, Callimaco, is, like Volpone, in love by hearsay with Lucretia, a beautiful, virtuous, and devotedly religious woman who has the misfortune to be married to an old, impotent, and jealous husband, Nicia. In order to gain access to Lucretia's bed Callimaco pretends to be a doctor able to cure what Nicia believes is his wife's inability to bear children. We see Nicia willingly consent to his own cuckolding in order to gain his ambition, an heir. The parallels with the mountebank scene in *Volpone* and Corvino's willing prostitution of Celia to Volpone in Act III, scene vii are obvious: but just as significant, perhaps, are the differences. The outcome of *Madragola* provides satisfaction for all the characters, even the duped. Volpone's attempt to win Celia, on the other hand, ends in disaster for himself. Furthermore, in choosing the role of mountebank rather than of doctor as Callimaco chose, Volpone has, in a sense, outdone his hero, for in taking on the role of mountebank he has also taken on the role of popular entertainer.

as something more elaborate than mere peddling is clear not only from
his lengthy patter but also from the fact that he takes Nano and Mosca
with him, as his accomplices. Presumably, these two are to carry on
some kind of 'act' while Volpone is elaborating on his oil. This becomes
clear, I think, when he asks Nano to sing the first song (II. ii. 120):
Volpone addresses him as 'ZAN FRITADA' which suggests that Nano is
playing a *dell'arte* role. Although *zanni* comes to be the name used for
stage servants in general, there is a character in the *dell'arte* scenarios
called Zanni who appears to be distinct from just a general servant.
Usually he has another name as well—as Zan Fritada whose part Nano
plays—and he appears always as the comic attendant, a clown who is
unlettered and uncouth.[17]

If we regard Volpone's performance as Scoto not simply as that of a
salesman but as containing, too, a rough attempt at presenting some
kind of popular scenario with recognizable characters, then the point of
the scene and the positions of Volpone and Celia become clear. For
Volpone's performance does not merely attract Celia's attention but,
we see, it actually includes her within the scenario itself. From Volpone's point of view, as would-be lover, and from ours, watching
Volpone playing two roles—fox and mountebank/lover—her response
is perfect. As she throws down her handkerchief she not only flatters
Volpone as lover, but she appears the conventional 'heroine' locked
in her tower by a jealous husband and responding to her lover who
sings to her beneath her window. Indeed, Corvino has seen the
act as a *dell'arte* scenario too; and he has characterized himself in
the role of the jealous husband, one of Pantalone's roles. As he beats
Volpone, Mosca, and Nano away from their stand outside his house
he says:

> Spight o' the deuill, and my shame! come downe, here;
> Come downe: no house but mine to make your *scene*?
> *Signior* FLAMINEO, will you downe, sir? downe?
> What is my wife your FRANCISCINA? sir?
> No windores on the whole *piazza*, here,
> To make your properties, but mine? but mine?
> Hart! ere to morrow, I shall be new christen'd,
> And cald the PANTALONE *di besogniosi*,
> About the towne.
>
>   (II. iii. 1–9)

Corvino defines Celia's part in the comedy as that of Francischina, the
willing maidservant, and Volpone's as that of Flavio, the lover, a role
made famous by Flamineo Scala, a member of the popular Gelosi

---

[17] See Nicoll, *Harlequin*, pp. 82–4 and H & S IX, p. 705, note to II. ii. 114 on Zan Fritada.

company.[18] Indeed, the similarity of the scene with aspects of the scenario *La Fortuna di Flavio*, the second in the collection published by Flamineo Scala in 1611, has been pointed out by Winifred Smith;[19] and although the plot of that scenario is far more elaborate than the mountebank scene in *Volpone* it is clearly this scenario that Corvino has in mind when he refers to Flavio, Francischina, and Pantalone, for it contains all these characters.[20] But we, the audience, see Celia in a different role. It has been pointed out that Jonson has conflated this scenario with aspects of another, entitled *Il pedante*, no. 31 in Scala's collection. In *Il pedante* the Captain woos Pantalone's wife, Isabella, from the *piazza* beneath her window and she drops her handkerchief to him.[21] So although Corvino sees his wife as 'playing' Francischina, Jonson's audience would recognize in her performance aspects of the beautiful Isabella as well. This double identity is, in itself, comic here; but it is also important in that it is developed later in the scene where Corvino brings his wife to Volpone's bedchamber.[22]

The irony and humour of the whole mountebank scene, which reflects on Celia herself, lies in the fact that her lover's eloquence has been merely an exhortation to buy quack medicine, and his love-songs have been merely Nano's advertising slogans. Volpone has been trapped into the debasement of language—and consequently into a ridiculous position here—by the very nature of the role (as mountebank) he has adopted. These are the 'love-songs' which woo Celia:

> *Had old* HIPPOCRATES, *or* GALEN,
> *(That to their bookes put med'cines all in)*
> *But knowne this secret, they had neuer*
> *(Of which they will be guiltie euer)*
> *Beene murderers of so much paper,*
> *Or wasted many a hurtlesse taper:*
> *No* Indian *drug had ere beene famed,*
> Tabacco, sassafras *not named;*
> *Ne yet, of* guacum *one small stick, sir,*
> *Nor* RAYMVND LVLLIES *great* elixir.

[18] See Duchartre, *Italian Comedy*, pp. 50, 87, 288. The Gelosi company revived its European tours in 1600 and continued playing until it was disbanded in 1604 on the death of its leading woman actress, Isabella. See also Barker, 'Three English Pantalones', Chapter V for a discussion of *Volpone* and the *commedia dell'arte*.

[19] Smith, *The Commedia dell'Arte*, pp. 187–95.

[20] For a translation see Salerno, *Scenarios*, pp. 11–21. The relation of the scenario to the mountebank scene in *Volpone* is discussed by Salerno on pp. 395–6.

[21] See Salerno, *Scenarios*, p. 405. The translation of *Il pedante* is on pp. 227–34.

[22] Each of the characters in the *commedia dell'arte* had certain stock characteristics and stock ways of behaviour which made them immediately recognizable to their audience. However, their actual roles varied from one scenario to the next, so that, for instance, Isabella is not always Pantalone's wife: sometimes she is his daughter, sometimes a widow, sometimes she is wooed by him.

> *Ne, had been knowne the* Danish GONSWART,
> Or PARACELSVS, *with his long-sword.*
>
> (II. ii. 120–32)

The doggerel of this is matched only by that of the song Nano and
Mosca sing later in the scene:

> *You that would last long, list to my song,*
> *Make no more coyle, but buy of the oyle.*
> *Would you be euer faire? and yong?*
> *Stout of teeth? and strong of tongue?*
> *Tart of Palat? quick of eare?*
> *Sharpe of sight? of nostrill cleare?*
> *Moist of hand? and light of foot?*
> *(Or I will come neerer to't)*
> *Would you liue free from all diseases?*
> *Doe the act, your mistris pleases;*
> *Yet fright all aches from your bones?*
> *Here's a med'cine, for the nones.*
>
> (II. ii. 191–203)

But the irony turns on Volpone too when we realize that he has confused
Celia's acting a part in his scenario with reality: that he has been as
completely overcome by her acquiescence as by her beauty. Volpone
and Mosca are now talking together:

> VOLPONE O, I am wounded. Mos. Where, sir?
>   VOLP Not without;
> Those blowes were nothing: I could beare them euer.
> But angry CVPID, bolting from her eyes,
> Hath shot himselfe into me, like a flame;
> Where, now, he flings about his burning heat,
> As in a fornace, an ambitious fire,
> Whose vent is stopt. The fight is all within me.
> I cannot liue, except thou helpe me, MOSCA;
> My liuer melts, and I, without the hope
> Of some soft aire, from her refreshing breath,
> Am but a heape of cinders.
>
> (II. iv. 1–11)

Is Volpone still playing Flavio? The extravagance of his response,
which appears to match that of his opening speech in the play, is now,
from his point of view, completely serious. In other words his role as
Scoto/Flavio has taken in even himself and his comedy has become
melodrama. Mosca points up this confusion in Volpone by his own
ironic detachment. He now begins to plot on his own, by inviting
Bonario to be present (in hiding) at the signing away to Volpone of his

inheritance by his father, Corbaccio. We do not yet see clearly what Mosca is up to, but through this growing assertion of independence we see clearly what is happening to Volpone.

Volpone's next and grandest plot is to enlist Mosca's aid in getting Corvino to bring Celia to him; this is also the culmination of Volpone's self-deception and the centre of Jonson's play.

III

Volpone's wooing of Celia in Act II, scene vii (ll. 133 ff.) has caused much controversy.[23] The difficulties most commonly experienced here seem to arise from a tendency to regard the scene, out of its context, as a kind of 'set piece'. Paradoxically, precisely because it *is* this we must consider it within the whole context of the play, as a climax very carefully and subtly worked for from the beginning. The song too which is at the centre of the scene lends itself to being regarded as an anthology piece, and this characteristic of the song is part of the significance of its inclusion in the scene.

When Celia and Volpone are left together we witness the third of Volpone's 'dramas'. The first, the duping of the birds of prey, was completely successful. The second, Volpone's wooing of Celia under the disguise of a mountebank, was successful from Volpone's point of view but from our point of view it was undermined by the irony of the conflict between act and situation, and by the irony in the conflict between the language Volpone speaks as Scoto and the intention of the language—as that of Celia's lover. Now when he is left alone with Celia Volpone believes he is not acting, he believes that he is being himself, that he is no longer the 'fox feigning dead', the old man made up by Mosca to look ill and dying. Now, he believes, he will appear to Celia as the Magnifico he really is and as the list of *dramatis personae* describes him. To woo her he will use the poetic and musical arts, the social manners, and the code of love-making which as a Venetian noble he 'inherits'. But what, we ask, *is* Volpone's real identity? When Volpone leaps out of bed and tells Celia that his revival is due to her 'beauties miracle' (I I I. vii. 146) we see him, and Celia sees him, as an old man still, with Mosca's ointment making his eyes and nose run. The fox has turned out to be the Venetian Magnifico: but who is this Magnifico? And who is Celia, how has our view of her changed since we saw her in the double role of Francischina and Isabella? While we may very well sympathize with Celia's abhorrence at, and reluctance to comply with, Corvino's command that she get into bed with Volpone, the sick and

---

[23] See, for instance, Enright, 'Poetic Satire', p. 211; Gianakaris, 'Ethical Values', p. 48; Thayer, *Ben Jonson*, p. 62. Knights, *Drama and Society*, pp. 156–7 points out in what way the derivative quality of Volpone's speech operates against it.

dying old man, when she is left alone with him and he leaps out of bed showing her he is by no means palsied and incapable, our response is one of amusement at them both rather than of sympathy with Celia. Once more, we feel, Volpone and Celia are acting: but this time something has gone seriously wrong for Volpone.

The scene between Volpone and Celia appears once more like a stock scenario from the *commedia dell'arte* repertoire, although this time neither of the characters is conscious of it. Volpone, the Venetian Magnifico, has no identity other than that of one of the most famous roles of the lecherous old Pantalone, Pantalone *inamorato*, the Magnifico of the *commedia*. Just as when he feigned sick Volpone mimicked Corbaccio, the decrepit, deaf old man, and mimicked him consciously, now it is Corvino who has given us the clue to Volpone's—this time unconscious—act. Celia too, in now revealing her 'identity' as Isabella—the role we, the audience, saw her playing in the earlier scene—is still playing a role. But this time Jonson develops the most notable stock qualities of this character: her virtue, her beauty, and her chastity. Her replies to Volpone are comic rather than pathetic, first because they insist on her identity as the *dell'arte* Isabella, and secondly because now, in a different 'scenario', she is forced to act a rather different Isabella from the one Volpone wooed in the *piazza*. The *Recueil Fossard*, a collection of illustrations of stock *dell'arte* characters and scenes, can provide us with a picture of almost this very scene. Even the words of Isabella, inset beneath the picture, summarize those of Celia to Volpone.[24] (See Pl. I.)

What is this role that Volpone, now unconsciously, plays? In many of the scenarios which survive for the repertoire of the *commedia dell'arte* Pantalone is a serious character and a nobleman, often specifically described as a Venetian Magnifico.[25] In his discussion of the character of Pantalone Allardyce Nicoll says that he is usually described as a 'vecchio', as an old man; but this does not, in the sixteenth century,

---

[24] Isabella's words may be translated: 'But why do you come to me, mad, infamous, and dishonest old man, and ask me over and over again to love you? Don't you know that before agreeing to your request I would much rather die a thousand deaths.' The role of Isabella in the *commedia dell'arte* was made famous by Isabella Andreini whose husband, Francesco, succeeded Flamineo Scala as manager of the Gelosi company. During her lifetime Isabella was honoured all over Europe for her beauty, her virtue, and her acting and celebrated by such poets as Ariosto, Giraldi, Guarini, and Marino; and at her death in childbirth at Lyons in 1604, the whole city turned out to pay her funeral honours. When *Volpone* was performed in 1605 the death of Isabella would still have been topical and her reputation still in the minds of Jonson's audience.

[25] For Pantalone as Magnifico see Duchartre, *Italian Comedy*, p. 184; Oreglia, *Commedia dell'Arte*, p. 78; Nicoll, *Harlequin*, p. 50. Nicoll refers to the scenarios in which Pantalone is Magnifico. References are to the collection of scenarios by Flamineo Scala, *Il teatro delle favole rappresentative* (Venice, 1611): *Il pedante* (Scala, 31), *Il fido amico* (Scala, 29), *Le disgratie di Flavio* (Scala, 35). For translations of these scenarios see Salerno, *Scenarios*.

necessarily mean someone *very* old.[26] Certainly, Pantalone is usually depicted as very agile. Professor Nicoll says that

in these prints, although he sometimes appears in indecorous and ridiculous situations, his general presentation is either in dignified posture or else in violent action. . . . In crouched attitude he circles, with almost animal ferocity, around the abject figure of a servant who has annoyed him; he displays the grace of a dancer as he leans sideways from a pointing companion or sweeps in courtly bow towards the object of his affections; even more vigorous, virile and masculinely active is his portrait as, arms widely outspread and cloak flying out behind him, he reaches forward with his right foot bent and left stretched out behind. There is nothing of decrepitude here.[27]

A typical pose, described in the last part of the passage above, is that of the famous actor Stefanello Bottarga in the role of Pantalone. (See Pl. II.) Pantalone is usually represented as rich and sometimes also miserly. He is often represented as the would-be lover, the rival of younger men in lust and intrigue; and the phallus was a common detail of his costume.[28] The audience of *Volpone* would not, of course, know that Jonson's list of *dramatis personae* described Volpone as a Venetian Magnifico; but then, in itself, this would not be a significant clue since many contemporary plays include Venetian magnificos who are not in any way to be associated with Pantalone.[29] However, Jonson's point could be made in performance by giving Volpone at least some of the distinctive clothes Pantalone always wore and some of his characteristic gestures and movements—which suggest an agility in keeping with his other title, the fox.[30]

[26] Nicoll, *Harlequin*, pp. 46–9.

[27] Nicoll, *Harlequin*, p. 49.

[28] See Duchartre, *Italian Comedy*, p. 29.

[29] For instance Brabantio in *Othello* is described in this way, and in *The Merchant of Venice*, III. ii. 281–5, Salerio, speaking of Shylock's bond, tells Bassanio that

> Twenty merchants,
> The Duke himself, and the magnificoes
> Of greatest port, have all persuaded with him;
> But none can drive him from the envious plea
> Of forfeiture, of justice, and his bond.

[30] Oreglia, *Commedia dell'Arte*, p. 80, describes Pantalone's typical appearance: 'Pantalone's costume is predominantly red. This is the colour of his woollen cap in the Greek style, his close-fitting jacket and his long, tight breeches. His robe is black but lined with red, with wide sleeves. . . . The face is bony, the eyebrows accentuated, the nose hooked. His hair flows down over his shoulders. Often the Magnifico plays to his public in profile, thus accentuating the comic effect produced by his jutting pointed beard, grey or white, and his long moustaches . . . He wears a purse in his belt and, in the sixteenth and seventeenth centuries, also a sword or dagger. He wears yellow mules in the Turkish style.'

The relationship of Volpone and Pantalone has also been seen by Barker, 'Three English Pantalones', Chapter V. Barker discusses the *commedia*'s magnifico as miserly and lustful, and goes on to illustrate these characteristics in the birds of prey as well, especially in Corvino and Corbaccio. He does not go on to discuss the specific use to which Jonson has put these borrowings and analogies.

So when Volpone leaps out of bed, thinking to invite Celia by his vigour and his accomplishments, he is simply—but unconsciously this time—taking on another role. Nor does he realize that Celia too is simply a 'stock' heroine and that the scenario in which each unconsciously acts is capped, in true melodramatic style, by Bonario's grand gesture, his leaping out from behind the arras in the nick of time to save Celia from rape (I I I. vii. 267–75). The comedy of the scene lies in its melodrama, a result of the complete lack of identity of all the characters and particularly of Volpone himself. It now seems doubly ironic that among the greatest delights Volpone can offer Celia—apart, of course, from his riches—are those of playing or acting other roles:

> my dwarfe shall dance,
> My eunuch sing, my foole make vp the antique.
> Whil'st, we in changed shapes, act OVIDS tales,
> Thou, like EVROPA now, and I like IOVE,
> Then I like MARS, and thou like ERYCINE,
> So, of the rest, till we haue quite run through
> And weary'd all the fables of the gods.
> Then will I haue thee in more moderne formes,
> Attired like some sprightly dame of *France*,
> Braue *Tuscan* lady, or proud *Spanish* beauty;
> Sometimes, vnto the *Persian Sophies* wife;
> Or the grand-*Signiors* mistresse; and, for change,
> To one of our most art-full courtizans,
> Or some quick *Negro*, or cold *Russian*;
> And I will meet thee in as many shapes . . .
> (III. vii. 219–33)[31]

Furthermore, Volpone's main argument in his initial persuasion of Celia is merely the argument Corvino himself gave her:

> '*Tis no sinne, loues fruits to steale;*
> *But the sweet thefts to reueale:*
> *To be taken, to be seene,*
> *These haue crimes accounted beene.*
> (III. vii. 180–3)

The scene completes Volpone's self-deception and this is the source of its humour. After Bonario's triumphant exit with Celia the scene dissolves: for us, in complete farce, for Volpone, in complete disaster. He cries out in anguish and despair:

> Fall on me, roofe, and bury me in ruine,
> Become my graue, that wert my shelter. O!
> I am vn-masqu'd, vn-spirited, vn-done,
> Betray'd to beggary, to infamy . . .
> (III. vii. 276–9)

[31] Cf. also III. vii. 146–53 and 157–64.

And immediately, Mosca enters. His words are in keeping with Volpone's melodrama, but also dangerously in mockery of it:

> Where shall I runne, most wretched shame of men,
> To beate out my vn-luckie braines?

(III. viii. 1–2)

We have passed the turning-point of the play: Mosca now has the upper hand, the flesh-fly is beginning to feed.

The practical dangers of adopting roles which finally take over one's identity are illustrated in the following scenes in which Volpone becomes more and more dependent on Mosca, and, of course, in the final outcome of the play. But the danger in a lack of personal identity is not expressed merely in the outcome of the plot; in the scene with Celia in particular, it is expressed by the complete lack of correspondence between words and meaning, by the fact that none of the normal relations of language to social values seems any longer to exist. In the end, Volpone in exasperation is driven simply to act:

> I should haue done the act, and then haue parlee'd.
> Yeeld, or Ile force thee.

(III. vii. 264–5)

This lack of correspondence between words and meaning is evident throughout the scene and may explain why some critics have been puzzled over the fact that, in extract and out of context, some of Volpone's poetry is undoubtedly fine and persuasive.[32] It is this point in particular that the song Volpone sings to Celia (III. vii. 165–83) supports and makes clear; and in this it extends the function of the songs Nano sang in the mountebank scene.

> *Come, my* CELIA, *let vs proue,*
> *While we can, the sports of loue;*
> *Time will not be ours, for euer,*
> *He, at length, our good will seuer;*

---

[32] See, for instance, Celia's protest:

> Is that, which euer was a cause of life,
> Now plac'd beneath the basest circumstance?
> And modestie an exile made, for money?

and Volpone's reply:

> I, in CORVINO, and such earth-fed mindes,
> That neuer tasted the true heau'n of loue.
> Assure thee, CELIA, he that would sell thee,
> Onely for hope of gaine, and that vncertaine,
> He would haue sold his part of paradise
> For ready money, had he met a cope-man.

(III. vii. 139–44)

> *Spend not then his gifts, in vaine.*
> *Sunnes, that set, may rise againe:*
> *But if, once, we lose this light,*
> *'Tis with vs perpetuall night.*
> *Why should wee deferre our ioyes?*
> *Fame, and rumor are but toies.*
> *Cannot we delude the eyes*
> *Of a few poore household-spies?*
> *Or his easier eares beguile,*
> *Thus remooued, by our wile?*
> *'Tis no sinne, loues fruits to steale;*
> *But the sweet thefts to reueale:*
> *To be taken, to be seene,*
> *These haue crimes accounted beene.*

(III. vii. 165–83)[33]

Part of the point of the song lies in the difference between what the song purports to be (and what it represents as an anthology piece) and what in its context it is. Quite clearly the song can be regarded seriously; that is to say, it is not a literary or musical parody in the way Hedon's or Crispinus's songs are. As a love-song the words are, in the best tradition, an imitation of a poem by Catullus: 'Vivamus, mea Lesbia'.[34] As a means of persuading Celia to make love Volpone's performance of the song follows the advice of those 'authorities' who write of the power of music to affect and persuade the listener, particularly to persuade her to love. Volpone's seizing his lute or viol and giving what appears to be an extempore and virtuoso performance of his song would simply underline his nobility, his courtliness, his art.

A setting of 'Come my Celia' by Alfonso Ferrabosco I I was published in his *Ayres* (1609), no. 6, for voice with lute and bass viol accompaniment. Ferrabosco's setting probably belongs to the first

---

[33] Volpone bursts into song again, later in the scene: ll. 236–9.

> *That the curious shall not know,*
> *How to tell them, as they flow;*
> *And the enuious, when they find*
> *What their number is, be pind.*

Jonson used these four lines later at the end of the poem in *The Forrest* which follows 'Song. To Celia' ('Come my Celia', *The Forrest*, no. 5). The poem is clearly intended as a continuation of no. 5, for it is entitled 'To the same', is in the same verse form, and, omitting the final four lines (from *Volpone*), has the same number of lines. In a performance of *Volpone* which used Ferrabosco's setting of 'Come my Celia' Volpone could sing these four lines to the music which sets the final lines of the previous song.

[34] For a discussion of the song's classical source see Sternfeld, 'Song in Jonson's Comedy'. Four years earlier Thomas Campion had published, in Rosseter's *Ayres* (1601), an imitation of the same poem by Catullus: 'My sweetest Lesbia'.

EXAMPLE 7. 'Come my *Celia*, let vs proue'

Come my *Ce* - *li* - *a*, let vs proue,

while wee may the sweets of loue, Time___

___ wil not be ours for eu - er, he at length___

_____ our good _____ wil se - uer.

Spend not then his _____ gifts in vaine,

Sunnes that set may rise a - gain, But _____

if we once loose this light, tis with vs

per- pe - tu - all night.

Why should wee de - ferre our ioyes, Fame and

'ru - mour are but toyes? Can - not we ____

____ de - lude the eyes of a few poore hous-hold

spyes, Or ____ his ea - sier eares ____ be - guile,

Thus re - mou - ed by our wile

Tis no sinne loues fruits to steale, But the sweet

theft to re - ueale, To be tak - en,

Alfonso Ferrabosco, *Ayres* (1609), no. 6, Sig. C. 1^v– C.2.

Note

10 tabl. IV: Ferrabosco gives c on course 2; trans. as b on course 2.

performance of the play, for in 1605 Jonson and Ferrabosco also began to collaborate in masques for court.[35] If Volpone sang accompanied he would have accompanied himself, and therefore both instrumental parts cannot belong to the play. The bass viol part reproduces the bass part of the lute accompaniment; and although in the main the lute part simply provides harmonic support it also contains some counterpointing of motifs in the vocal line and would be rather more interesting as accompaniment than the bass viol alone.[36] Ferrabosco's setting has probably been influenced by the ideals of the French academies and the *Camerata* which stressed the affective power of musical settings when they clearly expressed their text: the setting is partly declamatory in style, although less clearly so than some of the masque songs Ferrabosco wrote later. The relationship between the words and the music here is a vital and complex one. The setting pays more attention to the poetic form than do some, later, declamatory settings where the text is treated as if it were prose and little account taken of such matters as the sense of the poetic rhythms and the rhymes.

The first four and the second four lines of 'Come my Celia' are sung to the same music and therefore there is little opportunity for following in any but a general and metrical sense the meaning of the words. The melodic line is simple and symmetrical, the harmonic basis and the cadential points following the line structure of the poetry and containing only the simple modulation to the dominant key at the end of line 2 (line 6). The first part of the song is, then, predominantly musical in structure: even the syncopation of the melody with the accompaniment at bars 2–3, 7–8, and 10–11 serves a musical rather than a poetic function in pushing the melodic line on towards the end of the phrase rather than, for instance (as later in the song), emphasizing significant words. These first eight lines of Jonson's text are those which follow Catullus' poem closely: the rest of the poem maintains its spirit but refers more specifically to Volpone's and Celia's immediate situation. Catullus' poem was widely known and imitated in Jonson's time and the simple musical statement of these lines seems particularly appropriate to their almost proverbial character. By contrast, the setting of the following ten lines of the poem underlines their more specific reference to the dramatic situation, and what we are to believe is their extempore nature.

The song is divided into three sections, the second section setting lines 9–14 and the third, which is repeated, lines 15–18. The setting of

---

[35] The same setting, for voice and lute accompaniment, also occurs in British Library MS Add. 15117, f. 20ᵛ. See also Chapter I, n. 46.
[36] All the songs in Ferrabosco's *Ayres* give accompaniments for both lute and viol, the viol doubling the bass of the lute part as in 'Come my Celia'.

lines 9–14 still maintains a simple melodic vocal line following the line-structure of the poem, but the relation of music to text is rhythmically and harmonically more complex than that in the first part. Syncopation is used to point words and phrases (as at bars 27–8 and 31–3); and at the same time bars 29 and 31 balance one another musically. The verbal sense is further pointed up by the way the harmonic basis carries the verbal phrase forward at some cadences against the obvious pause in the melodic line, thus drawing attention to the poetic significance of the rhymes. The cadences at bars 29 and 34 are examples.

The third section of Ferrabosco's setting, lines 15–18 of Jonson's text, is to be sung twice, thus musically balancing the opening section. Here too Ferrabosco has imitated the sense of the words in a general way within a pre-eminently musical structure. Most striking are the rather jaunty sequence setting ''Tis no sin Love's fruits to steal' and the emphasis given to 'sweet theft' by the syncopation and the imitation in the accompaniment. The last two lines are repeated in Ferrabosco's setting, emphasizing ironically the lines in which Volpone is merely repeating Corvino's arguments to Celia. In the first statement of lines 17–18 Ferrabosco's accompaniment supports and underlines the poetic stress of the words—as at 'crimes' for instance. The repetition of these lines, in being mainly an extended final cadence, draws attention to itself as simple emphasis.

The setting of the song follows fashionable, and serious, ideals for setting words to music, and in performance would support in a subtle and quite sophisticated manner both the mood and the spoken rhythms of the text. It is a setting completely befitting the performance of a Venetian nobleman. But in its context the song is comic: not simply because the 'wisdom' of the text has already been suggested by Corvino himself, but more generally in that Volpone now has no personal identity. So the song, in itself a superb example of the 'eloquence' of music-for-words, and intended as a heightening of Volpone's persuasion, in fact deflates that persuasion. It is a mockery of itself, and Volpone's performance of it merely mimics himself. Furthermore, because of the way this scene with Celia caps the comedy of the earlier scene in which Volpone wooed Celia as a mountebank, we cannot, I think, resist comparing Volpone's love-song here with the 'love-songs' he had performed beneath her window. This song's traditions, source, and setting may be superior, but Celia responded to Nano's advertisement songs far more 'properly' than she responds to Volpone's eloquence now. The complete chaos of values which these two scenes point up, and which the songs in each support and clarify, underlies the comedy of the whole play.

La Donna Isabella and Pantalon Inamorato.

Stefanello Bottarga as Pantalone.

The Three Graces; detail from Botticelli's
La Primavera.

IV

As Volpone assumed roles, his downfall is precipitated by the roles' taking over his identity. This, of course, is made explicit by the court's judgement delivered on him at the end of the play: that since Volpone's wealth was gained

> By faining lame, gout, palsey, and such diseases,
> Thou art to lie in prison, crampt with irons,
> Till thou bee'st sicke, and lame indeed.
>
> (v. xii. 122–4)

But we see the beginning of this earlier, when he has returned safely from his first summons before the court:

> Well, I am here; and all this brunt is past:
> I ne're was in dislike with my disguise,
> Till this fled moment; here, 'twas good, in priuate,
> But in your publike, *Caue*, whil'st I breathe.
> 'Fore god, my left legge 'gan to haue the crampe;
> And I apprehended, straight, some power had strooke me
> With a dead palsey.
>
> (v. i. 1–7)

As the old tale has it, the wind is already changing and Volpone is to be stuck with the part he played. Mosca recognizes this when he says to Volpone:

> We must, here, be fixt;
> Here, we must rest; this is our master-peece:
> We cannot thinke, to goe beyond this.
>
> (v. ii. 12–14)

But Volpone is determined to go one step further; and like Reynard who is in danger when he steps outside his castle, Maupertuis, so Volpone goes too far in leaving his treasure and the keys of his house in Mosca's hands, giving out that he is dead, and then going into the streets disguised as a *commandator* to taunt the birds of prey with their loss of his wealth.

However, the ending has a double twist. Mosca misjudges in thinking he can finish Volpone's 'master-peece' for him. He fails to realize that he is not as completely independent as he believes (or as his soliloquy in III. i asserts). In his role as parasite, 'flesh-fly', he too has a part within the beast-fable. Like the birds of prey he finally succumbs to greed for Volpone's wealth and in this greed he fatally misjudges Volpone. In his last stand Volpone himself recognizes that his identity is no longer separable from his role. Faced with the choice either of a whipping for being a corrupt *commandator* or of punishment for his other impostures, he is forced to affirm his true identity when he throws off his disguise to reveal not, this time, the Venetian Magnifico, but the fox:

> The FOXE shall, here, vncase.
>
>   (v. xii. 85)

And so Volpone's own last words also act as a gloss on the judgement of imprisonment 'crampt with irons' which the *avocatori* pass on him:

> This is call'd mortifying of a FOXE.
>
>   (v. xii. 125)

We may recall at this point the moralistic commentary to the bestiary account of the fox who feigns dead and see that it has now been demonstrated, by Volpone himself, to be true. For both the literal and the 'moralized' fox are included within Volpone's 'mortification'. He is game caught and hung till it is high and a more tender delicacy; and the ending of the bestiary moralizing speaks of the need to 'mortify the doings of the foxy body'.[37]

But in the final analysis Volpone's last words push neither of these interpretations. We cannot sit smugly back in our seats and acquiesce in a simple judgement of wrong punished and virtue (Celia and Bonario?) rewarded. First of all, the court which judges Volpone, Mosca, and the birds of prey consists of some patently corruptible *avocatori* who find the truth only by the fact that Volpone reveals it. The play's criticism is not contained within the beast-fable but extended beyond Volpone himself to include a whole corrupt society. Although some are punished, we are still left with an endless vista of greed, of self-seeking, of shifting identity in order to gain something for oneself. Mosca's dizzying vision of a world consisting only of parasites and sub-parasites is no longer comic when it is all we are left with.

Finally, like Reynard who escaped from the judgement of the corrupt court, Volpone himself has the last word: in the Epilogue.

> The seasoning of a play is the applause.
> Now, though the Fox be punish'd by the lawes,
> He, yet, doth hope there is no suffring due,
> For any fact, which he hath done, 'gainst you;
> If there be, censure him: here he, doubtfull, stands.
> If not, fare iouially, and clap your hands.

We are at once transported back to the beginning of the play, and we experience relief that we can recover our initial simple delight in the rogue-hero, that it is, after all, 'just a story'. But in the very fact of making us 'fare iouially' and applaud Volpone, of making us laugh

---

[37] White, *Book of Beasts*, p. 54.

again with Volpone, Jonson has trapped us into laughing at ourselves in Volpone, into seeing ourselves in Volpone the actor, the role-player, the fox. This final twist would have a curious effect on an audience. We laugh loudly both with relief and in order to hide the fact that we *are* relieved. It is not the merry laughter of an audience at a romantic comedy which has the effect of drawing the audience together.[38] This laughter isolates us from those spectators sitting near us, for if we admit our relief we admit at the same time our sense of 'guilt', the degree to which we have been moved by the play. This means that even our pleasure in the rogue-hero is turned to a mockery of ourselves; for just as Volpone's adoption of roles, his acting, turned against him at the crucial point in his career—his seduction of Celia—so too does our response to the ending force us to recognize ourselves and our society in the images of deceit which the play has presented to us. Our identity, like that of Volpone in the scene with Celia, has become simply a reflection in a distorting mirror.

V

There is only one song in *The Devil is an Ass* (1616), and it is sung by Wittipol to woo the beautiful Mrs Fitz-dottrell. This song makes a point in the play similar to that of Volpone's song to Celia, in that it is comic only in its context. The incongruity of the situation in which the song is performed makes Wittipol appear—like Volpone in his singing to Celia—to be simply acting a part, simply mimicking. Furthermore, in its context the text of the song shows a debasement of the 'wisdom' which a love-song should express, and to this degree the performance of the song continues Jonson's criticism of society by criticizing its debasement of language. Wittipol's song makes an altogether simpler point, however, than the songs in *Volpone*; its function, although not strictly parodic, is much closer to that of Hedon's song in *Cynthia's Revels*. This is probably because the Wittipol sub-plot is only tenuously a part of the play's action, and so we cannot say that the song intensifies our understanding of the play's main point in the way the songs in Acts II and III of *Volpone* do.

[38] To some degree, of course, Volpone is simply making us aware of the usual response to satire. Jaques in *As You Like It* makes clear what this is when he says,

> And they that are most galled with my folly,
> They most must laugh. . . .
> He that a fool doth very wisely hit
> Doth very foolishly, although he smart,
> Not to seem senseless of the bob.
>
> (II. vii. 50–1, 53–5)

Volpone's Epilogue gives another twist to this truism and makes us acknowledge the truth of this personally.

The main action of the play concerns Meere-craft's schemes and his duping of Fitz-dottrell; Wittipol's gulling of Fitz-dottrell is a secondary plot. However, as L. C. Knights has pointed out, the play is not merely a succession of satirical sketches of contemporary economic and social life: it 'cuts beneath the superficial follies, the accidental forms, and goes to the root of the disease, shaping the material in the light of an humane ideal that is implicit throughout'.[39] This 'humane ideal' is implicit partly in the comedy provided by Fitz-dottrell himself and in our continually shifting evaluation of Meere-craft's 'projections'.[40] But it is implicit too in the Wittipol–Manly plot which brings the play as a whole closer to the techniques and values of *Volpone* than is usually recognized. In the Wittipol plot Jonson examines once again ideas of acting and of roles: although here the examination is less complex and less detailed than it was in *Volpone*.

The play opens in Hell where we see Pug, a devil, negotiating with Satan to be allowed to spend a month on earth. Pug is allowed to spend one day, in the body of a cut-purse who has been hanged that morning at Tyburn; and he is to be the servant of Fitz-dottrell, who has a desire to see the devil himself and who hires Pug because his name is Devil. The comparatively straightforward use which is made of Pug in the play has often been pointed out. This is simply the story of the Devil who visits earth for a day to try to win more souls for Hell and who ends up so foiled and beaten by the corruption of the world that he wishes for midnight to come quickly and for Satan to take him back again to Hell. Contemporary London is so wicked that it sees even the Devil merely as the elegant gentleman-usher, M. De-uile.[41] However, Wittipol's function in the play appears to complicate this quite simple moral point—that the vices of contemporary London outwit and outdo the Devil himself. After Pug has left Hell for earth we see Wittipol negotiating, through his acquaintance Ingine, with Fitz-dottrell for a quarter-hour's conversation with Fitz-dottrell's beautiful wife in exchange for his cloak. Fitz-dottrell, who is obsessed by clothes and appearances, is eager to have the cloak because he plans that afternoon to see the new play: *The Devil is an Ass*. Fitz-dottrell never gets to the play as he becomes further and further enmeshed in Meere-craft's schemes for making him the Duke of Drown'd Lands. In itself the device of Fitz-dottrell's wishing to see the play of which he himself turns out to be the main character may seem to make a fairly simple point and one which merely endorses the moral function of Pug in the play. Furthermore, Fitz-dottrell obviously does not regard his visit to the theatre merely as

[39] Knights, *Drama and Society*, p. 183.
[40] Ibid., p. 181.
[41] IV. iv. 198.

the visit of a spectator. He has said to his wife, in explanation of the new
cloak:

> Heere is a cloake cost fifty pound, wife,
> Which I can sell for thirty, when I ha' seene
> All *London* in't, and London has seene mee.
> To day, I goe to the *Black-fryers Play-house*,
> Sit i' the view, salute all my acquaintance,
> Rise vp between the *Acts*, let fall my cloake,
> Publish a handsome man, and a rich suite
> (As that's a speciall end, why we goe thither,
> All that pretend, to stand for't o' the *Stage*)
> The Ladies aske who's that? (For, they doe come
> To see vs, *Loue*, as wee doe to see them)
> Now, I shall lose all this, for the false feare
> Of being laught at?
>
> (I. vi. 28–40)

The play at which Fitz-dottrell was going to show off his fine new cloak
appears to move outwards from the theatre to encompass all London,
and Fitz-dottrell in his cloak becomes its main character. This device of
the cloak in which Fitz-dottrell is to attend the playhouse gives to *The
Devil is an Ass* a duality of perspective, so that *The Devil is an Ass* is both
the play *we* watch, an image of reality, and a play within the main play
which we only hear about and never see— until we realize that it *is* the
play we are watching. This ambiguity is not insisted on within the part
of the plot which deals with Meere-craft's schemes for Fitz-dottrell; but
it assists in sharpening our awareness of Wittipol's function as an actor
within Fitz-dottrell's world, who gradually becomes a disinterested
onlooker and finally becomes stage-manager of the 'play' which Fitz-
dottrell's world, the play *we* watch, gradually becomes. Wittipol's
function is, finally, similar to that of Crites; but it is less straightforward
in that, to begin with, he is too much involved in the essential failings of
Fitz-dottrell's London. That is to say, the values of the whole play are
rather more complex than simply those of Wittipol's ideal of love,
which develops into a kind of Platonism in Act IV, scene vi. In many
respects the play creates its values by the way it fluctuates between a
single and a double image: the play as an imitation of the real world and
the play as the play Fitz-dottrell wanted to see. Wittipol seems to be the
pivot on which this dual vision turns; and like Volpone's song to Celia
his song to Mrs Fitz-dottrell, in its context, assists in characterizing the
fluctuating yet still positive moral centre of the play.

In exchange for his cloak Wittipol is allowed to speak to Mrs
Fitz-dottrell for a quarter of an hour in the presence of her husband (I.
vi). However eloquent Wittipol's address might appear within the

blighted world of Fitz-dottrell's greed and folly, it is made ludicrous by the situation—the distance marked on the floor, the fact that Mrs Fitz-dottrell has been forbidden to answer, and Fitz-dottrell's jealous presence. Nevertheless, Mrs Fitz-dottrell is impressed by Wittipol's performance and manages to trick Pug into arranging a meeting between them, through the window of Mrs Fitz-dottrell's gallery which fortunately faces the window of Wittipol's friend Manly's room in Lincoln's Inn. But if the first meeting was ridiculous, the second meeting (ii. vi), of which Fitz-dottrell exclaims that he has been made a 'Cuckold,/Th⟨o⟩rough a casement' (iv. vii. 52–3), is far more so. It is made ridiculous both by the situation and by the fact that Wittipol takes himself too seriously to recognize the incongruity of his position, as he had recognized the incongruity of his earlier meeting with Mrs Fitz-dottrell. For Wittipol is unconsciously acting a part here: he regards himself as a perfect courtly lover and seems quite unaware that the situation undermines the seriousness of his intention. Only a short time before this scene we have seen Pug's unsuccessful attempts to seduce Mrs Fitz-dottrell (ii. ii. 12–15 and 72–86) and this must surely be in our minds too. To his own perception Wittipol's song at the window is sincere and perfect eloquence:

> *Doe but looke, on her eyes! They doe light—*
> *All that Loue's world comprizeth!*
> *Doe but looke on her hayre! it is bright,*
> *As Loue's starre, when it riseth!*
> *Doe but marke, her fore-head's smoother,*
> *Then words that sooth her!*
> *And from her arched browes, such a grace*
> *Sheds it selfe through the face;*
> *As alone, there triumphs to the life,*
> *All the gaine, all the good, of the elements strife!*
>
> *Haue you seene but a bright Lilly grow,*
> *Before rude hands haue touch'd it?*
> *Haue you mark'd but the fall of the Snow,*
> *Before the soyle hath smuch'd it?*
> *Haue you felt the wooll o' the Beuer?*
> *Or Swans downe, euer?*
> *Or, haue smelt o' the bud o' the Bryer?*
> *Or the Nard i' the fire?*
> *Or, haue tasted the bag o' the Bee?*
> *O, so white! O, so soft! O, so sweet is shee!*
>
> (ii. vi. 94–113)[42]

[42] At ii. vi. 13–22 we are told that Manly sings. This is probably the song Wittipol himself sings later in the scene. However, of the earlier song, Manly's song, Wittipol says that the words will 'goe vnto the ayre you loue so well' (ii. vi. 13). The music which exists for the song Wittipol sings at

Although the poem is better poetry than Hedon's song, its senti-ments, especially those of stanza two which is the only stanza set to music, are almost exactly the same; for we find the ideal lover's exalta-tion of the perceptions of the faculties of sight and hearing replaced here by the perception of the 'base' senses of taste, touch, and smell. On the other hand, Wittipol's song does not make use merely of clichés as Hedon's did: his images are precise, anchored in common homely experience in a way which creates its own values and poises the song, in its context in Act II, scene vi, between complete seriousness and farce. Whereas Hedon's performance was merely illustrative of his aimless character, Wittipol's situation is a potentially developing one, and one to which he himself is completely committed. Like Volpone's song to Celia, Wittipol's song comes as the culmination of the scene each sees as leading to the fulfilment of his ideal.

Like the setting of Volpone's song to Celia, the musical setting of Wittipol's song is an important part of its meaning. Wittipol's song, like Volpone's, is to be judged for itself, as an anthology piece, as well as for its incongruity in its context. This ambiguity in the performance of the song is summed up in the contrast between the idyllic final line:

O, so white! O, so soft! O, so sweet is shee!

and the entrance of Fitz-dottrell, unseen by Wittipol, behind his wife, with the bitter:

Is shee so, Sir? and, I will keepe her so.

(II. vii. 1)

A setting of the song occurs in several early seventeenth-century manuscripts. The earliest of these is British library MS Add. 15117, a manuscript collection which was possibly compiled no later than 1616, the year in which Jonson's play was performed.[43] The six other versions of this setting, all in later manuscripts, reduce the subleties of the 15117 version and can thus be assumed also to be later. The setting has been ascribed to Robert Johnson, who was writing a good deal of music for the King's Men at this time and also setting dance tunes for Jonson's

---

the end of the scene appears to have been written especially for those words. So, either Manly sings the *same* song, to the same tune, and we are to consider it a popular melody; or, the melody which exists for the words was not that intended for performances of the play; or, Manly sings a different song, to a different, popular melody. If this latter explanation is what Jonson intended then Manly's song is the only 'blank' song (i.e. the only song whose words are not given) in all Jonson's works. Because of this, it seems most probable that Manly's song is that which Wittipol sings later, and the first of the three suggestions is the most attractive.

[43] For a consideration of the manuscript collection and its possible connection with the London theatres see my discussion, Joiner, 'B.M. MS Add. 15117'.

EXAMPLE 8. 'Haue you seene but a whyte lillie grow'

Haue you seene but a whyte lil - lie

grow _____ be - fore rude hands had

toutcht it, haue you markt __ but __ the __ fall of the snow

be - fore — the earthe hathe smucht it, haue you felt the

woole of beu - er, or swans downe eu - er,

or haue smelt of the bud of the bryer or the nard in the fire

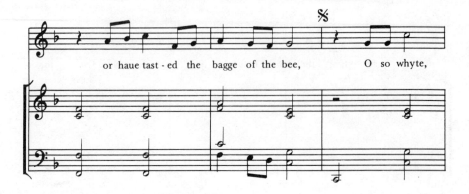

B.L. MS Add. 15117, f. 17ᵛ.

Notes.

3 voice VIII: MS gives the final note of the run as ♪.

3 tabl. I and II: MS = ♩ ♪ In I, beneath the upper note (c on course 1) a has been written.

6 voice III-VI: MS gives four semiquavers here while maintaining a semibreve in the accompaniment. I give these notes as quavers. An alternative would be to keep the semiquavers and alter I and II to ♪. and | in the tablature to ♪ The advantage of this would be that the piece would then end on the first beat of the bar instead of the 3rd, as in my transcription. The final note would then be a semibreve, as in the MS.

13 tabl. I-III: MS gives no note-values.

15 tabl. I-III, IV-VI: MS gives note-values as ♭♩. I transcribe as though ♭♩.

18 tabl. I: MS gives no note-value.

20 tabl. I-II: MS gives the following between I and II ⊞

20 tabl. II: MS gives ⟨c⟩ on course 5 as part of this chord.

masques; but there is no specific evidence that this song is his.[44] It is possible that the setting of Wittipol's song in British Library 15117, f. 17ᵛ is that which was sung in the first performances of the play, although neither this nor any of the other extant versions sets the first of the two stanzas Jonson's folio texts give.[45] All we have to go on is the fact that its occurrence in the British Library manuscript seems to be contemporary with the play, that no other settings of the song exist, and that this particular one was very popular. Furthermore, it seems appropriate within the context of the play itself. For the music complements the poetry in that it maintains the poetry's precarious balance—in its context—between the serious and the absurd. Like Ferrabosco's setting of 'Come my Celia', the setting of 'Haue you seene' is not strictly declamatory nor affective, but maintains what Campion called 'a manly cariage, gracing no word, but that which is eminent, and emphaticall'.[46] The musical shape of the setting follows the verbal phrases more closely than is the case in some of Dowland's dance ayres, for instance; and this impression is reinforced, perhaps, by the fact that the lute accompaniment is simple and chordal, supporting the vocal line mainly harmonically rather than mingling with it as an equal part. The setting thus illustrates the ideal relationship of music to words first advocated by the Platonic French academies and the *Camerata*, a relationship which gives the song affective power. By giving to the series of rhetorical questions of which the poetry consists a melodic rather than a declamatory setting which would harden and inflate the poetry, the song succeeds in creating a stasis in the ludicrous action we have just witnessed,[47] in creating an ideal moment which, while it lasts, is convincing to us. Certainly, Wittipol has the last word in the episode; and although these final words have an exaggerated anguish and are made comic too by the fact that, in a different building, he is helpless, they are at least partly justified by the unfortunate position of Mrs Fitz-dottrell. Wittipol says of Fitz-dottrell:

> O! I could shoote mine eyes at him, for that, now;
> Or leaue my teeth in'him, were they cuckolds bane,
> Inough to kill him. What prodigious,
> Blinde, and most wicked change of fortune's this?

[44] Cutts, *La Musique*, p. 152 ascribes the song to Robert Johnson purely on stylistic grounds. In *La Musique*, he has transcribed two versions, that in B. L. MS Add. 15117 and a version in New York Public Library, Drexel MS 4175, no. 49 (see pp. 54–6). The list of settings is given on p. 150.

[45] For details of printing see H & S vi, pp. 145–61 Jonson included both stanzas of the poem as no. 4 in his 'A celebration of Charis in Ten Lyrick Peeces' in *The Underwood* (1640).

[46] See above, p. 42

[47] Jonson's stage direction for II. vi. 70–80 is: '*He growes more familiar in his Courtship, playes with her paps, kisseth her hands, &c.*' We remember that the lovers are at windows on opposite sides of the street.

I ha' no ayre of patience: all my vaines
Swell, and my sinewes start at iniquity of it.
I shall breake, breake.

(II. vii. 17–23)

It is Fitz-dottrell who is made to look the more foolish by his jealous striking of Wittipol's 'mistress'—his own wife.

Because the whole episode reminds us in many ways of Volpone's wooing of Celia and his 'discovery' by Bonario, the important differences become apparent. The main difference, of course, is that Mrs Fitz-dottrell is no Celia, for she chooses and expresses values for herself; nor is Wittipol a Volpone, trying merely to add a beautiful mistress to his spoils. Thus, the plotting of the two against Mrs Fitz-dottrell's foolish and self-centred husband makes the comedy of the wooing scene dynamic, a potentially developing situation.

When we next see Wittipol he is again plotting to delude Fitz-dottrell and to gain an interview with Mrs Fitz-dottrell, this time disguised as the Spanish lady, the 'President', the '*Law*' and the '*Canon*' (II. viii. 32) of women of fashion. The absurdity of the plot falls not only on Fitz-dottrell but also on Wittipol himself. In his ludicrous disguise (Lady Taile-bush sees him as 'the very *Infanta* of the *Giants*', IV. ii. 71) he attempts to seduce Mrs Fitz-dottrell by taking her aside to another room to read to her. This scene (IV. vi) which is the culmination of his absurdity is also the scene of his 'education'. In performance, moreover, it might be regarded as parallel to the scene in which Wittipol woos Mrs Fitz-dottrell through the window; although this time it is not Fitz-dottrell himself who is concealed and then stands behind unnoticed, but Wittipol's friend Manly. Manly's part in the play is small and he is scarcely independent of Wittipol himself.[48] He advises Wittipol to help Mrs Fitz-dottrell against her husband rather than seduce her; for in becoming disillusioned about his own mistress, Lady Taile-bush, he has also become more idealistic. Manly's advice to Wittipol here may be seen as a development of the earlier, parallel, scene where he first sings Wittipol's song and then slips away. Now, the positive values of that song—as a courtly and aristocratic art—are developed from this, later scene as responsible action.

With the aid of both Manly and Mrs Fitz-dottrell Wittipol now becomes completely the 'stage-manager' and the play becomes his 'play' when the ass (Fitz-dottrell) becomes the Devil (v. viii). 'How now, what play ha' we here?' Wittipol asks as Fitz-dottrell, pretending to be possessed by the Devil, lies in bed foaming at the mouth and

---

[48] See Thayer, *Ben Jonson*, p. 168, who suggests that Manly is Wittipol's conscience, his *alter ego* which is developed through the play.

chanting nonsense rhymes. Wittipol answers himself: 'The *Cockscomb*, and the *Couerlet*' (v. viii. 39–40).

Manly, who has little individuality in the play, has most of the speaking in the final scene: Wittipol himself says little. In this, Jonson has avoided giving Wittipol the limiting didacticism of a character like Crites. To a degree he has left our impression of Wittipol free of moralizing and maintained in this way the dual-play effect.

Although we are not, then, given a solution to the world in which the Devil is an ass and in which the ass plays devil, nevertheless, in the contrast of Wittipol's growing self-awareness in the final scenes with Fitz-dottrell's final disintegration into feigned madness and incoherent raving, we are shown where a solution may be sought. It is to be found in poetry, eloquence, in the theatre itself. It is not to be found in the theatre as Fitz-dottrell sees it, where he himself takes the main part, but in Jonson's theatre which 'holds the mirror up' to Fitz-dottrell's world and shows 'the very age and body of the time his form and pressure'.[49]

VI

As anthology pieces both Volpone's and Wittipol's songs illustrate some of the important values which lie behind their plays; values of an aristocratic society, values which see in man's ability to communicate effectively by poetry and music those qualities which place him in harmony with the divine cosmic plan. But in both plays this point is enacted in the pattern of the whole play rather than stated; in the particular contexts the wisdom of the songs' composers and performers is shown to be flawed and we thus have mimicry rather than eloquence.

Between *Volpone* and *The Devil is an Ass* Jonson was writing not only plays but also masques for the court. In his masques he drew more heavily and more explicitly on those values of a Platonic courtly ideal which lay behind his use of song in the plays we have looked at so far, and informed, especially, his use of song in *The Devil is an Ass*. Before I turn to Jonson's masques, however, I consider, in the chapter which follows, some of these ideas and values within their sixteenth-century context.

[49] *Hamlet*, ii. ii. 24.

PART TWO

4

A Renaissance Courtly Ideal: Castiglione's Book of the Courtier

So FAR we have considered the more moralistic, the more strictly satirical aspects of Jonson's work: his concern with 'men, manners and morals'. The virtues and values outlined for us in the Dedication of *Volpone* and demonstrated in that play (and, we have seen, in earlier plays) derive from a classical humanism: indeed, they derive largely from Horace. Further, Jonson's use of music and song both in the early plays for the children's theatre and in the comedies from *Volpone* to *The Devil is an Ass* supports the strong moralistic bias of his ideas about the value of poetry. In these plays song is used to demonstrate his assertion that the good poet and the good man are necessarily one: the affected man, the fop or charlatan, can merely plagiarize. Hedon and Amorphus's songs in *Cynthia's Revels*, or Crispinus's songs in *Poetaster*, illustrate the absurdity of the affected man who attempts to become a poet; and Jonson's satire of Ovid and his literary group in *Poetaster* stems from the same belief. On the other hand, song is used in *The Devil is an Ass* not so much as satire as to make clear the equivocal position of Wittipol: the sensitive man, aware of the follies of his own society but not yet fully aware of himself. Later in the play Wittipol learns to reach a position of control, which Jonson shows us as self-control; a position very similar to Clerimont's in Act, I scene i of *Epicoene*. Like Clerimont, Wittipol is now able to manipulate, to some degree, the action of his play.

In *Volpone*, as in *The Devil is an Ass*, Jonson's use of song is not direct social satire—in the way Hedon's or Amorphus's or Crispinus's songs are. Volpone's song to Celia and Wittipol's song to Mrs Fitz-dottrell are comic, not so much in themselves, as that they are out of place. In each case the characters are blind to the reality of their situations, and unaware of the incongruity of the songs in their contexts. In particular, Volpone's song to Celia (like Wittipol's song to Mrs Fitz-dottrell) allows us both to admire and to condemn. The song to Celia, together with the songs in the mountebank scene, are, however, more important to the play as a whole than Wittipol's song; and this is because the songs in *Volpone* are not simply isolated illustrations of the play's comic mode, but are essential to that play's demonstration of the discrepancy between intention and act, between words and meaning. Wittipol's and

Volpone's songs are satiric only in their contexts; and the failure of these characters to realize for us an image of the Renaissance courtier each emulates makes them appear ridiculous. In other words, like Clerimont's song in scene i of *Epicoene*, the ideal image stands behind the scene as some measure of value within the play.

This chapter will consider the values on which these songs and their functions in the plays are based. The discussion which follows will be largely of one work, Castiglione's *Il libro del cortegiano*, first published in Venice in 1528 and translated into English by Sir Thomas Hoby in 1561. There is no doubt of the extreme popularity of the work: the sixteenth-century Italian editions are too many to enumerate, and it was well known among cultured Englishmen before Hoby's translation.[1]

I

The Book of the Courtier has been regarded chiefly on the one hand as a handbook of court etiquette and behaviour and on the other hand as a source, in Bembo's speech at the end of Book IV, for popular Renaissance Platonism. It was one of several etiquette books in the sixteenth century, and certainly in Europe it vied with another, more strictly 'handbook' sort of work, della Casa's *Galateo*, which was also widely translated. The form of Castiglione's work is unusual, for it is not simply a catalogue of the manners and customs of polite society. The work is an idealized record of discussions that took place on four consecutive evenings among the courtiers at the ducal palace of Urbino; discussions of the nature, function, and manners of an ideal courtier. Thus the work is in one sense an historical record; but more important than this it has an artistic coherence and unity which makes it also a presentation in a literary form of the precepts for the ideal courtier put forward in the discussions. It becomes a demonstration itself of the ideal of the court and its courtiers. Castiglione obviously regarded himself as writing something more than just a handbook of social etiquette: for he penetrates well below the surface of mere social politeness. The book is concerned with larger issues, with the meaning of man in society and his place in the universe. It views courtly arts and skill as part of the moral and aesthetic whole which, ideally, he believed, man's life should be. Indeed, what contributes largely to its coherence is Castiglione's sympathetic sharing and understanding of the Renaissance concern with the ambiguity of man's nature. The old medieval acceptance of the Chain of Being is coming to be redefined: man is still merely a link in this great chain, but he has become, as it were, the central link; his moral responsibilities are more sharply evident. Man is now regarded

[1] Einstein, *Italian Renaissance in England*, Chapters 2 and 3.

as being 'set . . . at the world's centre that . . . from thence [he may] more easily observe whatever is in the world'. Man is made 'neither of heaven nor of earth, neither mortal nor immortal' but has 'the power [either] to degenerate into the lower forms of life, which are brutish' or 'out of [his] soul's judgment, to be reborn into the higher forms which are divine'.[2] By the exercise of his 'soul's judgment' man will recognize the order and beauty of God's universe, and he will seek unceasingly to imitate this order and beauty in his own life. It is this doctrine which may be regarded as the basic conviction of Castiglione's work; and in his long discourse, at the end of Book IV, of man's place in the universe, Bembo makes explicit the assumptions underlying the whole of *The Courtier*. Bembo follows very closely the ideas of the Renaissance Platonists; but the value of his exposition for us lies not so much in its ideas, but in the way in which those ideas are expressed. First, however, I look at these ideas, and later consider in what ways they become part of the book's artistic coherence and its significance.

Bembo speaks of 'the state of this great Inginn of the world, which God created for the helth and preservation of every thing that was made' and observes that 'these thinges . . . have . . . suche beawtie and comelinesse, that all the wittes men have, can not imagin a more beawtifull matter'. This 'Inginn' is the perfection of goodness and beauty. This is made explicit when, in comparing the universe with man 'which may be called a litle world', Bembo concludes that 'Good and beawtifull be after a sort one selfe thinge, especiallie in the bodies of men: of the beawtie wherof the nighest cause . . . is the beawtie of the soule: the which as a partner of the right and heavenlye beawtie, maketh sightlye and beawtifull what ever she toucheth . . .".[3] The body is an expression of the soul in the way that the visible and natural universe is an expression of God's goodness, of the harmony of the universal order.

'Good and beawtifull be after a sort one selfe thinge': if the ideal courtier will recognize this truth about 'this great Inginn of the world', a truth about the harmony and interdependence of the spiritual world and the natural (or sensual and experiential) world, then he has in the 'great Inginn' a perfect model for his own life and for every aspect of his life. It is clear throughout that the courtiers at Guidubaldo's court recognize this.

Bembo's words appear to provide a synthesis of what had often seemed in the middle ages to be dual and opposed aspects of life, an opposition of transcendental and empirical experience and knowledge.

[2] Pico della Mirandola, 'On the Dignity of Man', trans. Forbes, p. 225. Pico is one of the most important of the Italian Platonists.
[3] *The Courtier*, IV; pp. 349 and 350.

Such a dualism is evident, for instance, in endless debates about the relative merits of the contemplative and active lives, the life of the philosopher-saint or the life of the soldier-statesman. The topic is also discussed at some length by the courtiers at Duke Guidubaldo's court. But the debate here differs from the medieval debates on the subject, and the difference is perhaps most succinctly defined by Bembo's statement that 'Good and beawtifull' are 'one selfe thinge'.

In the middle ages 'beauty' does not have the high moral status which the Renaissance Platonic philosophers, following Plato's *Phaedrus*, gave it; and so the dichotomy between the sensual and the spiritual realms of experience is absolute. Bembo's remark, on the other hand, reminds us of the value the Renaissance gave to the artist, as co-creator of the universe, the man who understood the divine plan by contemplation of the created world around him and who imitated this plan in his own medium—whether poetry, painting, sculpture, music, or architecture. As man can imitate his Creator in the liberal arts, so too can life itself become an art, so that action within the created universe necessarily takes on a moral quality which may be judged simultaneously by aesthetic standards. Life as an art is perhaps the main theme underlying Castiglione's book. The end, therefore, of all action is a greater understanding of the absolute moral and aesthetic value of God's universe; contemplation of the Heavenly Beauty is reached through participation in, and an understanding of, the creation. This gives a perspective rather different from the medieval one to the debate about action and contemplation in *The Courtier*. Lord Octavian, discussing a remark of Duke Fredericke's, says:

But the ende of the actyve or doinge lief ought to be the beehouldinge, as of warr, peace, and of peynes, rest. Therfore is it also the office of a good Prince so to trade his people and with such lawes and statutes, that they maye lyve in rest and in peace, without daunger and with encrease of welth, and injoye praisablye this ende of their practises and actions, which ought to be quietnesse.

(IV; p. 318)

Although of course the Lord Octavian does primarily mean a literally and materially peaceful existence the passage seems to take us further. It carries us forward to Bembo's philosophical discourse about the nature of the universe. Bembo speaks of 'the high mansion place where the heavenlye, amiable and right beawtye dwelleth, which lyeth hid in the innermost secretes of God, least unhalowed eyes shoulde come to the syght of it'; he says that 'there shall we fynde a most happye ende for our desires, true rest for oure travailes, certein remedye for myseryes, a most healthfull medycin for sickenesse, a most sure haven in the troublesome stormes of the tempestuous sea of this life'.[4] We cannot say that he is placing a doctrine of Absolute Virtue over against one of worldly aspiration such as Octavian has spoken of. Rather, he is speaking of a concept of Absolute Virtue, of which the Lord Octavian's is the imitation in human affairs. For, in a personal sense, Octavian's state of 'quietnesse' is a state of perfect freedom, a state of perfect understanding of, and harmony with, the whole of the created universe; it is a state of mind, removed from the immediate and temporal exigencies imposed by human society in a state of unrest or disruption.

II

One of the main emphases of the final Book of *The Courtier*, and one which finally emerges as of underlying importance to the whole, is the emphasis laid on communication. In the early part of Book IV, for instance, the ideal courtier is spoken of as the adviser of the Prince, someone who can communicate an understanding of virtue and goodness. The primary form of communication is, of course, discourse or speech; but the whole argument of the work makes clear that speech is by no means the only means of communication. All the liberal arts, all the accomplishments of the courtier will express him.[5] So, while a good deal of importance is given in the discussions to discourse, and while, indeed, the whole form of the book, as dialogue, and the tenor of this dialogue, point to the importance of eloquence, the terms in which the debates on language are carried out are those also used in discussing other liberal arts which are regarded as expressing an understanding of the universe: in particular, the arts of music and dancing.[6] The implications of the courtiers' discussion of the value of eloquence are important then, because while their definition of eloquence refers explicitly to language and speaking (to oratory, poetry, and conversation), implicitly it includes all the arts which the ideal courtier must acquire. Underlying the discussion of all the liberal arts is a single set of assumptions about their value. In stressing communication as the supreme significance of the arts, the courtiers in fact stress the primary importance of the listener's response.

[4] *The Courtier*, IV; p. 361.

[5] Cf. Mazzeo, *Renaissance and Revolution*, pp. 147–8.

[6] The importance of speech and the arts of oratory was not, of course, an exclusively Renaissance emphasis. Although the Platonic philosophers of the Renaissance viewed eloquence in a manner rather different from that of the medieval philosophers, it had a similar significance as defining man as distinct from animals. Renaissance writers nearly always couple discourse or speech with Reason, that faculty whereby man comprehends the universe around him—what Hamlet calls 'god-like reason', the ability of 'looking before and after'. (See *Hamlet*, IV. iv. 36–9 and I. ii. 150 where Hamlet speaks of 'a beast that wants discourse of reason'.) It is the poet, Jonson says, who is 'arbiter of nature': 'Dedication' of *Volpone*, ll. 27–8. Ficino described 'discourse' as 'the messenger of reason'. See *Five Questions*, trans. Burroughs, p. 206.

This view which gives great importance to art is intimately related to the aesthetic world-view which was the basis of Renaissance Platonist thinking. Perhaps the interrelationship of the value of communication and an aesthetic world-view is most clearly summed up in one of the most popular Renaissance images and one which is extremely ancient: the dance of the Three Graces. In Renaissance Platonic thought the Three Graces symbolize the triadic nature of Love, or God; and their dance in a circle symbolizes the unity in their trinity. Love, the middle dancer in the group, looks towards Pleasure though first directed and inspired by Beauty. Plate III shows the dance of the Three Graces from Botticelli's *Primavera*. In Botticelli's painting the whole group is presided over by Venus, the goddess of love.[7] So, Beauty comes from God, and man, inspired and moved by love of beauty, returns to God through Pleasure in Beauty. Such a philosophy which is both aesthetic and moral lays emphasis on the affective qualities of art.

The Renaissance Platonist philosophy of Love on which the arguments in *The Courtier* are based was expressed most clearly by Ficino in his *Commentary* on Plato's *Symposium*. In a passage in this *Commentary* he explains the relation between Love and Beauty like this:

For shame frightens men away from evil deeds, and the desire of being superior summons them to good deeds. Nothing lays these two before men more sharply and clearly than Love. When we say Love, we mean by that term the desire for beauty, for this is the definition of Love among all philosophers. Beauty is, in fact, a certain charm which is found chiefly and predominantly in the harmony of several elements. This charm is three-fold: there is a certain charm in the soul, in the harmony of several virtues; charm is found in material objects, in the harmony of several colours and lines; and likewise charm in sound is the best harmony of several tones. There is, therefore, this triple beauty: of the soul, of the body, and of sound. That of the soul is perceived by the mind; that of the body, by the eyes: and that of sound, by the ear alone . . . Since . . . Love is the desire for enjoying beauty, Love is always limited to [the pleasures of] the mind, the eyes, and the ears. . . . desire which arises from the other senses is called, not love, but lust or madness.[8]

The perception of beauty depends on communication: the soul becomes aware of beauty and attains to a state of Love only in so far as it is aroused by Reason or the higher senses of sight and hearing. Ficino makes a linguistic connection between the Greek word 'to call' and the Latin word for 'beauty'.[9]

. . . that beauty [which] greatly arouses the soul, is called κάλλος 'arousing',

---

[7] For a full discussion see Wind, *Pagan Mysteries*, in particular pp. 36 f.

[8] Ficino, *Commentary on Plato's 'Symposium'*, trans. Jayne, p. 130.

[9] The linguistic relationship is, of course, Ficino's and cannot be taken literally.

from the Greek word κάλέω which means *to call*: κάλλος in Greek is equivalent to *pulchritudo* in Latin.[10]

The discussion of rhetoric, or eloquence, in *The Courtier* is at first practical: the courtier must avoid affectation,[11] and there is some difference of opinion whether or not 'auncient Tuscane wordes' are more suitable in both writing and speaking.[12] Count Lewis has the final word, saying:

> Therfore woulde I (for my parte) alwayes shonne the use of those auncient woordes, except it wer in certayne clauses, and in them very seldome. And (in my judgement) he that useth them otherwise, committeth a no lesse errour, then whoso would to folowe them of olde time, fede upon maste, where he hath now aboundance of corne founde oute.
>
> (1; p. 69)

The Count's advice on speaking emphasizes plainness, that the 'wisdom', the subject-matter of the communication must shine through the speech and not be clouded and confused by his own mannerisms and affectations:

> Then must he couch in a good order that he hath to speake or to write, and afterward expresse it wel with wordes: the which (if I be not deceived) ought to be apt, chosen, clere, and wel applyed, and (above al) in use also among the people: for very suche make the greatnes and gorgeousnes of an Oracion, so he that speaketh have a good judgement and heedfulnes withal, and the understanding to pike such as be of most proper significacion, for that he entendeth to speake and commend, and tempring them like wexe after his owne mynde, applyeth them in suche parte and in suche order, that at the firste showe they maie set furth and doe men to understand the dignitie and brightnes of them, as tables of peincting placed in their good and naturall light.
>
> (1; pp. 69–70)

The end of eloquence is not, therefore, beauty of speech in itself, but rather to make the listener as little aware of eloquence, for its own sake, as possible: 'at the firste showe' to 'doe men to understand the dignitie and brightnes' of the matters the speaker wishes to communicate.

Throughout this discussion, in emphasizing the importance of communication, Count Lewis emphasizes the response of the listener. Further on in the same discussion he makes the importance of the way in which the listener responds quite clear. He wishes his ideal orator

> to have the understanding to speake with dignitie and vehemency, and to raise those affections which oure mindes have in them, and to enflame or stirre them accordinge to the matter: sometime with a simplicitye of suche meekenesse of

---

[10] Ficino, *Commentary on Plato's 'Symposium'*, trans. Jayne, p. 167.

[11] Hoby's word is 'curiosity'. *The Courtier*, 1; pp. 59 f.

[12] *The Courtier*, 1; pp. 63–9.

mynde, that a man would weene nature her self spake, to make them tender and (as it wer) dronken with sweetnesse . . .

(i; pp. 70–1)

In emphasizing the response of the listener, rather than, for instance, the virtuosity of the speaker, Count Lewis sees rhetoric (which would include general conversation, poetry and literature, or formal oration) of value primarily as a means of understanding experience.[13]

Such a view of rhetoric makes the assumption that the 'vehemency' of the speech and its power to 'raise [the] affections' indicates the moral value, or truth, of what is being said. It implies that the 'wisdome' to be communicated will contain a universal truth. The Count says that the eloquent speaker will make his listeners 'weene that nature herself spake'.[14] The assumption is never questioned in *The Courtier*; but the recognition that the affections may be stirred by less than universal truth posed a dilemma for later, post-Reformation followers of the Platonic aesthetic. For instance, in his *Apologie for Poetrie* (1581–3), Sidney uses arguments for the value of poetry which often come very close to those Count Lewis uses: one example is his famous description of poetry as a picture, not in the ordinary sense of something visually perceived but in the sense that the effect of poetry on the listener is, like that of a picture, immediate, that it may 'strike, pierce [and] possesse the sight of the soule'.[15] Further, his often-quoted phrase of 'teaching by delighting' indicates both the moral and aesthetic qualities of poetry. Similarly, the 'golden world' of poetry of which Sidney speaks is not to be regarded as an escape world of pleasant fiction to be set over against a harsh world of reality or fact;[16] for, Sidney says, 'That imitation, wherof Poetry is, hath the most conueniency to Nature of all others.'[17] However, Sidney is trapped in his argument in a way Castiglione's courtiers are not, for although he suggests that Poetry complements the 'brasen' world of History and action, that the 'golden world' is a world of knowledge of Truth beyond the small demands and irrelevancies of Time and History, a world which '[lifts] vp the mind from the dungeon of the body to the enioying his owne diuine essence',[18] nevertheless, he is forced to admit that History's 'brasen' world is also the 'too much

---

[13] He does not by any means belittle the great art of the successful orator, however. The conclusion of this passage says that this orator will have 'suche conveiaunce of easinesse, that whoso heareth him, maye conceyve a good oppinion of himselfe, and thinke that he also with very litle a doe, mighte attaine to that perfection, but whan he commeth to the proofe shall finde himselfe farre wide' (p. 71).

[14] For a detailed and lucid discussion of this aspect of the Renaissance theories of rhetoric see Alpers, *'Faerie Queene'*, Chapter I, pp. 9 ff.

[15] *Apologie*, ed. Smith, i, p. 164.

[16] *Apologie*, ed. Smith, i, p. 156.

[17] *Apologie*, ed. Smith, i, p. 173.

[18] *Apologie*, ed. Smith, i, p. 161.

loued earth', that nature herself is imperfect, and that man's attachment to sensual beauty is at odds with his recognition of the Dvine Idea.[19]

This dilemma is one which arises again and again in late sixteenth-century English discussions of eloquence, or the 'stirring of affections'. But for Castiglione's courtiers the problem does not arise, and the other liberal arts, in particular music and dancing, are discussed at some length and in terms similar to those used in the discussion of rhetoric. The fact that these arts are regarded as related is important. I shall consider music first.

III

Like the discussion of rhetoric, the discussion of music touches on the more practical aspects first. The discussion of music's value to the courtier begins as a series of general and derivative statements: indeed, Castiglione at this point merely sets out the usual Renaissance arguments on the subject. The acknowledgement by the courtiers of music's value, when compared with the intensity and seriousness of their consideration of eloquence, appears perfunctory. Count Lewis says:

> . . . it hath bene the opinion of most wise Philosophers that the world is made of musick, and the heavens in their moving make a melody, and our soule [is] framed after the very same sort, and therfore lifteth up it self and (as it were) reviveth the vertues and force of it with musick . . .
>
> (I; p. 89)[20]

He then goes on to cite Plato and Aristotle, saying that they 'declare with infinite reasons the force of musicke to be to very great purpose in us, and for many causes (that should be to long to rehearse) ought necessarilye to be learned from a mans childhoode . . .'.[21] Although Count Lewis's claim that music 'reviveth the vertues' of the soul is similar to that made for eloquence, its similarity is in its statement only. At this point it carries no particular conviction—either for the Count or for us. However, the discussion of music is resumed on the second night, in Book II, and now the discussion centres on the kind of music the ideal courtier should practise, and the kinds of instruments suitable for him to perform on.[22] Lord Fredericke speaks like this of the occasions for 'practising' music:

---

[19] *Apologie*, ed. Smith, I, p. 156.
[20] Cf. Pietzsch, *Die Klassifikation*, pp. 40–2; Spitzer, 'World Harmony'.
[21] *The Courtier*, I; pp. 89–90.
[22] *The Courtier*, II; p. 118. The suitability of certain instruments for aristocratic performance was a much debated topic in sixteenth-century etiquette. Sir Fredericke specifically states that the courtier should not 'meddle' with 'the instrumentes that Minerva and Alcibiades refused, because it seemeth they are noisome', and Hoby's marginal gloss at this point indicates that he thinks Fredericke refers to 'Shalmes. Dulcimers. Harpe'. His objection to the shawm and the harp may

But especiallye [these sortes of musike] are meete to bee practised in the presence of women, because those sightes sweeten the mindes of the hearers, and make them the more apte to bee perced with the pleasantnesse of musike, and also they quicken the spirites of the verye doers.

(II; p. 119)

Although Lord Fredericke is speaking of a social art and referring to a social context his words now carry more conviction than did Count Lewis's earlier citing of Plato and Aristotle. In the consideration of music as an expression of, and an enticement to, love we are reminded of the more serious discussion the previous night of eloquence as a means of comprehending Virtue, Goodness, Beauty, and we are carried forward too to Bembo's discourse, in Book IV, of the Form of Goodness and Beauty which is Love. There it is made quite clear that there is no antithesis between this earthly love and transcendental Love of which Bembo speaks; for he says that this earthly love is 'the lowermost steppe of the stayers, by the which a man may ascende to true love'.[23] That the power of music is similar to that of eloquence, that its value lies in its power to move the listener to an understanding of Virtue and Love, is endorsed when we recall a comment of Count Lewis's on the previous night, in the midst of the discussion of eloquence and rhetoric:

Mark me musick, wherin are harmonies somtime of the base soune and slowe, and otherwhile very quicke and of newe divises, yet do they all recreat a man: but for sundrye causes, as a manne may perceive in the maner of singinge that Bidon useth, which is so artificiall, counninge, vehement, stirred, and such sundrye melodies, that the spirites of the hearers move al and are enflamed, and so listening a man would wene they were lifte up in to heaven. And no lesse doeth our Marchetto Cara move in his singinge, but with a more softe har-monye, that by a delectable waye and full of mourninge sweetnesse maketh

---

be because they were considered the instruments of professional musicians, men with merely a craftsman's ability and without the higher, theoretical knowledge which distinguished the aristoc-rat. Castiglione's reference to 'the instrumentes that Minerva and Alcibiades refused' may be a reference specifically to the flute or to wind instruments in general. The lesson of Marsyas in the story of Athena and Marsyas as told by Ovid in his *Metamorphoses*, VI, was one which the Renaissance writers on etiquette took to heart. The position is clearly indicated in this annotation of the story by George Sandys in the 1632 edition of his translation: 'This story is seconded by another of the excoriating of *Marsyas*: a Musician excelling in wind instruments; and called a Satyre, for his rude and lascivious composures: who finding the flute, which *Minerua* cast away, when she beheld in the riuer how the blowing thereof distorted her visage, was the first of mortalls that played thereon: and so cunningly, that he presumed to challenge *Apollo* with his Harpe: by whom overcome, he had his skinne stript ouer his eares by the victor. It is said that *Minerua* threw the flute away, not only for deforming her face, but that such musique conferreth nothing to the knowledge of the Mind; presented by that Goddesse, the patronesse of wit and learning' (p. 224, Sig. 2B.4ʳ).

[23] *The Courtier*, IV; p. 346.

tender and perceth the mind, and sweetly imprinteth in it a passion full of great delite.

(I; p. 75)[24]

Here where music is specifically referred to as a form of 'eloquence' the flat statements of popular Renaissance musical theory catch fire.

IV

In speaking of the effects on the listener both of rhetoric and of music we have seen that Castiglione's courtiers emphasize immediacy of perception, their powerful and sensuous quality. We observed that this kind of perception is likened to the state of ecstasy which Bembo describes in Book IV, the perception of Love itself. In Book IV Bembo speaks of the power of Love like this:

> Thus the soule kindled in the most holye fire of true heavenlye love, fleeth to coople her selfe with the nature of Aungelles, and not onlye cleane forsaketh sense, but hath no more neede of the discourse of reason, for being chaunged into an Aungell, she understandeth all thinges that may be understoode: and without any veile or cloude, she seeth the meine sea of the pure heavenlye beawtye and receiveth it into her, and enjoyeth that soveraigne happinesse, that can not be comprehended of the senses.

(IV; p. 360)

This is the Divine Love, the Virtue which orders and guides the universe: 'the beawtye unseperable from the high bountye, which with her voyce calleth and draweth to her all thynges . . .'.[25] This spiritual exaltation, the understanding of heavenly beauty, has on those who can attain to it an effect similar to the effects Count Lewis attributed to eloquence. The Count said that the eloquent courtier might speak 'sometime with a simplicitye of suche meekenesse of mynde, that a man woulde weene nature her self spake, to make [the affections] tender and (as it wer) dronken with sweetenesse',[26] Bembo's prayer to Love is 'Make us dronken with the bottomelesse fountain of contentation'.[27]

V

The effects on the listener of rhetoric and music are spoken of in very similar ways in *The Courtier*. The consideration of music as an art the courtier should learn shows influence both of the medieval *amour cortois* and of the Renaissance Platonic philosophy. The discussion of music

---

[24] Marchetto Cara (b. Verona? d. Mantua, *c.*1527) was famous in his day as a lutenist and composer and is remembered chiefly for his development of the *frottola* form. He was lutenist and composer at the court of Mantua from 1495 to 1525.

[25] *The Courtier*, IV; p. 360.

[26] *The Courtier*, I; p. 71.

[27] *The Courtier*, IV; p. 362.

and love begins as a discussion of traditional ideas surrounding courtly love; but in *The Courtier* the ideals of courtly love are merged with the Platonic concept of ideal Love and the former is regarded as the first step towards the latter, rather than as something distinct. So too in the discussion of music. What begins as a lover singing love-songs to his mistress becomes part of a cosmic philosophy, where music is related to the heavenly harmony and has a significant role in the lives of men.

Music was an important art to the Renaissance Platonists. The best discussion of the Renaissance attitude to music is that by D. P. Walker in his *Spiritual and Demonic Magic from Ficino to Campanella*. Dr Walker points out the particular importance of music in a philosophy which believed, as one of its basic tenets, in a world ruled by the fixed stars and the seven planets. Music was thought to have special efficacy in capturing and directing planetary influence and Dr Walker sees this theory as based on two separate but ultimately related principles.[28] The first of these is the ancient theory, which derives from Plato's *Timaeus* and which was popularly held throughout the middle ages, of the relationship between man and the universe, the microcosm and the macrocosm, the *musica humana* and the *musica mundana*. Both microcosm and macrocosm are constructed on the same harmonic proportions.[29] It is to such a belief that Count Lewis refers when he says that 'the world is made of musick . . . and our soule [is] framed after the very same sort' in the passage quoted above.[30] The second principle Dr Walker points to is the ancient belief that music imitates emotions and moral attitudes, a belief which is expressed in Plato's discussion of the Greek modes in his *Republic*.[31] This is related to the idea of world harmony by the fact that the planets themselves were believed to contain the particular moral qualities of the god after whom they were named, and thus music could imitate not simply the universal harmony but the quality of a particular planet and so affect the spirit of the listener with the influence of that planet. It is this celestial or divine power with which the 'mimetic' theory endows music that Count Lewis refers to in the passage quoted on p. 124, when 'the spirites of the hearers move al and are enflamed, and so listening a man would wene they were lifte up in to heaven'. So, by performing or listening to music of particular moral and affective qualities a person can become more Jovial, Venereal, Solarian, or Mercurial. Dr Walker quotes a passage, in translation, from Ficino's

[28] Walker, *Spiritual Magic*, p. 14.
[29] Cf. Lorenzo's speech to Jessica in *The Merchant of Venice* (v. i. 70–89) about 'the man that hath no music in himself', and also Donne's Holy Sonnet V: 'I am a little world made cunningly/Of elements, and an angelic sprite . . .'
[30] See p. 123. *The Courtier*, i; p. 89.
[31] Plato, *Republic*, iii. 398–9. Plato follows Damon, a fifth-century Athenian educational theorist. For a discussion of Greek musical theory before Plato see Lasserre. *Plutarque de la musique*.

De Triplici Vita (III. xxi) which gives 'rules' for composing astrological music:

1. Find out what powers and effects any particular star has in itself, what positions and aspects, and what these remove and produce. And insert these into the meaning of the text, detesting what they remove, approving what they produce.

2. Consider which star chiefly rules which place and man. Then observe what modes (*tonis*) and songs these regions and persons generally use, so that you may apply similar ones, together with the meaning just mentioned, to the words which you wish to offer to these same stars.

3. The daily positions and aspects of the stars are to be noticed; then investigate to what speech, songs, movements, dances, moral behaviour and actions, most men are usually incited under these aspects, so that you may make every effort to imitate these in your songs, which will agree with the similar disposition of the heavens and enable you to receive a similar influx from them.[32]

Ficino ascribes particular kinds of music only to the four planets whose influence is benign: i.e. the Sun, Jupiter, Venus, and Mercury. He says that Saturn, Mars, and the Moon have only 'voices' and not music.[33] Ficino also lists at this point the kinds of music appropriate to the benign planets:

Jupiter: music which is grave, earnest, sweet and joyful with stability.
Venus: music which is voluptuous with wantonness and softness.
Apollo (the Sun): music which is venerable, simple and earnest, united with grace and smoothness.
Mercury: music which is somewhat less serious (than the Apolline) because of its gaiety, yet vigorous and various.[34]

Of all the planetary influences captured or imitated by the musician that of the Sun (Apollo) is especially beneficial to man. In Ficino's philosophy the Sun holds a very important place. It is the middle, or fourth, of the seven planets in the Ptolemaic system; and it is also the source of life and light and therefore was regarded as the metaphorical centre of the universe. It is often used as a metaphor for God or Christ.[35] The Sun, or Apollo, is also the god of music; and so music as a means of leading men to gnosticism is particularly important. Ficino's music was monodic and aimed at clear expression of the text, an ideal which was followed by the late sixteenth-century music theorists. For Ficino, as for

[32] Ficino, *Op. Omn.*, pp. 562–3. The passage is quoted in Walker, *Spiritual Magic*, p. 17.
[33] Ficino, *Op. Omn.*, p. 563. Walker, *Spiritual Magic*, p. 17.
[34] Ficino, *Op. Omn.*, p. 563. Quoted in Walker, *Spiritual Magic*, p. 17.
[35] It is thought that it was his belief that the sun was the metaphorical centre of the universe which led to Copernicus's hypothesis that it is, in fact, the centre of the universe. Copernicus's scientific interests seem, in any case, to have been sparked off by his philosophical interest in the Hermetic writings.

the later theorists, the text was of supreme importance: in the passage quoted above which gives his 'rules' for composing planetary music it is obvious that he is writing of song rather than purely instrumental music. The reason for placing the first importance on the text was that the text carried intellectual content and could influence the mind, whereas music alone reached only the spirit. Words and music together thus were thought to be particularly effective because the words addressed the mind while the music affected the sense and the lower parts of the soul, the imagination or phantasy. Thus a song, words and music together, was believed to affect the whole man—mind as well as body and spirit.[36]

Ficino explained the powerful affective qualities of music by the fact that the sense of hearing, by which music is perceived, stands in the Platonic hierarchy of the senses between sight—the sense closest to Reason, the higher faculty of man—and the baser senses, of taste, touch, and smell. This is the passage, from the *Commentary on the 'Symposium'*.

Hence it also happens that touch, taste, and smell sense only what is very near them, and they are very much affected in the process of sensation . . .

Hearing, however, recognizes still more remote things and so it is not so limited. Sight perceives even farther than hearing and catches in a moment what the ear catches only with time, for lightning is seen long before the thunder is heard.

Reason catches the most remote things of all, for it perceives not only what is in the world and the present, as the senses do, but also what is above the heavens, in the past, and in the future.

From this it is apparent to anyone that of those six powers of the soul, three pertain to body and matter, that is, touch, taste, and smell; but the other three, that is, reason, sight, and hearing, pertain to the soul . . .[37]

Of all the senses, Sight is closest to the soul because, Ficino explains, an image perceived by the eye is 'incorporeal' and therefore most like the soul itself. He explains that 'the small pupil of the eye' can 'take in the whole heavens' and this is similar to the way the soul 'in a single point, takes in the whole breadth of the body in a spiritual way and in an incorporeal image . . . [I]t is the incorporeal quality which pleases.'[38] Ficino makes a distinction between the external, material world which is in continual motion (motion is how Ficino defines life) and the soul which is in a state of perfect rest outside time. The link between the two states, he says, is Hearing, which stands between the bodily and spiritual perceptions and partakes of both. Ficino calls the link between

---

[36] Walker, *Spiritual Magic*, p. 21.
[37] Ficino, *Commentary on Plato's 'Symposium'*, trans. Jayne, p. 166.
[38] Ficino, *Commentary on Plato's 'Symposium'*, trans. Jayne. p. 168.

soul and body the *Spiritus* which, he says, consists of air, the same substance as sound, which he defines as movement in air. Therefore sound has direct contact with the *Spiritus* whereas Sight, which is related to light, does not. In this way sound can be thought to form a link between the spiritual and the created worlds. Ficino describes music as 'spherical motion' and this description aptly characterizes his idea of music as participating in both the spiritual and external worlds.[39] For the sphere, like the circle, has always been regarded as a symbol of perfection, of timelessness, or eternity;[40] and, of course, motion involves time. The term 'spherical motion' thus provides an image with a meaning similar to that of the visual image of the Three Graces, dancing in a circle.

In the discussion both of rhetoric and of music in *The Courtier* Castiglione uses tactile and sensual images to suggest the effect of 'eloquence' on the listener; but when speaking of rhetoric he also uses the common Renaissance image (from Horace's *Ars Poetica*) of *ut pictura poesis*, the idea of the immediacy of perception by sight, the sense which stands closest in the Platonic hierarchy to Reason and understanding.[41] In this way, the exaltation by Renaissance musical philosophers of words and music as an ideal union can be understood. The images by which their effects are described in *The Courtier* make clear that the two together exemplify a link between soul and sense, one which is basic to the Renaissance Platonist aesthetic and ethical philosophy of the universe. Thus a song, for instance, can be regarded as an imitation of the divine macrocosm.

When the courtiers consider the place of music in education in Book I I, Lord Gaspar Pallavicin observes: 'There are manye sortes of musicke aswell in the brest, as upon instrumentes, therfore would I gladly learne whiche is the best . . .' Lord Fredericke replies:

Me thinke . . . pricksong is a faire musicke, so it bee done upon the booke

---

[39] The passage occurs in Ficino's *Commentary on Plato's 'Timaeus'*, and is quoted in Walker, 'Ficino's *Spiritus* and Music', p. 137. 'Musical consonance occurs in the element which is the mean of all [i.e. air], and reaches the ears through motion, spherical motion: so that it is not surprising that it should be fitting to the soul, which is both the mean of things, and the origin of circular motion. In addition, musical sound, more than anything else perceived by the senses, conveys, as if animated, the emotions and thoughts of the singer's or player's soul to the listeners' souls; thus it preeminently corresponds with the soul. Moreover, as regards sight, although visual impressions are in a way pure, yet they lack the effectiveness of motion, and are usually perceived only as an image, devoid of reality: normally therefore, they move the soul only slightly . . . But musical sound by the movement of the air moves the body: by purified air it excites the aerial spirit which is the bond of body and soul: by emotion it affects the senses and at the same time the soul: by meaning it works on the mind . . .' The passage in Ficino which refers to 'spherical motion' reads: 'Musicam consonantiam in elemento fieri omnium medio, perqúe motum, et hunc quidem orbicularem ad aures peruenire' (*Op. Omn.* ii, p. 1453).

[40] Cf. Lowinsky, 'Physical and Musical Space', p. 61.

[41] Count Lewis compared the effect of eloquence to 'tables of peincting', *The Courtier*, i; p. 70.

surely and after a good sorte. But to sing to the lute is muche better, because al
the sweetenesse consisteth in one alone, and a manne is muche more heedefull
and understandeth better the feate maner and the aer or veyne of it, whan the
eares are not busyed in hearynge any moe then one voyce: and beesyde everye
little erroure is soone perceyved, which happeneth not in syngynge wyth
companye, for one beareth oute an other. But syngynge to the Lute wyth the
dyttie (me thynke) is more pleasaunte then the reste, for it addeth to the
wordes suche a grace and strength, that is a great wonder.

(ii; p. 118)[42]

The other most important accomplishment, together with rhetoric
and music, for Castiglione's ideal courtier is dancing. For, like music
and rhetoric, dance is regarded as an art which imitates and expresses
the order and harmony of the universe; and from a philosophical point
of view it shares some characteristics with music which accompanies it.
Just as the art of music is regarded as imitating the cosmic music, the
harmony of the nine spheres, so too the art of dance is regarded as
imitating the eternal movement of the spheres, the cosmic dance.[43]

The extension of the philosophical ideas about dance to its social
implication is perhaps most clearly summed up in another Renaissance
'handbook' of courtly behaviour, written thirty years earlier than
Hoby's translation of *The Courtier* but obviously influenced by Castiglione's work. This is Sir Thomas Elyot's *The Boke named the Gouernour*
(1531).[44] Elyot sees in the 'associating of man and woman in dancing,
they both observing one number and time in their movings' an expression or imitation of the unity of all virtues, virtues which, he says, in
man or woman separately can never be complete.[45] Thus, dancing as a

---

[42] Castiglione refers to the 'uiola' and in each case Hoby translates this as 'lute', possibly
because this instrument was more commonly used as an accompaniment to English solo song at
the time of the translation. Castiglione's version of the passage begins like this:
'Bella musica rispose M. Feder. parmi il cantar bene à libro sicuramente, & con bella maniera: ma
anchor molto più il cantare alla uiola: perche tutta la dolcezza consiste quasi in un solo: & con
molto maggior attention si nota, & intende il bel modo . . .' The rather obscure passage in Hoby's
translation which begins: 'But syngynge to the Lute wyth the dyttie . . .' is like this in Castiglione:
'ma sopra tutto parmi gratissimo il cantare alla uiola per recitare: il che tanto di uenustà, &
efficacia aggiunge alla parole, che è gran maraviglia.' (*Il libro del cortegiano*, Venice, 1545, Libro ii,
Sig. D.8ᵛ.) Castiglione clearly has in mind a declamatory style of singing.

[43] Sir Thomas Elyot, in *The Governor*, speaks of the dance of the stars like this: 'The interpreters
of Plato do think that the wonderful and incomprehensible order of the celestial bodies, I mean
stars and planets, and their motions harmonical, gave to them that intensity and by the deep
search of reason behold their courses, in the sundry diversities of number and time, a form of
imitation of a semblable motion, which they called dancing or saltation.' (Book i, Everyman edn.,
p. 73.) Plato regarded dance as mimetic action. He believed that music not intended as accompaniment for words should be accompaniment for dance. See *Laws*, ii. 669. McGowan, *L'art du ballet de
cour*, discusses theories of dance in the later sixteenth century, pp. 17–27. She makes the point that
the phrases 'harmony of the spheres' and 'dance of the stars' were virtually interchangeable in
Renaissance thought.

[44] See also Davies's 'Orchestra' (1594).

[45] Elyot, *Governor*, i; p. 77.

courtly and social activity, like music and eloquence, prepares the mind for the recognition of Virtue since it imitates Virtue itself.

VI

The first three Books and part of Book IV of *The Courtier* deal with the social attributes of the ideal courtier, although we have seen that these are imaginatively related at almost every point to an ideal of more importance than merely social accomplishment; or rather, social accomplishment takes on more than a merely transitory significance in this context. The work ends with a statement of the view of the universe which underlies the whole work, the Platonic discourse on Love by Bembo. This gathers together and makes explicit the significance of each of the courtier's social accomplishments. Furthermore the connections between the social and the philosophical aspects of the ideal courtier's 'arts' are shown us in another way. Castiglione forestalls our questions about the relevance of all these 'arts' to the courtier's acknowledged position and chief function as adviser to the Prince by having Lord Gaspar Pallavicin pose these questions before we do. After the discussion of the way in which the courtier will serve his Prince, Lord Gaspar says:

I had not thought oure Courtier hadd bene so woorthy a personage. But sins Aristotel and Plato be his mates, I judge no man ought to disdeigne his name anye more. Yet wott I not whether I may beleave that Aristotel and Plato ever daunsed or were musitiens in all their lief time, or practised other feates of chivalrye.

(IV; p. 340)

The Lord Octavian answers Gaspar by saying that however grave and serious a philosopher the courtier may be, nevertheless these social attributes should be his, for they are not contrary to 'goodnesse, discreation, knoweleage and will, in all age, and in all time and place'.[46] But Lord Gaspar's objections are not to be satisfied by this general reproof and he goes on to mock at and to question the ideal that has been set up:

Then the L. GASPAR: I remember (quoth he) that these Lordes yesternight reasoninge of the Courtiers qualities, did alowe him to be a lover, and in makinge rehersall of asmuche as hitherto hath bene spoken, a manne maye pike out a conclusion, That the Courtier (whiche with his worthynesse and credit must incline his Prince to vertue) must in maner of necessitie be aged, for knoweleage commeth verye syldome times beefore yeeres, and speciallye in matters that bee learned wyth experyence: I can not see, whan hee is well drawen in yeeres, howe it wyll stande well wyth hym to be a lover, considerynge (as it hath bine said the other night) Love frameth not with olde men, and the

---

[46] *The Courtier*, IV; p. 340.

trickes that in yonge men be galauntnesse, courtesie and precisenesse so acceptable to women, in them are meere folies and fondnesse to be laughed at ... Therfore in case this your Aristotel an old Courtier were a lover, and practised the feates that yong lovers do (as some that we have sene in our daies) I feare me, he woulde forgete to teache his Prince: and paraventure boyes would mocke him behinde his backe, and women would have none other delite in him but to make him a jesting stocke.

(IV; pp. 340–1)

Gaspar is at once refreshingly down-to-earth, and at the same time his words serve to lay emphasis on Bembo's reply which follows and takes up most of the rest of Book IV; a reply which demonstrates the limitations of Gaspar's criticism and defines clearly, for Gaspar and for us, the value and point of the earlier discussions. Bembo's argument for the 'courtier not young' (whom Gaspar scornfully called 'this your Aristotel an old Courtier') is based on the thesis that this courtier no longer needs to practise the active or social manifestations of Virtue which would lead him to an understanding of the Universal Harmony, for, Bembo says, he is now able to perceive it directly. The whole emphasis of Bembo's discussion, then, is not so much one which defines an antithesis between this kind of 'wisdom' and those social accomplishments which the group has previously discussed, as one which defines his concept of knowledge, understanding, and wisdom, as a 'stair'. When he begins his discussion of Love by saying that 'Love is nothinge elles but a certein covetinge to enjoy beawtie' he makes clear that this 'covetinge' manifests itself in all kinds of love. 'In oure soule,' he says, 'there be three maner wayes to know, namelye, by sense, reason, and understandinge.' And although the main part of his discussion is of 'understanding, by the which man may be partner with Aungelles', nevertheless it is always clear that this highest means of perception by the human soul is dependent also on the other two.[47] In this way Bembo's discussion is clearly a development of what has gone before and it is not possible to separate the practical, 'handbook' aspects of *The Courtier* from the larger philosophical problems with which Bembo now deals. Castiglione obviously wished to stress the philosophical aspects of his book. This was more important to him than that it should be regarded as setting out a detailed programme for the way the ideal courtier must advise his Prince.[48]

The intimate relationship of the social accomplishments of the courtier and the complete significance of his life is demonstrated also by the design of the book itself. As Castiglione presents it, Duke Guidubaldo's

---

[47] *The Courtier*, IV; pp. 342–3.

[48] This point is made in detail by Mazzeo, *Renaissance and Revolution*, pp. 134–5. Mazzeo makes clear the distinction between Castiglione's work and more 'practical' works such as Machiavelli's *Il Principe*.

court and the conversations that take place there are themselves a demonstration of the precepts the book expounds. The ideal courtier 'created' by the discussions and the ideal lady who is to be his mistress are each an image of the best attributes of the people who create them. While it may seem to us, as it seemed to Lord Gaspar, that these ideal figures are too good to be true, we also realize that their 'creators', even Lord Gaspar himself, express in themselves and in their conversations the perfect balance of art and nature which is the basis of their ideal. It is in the whole tenor of the conversations, rather than in any 'rules' for behaviour that are set out, that the 'artificial' and the lived worlds meet. The literary form of the work is important in helping to create this impression of a Utopia which once existed and could exist again; and in this respect the emphasis laid on context—of time and place—seems significant. The discussions themselves are simple narrative in form: indeed, they purport to be almost historically accurate. However, formal aspects of the book, by deliberately distorting this basic concept of a narrative or historic time-sequence, convey a further dimension which is an important facet of the book's meaning.

In one respect, the narrative or historical sequence of the book is stressed: these are, for example, real people and the lapse of time between evenings is made clear, partly by the fact that a different aspect of the subject is treated each night. But it is also clear that the whole 'action' takes place in a sphere removed from a direct presentation of temporal reality: one critic has aptly described this aspect of the work as Arcadian.[49] The magnificent palace of the Duke and the conversations of the Duchess and her friends seem deliberately cut off from historical reality. The description Castiglione gives of the Duke's palace near the beginning of the work exemplifies these qualities.

This man [i.e. Duke Frederico, Guidubaldo's father] among his other deeds praisworthy, in the hard and sharpe situation of Urbin buylt a Palaice, to the opinion of many men, the fayrest that was to be founde in all Italy, and so fornished it with everye necessary implement belonging therto, that it appeared not a palaice, but a Citye in fourme of a palaice, and that not onelye with ordinairie matters, as Silver plate, hanginges for chambers of verye riche cloth of golde, of silke and other like, but also for sightlynesse: and to decke it out withall, placed there a wonderous number of auncyent ymages of marble and mettall, verye excellente peinctinges and instrumentes of musycke of all sortes, and nothinge would he have there but what was moste rare and excellent.

(1; pp. 29–30)

In one sense the description of Guidubaldo's court is a literal one, a simple description of a sumptuous palace, although at this level it

---

[49] Mazzeo, *Renaissance and Revolution*, p. 134.

remains very generalized. Within a literary convention and literary context the description is idealized, and in this sense is not unspecific. The way in which the palace is described and the aspects which Castiglione selects to describe for us are part of a conscious and artistic control, something more than simple historical narrative and accuracy.

However, both here and throughout, *The Courtier* also insists on claiming historical truth and hence a part of narrative time. It is balanced between reality and an ideal, while at the same time the reader is made aware of the discrepancy between these two. Indeed, the discrepancy between the 'litle world' of the 'Citye in fourme of a palaice' (a description at once comprehensive and limiting) and the world of real cities, is pointed out explicitly at the opening of Book I V, before the description of the final evening of the discussions at the palace and Bembo's philosophical discourse. At this point Castiglione defines the lapse in time between the discussions' taking place and his writing of them. Here he notes, for the first time, the most pressing distinction between reality and the ideal. It is the 'real' world, the world from which he himself is writing, which causes 'a bitter thought that gripeth me in my minde, and maketh me to call to remembraunce worldlie miseries and our deceitfull hopes, and how fortune many times in the verie middes of our race, otherwhile nighe the ende disapointeth our fraile and vaine pourposes . . .'.[50] The ideal is contained within the palace and defined by the description of it in Book I.[51] Once the limits of human time, which is felt as a pressing sequence of events having no regard to personal interpretation, have been established, so that what we have seen already of Guidubaldo's court and seen already as unquestionably good becomes now 'our fraile and vaine pourposes'; once these limits have been defined, the Fourth Book can go on to define in Bembo's discourse the extreme limits also of an ideal realm (and this too is created by the courtier's arts), where time exists only as a personal affair and is, hence, irrelevant. The limits are this state of perfect stasis, which is itself limitless. But his state of ecstasy is not simply described; it is even attained as Bembo tells of it. Despite Lady Emilia's gently amused awareness of Bembo's state of ecstasy when she 'tooke him by the plaite of hys garment and pluckinge hym a litle, said: Take heede (M. Peter) that these thoughtes make not your soule also to forsake the bodye',[52] it is also clear that the 'LADY EMILIA . . . together with the rest gave most diligent eare to this talke'.[53] Indeed, she, with the others, has been so rapt that no one realizes that day has come while

[50] *The Courtier*, IV; p. 293.
[51] *The Courtier*, I; pp. 29–30: see above.
[52] *The Courtier*, IV; p. 363.
[53] Ibid.

they have been listening and that they have been up all night. Love of the Good and the Beautiful can inspire the lover, as it has inspired Bembo, and can make of him a poet whose eloquence may create this temporally perfect state, a state where time does not seem to pass.[54] The state of ecstasy which Bembo has reached and which he has created in his listeners is a state of awareness which we now set alongside Castiglione's opening of Book I V, his 'bitter thought that . . . maketh me to call to remembraunce worldlie miseries and our deceitfull hopes'. Bembo's listeners have been so taken out of themselves that they forget temporal demands: 'And not one of them felt any heavinesse of slepe in his eyes, the which often happeneth whan a man is up after his accustomed houre to go to bed' (I v; p. 365). It seems significant that between the beginning of the First Book, where the setting of the Duke's palace and the 'situation' of Urbino are described (at least on one level) factually, and the end of the Fourth Book, the setting of the palace is not mentioned. Now we find that the opening description of the setting has been transmuted by the vision of an ideal state. Now too the tension which exists, to some extent, throughout—and which is made beautifully explicit by the Lady Emilia's gesture as Bembo breaks off—between narrative time and another kind of time is resolved. The palace has indeed become a 'Citye', and the world outside it embodies too the order and proportion, the perfect union of art and nature, which until now has been confined to a seemingly purely literary discussion:

> Whan the windowes then were opened on the side of the Palaice that hath his prospect toward the high top of Mount Catri, they saw alredie risen in the East a faire morninge like unto the coulour of roses, and all sterres voided, savinge onelye the sweete Governesse of the heaven, Venus, which keapeth the boundes of the nyght and the day, from whiche appeered to blowe a sweete blast, that filling the aer with a bytinge cold, begane to quicken the tunable notes of the prety birdes, among the hushing woodes of the hilles at hande.
>
> (IV; p. 365)

The passage has many literary antecedents; but specifically it may remind us of the opening of the Tenth Day of Boccaccio's *Decameron*

---

[54] Cf. the following poem by Michelangelo which contains, 'in little', the essence of Bembo's thesis:

> In me la morte, in te la vita mia;
> tu distingui e concedi e parti el tempo;
> quante vuo', breve e lungo è'l viver mio.
> Felice son nella tuo cortesia.
> Beata l'alma, ove non corre tempo,
> per te s'è fatta a contemplare Dio.

'In me death, in you my life. You mark and grant and separate time; as you wish, short or long is the pace of my life. Happy am I in your courtesy. Blessed the soul in which time does not run. By you it is made to look upon God.'   (*Penguin Book of Italian Verse*, p. 164.)

where the stories and dancing from the night before have continued so late that the sun is beginning to tint the morning sky before the group retires.[55] It is, indeed, the fact that the ending of *The Courtier* clearly belongs within a tradition that sharpens its significance in its context here. For Castiglione's description of the morning is not merely an indication that Bembo's story has so engrossed them that the night has passed without the courtiers' realizing it: in its humanizing of nature, its pastoral-idyllic character, it reflects an attitude towards the world beyond the castle which may be seen as specifically exemplifying Bembo's philosophy. The description is, then, extremely 'artificial'; but at the same time this 'artifice', as an attitude to life, has been shown to be more personally valuable than simple temporal reality could be. The perfect relation between art and nature which *The Courtier* advocates throughout, and the social aspects of which are shown in the discussions, is demonstrated finally as the windows of the palace are opened to let in the morning sun.

VII

Jonson himself said that 'without Art, Nature can ne're bee perfect; &, without Nature, Art can clayme no being'.[56] His masques in particular, and his later plays, express and in their own way renew ideals of a perfect union of art and nature such as is shown to us in *The Courtier*. The Jonsonian masque celebrates the court. The values of the ideal court, Jonson believes, are not only the practical and civic ones of wise and tolerant governance, but are also larger, spiritual values which include an understanding of the human condition as the Renaissance Platonist tradition viewed it. The ideal monarch is regarded as the Platonic philosopher-king, a mirror of God's own 'heavenlye reason and understanding',[57] and his court is the centre of learning and of the liberal arts. The *raison d'être* of the Jonsonian masque is the celebration of the court's virtues. In his Dedication of *Volpone* Jonson said that the

---

[55] The Ninth Day ends like this: '. . . appresso alla quale, per ciò che già molta notte andata n'era, comandò il re che ciascuno per infino al giorno s'andasse a riposare.' The Tenth Day, which follows directly, begins: Ancora eran vermigli certi nuvoletti nell 'occidente, essendo già quegli dello oriente nelle loro estremità simili ad oro lucentissimi divenuti, per li solari raggi che molto loro avvicinandosi li feriono, quando Panfilo levatosi, le donne e' suoi compagni fece chiamare. (Which being fully finished, the King gave order, that everie one should repaire to their Chambers, because a great part of the night was already spent.

Already began certaine small Clouds in the West, to blush with a Vermilion tincture, when those in the East (having reached to their full heighth) looked like bright burnished Gold, by splendour of the Sun beames drawing neere unto them: when Pamphilus being risen, caused the Ladies, and the rest of his honourable companions to be called.) Boccaccio, *Decameron*, a cura di Bianchi, pp. 669–70. Trans. anon., 1620, pp. 191–2.

[56] Jonson, *Discoveries*, ll. 2503–4. H & S VIII, p. 639.

[57] *The Courtier*, IV; p. 314.

Poet is a teacher of 'things diuine, no lesse then humane';[58] and through the masque form Jonson could demonstrate in a more practical way the ideals expressed by works such as *The Courtier*: more practical, in the sense that the masque literally brings together, within a single form—the artistic creation—a synthesis of music, poetry, and dance, and includes the audience too, in the social dances or revels with which it concludes. In his development of the court masque Jonson draws together all the arts to create an image or emblem of the macrocosm itself.

[58] *Volpone*, Dedication, l. 28.

5

Jonson's Masques I

Orpheus with his lute made trees,
And the mountain tops that freeze,
   Bow themselves when he did sing:
To his music plants and flowers
Ever sprung; as sun and showers
   There had made a lasting spring.

Everything that heard him play,
Even the billows of the sea,
   Hung their heads and then lay by.
In sweet music is such art,
Killing care and grief of heart
   Fall asleep, or hearing, die.
             (Shakespeare, *Henry VIII*, iii. i. 3–14.)

IN THE Renaissance the figure of Orpheus was, perhaps, the most often invoked of all classical figures. He represented the ideal and perfect orator, the man whose eloquence could move even inanimate nature. His power lay not simply in eloquent speech: it was 'with his lute' that he had the power to make nature 'bow'. From a literal point of view, Orpheus is simply a magician: his power is magical and fantastic, he makes the inanimate behave as if alive. But Shakespeare's poem points to a deeper, more imaginative response to the natural world. It is the response of the reader himself. He is not simply the cynical onlooker at a magician's tricks, or the dispassionate hearer of a fantastic story. Orpheus' music does not merely affect or change what we had thought was inanimate nature. Rather, it shows us a truth about 'inanimate' nature and about ourselves: from *our* point of view his music has the power to create a state in which 'sun and showers/There had made a lasting spring'. *Our* response is inevitably involved. In his music there is 'such art' that the whole temporal and natural world is transformed—not changed (as a literal response to the poem suggests), for it is rather we, the listeners, who are changed. The pressing exigencies of time—'Killing care' and 'grief of heart'—pass away, 'fall asleep', or 'die'. Orpheus' singing can teach us to regard ourselves, and our position within the natural and temporal universe, in a new and significant way. In re-creating for us the natural universe, Orpheus' music so perfectly imitates the universal harmony that we are made to perceive and to believe in the reality of a world not subject to time or change. Orpheus not only affects his listeners with the sheer beauty of sound he makes: in being the perfectly eloquent man he is also perfectly wise. Orpheus is not simply a magician; he is a *magus*.

This chapter and the next consider the particular problems and values of Jonson's masques for court. I have called Shakespeare's poem to the reader's mind at this point for two reasons: first it sums up, as it were, the essential qualities of *The Courtier* and thus acts as a bridge between our consideration of that work and Jonson's masques, works of a quite different kind but influenced by the values for which *The Courtier* stands. Second, the quality about the eloquence of Orpheus to which Shakespeare's poem points most clearly is the significance of the listener's response. We recognize that this response may be, though perhaps only initially, a dual one. We can choose the cynic's view of Orpheus as a magician; or we can choose to commit ourselves to the vision he creates for us. The Renaissance saw this kind of commitment as a recognition of Truth and Wisdom. In the end, there is to be no choice: Bembo's audience was compelled by *his* discourse, by his vision. But the possible duality of response suggested by our reading of Shakespeare's poem epitomizes problems which the masque form creates. Shakespeare's poem demonstrates the, at best precarious, balance which the masque-writer—or 'inventor'[1]—maintains; a balance between the perfect response, the recognition of the 'lasting spring', and the cynic's response of 'merely magic, merely fantasy' as he turns away. For if the masque is to come alive it depends, more than any other form, on a sympathy between its actors and its audience where each takes on, partially, the role of the other. The masque has the qualities of both 'game', in which all take part, and 'show', in which actors and audience are divided.[2] It is the relation between actor and audience which constitutes for Renaissance theorists the potential supremacy of the masque as an ideal art form. It also contributes to its destruction.

I

Ben Jonson developed the masque form at James's court into something quite different from, and far more sophisticated than, the early Tudor and Elizabethan masque.[3] The origins of the masque in mum-

---

[1] Jonson uses this term frequently in distinguishing the 'show', the aspects which appeal to the senses, and the intellectual significance of the masque which lasts beyond the single occasion. It is this latter which is the 'invention'. He refers to himself as masque 'inventor' in several descriptions of his masques. Jonson's use of the term is discussed in detail by D. J. Gordon, 'Poet and Architect'.

[2] Cf. Welsford, *Court Masque*, Chapter XIII.

[3] For a discussion of the usual structure or form of the Stuart masque see Sabol, *Songs and Dances*, Introduction, p. 1. The usual form of the Jonsonian masque is discussed below.

mings and seasonal festivities have been well documented;[4] and indeed one of the strengths of the form as Jonson conceived and developed it was that it maintained its traditional functions and to some degree its traditional forms. However, under James, the masque became a far more formal affair, largely through the influence of Jonson himself, although it is clear that this was to James's own liking and may have been by his direction.[5]

Jonson's masques all followed a similar pattern. The masque began with speeches explaining the plot or setting, rather in the manner of the speeches of the Presenter of earlier Tudor masques. In his later masques where he introduced an antimasque, this usually preceded the main masque and by its dramatic action—in opposition to the mythic ideal of the masque itself—usually made the formal introductory speeches unnecessary. There usually followed some kind of visual revelation and songs of celebration. These in turn were followed by the masque dances, elaborate figure dances illustrating in their choreography the central philosophical point of the masque. Jonson's masques usually had three main-masque dances, occasionally four; and these either followed directly one after another or were separated by songs intended to make a complementary point. After the masque dances, and songs which recognized the monarch and courtiers seated in the hall, the masquers descended from the stage and took partners from among the audience. The social dances which followed were the revels. They usually began with one, or several, pavanes, slow stately dances in quadruple time and often referred to in masque texts as the 'measures'. These were followed by livelier dances: galliards, corantos, voltas. The length of time the revels took was not fixed; sometimes they lasted an hour or more. But their end was usually marked by one of the actors in the masque drawing attention to the lateness of the hour or the elegance of the dancers, and the whole 'performance' finished with the masquers returning to their set, on-stage, in a final masque dance and the singing of a song which reiterated the theme of the masque.

The main point of the Jonsonian masque was celebration—of the King, his court, and the society of which he was head. Earlier Tudor masques provided the traditional basis of spectacle, music, song, dance and often some kind of allegorical significance on which Jonson could build an art form which was more formalized, more sophisticated, and more philosophical in intention. In particular, the revels, or social dances in which all the courtiers joined and which had always been a special feature of the masque and often its *raison d'être*, were given a new

[4] See Brotanek, *Die englischen Maskenspiele*: Reyher, *Les Masques anglais*; Welsford, *Court Masque*.
[5] See below, p. 146 and cf. Orgel, ed., *Complete Masques*, Introduction, p. 3. James had obviously disliked Daniel's *Vision of the Twelve Goddesses*, presented at court in 1604.

meaning. In making these a more integral part of the masque's philosophical significance, rather than something merely tacked on to the end of a 'performance' or 'show', Jonson gave the revels a moral function; and thus the participation of the audience in the masque had a significance beyond that imposed by the boundaries of 'game'.

The Jonsonian masque is clearly influenced by Renaissance Platonist ideals, ideals expressed particularly by the French academies of the later sixteenth century and put into practice in the French *ballets de cour*. Devised in association with Inigo Jones (as set-designer), who early in his career was interested in Italian artistic theories and was widely travelled,[6] and with, among others, Alfonso Ferrabosco II, Robert Johnson, and Nicholas Lanier (as musicians and composers), all of whom were interested in Continental theories of setting words to music, Jonson's masques seem aimed at fulfilling the Renaissance Platonist ideal of a perfect composite art form, giving equal importance to all the arts, and through the expression of what were regarded as certain philosophical truths, affecting and moving the spectators to virtue and understanding.

Sixteenth-century theorists saw parallels between various art forms and sought with the aid of classical theory to extend these as far as possible. Some of these parallels are evident in Castiglione's *Courtier*: for instance, the relation between the visual arts and poetry, and the related effects believed to be produced by certain kinds of music and eloquence. Similarly, music and dancing were regarded as very closely related, especially when the dance was some kind of mimetic action. In each case, the correspondences between various art forms were based not so much on aesthetic similarities as on the moral significance of each art—as imitating the supreme art of the universe itself—and on the idea of the divinity of the artist.[7] Such a theory of a union of all art forms as an image of the divine macrocosm lay behind the famous *Balet comique de la reine*, presented in 1581 as part of the celebrations at the French court for the marriage of the Queen's sister, Marguerite de Vaudemont, and the Duc de Joyeuse, a favourite of Henri III.[8] The whole *Balet* was planned by Baltasar de Beaujoyeulx, a musician at court, but the work was a composite one, involving several collaborators. The poems, on subjects set by Beaujoyeulx, were by La Chesnaye, the music by Lambert de Beaulieu, and the scenery by Jacques Patin. Beaulieu, in particular, is known to have had close

---

[6] For details see Summerson, *Jones*, pp. 15–16, 35–7 and Yates, *Theatre*, pp. 8of.

[7] See McGowan, *Ballet de cour*, Chapter I.

[8] See Yates, *French Academies*, pp. 237 f. and McGowan, *Ballet de cour*, pp. 42–7. Jonson possessed a copy of the masque description.

associations with de Courville, co-founder with Baïf of the *Académie*; and the theories of the *Académie* obviously lay behind the place given to music and his settings of the poems.[9] The theme of the *Balet comique*, expressed in several elaborate and complex levels of allegory, was one perennially discussed in the *Académie*: that of the establishment of reason and harmony and subjugation of the 'beasts' of the passions.[10] The *Balet comique* is important as one of the most significant attempts by members of the *Académie* to establish a 'perfect' composite art form and it is of interest here in that it clearly had great influence on the Jacobean masque in England. Jonson's masques, in particular, appear to owe a good deal to the ideals and sometimes even the details of the *Balet comique*. His *Masque of Blackness*, the first full masque he wrote for James's court, uses the same mythological sources and some very similar allegorical devices.[11]

One other feature which Jonson and Jones developed from the European masques, and from the *ballet* in particular, was the use of perspective sets rather than dispersed scenery. In earlier, Tudor, masques, the scenery was usually dispersed about the hall and the masquers moved from one 'set' to another; or the masquers were drawn into the hall on pageant cars which also contained the scenery for their part of the allegory. The *Balet comique* actually illustrates a transitional stage in the use of the masque sets and scenery, for it used both dispersed sets—at the sides of the hall—and a perspective set, at one end. All Jonson's masques used a fixed stage with a set intended to be viewed from one point only, the throne of state; and thus the picture element,

---

[9] See Yates, *French Academies*, p. 238.

[10] See Yates, *French Academies*, p. 240.

[11] The objection sometimes offered that Jonson's masques differed in aim from those inspired by the French *Académie* because of Jonson's continual insistence on the supremacy of the poet over the other collaborators is not convincing, not at least as regards his earlier masques. Although Jonson claims the honour of the 'invention' for himself, the extant descriptions of his early masques give full credit to the sets, the costumes, the choreography, and the music and make clear that these were integral to the whole. J. P. Cutts has suggested (in 'Le Rôle de la musique dans les masques de Ben Jonson') that Jonson's masques appear to give least importance to music because it was always associated with either song or dance and rarely given a place on its own; and this would imply, he believes, that Jonson viewed the aims of his masques as somewhat different from those of the French *ballets de cour*. It is true that Jonson's masques very rarely use instrumental music on its own: when they do it is usually described as 'loud music' or 'loud and full music' and was obviously intended to cover up the creaking of moving machinery. See, for example, *Beauty* where loud music played as the 'whole *Iland* mou'd forward, on the water' (ll. 256–7); *Haddington Masque* where '*with a lowd and full musique, the Cliffe parted in the midst, and discouered an illustrious* Concaue . . .' (ll. 264–5); or the appearance of *Fama Bona* in *Queens*, who 'after the Musique had done, wch wayted on the turning of the *Machine* [ie. the *machina versatilis*, the Throne], calld from thence to *Vertue*, and spake . . .' (ll. 455–6). Such music may have been no more than a few notes on oboes or trumpets. Cutts's suggestion was countered in a general way by Jean Jacquot, who pointed out that far from implying a lack of interest in Renaissance Platonist theories of music, Jonson's coupling of music with either dance or words actually illustrates his thinking in line with the ideals of the *Académie*. See the report of the discussion at the end of Cutts's paper, pp. 302–3.

framed by a proscenium arch, took on a far more important role than it had in earlier masques.[12] For instance, by clearly separating the masquers from the audience seated in the hall, Jonson and Jones gave to any action which took place in the hall rather more emphasis than it had had in, say, the Tudor interlude where action among the audience was very common.[13]

However, in making the masque more formalized and more elaborately philosophical than earlier masques had been, Jonson faced some artistic problems. The revels, the social dances, were still the centre of the masque; if anything, they became more significant as the masque itself took on a new kind of seriousness. But their function as 'game' had changed somewhat, for they had become, at least conceptually, part of the masque's expression of an ideal world and now signified the translation of the masque's myth into the reality of the court. But how was the 'inventor' to include aesthetically within the masque's image of an ideal state the actuality of James's court; how was he to prevent the masque from breaking into two distinct parts—the masque-proper and the revels? How was he to reconcile convincingly a particular occasion or festivity—and all the enormous cost, extensive preparation of performers, magnificence of scenery, was for one night's pleasure only—how, then, to reconcile this with an image of a permanent and lasting philosophical truth? These were problems which Jonson faced when he began writing masques, and they were problems that were to occupy him for nearly thirty years.

In the introductory comments to the text of one of his earliest masques at James's court, *Hymenaei* (1606), Jonson makes this statement about masques:

though their *voyce* be taught to sound to present occasions, their *sense*, or doth, or should alwayes lay hold on more remou'd *mysteries*.

(ll. 17–19)

Although a particular masque was, primarily, celebrating a particular courtly occasion, Jonson says that the masque was to express not merely the single occasion but rather its essence. The occasion's significance as a courtly and social event was most important to him, its meaning and value within the ordered society, this kingdom of the 'little god'.[14] These matters are the 'more remou'd mysteries' to which Jonson refers, what he elsewhere calls the 'soul' of the masque. Thus,

---

[12] For instance, in the description of *Blackness* Jonson tells us: 'These thus presented, the *Scene* behind, seemed a vast sea (and vnited with this that flowed forth) from the termination, or *horizon* of which (being the levell of the *State*, which was placed in the vpper end of the hall) was drawne, by the lines of *Prospectiue*, the whole worke shooting downewards, from the eye; which *decorum* made it more conspicuous, and caught the eye a farre off with a wandring beauty' (ll. 82–9).

[13] See Craik, *Tudor Interlude*, Chapter I.

[14] James I and VI, *Basilicon Doron*, ed. Craigie, I, pp. 24–5.

the masque celebrated the court of James as an image of the Divine Harmony; and it depended for its full meaning on the recognition of this by all taking part. Emphasis was placed on the revels, for these dances were the spectators' 'acknowledgement' of the masque's affective power. We might say that the basic tenet of the Jonsonian masque was that the proscenium arch which separated the masque from its audience, myth from reality, existed to be broken down. The success with which the audience could be included within the masque's meaning must be a major criterion for judging the success of the whole.

There is a further problem. The masque's meaning depended to a large extent on the right response of the audience; or rather on the audience's recognition that it was not really audience in the sense simply of onlooker, but that it too had a part to play. Although ideally, of course, this was simply a recognition that the masque was the audience's own image, in fact this could never have been the case. The aesthetic unity would have been threatened because the audience in the banqueting hall would not necessarily have acknowledged either the fiction or the philosophical truth of their inclusion; and the dancing space for the revels in fact hovered between fiction and reality. Too heavy a responsibility for the masque's success was placed on the audience; and although this was always courtly and aristocratic even such exalted human nature must have been at times only human! Precisely because the masque was not self-contained, because in including the audience it could not help but share its transitory and temporal quality nor help but acknowledge that it was only a single evening's pleasure, the masque contained within itself an antinomy which could never be successfully resolved. Jonson could not ignore the masque's transitory quality. His courtly audience may at times have come close to his ideal audience, an audience which responded perfectly to the philosophical and transcendental intentions of the masque and was significantly affected and instructed by its truths in a way which lasted beyond the single evening, but still he recognized that most of the time many among them inevitably would not understand his meaning. Even early in his career, in his description of the arch at Fenchurch, designed as part of the Entertainment for James's coronation in 1603, he recognized that most of the spectators regarded the arch not as part of the allegory of the entertainment but only as a passing wonder, something to be admired and forgotten. Any 'more remou'd mysteries' were not understood. So his elaborate description of the arch concludes:

And for the multitude, no doubt but their grounded iudgements did gaze, said it was fine, and were satisfied.

(ll. 265–7)

Jonson's recognition that the 'grounded iudgements' of the 'multitude' were also to be found among James's courtiers is expressed very clearly in one of his most successful masques, *Pleasure Reconciled to Virtue* (1618). In a sense this masque was 'about' the significance of the masque form; Daedalus the supreme artist instructed the masquers in their dances. Daedalus' first song ended with a very sharp statement reaching to the core of the masque and its dilemma:

> *For Dauncing is an exercise*
> *not only shews ye mouers wit,*
> *but maketh ye beholder wise,*
> *as he hath powre to rise to it.*

(ll. 269–72)

It was not only the 'wit' of the 'mouer' but the 'powre' of the beholder to understand its meaning which was important in the masque. The part that the audience played was essential to its truth. The audience must enter into the spirit of the masque and in order to do this must understand the 'Truth' of its 'invention'. As in a game the spoil-sport is far more hated than is the cheat, for the spoil-sport breaks the magic circle and his response is the cynic's response of 'mere fantasy, mere fiction';[15] so in the masque. But where the enclosed and strictly formal-ized 'play'-world, the world of art, was synonymous with, and rep-resented what was regarded as, a fundamental philosphical truth, then the cynic was not merely the spoil-sport, he was the ignorant and dangerous man. He could be likened to the man Lorenzo speaks of who 'is not moved with concord of sweet sound', the man 'fit for treasons, strategems, and spoils', whose 'affections' are 'dark as Erebus'.[16]

In the final analysis the masque inventor, like any artist, had to admit that he had no absolute control over his audience's receptivity and powers of understanding and hence no real control over their part in the total artistic fiction. To a greater extent than a play, a Jonsonian masque depended for a large part of its meaning, indeed its whole meaning, on its affective qualities, on the power it contained of moving the audience to understanding; otherwise, it became mere extravaganza, an elaborate show. The 'wisdom' of its ideal, the 'lasting spring', had in the end to be created by a conscious effort of the audience's will. It is ironic that, during the revels of *Pleasure Reconciled*, the very masque which makes this point clear, we are told that the courtiers 'being well nigh tired . . . began to lag, whereupon the king, who is naturally choleric, got impatient and shouted aloud Why don't

---

[15] Cf. Huizinga, *Homo Ludens*, p. 30.
[16] Shakespeare, *Merchant of Venice*, v. i. 69–88.

they dance? What did they make me come here for? Devil take you all, dance.'[17]

II

The following discussion considers some of Jonson's masques in detail and his solutions to the problems I have looked at briefly. I attempt to trace Jonson's development of the form from the early masques without antimasques to the later masques with elaborate stage sets, and to consider the significance of his incorporating in these later masques more and more of the elements of traditional festivals, mummings, and disguises. The early masques, however, represented an almost complete break, something quite new.

James employed Samuel Daniel to write the masque for Christmas of 1604. This was *The Vision of the Twelve Goddesses*, a masque following the allegorical and processional style which had been popular in England for years.[18] James was dissatisfied with the masque and the commission was given to Jonson the following year. Jonson's first masque, *The Masque of Blackness*, was new in that its 'action' was confined to a stage at one end of the hall, except for the revels themselves, the dances in which all the court joined when the masquers stepped down from the stage. This meant that the stage provided a focal point for the audience and thus the sets could provide a more complex emblematic and symbolic complement to the masque 'action' than was possible in a procession-style masque. The *Masque of Blackness* was written for Queen Anne and her ladies, for Twelfth Night, 1605. The Queen had requested that it contain something novel, and wished that she and her ladies be masked as 'Black-mores'.[19] Around this command Jonson had to construct a 'story' which would compliment the Queen and James and also include the Queen as a blackamoor within its fiction. Briefly, the theme or 'story' of the masque is as follows. The Queen and her ladies were to represent the twelve daughters of Niger. They are black and have always believed that their blackness was a sign of the Sun's 'feruent'st loue,' the Sun who is 'the best iudge, and most formall cause/Of all dames beauties'.[20] However, they have grown sad because

---

[17] Orazio Busino, chaplain to the Venetian Embassy in London, in *The Calendar of State Papers, Venetian*, xv (1909), pp. 111–14. Trans. in *A Book of Masques*, pp. 232–4. Busino gives a detailed account of the whole performance which complements Jonson's own text.

[18] See Orgel, ed., *Complete Masques*, Introduction, p. 3.

[19] See *Blackness*, l. 22. The 'disguise' was not favourably received. H & S x, p. 448 quote from Carleton's letter to Sir Ralph Winwood describing the occasion: 'Instead of Vizzards, their Faces, and Arms up to the Elbows, were painted black, which was Disguise sufficient, for they were hard to be known; *but it became them nothing so well as their red and white, and you cannot imagine a more ugly Sight, then a Troop of lean-cheek'd Moors*. . . . [The Spanish Ambassador] took out the Queen, and forgot not to kiss her Hand, though there was Danger it would have left a Mark on his Lips.'

[20] ll. 141–2.

it is rumoured that black is not after all the 'perfectst beauty'. One evening as they are bathing in their Lake they see in the water a vision which tells them that if they will find the source of a superior beauty they must seek a land whose name ends with 'tania':

> *where bright* Sol, *that heat*
> *Their blouds, doth neuer rise, or set,*
> *But in his Iourney passeth by,*
> *And leaues that* Clymat *of the sky,*
> *To comfort of a greater* Light,
> *Who formes all beauty, with his sight.*

(ll. 190–5)

So they have set out with their father Niger to find this land, and the masque treats of their arrival in Britain—'Britania'—and their recognition of James as the other Sun, which does not scorch them black but whose 'rays' purify and make more beautiful and perfect everything about him.

Jonson's printed description of the masque begins with a detailed exposition of the nature of the masque set and of the costumes of the masquers and actors in the masque.[21] The set and costumes were designed by Inigo Jones. Since the masque form was, fundamentally, symbolic or emblematic every aspect of the set conveyed the theme, or 'invention', of the whole. When the King and courtiers first entered the hall they saw a curtain painted to represent a 'Landtschap, consisting of small woods, and here and there a void place fill'd with huntings'.[22] At the beginning of the masque this painted curtain 'fell', we are told, and revealed a seascape, not a painted scene this time but a moving set.

With the dropping of the curtain to reveal the sea with the masquers and their attendants the masque began. A Triton and two sea-maids sang a song welcoming 'the *Orient* floud/Into the *West*'.[23] Jonson gives detailed descriptions of the seascape, the actors, and masquers, for the set and the figures in it contained the essential meaning of the masque. He tells us that the waves of the sea 'seemed to moue, and in some places the billow to breake, as imitating that orderly disorder, which is common in nature';[24] he describes in detail how the sea-horses, the Tritons, and the figures of Oceanus and Niger were placed in the set, and expands on the central 'great concaue shell, like mother of pearle,

---

[21] The 'actors' are distinguished here from the masquers in that their parts were speaking or singing ones and were usually taken by professional actors or musicians. The masquers, on the other hand, were nobles—in this masque, the Queen and her ladies—and they did not speak. Usually the actors in the masque did not leave the masque set as the masquers themselves did.

[22] ll. 24–6.

[23] ll. 98–9.

[24] ll. 27–30.

curiously made to moue on those waters, and rise with the billow'[25] which contained the twelve masquers, the daughters of Niger. The actors and masquers were not regarded as separate from this setting: their costumes represented in style and colours the predominant attributes of the element each acted. Oceanus was presented 'in humane forme, the colour of his flesh, blue; and shaddowed with a robe of sea-greene; his head grey; and horned . . .'; Niger was 'in forme and colour of an *Æthiope*; his haire and rare beard curled, shaddowed with a blue, and bright mantle . . .'.[26] These were not anthropomorphic figures so much as embodiments of the emblematic qualities of the set. That the set itself was emblematic is clear from Jonson's description of it as imitating the essence of nature by means of art. He points, for instance, to the 'orderly disorder' of the sea, or the 'extravagant order' of the arrangement of the masquers within their shell.

The pictorial aspect of the masque consisted of two scenes, the first a painted, static, but idealized landscape, the second a moving seascape peopled by mythological characters. The use of sea scenes, water devices, mechanical waves and fountains in court festivities and masques was very popular in both France and Italy in the late sixteenth century and Jonson and Jones may have been influenced by developments in stage machinery in their choice of a basic theme.[27] But probably a more important influence in the choice of a sea setting was the metaphorical richness of water images and the philosophical significance given to sea and earth mythology by Renaissance Platonism. The mythology is basic to the *Balet comique*, for instance, in its use of the Circe and Ulysses fable; for Circe is the daughter of the Sun and granddaughter of the Ocean and hence signifies 'the mixture of the elements which comes about through the movement of the Sun who is the father of form, and of Perseis [her mother] the mother [of] matter'.[28] So the set of the *Balet comique* incorporated a fountain placed close to Circe's sunlit garden, and the garden and the fountain together symbolized her significance for the masque. She represented the natural world, the continuing cycle of generation and death, the continuous transformation of the elements. And the 'action' of the *Balet* was based on the conflict between Ulysses, who represented reason and the power of the soul, and Circe, who signified the 'natural man'. Ulysses' companions, turned to beasts by Circe's power, represented in their relation to Ulysses on the one hand and to Circe on the other 'the powers and faculties of the soul

---

[25] ll. 59–61.

[26] ll. 44–6 and 50–2.

[27] See Rousset, 'L'Eau et les tritons'. For a discussion of the machines which moved the waves see Nicoll, *Stuart Masques*, p. 59.

[28] The allegorical exegesis is given on pp. 74[r]–75[v]. The passage is translated and quoted by Yates, *French Academies*, p. 240.

conspiring and according with the affections of the senses which are not in obedience to reason'.[29]

In Jonson's description of *Blackness* we can see certain basic similarities between his 'invention' and that of the *Balet comique*. Both the natural and mythological qualities of the sun and the ocean were made clear in the masque set and in the speeches of Oceanus and Niger which opened the masque. The daughters of Niger are described as beloved of the sun who 'in their firme hiewes, drawes/Signes of his feruent'st loue; and thereby shewes/That, in their black, the perfectst beauty growes'.[30] Oceanus, who rode a sea-horse beside Niger, represented in Greek mythology the cosmic life source from which all life flows. That the set and the figures in it represented more than simply the elemental forces of nature, however, is made clear by Jonson's detailed description. Oceanus symbolized not simply physical generation and creation but spiritual life as well: he carried a trident which was associated in Renaissance emblem books with the preaching of Christianity.[31] And when Niger was describing how his daughters were favoured by the Sun he pointed out that their physical appearance was merely the outward sign of their spiritual excellence:

> Since the fix't colour of their curled haire,
> (Which is the highest grace of dames most faire)
> No cares, no age can change; or there display
> The fearefull tincture of abhorred *Gray*;
> Since *Death* her selfe (her selfe being pale and blue)
> Can neuer alter their most faithfull hiew;
> All which are arguments, to proue, how far
> Their beauties conquer, in great beauties warre;
> And more, how neere *Diuinitie* they be,
> That stand from passion, or decay so free.
>
> (ll. 145–54)

The 'progress' of the masque, from the journey in search of the answer to the riddle to the recognition that the daughters of Niger had arrived in Britania, the 'progress' from the masque set to the dancing-floor of the hall where the revels took place, was presented in the masque as a progression from elemental life to spiritual life, from a recognition of the elemental forces of nature to an understanding of the metaphorical significance of water and the sun. The spiritual qualities imaged by the mythological significance of water were demonstrated in the elaborate figure dance which the masquers performed as they

---

[29] *Balet*, p. 74^{r-v}. Trans. and quoted in Yates, *French Academies*, p. 240.
[30] ll. 142–4.
[31] See Yates, *French Academies*, p. 242, n. 4.

stepped ashore. The spiritual qualities imaged by the Sun were
revealed when the masquers recognized James seated in the centre of
the hall: James that 'temperate' sun who 'refines/All things, on which
his radiance shines'.[32]

Jonson's description of the first masquers' dance (in this masque
there were only two) tells us that *'euery couple (as they aduanced) seuerally*
[presented] *their fans: in one of which were inscribed their mixt* Names, *in the
other a mute* Hieroglyphick, *expressing their mixt qualities'*.[33] The meaning
of these 'hieroglyphicks' which Jonson sets out for the reader has been
discussed in some detail by D. J. Gordon.[34] The six pairs of masquers
were led by the Queen and the Countess of Bedford representing
respectively Eurphoris, fertility, and Aglaia, the first of the three
Graces who is specifically associated by Ficino with Splendour or
beauty of spirit.[35] So the couple who led the dance symbolized 'a royal
and spiritual beauty fertilizing the earth'.[36] The other pairs of dancers
represented various qualities of the element water, but at the same time
their 'hieroglyphicks' also implied water's spiritual and symbolic qualities. The whole dance probably also alluded to the specific qualities of
England's climate as moderating and tempering the fiery heat of the
east.[37] The dance, then, expressed the masque's 'invention': it expressed the union of east and west, of the fiery sun and water; and it
symbolized the flux of life, the continual 'dance' of the elements forming
and reforming yet always the same. Finally and most importantly it
expressed and recognized the spiritual or metaphorical significance of
the images of Sun, Water, and Life. The union of east and west, of life
and Life, was completed as the masquers stepped out of their masque
set to dance with James's courtiers. The masque's emphasis on
James as the spiritual and refining Sun suggests that, like the *Balet
comique*, *Blackness* may have been conceived as a kind of talisman
—to draw down the benign influences of the sun on James and his
court.[38]

So far we have concentrated on the basic theme or philosophical
emblem of the masque as embodied in its visual and choreographic
aspects. The music which accompanied the masque dance was
regarded philosophically as inseparable from the meaning of the dance
itself. This means that aesthetically it needed to provide little more

[32] ll. 264–5.
[33] ll. 266–9.
[34] Gordon, *'Blacknesse* and *Beautie'*, pp. 125–7.
[35] Gordon, *'Blacknesse* and *Beautie'*, p. 127. Cf. *Beauty*, ll. 180–3 where Splendor is one of 'the
figures representing the Elements of Beauty'.
[36] Gordon, *'Blacknesse* and *Beautie'*, p. 127.
[37] Ibid.
[38] For a discussion of the *Balet comique* as a talisman see Yates, *Bruno*, p. 176.

than a rhythmic emphasis.[39] But the masque apparently gave equal importance to speech and song, and these must be considered with the more formal, aesthetic qualities of the masque, as they expressed its emblem and its philosophical basis.

The masque opened with a song in three parts, performed by a Triton and two sea-maids. Sirens were traditionally associated with the power of music, although usually in a 'bad' sense as representing the allurements of the flesh. In his use of sirens here Jonson appears to have been influenced by the use of sea-sirens in the *Balet comique* where their singing was regarded as having influence for good, probably by confusion of their name with the 'good' sirens, daughters of one of the Muses, who guide the celestial spheres and create the heavenly harmony.[40] Tritons were regarded as the male counterpart of the sirens of the sea and so were also associated with affective music. They were believed to have human voices.[41] The opening song of *Blackness* was, then, celebration, and at the same time the power of the sirens' music must have been intended to 'draw' the audience into an understanding of the emblem of the masque. The long speeches between Oceanus and Niger which followed and described how and why the daughters of Niger had come to Albion must, then be regarded not so much as the simple traditional statement of the 'plot' or situation by a Presenter before the masque began, but rather as a kind of extension of, or complement to, the whole 'invention' of the masque of which the audience would already have been made aware in their response to the visual set and to the song which opened the masque. The relation of the speeches of Oceanus and Niger to the visual set and the song implies that the progress of the masque, from the falling of the curtain on which the landscape was painted to the revels and the final masque songs, could not be regarded as corresponding to a sequence of fictional events. There was, of course, a temporal dimension in the masque, and this was specifically recognized at the end when, at the conclusion of the revels, Æthiopia reminded the Nymphs that 'the night growes old'.[42] But the

[39] A study of the music for the masque dances discussed in this and the following chapter shows that the music is fairly uniform in structure, most being in duple metre, sometimes with a contrasting section in triple metre. Occasionally double rhythms occur, a superimposing of duple and triple time. This is evident in the dance of the Humours and Affections in Hymenaei and in the witches dances in *Queens* (see below). B.L. MS Add. 10444, which contains many of these dances, gives no indications of the tempo or the style of the dances: these can only be guessed at from the sketchy outlines. See also Sabol, *Songs and Dances*, p. 2. Sabol transcribes and edits many of the dances from this manuscript. For a further discussion see his notes on individual dances, pp. 168 f.; Lawrence, 'Notes on a Collection of Masque Music'; Cutts, 'Jacobean Masque and Stage Music'; 'Le Rôle de la musique dans les masques de Ben Jonson'; Willetts, 'Sir Nicholas Le Strange's Collection of Masque Music'.

[40] See Yates, *French Academies*, pp. 241–2.

[41] Yates, *French Academies*, p. 242, n. 4.

[42] l. 325.

temporal dimension was mainly that of verbal, musical and scenic 'events': while the total significance of these was to be a kind of gradual realization within the mind of the audience of the single 'invention' of the masque. So the whole masque was an elaboration on the significance of the first idealized landscape, 'Britania' ruled by James. The masque was to represent the elaboration in the audience's minds of a single philosophical truth, a single emblem.[43] So too the development of the masque to include the audience—in the dances of the revels—was presented fictionally as spatial rather than temporal: the masque set was enlarged to include James's court.

Because the response of the audience was an aspect of the masque's form the affective quality of each of the arts which made up the whole was obviously regarded as important. Because the powers of music to affect the listener were highly regarded within the Platonic philosophy the nature of the songs is of particular interest. We have already considered the opening song in its context both as celebration and as suggesting the relation of the emblem set to the audience. No music exists either for this song, for the song sung during the revels, or for that which concluded the masque. But music by Ferrabosco does survive for the song which followed the masque dance and preceded the revels, and we could assume that the others, if they were also set by Ferrabosco, would have been similar in style.[44]

> Come away, come away,
> We grow iealous of your stay:
> If you doe not stop your eare,
> We shall haue more cause to feare
> *Syrens* of the land, then they
> To doubt the *Syrens* of the sea.
>
> (ll. 295–300)

The song has been set in a style which might be described as at least partly declamatory, in keeping with the instructional rather than lyric nature of its text. This style is clear, for instance, in the opening motif and the fact that the musical rhythm and accentuation closely follow

---

[43] Alpers, 'Narrative and Rhetoric', p. 392 points to a similar relation between art and audience in the poetic mode of *The Faerie Queene*.

[44] A variety of musicians was commissioned to work with Jonson in his masques. Usually if more than one composer was employed, one wrote the music for songs, the others composed the dance music. However, this was not invariably the case and indeed may have been less frequently so than we assume, for we have in most cases only accounts to work from and their evidence is not always very specific. Where Jonson mentions a composer by name, as he several times refers to Ferrabosco's work for his early masques, he does not refer specifically to the settings of songs, although his praise usually refers to music for songs rather than for dances. The dances are mentioned only as choreography. The music for 'Come away' was published in Ferrabosco's *Ayres* (1609), no. 3 and a treble and bass version occurs also in Christ Church, Oxford, MS Mus. 439, p. 31. See also Sabol, *Songs and Dances*, p. 25.

EXAMPLE 9(a). 'Come away'

Come a - way, come a - way, we grow

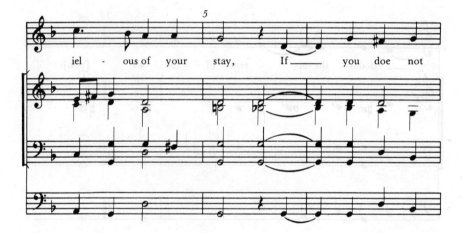

iel - ous of your stay, If_____ you doe not

stoppe your___ eare, we shall haue more cause to

Alfonso Ferrabosco, *Ayres* (1609), no. 3, Sig. B.2.

Note.

The bass viol part writes the repeat in full although it is the same as the first time with the exception of bar 8 (second time) where the third and fourth beats are given as a minim on G.

EXAMPLE 9(b). 'Come away'

jel - ous of yor staye If___ you doe not stopp your___

eare we shall have more cause to feare Sir - ens of the land then

they to doubte the Sir - ens of the sea.

Christ Church MS Mus. 439, p.31.

Note.

14, Treble I: MS = minim.

the spoken rhythm of the words. Furthermore, the musical shape of the whole, the balancing of phrases, and the melodic line itself are clear and quite simple. Ferrabosco has created a balance between the expository content of the verse and the music. Yet the whole song is quite clearly a musical structure, one which complements the formal, poetic qualities of the text expressed mainly in its rhyming couplets. Pointing of the text is created by a simpler use of devices similar to those in the setting of 'Come my Celia': syncopation in the melody and allowing the harmonic structure to direct the flow of the text, sometimes against obvious cadence points in the melodic line. Despite the brevity and simplicity of this song it is worth pausing to consider its construction because many masque songs posed similar problems for the composer. The verse of many masque songs, like the verse of this song, is not lyric but expository or instructional; and the composer has not, therefore, within the verse itself any guide as to tone or feeling or 'mood'. The problem is solved later by the use of recitative, although the introduction of this into masque appears to have given music's significance within the masque form a different emphasis. Recitative, or even a fairly free declamatory setting, does not take account of the poetic structure of the words but treats verse and prose alike. It seems that Ferrabosco's settings of the songs in Jonson's early masques strike a nice balance between the ideal of heightened speech and a musical shape which complements the poetic structure. Ferrabosco's masque songs support the philosophic basis of the masque: for the poetry is not to be regarded as dramatic or narrative but as an aspect of an emblem created by several art forms equally. In these songs the philosophic importance of the music—as formal and imitative of a universal pattern—is to be equally important with its function as eloquence.

In 'Come away' Ferrabosco sets the first couplet of Jonson's text, a simple statement, by two balanced musical phrases. But at bar 8, the grammatical sense invites only a slight pause—because of the rhyme—and this is supported by the perfect cadence in D major which becomes a perfect cadence in G minor before the next line of the verse begins so that the modulation and cadence at 'your eare' is felt as merely temporary, as pressing forward. The musical phrasing of the second couplet of the text balances that of the first: but a more dynamic quality which the words demand is conveyed in the treatment of the cadences—at bar 8, as we have seen, and particularly at bar 10, 'to feare'. Here the enjambment in the text (ll. 4–5) is complemented by maintaining the tonic harmony throughout the bar. Ferrabosco imitates musically the conflict between the poetic sense of the final two couplets and the grammatical sense of their statement by his simple harmonic treatment and by using the same rhythmic pattern for each of the last two lines of text but distorting the emphasis by syncopation. Thus bar 10 II to bar 12 I is reflected in bar 13 II to bar 15 I, and the link is created by the rhythmic treatment of the simple modulation at bar 12 where the equal (minim) notes in the melody stabilize the double harmonic implications of the dotted minim accompaniment. The importance of this final couplet in the song's context in the masque is reflected in the way Ferrabosco has emphasized the balance between sea Sirens and land Sirens (the courtiers), and in the fact that in the musical setting this section is to be repeated. In the other extant version of this song, that in Christ Church manuscript Mus. 439, this musical support for the rhyming couplet—by the rhythmic balancing of the phrases while the syncopation shifts the verbal emphasis—is lost by the insertion of the minim rest at bar 13 I. This rest not only disturbs the sense but makes the balance of the couplet more rigid by over-emphasis. Here the rhythm of 'doubte the Sirens of the sea' is an exact reflection of 'Sirens of the land then they'.

The song, as it occurs in Ferrabosco's *Ayres*, may be said to represent a heightening of natural speech. Its function in the masque context was to persuade the masquers not to be tempted by the courtiers but to remain within the masque set. The masquers took no notice of the instruction, for immediately the song was finished they stepped down and chose partners from among the audience. The revels now began and, we are told, they consisted of *'seuerall* measures, *and* corranto's'. But this was not the end of the masque. As the revels were drawing to a close the masquers *'were againe accited to sea, with a* song *of two* trebles, *whose cadences were iterated by a double* eccho, *from seuerall parts of the land'*.[45] The song, 'Daughters of the subtle floud'(l. 305), was sung by the masque 'actors'. The song reminded the masquers that they were of a different element from the courtiers and therefore should not 'let earth longer intertayne' them. If the courtiers really belonged in the same element as the masquers they would follow them back to the sea. Of course the courtiers did not do so and so the final stanza pointed out the difference between courtiers and masquers:

> They are but earth,
> And what you vow'd was water.
>
> (ll. 321–4)

So although the court, by participating in the revels, was complementary to the masque's perfected world, nevertheless there remained the sense that the imperfections of the real world, a world subject to time, would weaken the virtues of the other; and hence as 'the night [grew] old' the masquers had to return to their set. Still, the masque ended with a recognition of the complementary nature of two worlds rather than an affirmation of their separateness: Albion (or James) was now described as 'Neptune's sonne'.

III

Blackness was published in quarto in 1608 together with the *Masque of Beauty* which was performed in 1608. This latter masque was also written for the Queen, who had requested a sequel to *Blackness*. The transformation of blackness to beauty which was promised the daughters of Niger at the end of *Blackness* was now to take place, and Jonson excused the delay of three years by the fact that four more of Niger's daughters, also wishing to be transformed, had made Night envious and caused her to imprison them in darkness on a floating island. They

[45] ll. 302–4.

were to be released only by the other twelve who had been all this time
wandering at sea in search of them. *Beauty* made use of the same
Platonic concept of James as alchemist–sun–king, whose island was a
little world of perfect harmony and governed by Love.[46] It was his
power, indeed, which—both figuratively and literally—created the
masque.

    Beauty was simpler in structure than *Blackness* and Jonson achieved
this largely by the way in which the masque was presented. The first set
the audience saw was simply '*a curtaine . . . (in which the* Night *was
painted)*'[47] and the distinction between stage and audience was broken
down by the fact that the first Presenter of the masque, Boreas, the
North Wind, addressed Ianuarius who was seated in the hall among
the audience and who presided over the whole masque. Boreas came in
looking for King James, and was asked by Ianuarius to explain the two
years' delay of the daughters of Niger in returning to James's court. So
in this masque the audience was not required to understand the introductory and explanatory speeches in relation to a specific emblem
set—as was the case in the opening of *Blackness*. Ianuarius, as he himself
said, belongs to 'feasts,/Freedome, and triumphs; making Kings his
guests',[48] and thus, as in traditional Christmas festivities, the audience
was included in the 'game' from the outset.

    When Boreas' narration was over and Ianuarius was cursing him as
the bringer of bad news, suddenly another figure appeared; now Vulturnus, the South Wind, entered the hall:

> All horrors vanish, and all name of *Death*,
> Be all things here as calme as is my breath.
> A gentler *Wind* VVLTVRNVS, brings you newes
> The *Ile* is found, and that the *Nymphs* now vse
> Their rest, and ioy.
>
>   (ll. 117–21)

Vulturnus, the foregoer of the spring, of new life and new birth, belongs
to winter festivities; but at the same time he symbolizes the spiritual
spring, the spiritual new life which was basic to the 'invention' of the
masque. Vulturnus told the audience that 'The *Nights* black charmes
are flowne'[49] and described the Isle and the Throne that the nymphs'
queen had built for them, a 'new *Elysium*', a springtime world of Beauty
and Love. This 'Elysium' was now floating towards Britain, and was
the 'miracle' which James himself—'great *Neptunes* sonne'—had
wrought.[50]

[46] For a full discussion of the symbolism and imagery see Gordon, '*Blacknesse* and *Beautie*'.
[47] ll. 161–2.
[48] ll. 50–1.
[49] l. 121.
[50] ll. 137–60.

At this point the curtain of Night was drawn aside and the island 'discouer'd' to 'loud Musique'.[51] The barriers between the emblematic masque set and the audience of whom it was an emblem were broken down by making the recognition that '*Nights* black charmes are flowne' a recognition from among the audience. In making all narration in this masque come from characters outside the set, among the audience, Jonson explicitly recognized that the audience too was part of a fiction. *Blackness*, by contrast, did not acknowledge that the audience had this special function.

The musicians, the spirits of 'Orpheus, Linus and the rest', came forth from their arbours on the island and sang the introductory song: 'When *Loue*, at first, did mooue' (l. 281). As in *Blackness* the musicians here were part of the fiction of the masque set; but, unlike *Blackness*, the masque-proper depended far more simply on picture, song, and dance. Jonson describes the visual emblem of the masque—the island and the throne—in great detail and it is clear that the songs and dances supported and expanded the symbolic qualities of the set.[52]

The masque dances and the dances of the revels were interspersed with songs which celebrated and praised the beauty of the dancers and propounded the Platonic theme of the masque—the relationship between Beauty and Love. By interspersing songs in the dances of the revels as well as in the masque dances, Jonson emphasized that the masque set and the court were, and had been from the beginning, one. The audience would not have felt the 'discovery' of the court as part of the masque as strongly as it would have done in *Blackness*: nor would it have been jolted by the recognition of James as Sun, as the supreme alchemist who turned 'blackness' to 'beauty', chaos to love, for here he was the 'creator' of the masque. The masque-world did not so much come to include his court as grow from it.

Music survives for five songs in the masque: all by Ferrabosco and published in his *Ayres*.[53] The first of these, 'So beautie on the waters stood' (l. 324), was sung in celebration of the sixteen lady masquers as they stepped ashore and danced their first masque dance, a figure dance, directed by the choreographer, Thomas Giles, who was playing the part of Thames welcoming the 'Nymphes' to Britain. We are told that the masquers ended their dance 'in the figure of a *Diamant*, and so,

---

[51] The Throne and the costumes of the masquers are described in great detail by Jonson. See H & S vii, pp. 186–90.

[52] See also Gordon, '*Blacknesse* and *Beautie*', pp. 128–38.

[53] 'So beautie on the waters stood', l. 324; the three songs 'If all these CVPIDS', 'It was no politie', 'Yes, were the *Loues*', ll. 340–63; 'Had those, that dwell in error foule', l. 368; Ferrabosco, *Ayres*, nos. 21, 18–20, 22. These are reproduced in Sabol, *Songs and Dances*, pp. 34–9. The three songs, ll. 340–63, also occur, in treble and bass only, in Christ Church MS Mus. 439, pp. 93, 94, 96.

EXAMPLE 10. 'So beautie on the waters stood'

So beau-tie on the wa-ters stood,

when Loue had se-uer'd earth from floud,

So when hee part-ed ayre from fire,

Alfonso Ferrabosco, *Ayres* (1609), no, 21, Sig. G.2.

Note.

29a, tabl.: MS gives no chord for this bar.

standing still, were by the Musicians, with a second *Song* (sung by a loud *Tenor*) celebrated'.

> So beautie on the waters stood,
> When *loue* had seuer'd earth, from flood!
> So when he parted ayre, from fire,
> He did with concord all inspire!
> And then a *motion* he them taught,
> That elder then himselfe was thought.
> Which thought was, yet, the child of earth,
> For *loue* is elder then his birth.

(ll. 325–32)

Ferrabosco's very simple setting of the text takes full account of the form and the structure of the verse. The music can only be said to be

declamatory in the sense that it follows, on the whole, the spoken
rhythm of the words and the melody is underlined by a fluid, yet
harmonically very simple, accompaniment. Ferrabosco has represented Jonson's balancing of the first couplet against the second by
setting them to the same music; and this first section itself consists of a
melodic balancing of two very simple phrases. As in the song in
Blackness ('Come away') Ferrabosco emphasizes the philosophical
significance of the text for the masque by setting it in a simple and
formal way. The third couplet (ll. 5–6), which develops the statement
of the first two, is treated in a freer melodic line, imitating the word
'motion'. But, as Jonson's final couplet suggests the paradox and the
cycle of the birth of Love, so Ferrabosco's setting returns in the final
section to the simple rhythmic patterns and tonic key of the opening
section so that it reflects in its form the point of the text. The words and
their meaning are thus clearly expressed by and within the simple
musical structure.

After the song was over the masquers danced their second masque
dance and then stepped into the hall to dance with the audience. The
revels, we are told, *'to give them* [ie. the dancers] *respite,* [were] *intermitted
with song'* (ll. 338–9). In performance these songs presumably followed
one another directly; the first two were sung by trebles, the third by a
tenor.

> If all these CVPIDS, now, were blind
> > As is their wanton *brother*;
> Or play should put it in their mind
> > To shoot at one another:
> What prettie battaile they would make,
> > If they their obiects should mistake
> And each one wound his *mother*!

Which was seconded by another treble; thus,

> It was no politie of court,
> > Albee' the place were charmed,
> To let in earnest, or in sport,
> > So many *Loues* in, armed.
> For say, the *Dames* should, with their eyes,
> > Vpon the hearts, here, meane surprize;
> > Were not the men like harmed?

To which a tenor answer'd.

> Yes, were the *Loues* or false, or straying;
> Or *beauties* not their beautie waighing:
> But here, no such deceipt is mix'd,
> Their flames are pure, their eyes are fix'd:
> They doe not warre, with different darts,
> But strike a musique of like harts.

In the first two of these songs the division in the musical sections, the modulations, and the shifts in tempo and rhythmic pattern correspond to the sense of the text. So, for instance, in 'If all these Cupids', the formal musical simplicity of bars 1–10 complements the expository character of the first four lines of the verse, while the second section—in its shift of key and its more fluid melodic line—supports the sense of the second part of the poetry. Ferrabosco's setting picks up the suggestion of humour in the text in the melisma on 'wanton' (bars 4–5) and the falling sequence (bars 16–20)—emphasized by the way it readjusts the rhythm at bars 18–19—on 'and each one wound'. In the second song, 'It was no politie of court', Ferrabosco uses a similar device to emphasize the implied humour in the words and the unlikeliness, in the context, of the song's proposition, by the way the figure (bar 18—'vpon the') is repeated with a different rhythmic and harmonic sense in the following bar (19–20—'meane surprise'). The reiteration of the question (bars 20–4) by means of a sequence is a fairly obvious instance of matching a rhetorical with a musical device. The answer to both songs, an answer which points up the frivolity of their suggestions, is made by a tenor, in the third song: 'Yes, were the *Loues* or false, or straying' (l. 358). The setting of the opening couplet is deliberate, slow, and built upon a very simple and unadorned harmonic accompaniment. The following lines, which expand the statement of the first two, are set to a more fluid melodic line, which also makes use of sequences to point up the main emphases of the verse. The final section of the song (bars 19–37), which contains the culmination of the group of three in praising both the masquers and the dancers in the revels, makes far more use of melismatic passages, especially in the repetition of the words of the final two lines (bars 29–37). In breaking away from the ponderous and serious declamation of its opening the final section reflects, in an essentially lyric style, the joy in the recognition that Beauty and Love are here, in James's court, and that the revels essentially express this.

The version of this group of three songs which occurs in the Christ Church manuscript Mus. 439 is only treble and bass but is essentially Ferrabosco's music. The version is interesting because of the lavish amount of ornamentation suggested in the vocal line, particularly in 'If all these cupids'. The song may very well have been performed in the masque in this way: and if this was so we might conclude that virtuosity of musical performance was as important as the philosophical and discursive nature of the poetry. As it is indicated here, however, the elaborate ornamentation would not obscure the basic musical shape of the work nor the significant relationship of the words to the music.

After these songs the revels continued with renewed energy in 'galliards' and 'coranto's'. The ending of the revels was marked by another

EXAMPLE 11(a).

'If all these *Cupids*' First Part

If all these *Cu - pids* now were blinde, as

is their wan - ton broth - er, Or play should

put it in their mindes, to shoot at one an -

oth - er, What pre - ty bat - taile they would make if

they their ob - iects should mis - take,

and each one wound, and _____ each one wound

his moth - er [moth - er.]

Alfonso Ferrabosco, *Ayres* (1609) no. 18, Sig. F.2^v.

'It was no pollicie of court' Second Part

It _____ was no pol - li -cie _____

of court, al - though the place be charm -

10

ed, To let in earn - est or in sport,

so ma-ny loues _____ in

15

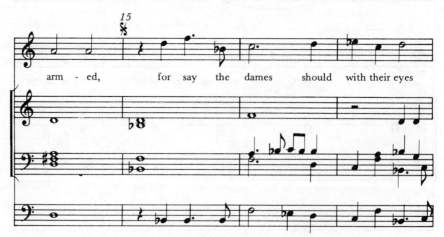

arm - ed, for say the dames should with their eyes

vp - on the   hearts   here   meane   sur - prise,   were__

__ not the   men,   were   not the   men   were __

__ not   the   men __   like   harm - ed.

Alfonso Ferrabosco, *Ayres* (1609), no. 19, Sig. G.1.

'Yes were the loues' Third Part

Yes were the loues or false or stray - ing, or beau - tie

not their beau - tie way - ing, But

here no ____ such de - ceipt is

mixt, their flames are ____ pure

____ their ____ eyes are

they   doe not   warre   with   dif -

frent   darts,   but   strike   a

mu   sicke   of   like   hearts.

Alfonso Ferrabosco, *Ayres* (1609), no. 20, Sig. G.1^{v}.

EXAMPLE 11(b).

'If all these cupides'

wound   and ___ each one wound   his moth-er

[what]   [moth-er.]

his   moth-er

Christ Church MS Mus. 439, p.93.
Note.
20b Bass: MS = ♮ No treble given.

'It was no pollicie of court'

It ___   was   no   pol - li - cie ___   of

court,   al - though the place   be charm - ed: to

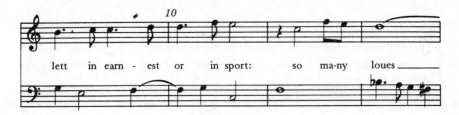

lett   in earn - est   or   in sport: so   ma-ny   loues ___

Notes.

Christ Church MS Mus. 439, p.94.
22 Bass: Between II and III MS = (♪) on f. sharp
26b Treble: MS =
26b Bass: MS =

'Yes weare the loues'

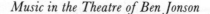

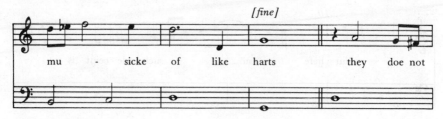

Christ Church MS Mus. 439, p.96.

Note.

The setting appears to be incomplete: it occupies the whole of p. 96 and the following leaf may have been torn out. However, a repeat from bar 24 after bar 33 to bar 28 makes sense and simply this may have been intended.

song, '*by the first tenor*', once more celebrating the lady masquers and to which they responded by performing their third masque dance, '*most elegant, and curious . . . and not to be describ'd againe, by any art, but that of their owne footing*'.[54] The setting for this song too was published in Ferrabosco's *Ayres*.

> Had those, that dwell in error foule,
> And hold that women haue no soule,
> But seene these moue; they would haue, then,
> Said, *Women were the soules of men.*
> So they doe moue each heart, and eye
> With the *worlds soule*, true *harmony.*

In some respects this setting is closer to declamatory ayre than those for the songs earlier in the masque. The statement of the text is expressed very simply in a melody which, in the first section at any rate, is merely an elaboration of a simple harmonic bass. However, the rhythmic pattern does not follow the normal spoken accentuation and in this way Ferrabosco allows the music to express the words while drawing attention to the musical shape. The treatment of 'error' (bars 3–4) is an obvious example, but the rhythmic emphasis of 'no soul' (bars 8–9) is a more subtle instance, as is the way the insistence on the

[54] ll. 375–7.

EXAMPLE 12. 'Had those that dwell in error foule'

Alfonso Ferrabosco, *Ayres*, no. 22, Sig. G.2^V.

tonic chord at the end of section one and the beginning of section two (bar 10) helps to point the fact that grammatically there is no long pause at 'soule'. In the second section the cadence at bars 12–13 points up the enjambment in the text, and the following statement—'women were the soules of men'—is reflected in the setting's very simple harmonic and melodic treatment. A recognition of the point of the words without attempting direct declamation (as at bars 8–9, 12–13) is evident too in Ferrabosco's treatment of the last two lines. Musically, the phrases which set each of these lines are almost exactly the same, although in different keys—bars 19–20 are reproduced a fifth lower in bars 22–3. However, the syncopation and the brief modulation to E flat major at bar 22 push the emphasis on to 'world's soul' whose sense is complemented and reinforced by the melismatic treatment of 'harmony' above the simple and stable perfect cadence. In this way Ferrabosco has used a variation of a very simple sequential musical device which makes clear the relation Jonson's text makes between the two lines of the final couplet.

In all these songs Ferrabosco's settings both emphasize and complement the philosophical content of the words. As heightened eloquence they belonged in the fictional ideal of the masque set, the permanent springtime created by Love and Beauty, and as affective music they were to draw the audience to an understanding of its own relationship to the masque's emblem.

Jonson regarded *Blackness* and *Beauty* as complementary, and the relationship of one to the other is an important aspect of their meaning. 'Beauty' grows out of 'Blackness', and so Jonson had the inevitable lapse of time between the performances of the masques described as a state of suspended being. Beauty was not destroyed but simply obscured for a while by Chaos and Night which symbolized the more mundane or aimless aspects of life. For Love and Beauty, according to Ficino who is following Hermes Trismegistus in this, were placed in the heart of Chaos itself; and it was the power of Love and Beauty to banish Chaos which was celebrated in the two first songs in *Beauty* (ll. 281 and 324). So, Night must 'yield to light/As *Blacknesse* hath to *Beautie*'. In *Blackness* the 'progress' of the masque illustrated the Platonic relationship between physical life and spiritual Life, between the sun which 'drawes' in the Aethiopes' 'hiewes' 'signes of his feruent'st loue' and the 'sunne' which is 'temperate, and refines/All things, on which his radiance shines'.[55] In *Beauty* this illustration was completed and at the same time its larger, cosmic implications expressed by drawing comparison with the creation of the world. At the end of *Beauty* the masquers returned to their throne which 'had a circular motion of it owne, imitating that which we call *Motum mundi*, from the *East* to the *West*';[56] and the song which concluded the masque was a prayer that the qualities the masque 'invention' expressed might continue to reign in James's court.

In the speech by Ianuarius which ushered the masquers back to their throne Jonson made clear the importance of these seasonal festivities:

> Long may his light adorne these happy *rites*
> As I renew them; and your gracious sights
> Enioy that happinesse, eu'en to enuy, 'as when
> *Beautie*, at large, brake forth, and conquer'd men.
>
> (ll. 392–5)

---

[55] *Blackness*, ll. 142–3; ll. 264–5.
[56] *Beauty*, ll. 257–8.

James's court was to belong both to the changing seasons over whose passing Ianuarius presides, and to the spiritual peace expressed by the Arcadian world of eternal springtime: 'The '*Elysian* fields are here' were the masque's last words.

IV

Hymenaei, written two years earlier than *Beauty* for the marriage of the Earl of Essex and Frances Howard, was similar in conception to *Beauty* and may, indeed, have suggested *Beauty*'s more ambitious demonstration of a philosophical idea. The 'invention' of the masque was the significance of the marriage rites which 'celebrate the happinesse of such as liue in that sweet *vnion*, to the harmonious lawes of Nature and Reason'.[57] Whereas in *Beauty* Night and Chaos complemented Beauty and Love, so in *Hymenaei*, after Hymen's first speech which recognized James as the 'more then vsuall light' who presided over these 'Rites', the Globe which was the central device in the set, '*figuring Man*', opened '*with a kind of contentious Musique*' and eight men issued forth representing the four Humours and Affections.[58] Hymen called on Reason to 'Looke forth' and 'instruct their darknesse', and Reason, who was '*seated in the top of the* Globe (*as in the braine, or highest part of* Man)', descended and spoke to the Humours and Affections who sheathed their swords and retired to the sides of the stage 'amazed'.[59] Although many commentators regard the dance of Humours and Affections as Jonson's first antimasque it was not an antimasque in the sense that Jonson used the word in *Queens* and later masques: the dancers were not professional actors, they had no speaking parts, and they later joined in the revels. Nor was it similar to the exchange between Ianuarius and Boreas, for it was included within the masque and was part of its emblem set. The distinction between this dance and antimasque as Jonson later developed it may seem a fine one but it is nevertheless formally significant. The Humours and Affections were represented as part of man, who also includes Reason. The balance of the affections and reason creates in man the proper state for Love and a true Union at Hymen's altar. After the descent of Juno this love could be celebrated in the songs and dances of the masque. The point of the masque, then, was the understanding of the proper place in the 'microcosme' of the Humours and Affections, and, as in *Blackness*, this was created first of all in the emblem stage-set and then re-enacted by the whole of James's court in the revels. But, unlike *Beauty*, this emblem included and allowed for 'contentious' factors in human existence: the mundane

[57] *Hymenaei*, gloss to l. 112.
[58] l. 83; ll. 109–12.
[59] ll. 126–7; ll. 129–30; l. 157.

aspects of the court could be more readily included within the masque's meaning since they were already included within its emblem set. The wild contentious music to which the Humours and Affections danced was a destruction of Order but a destruction made within the terms of Order itself—that is, as dance only, and not as a dramatic mode.

No music exists for the songs in *Hymenaei*, but this is the earliest of Jonson's masques to which music for the masque dances can be fairly certainly ascribed. The music occurs in treble and bass only in the manuscript collection of masque music in British Library MS Add. 10444. The music in this collection is for the dance of Humours and Affections and for the three main-masque dances.[60] The dance music survives in this manuscript only as treble and unfigured bass so it is difficult to gain any very clear idea of how it must have sounded in performance: certainly, the music here bears little relation to Jonson's descriptions in the masque text. The dance of Humours and Affections out of their 'Microcosme, *or* Globe', for instance, is described as having been accompanied by 'a kind of contentious Musique'—music obviously intended, as was the choreography, to symbolize man as chaos when not controlled by Reason.[61] The music entitled 'Essex Anticke Masque' in British Library MS Add. 10444 does not give any indication of 'contentiousness'. Such effect must have been created by the 'orchestration' of the dance music: loud or harsh-sounding instruments such as sackbutts, trumpets, or cornets could have been used here, or perhaps 'contentious' refers to some kind of elaborate polyphonic treatment of the dance music.

The very simple form in which the music survives in the British Library manuscript can give only the merest hint of what the audience at Whitehall would have heard. The British Library manuscript treble and bass parts may be part of an incomplete set; or the form in which the music occurs may be explained by what seems to have been a common procedure in preparing the music for the masque dances. The accounts for some masque payments survive and from these we can see that it was customary to pay one person to compose the dance music and another to set the music to the violins, or other instruments.[62] It

[60] B.L. MS Add. 10444, nos. 92–5, ff. 42 and 92: 'Essex Anticke Masque'; ff. 42ᵛ and 92: 'The first of my Lord of Essex'; ff. 42ᵛ and 92: 'The second'; ff. 42ᵛ–43 and 92ᵛ: 'The Third'. See also Sabol, *Songs and Dances*, pp. 144–9. Versions of the antimasque and main masque dances were printed in Adson's *Courtly Masquing Ayres* (1621), all à 5, as numbers 4, 5, 6, 7.

[61] See Gordon, 'Jonson's Masque of Union', pp. 112–3.

[62] Accounts survive for *Oberon* and *Love Freed* and are quoted in H & S x, pp. 521 and 528. The records of payments for *Oberon* in the Pell Order Book make the distinction thus:

To M. Robert Iohnson for making the Daunces xxˡⁱ
Thomas Lupo for setting them to the violins Cˢ

The accounts for *Love Freed* tell us that Thomas Lupo was again paid five pounds 'for setting the dances to the violens'.

EXAMPLE 13. Essex Anticke Masque

20

B.L. MS Add. 10444, *ff.* 42 and 92.
Note.
15 and 19, Bass: Time signature = 3

seems that a composer did not have sole responsibility for writing and orchestrating the dance music but that the final instrumental score would represent the collaboration of a least two people. Such a method of providing instrumental music may seem arbitrary, but it could be compared with Robert Russell Bennett's orchestrations of songs for many Broadway musicals in the 1950s. In the case of the masque dances the music itself was clearly of secondary importance to the symbolic meaning of the dance—of which the music provides only a part. In the 'Essex Anticke Masque' a 'contentious' quality in the actual choreography may be clearly enough indicated by the shifts in key and the overlapping rhythms which are evident in the extant music even in its very sketchy form. When he describes the three main-masque dances Jonson mentions the instruments used in the performance of the first, which was 'led on by ORDER, the seruant of REASON' and was accompanied by *'a rare and full musique of twelue Lutes'.*[63] Here the philosophical significance of the instruments was important in the same way as was the symbolic nature of the choreography; the description does not give us any real indication of how the music sounded, and indeed, as it exists in its sketchy form, it appears very little different in style from that of the other two main-masque dances. These other two are described purely as choreography:[64] it is the combination of music and dance as a symbol of man's relation to the cosmos which is important.

[63] *Hymenaei,* ll. 271–2.
[64] ll. 310–18; ll. 399–401.

EXAMPLE 14.

The first of my Lord of Essex

B.L. MS Add. 10444, *ff.* 42^v and 92.

The second

B.L. MS Add. 10444, ff. 42^v and 92^v.

Note.

7 , Treble II: MS=B

8, Bass, MS = minim.

The Third

B.L. MS Add. 10444, *ff.* 42^v - 43 and 92^v.

V

One of Jonson's most widely acclaimed developments of the masque form was the introduction of an antimasque in the *Masque of Queens* (1609). The Queen, who was to be the chief masquer, had 'commaunded [Jonson] to think on some *Daunce*, or shew, that might præcede hers, and haue the place of a foyle, or false-*Masque*'.[65] The origin of the antimasque is obscure: Enid Welsford points out that grotesque dances and contrasts were common in Tudor mummings and both these dances and their performers were sometimes referred to as 'antics'.[66] Although we recognize the formal and practical distinction, and Jonson himself makes clear the difference of this new antimasque in *Queens* from anything either he or others had previously devised,[67] the dance of Humours and Affections in *Hymenaei* must later have been regarded as belonging to the antimasque tradition, for its music is entitled 'Essex Anticke Masque'. In the *Haddington Masque* (1608), written for the marriage of Viscount Haddington and Elizabeth

[65] ll. 12–13.

[66] *Court Masque*, p. 184.

[67] Jonson wrote of this new antimasque in his introduction to the masque text: 'I was carefull to decline not only from others, but mine owne stepps in that kind, since the last yeare I had an *Anti-Masque* of Boyes,' (*Queens*, ll. 14–16.)

EXAMPLE 15(a). 'Why stayes the bride groome to inuade'

you a vir - gin say,   To - mor - row

15

rise,   the   same   your   moth – er   is,   and

20

vse   a   nob - ler   name,   speed   well   in   hy - mens

Alfonso Ferrabosco, *Ayres* (1609), no. 11, Sig. E.1.

EXAMPLE 15(b). 'Why stayes the bridgrome to invade'

name _____ speed well in hy - mens warr

that what you are by yor per - fect - ions

we and all may

see.

Christ Church MS Mus. 439, pp. 60-1.

Ratcliffe the year before *Queens*, Cupid was discovered 'attended with
twelue boyes, most antickly attyr'd, that represented the sports, and
prettie lightnesses, that accompanie Loue'.[68] These danced '*a subtle
capriccious Daunce, to as odde a* Musique, *each of them bearing two torches,
nodding with their antique faces, with other varietie of ridiculous gesture*'.[69] In
both this masque and *Hymenaei*, however, these 'antic' characters represented an aspect of the theme of the main masque and were not
directly opposed to it; in each case the 'antic' figures joined in the main
masque dances.[70] In calling his antimasque to *Queens* a 'foyle, or
false-*Masque*' Jonson seems at pains to make clear that this was not
merely an entertainment tacked on to the masque but an integral part
of it. The antimasque for *Queens* was to represent a complete opposition
to the theme of the main masque: the witches represented 'the opposites
to good *Fame*'.[71] The scene was set as 'an ougly *Hell*: wch, flaming
beneath, smoakd vnto the top of the Roofe', and the witches 'came forth
from thence' to 'a kind of hollow and infernall musique'.[72] Unlike the
Humours and Affections of *Hymenaei* or the boys of the *Haddington
Masque*, the witches not only danced but spoke. Their dances, like the
dance of the Humours and Affections, were probably characterized as
'antick' more by the wild gestures of the dancers and the use of

---

[68] *Haddington Masque*, ll. 158–60. It is to this antimasque that Jonson refers in the introductory
passage to *Queens* quoted in note 67. I do not consider the *Haddington Masque* in detail here because
in design it is similar to *Hymenaei*, and also because masques celebrating a specific occasion,
particularly a wedding, do not pose the same problems as the masques written simply as part of
seasonal festivities. Both Jonson's marriage masques ended with an Epithalamion, a song in
praise of the bride and bridegroom, and since its main purpose was to send them to bed obviously
there were not the same formal and philosophical difficulties sometimes apparent in the endings of
other masques. Music exists for the Epithalamion of the *Haddington Masque* in Ferrabosco's *Ayres*
(1609), no. 11. The words in this version are taken from stanza 5 only of Jonson's text: 'Why stayes
the *Bride-grome*'. It is not clear whether the whole was sung or not: in the verse preceding the
Epithalamion to *Hymenaei* (l. 434) Jonson rather ruefully remarks that '*onely one staffe was sung*',
although he prints the whole poem. A very ornate version of 'Why stayes the *Bride-grome*' exists
in Christ Church MS Mus. 439, pp. 60–1, and the occurrence of the same stanza of the song in this
mauscript may support a suggestion that only this stanza was sung. For a discussion of this
manuscript collection as representative of a choir-school repertoire and of the importance in this
context of the ornate version of Ferrabosco's setting, see my article, 'Christ Church MS Mus 439'.
The song is also printed in Sabol, *Songs and Dances*, pp. 40–1, the version from the *Ayres*. There
exists a setting by Henry Lawes of the lyric '*Beauties*, have you seen a toy' (ll. 85 ff.), but the setting
is late and the masque text suggests that this was not sung: see l. 84. Lawes's version occurs in New
York Public Library, Drexel MS 4257, no. 37; B.L. MS Add. 11608, f. 81; B.L. MS. Add. 53723
(formerly Loan MS 35) no. 67; Lawes, *Second Book of Ayres and Dialogues* (1655), p. 41; Lawes, *Select
Ayres and Dialogues*, 11 (1669), p. 75.

[69] *Haddington Masque*, ll. 171–4.

[70] Enid Welsford also points out the probable influence on the antimasque of *Queens* from the
French ballet-masquerade, in particular *Le Ballet de la Foire Saint-Germain*. See *Court Masque*, pp.
184–5.

[71] *Queens*, ll. 18–19.

[72] ll. 24–6 and 29–30.

EXAMPLE 16(a). The wyche

B.L. MSS Add. 17786–9 and 17791, *f.* 5 in each part-book.

EXAMPLE 16(b).

The first witches dance

B.L. MS Add. 10444, *ff*. 21, 74[v].

Note.

5 Bass II: MS = c

The second witches Dance

B.L. MS Add. 10444, *ff.*21ᵛ, 75.

Note.
10 Treble II: MS = E
15 Bass I—III: MS =

EXAMPLE 16(c). The wiches Daunce

B.L. MS Add. 38539, *f*.4.

Note.

40–41a: The piece in the MS ends at bar 41a and there is no indication of first and second time bars. Their addition here is editorial; but they seem necessary as 41a cannot be the final bar of the piece.

EXAMPLE 16(d). ye witches dawnce

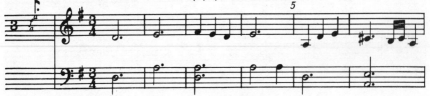

Trinity College, Dublin, MS D.1.21, p.65.

Note.

Lute tuning = D A d a d'g'

EXAMPLE 16(e). The Witches daunce in the Queenes Maske

Robert Dowland, *Varietie of Lute-Lessons* (1610), Sig. P. 2ᵛ.

Note.

9 Treble II: Lower note of chord given as F natural.

EXAMPLE 16(f). [The second witches' dance]

Christ Church MS Mus. 92, *ff.* 15–15^{v}.

Notes.

15 Bass I: upper note = minim
20 Treble IV–VII = semiquavers
25 Treble I: = minim
32 Treble and Bass = minims
33 Bass I: lower note = minim on A
34 I: upper note = minim
39 Bass I: lower note = minim
40 Bass: upper and lower notes = minims.

cf. Cutts, J.P., *La musique de la troupe de Shakespeare*, pp.16 and 126.

loud-voiced instruments than by any attempt to represent the grotesque or the strange in the music itself, although here too the music
suggests, rhythmically, complicated choreographic patterns.[73]

In the antimasque of witches most of the dialogue is a kind of
incantation which might be regarded as correlative with the dances
themselves: the effect of the verses is cumulative rather than dramatic.
Where the dialogue does become 'dramatic' (in the sense that it promotes some kind of action) as, for instance, when the Dame addresses the
Hagges, the heroic couplets seem to foreshadow and deliberately mock
the speeches of Heroique Virtue and Fame. The rhythm of the Dame's
speeches distorts the formal and static qualities of the couplets as they
are later used so that the rhymes are almost lost in the reading.[74] The
opposition of antimasque to main masque was to be absolute: 'the
whole face of the *Scene* alterd; scarse suffring the memory of any such
thing: But, in the place of it appear'd a glorious and magnificent
Building, figuring the *House of Fame* . . .'[75] However, Jonson's two sets
did not in fact represent clear opposites to one another. The witches

---

[73] See the description of the second witches' dance, ll. 344 ff., and Jonson's recognition of 'the
Maker of the *Daunce*, *Mr. Hierome Herne*' rather than any mention of the composer of the dance
music. This grotesque dance is quite clearly to be regarded as the opposite of the elaborate
'hieroglyphs' and symbols which the main-masque dance patterns created. Music for both the
witches' dances (ll. 43 and 344) occurs in B.L. MS Add. 10444, ff. 21 and 74ᵛ, 21ᵛ and 75. There is
music for the first dance only in lute arrangements in Robert Dowland's *Varietie of Lute-Lessons*
(1610), Sig. P.2ᵛ, in B.L. MS Add. 38539, f. 4, and in Board MS (in the private collection of Mr
Robert Spencer), f. 26. This version has been copied from Robert Dowland's *Varietie of Lute-Lessons*,
even including Dowland's error, bar 9. In bar 14, Board omits the lower note from the chord
immediately before the double bar. There is an arrangement for lyra viol in William Ballet's Lute
Book (Trinity College, Dublin, MS D. 1. 21), p. 65. There is a five-part consort version of the first
dance in B.L. MSS Add. 17786–9 and 17791, i–v, f. 5, entitled 'The wych', and another consort
version in William Brade's *Newe ausserlesene liebliche Branden* . . . (Hamburg, 1617), entitled 'Der
Hexen Tanz' (no. XLIX). There is a version of the second witches' dance only in Christ Church,
Oxford, MS Mus. 92, ff. 15–15ᵛ.

J. P. Cutts, 'Robert Johnson and the Court Masque', p. 114, remarks that a second witches'
dance is not referred to in Jonson's text and that if one had been performed Robert Dowland would
have published it with the other dances for this masque in his *Varietie of Lute-Lessons*. He believes
that the piece described as the second witches' dance (in B.L. MS Add. 10444 and Christ Church
MS Mus.92) belongs to a play, possibly *Macbeth*. Cutts bases his assumptions on his interpretation
of Jonson's opening description of the masque (H & S vii, pp. 282–3). He regards the entrance of
the witches (ll. 29–30) as accompanied by the 'spindrells, timbrells, rattles, or other *veneficall*
instruments' and therefore as noise and gesture rather than the dance given as the witches' dance.
Jonson's text describes, however, a dance *after* the witches' entry (ll. 43 f.), and it seems from his
description that this dance was different from their entry: 'These eleven Witches beginning to
daunce . . .'. I suggest that the music for the first witches' dance belonged here and that for the
second at l. 344.

[74] The qualities of Virtue and Fame are found together in the emblem in honour of Sir Thomas
Chaloner in *Minerva Brittanna* (London, 1612). This is pointed out by Bergeron. 'English Civic
Pageantry', pp. 180–1, who says that Dekker was the first to make the association of Virtue and
Fame—in the Lord Mayor's Show of 1612. Jonson's masque three years earlier may well be the
first.

[75] ll. 357–60.

and their hell may have been intended to symbolize moral evil, as Jonson tells us, but the mode of the whole antimasque was far more dramatic than that of the main masque, which depended almost entirely on its visual aspects, that is, the emblem set, for its meaning. The witches' dances, too, characterized or illustrated their moral deformity while the dances of the main masque depended far more on symbolic choreography for their meaning. Of the third of these masque dances, especially, we are told 'a more *numerous* composition could not be seene'; and that it was

graphically dispos'd into *letters*, and honoring the Name of the most sweete, and ingenious *Prince, Charles, Duke of Yorke* wherin, beside that principall grace of perspicuity, the motions were so euen, & apt, and theyr expression so iust; as if *Mathematicians* had lost *proportion*, they might there haue found it. The *Author* was Mr. Tho. *Giles.*[76]

(ll. 750–6)

As in *Blackness*, the main masque was simply an expansion of the emblem itself. But the balance between masque and antimasque could not have been equal. Jonson says that the antimasque vanished, 'scarse suffring the memory of any such thing': but that the memory *did* remain is evident—even in a single respect—from the number of sources which reproduce one of the witches' dances. In effect, if not in design or intention, the antimasque of witches was a little drama in itself, and this would have laid too much stress by contrast on the purely moralistic significance of the House of Fame, emphasizing the audience as spectators rather than as participators.

This point may become clearer when we examine the effect of the only song for which music still survives: 'When all the Ages of the earth' (ll. 737–48), which was set by Ferrabosco and printed in his *Ayres*, no. 23. The song was sung during the revels and introduced the third masque dance.

When all the Ages of the earth
Were crown'd, but in this *famous birth*;
And that, when they would boast theyr store
Of *worthy Queenes*, they knew no more:
How happier is that *Age*, can giue
A *Queene*, in whome all they do liue!

[76] Music for the three masque dances occurs in a lute arrangement in Robert Dowland's *Varietie of Lute-Lessons* together with the first witches' dance. Another lute version of the third mainmasque dance (with divisions different from Dowland's) occurs in the Board MS, f. 41, untitled. There is a set of three dances in B.L. MS Add. 10444, ff. 10ᵛ and 65ᵛ, 11ᵛ and 66ᵛ, 12ᵛ and 67, entitled respectively: 'The Queenes Masque. the first', 'The Queens Maske. the second', and 'The Queenes third Masque'. These are different from the three Queen's Masque dances in Dowland's *Varietie*. The Dowland versions are more likely to belong to *Queens* because of their grouping with the first witches' dance. The dances in the B.L. manuscript, then, belong to another masque of Queen Anne's. Since they occur early in the manuscript and since the dances seem to be roughly in chronological order there, they may very well belong to either *Blackness* or *Beauty*.

EXAMPLE 17(a).

The first of the Queenes Maskes

Robert Dowland, *Varietie of Lute-Lessons* (1610), Sig. P.1ᵛ.

Note.

15 Treble IX and X = 𝅘𝅥 (𝅘𝅥𝅮)

The second of the Queenes Maskes

[Sig P.2]

Robert Dowland, *Varietie of Lute-Lessons* (1610), Sig. P.1^v – P.2.

Note.

5 Treble II and III = ♪ (♪)

20: Treble IV = e on the g string. I transcribe as d.

21: Treble I= ♪ (♩)

The last of the Queenes Maskes

Robert Dowland, *Varietie of Lute-Lessons* (1610), Sig. P.2.

Note.

5 Treble I-II, note-values =

12 Treble IV: upper note of chord given as G.

EXAMPLE 17(b).

[The third dance from *Queens*]

Board MS, *f.* 41 (untitled)

Notes

5 Bass I and II: MS gives open string and fret d on string 5.

7 MS gives no note values for this bar

8 MS = I-II

11 MS gives not values for the first two chords as

12 Treble VII: MS =

EXAMPLE 18.

The Queenes Masque. the first

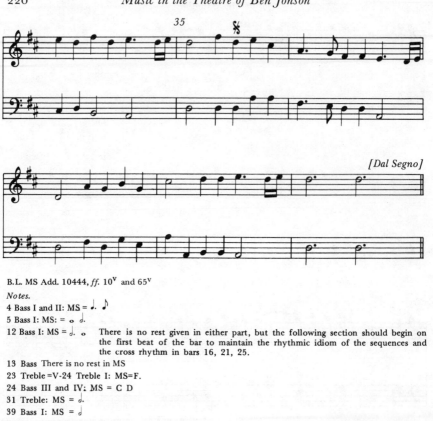

B.L. MS Add. 10444, *ff.* 10ᵛ and 65ᵛ

Notes.

4 Bass I and II: MS = ♩. ♪

5 Bass I: MS: = 𝅝 ♩.

12 Bass I: MS = ♩. 𝅝   There is no rest given in either part, but the following section should begin on the first beat of the bar to maintain the rhythmic idiom of the sequences and the cross rhythm in bars 16, 21, 25.

13 Bass There is no rest in MS

23 Treble =V-24 Treble I: MS=F.

24 Bass III and IV: MS = C D

31 Treble: MS = ♩.

39 Bass I: MS = ♩

The Queens Maske. the second

B.L. MS Add. 10444, *ff.* 11^V and 66^V.

Notes.

17 II : MS gives no rests in either part.

30, Treble, between III and IV gives:

Since the inclusion of this not only upsets the bass part but also the phrase length it has been omitted as the simplest and most likely scribal error in an otherwise difficult passage.

32 II : MS gives no rest in either part.

51 Treble II: MS =

The Queenes third Masque

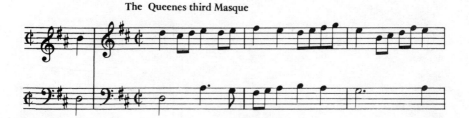

B.L. MS Add. 10444, *ff.* 12ᵛ and 67.

Notes.

5 Bass II : MS = G
6 Bass I: MS = G
10 Treble and Bass: MS = ♩.
14 Treble and Bass: MS = ♩
19 Treble IV - VI: MS = ♩ ♫
21 Treble and Bass: MS has three beats only.
29 Treble VI - VIII: MS = ♩. ♫
30 Time signature (31) precedes I in treble and III in Bass.
34 Treble I: not in MS

EXAMPLE 19(a). 'If all the ages of the earth'

Alfonso Ferrabosco, *Ayres* (1609), no. 23, Sig. H.1.

EXAMPLE 19(b). 'If all the ages of the earth'

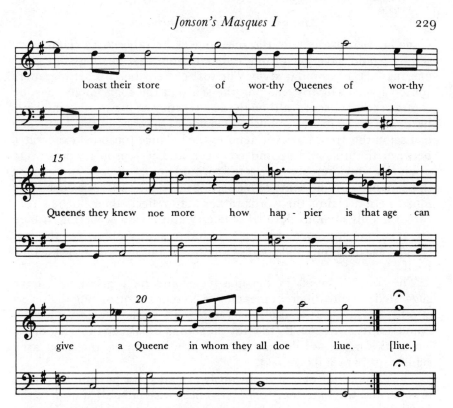

boast their store of wor-thy Queenes of wor-thy

Queenes they knew noe more how hap - pier is that age can

give a Queene in whom they all doe liue. [liue.]

Christ Church MS Mus. 439, p. 95. *Note.* 22b Treble and Bass: MS = ♩

In the earlier masques, songs sung during the revels served the purpose of reminding the audience that as participators in the revels they were also participators in the masque and thus part of the meaning of the masque's emblem. But because of its placing the effect of 'When all the Ages of the earth' must have been different. The words of the song sum up the theme of the main masque: that Queen Anne and the age in which she lives crown all former ages and that she gathers within her virtue the virtue of all former queens. So the song celebrated the Queen who crowned the pyramid of masquers in the House of Fame and 'of whose dignity, and person the whole *scope* of the *Invention* doth speake throughout'.[77] The Queen was now actually dancing in the revels; but because the structure of the masque, with its dramatic antimasque, emphasized the passive role of the audience—as spectators—the song must more obviously have celebrated the 'illusion' of the House of Fame, the world *behind* the proscenium arch, and cannot clearly have addressed the audience or acknowledged its response. The link between the masque emblem and the court would have seemed now only

[77] ll. 656–7.

nominal. Because of this the meaning of Ferrabosco's declamatory setting would have been quite different from that of songs in earlier masques set in a similar style. The text of Ferrabosco's setting alters Jonson's verse slightly, making the sense of the song for its masque context rather obscure, although the alteration of the words may have been made only for the published version of the song in the *Ayres*. The text set in the *Ayres*, however, ignores the balance Jonson's text creates between the first and second couplets; and if Jonson's words were originally sung, Ferrabosco's setting would not have clearly supported this balance. Unlike some of his settings of earlier masque songs, the music here declaims the words rather than reflects their poetic structure, the only obvious parallel of poetry and music occurring at bars 16–22 where the harmonic and rhythmic shift emphasizes the last couplet as containing the point of the song—and indeed of the masque itself.

The song's context in the masque would have given it, I have suggested, a quite different meaning from songs sung during the revels of other masques. It would have remained a virtuoso piece, a performance for its own sake. By the way the setting breaks up the sense of the words the music would not have clearly supported the song as a significant part of its context.

The antimasque of *Queens* obviously extended the possibilities of the masque and was extremely popular. There was, after all, a limit to the number of times one could go on showing, by emblems, that James's court was Elysium. But the antimasque of *Queens* pointed to a further problem of the masque as a form: what kind of illusion was the masque to be in relation to its audience? From now on Jonson seems to have been seeking a way not only to include the court within the masque fiction but to include the antimasque as well, while keeping some of the very popular dramatic elements of the witches' antimasque. He had already examined one possibility tentatively in the figure of Ianuarius: that is, the possibility of confining the 'dramatic' action to more clearly 'antick' figures, figures not (as the witches were) from drama, but from mummings, disguises, and interludes, figures who traditionally were expected to appear in the audience itself. In this way—as in *Beauty*—Jonson could acknowledge more explicitly that the audience was itself part of a fiction. But in doing this he was in some respects compromising one of the most vital functions of the masque as it appeared in *Blackness*, for example; that is, the explicit recognition of the power of the masque to affect its audience and move its members to an awareness of their own part in the 'truth' symbolized by the masque itself and of the divine ordering of James's kingdom.

The success of *Blackness* must have been at least partly due to the relation of masque and audience. At first the courtiers were simply themselves, citizens of Jacobean London. Then at the climax of the masque the audience was also recognized as belonging within the masque's meaning. The revels in *Blackness* represented the audience's recognition of its spiritual similarities with the masque and were not merely a literal expansion of the stage. This appears to have been an ideal relationship between masque and audience.

6

Jonson's Masques II

A STUDY of the masques beyond *Queens* makes clear various ways of treating the problem of form which the relation between masquers and audience in effect created. Ideally the audience's joining in the revels was their recognition of, and assent to, the Truth of the masque's emblem. In practice, however, the participation of the courtiers would have increasingly weakened the virtues of the masque's perfected world and the ending was often a kind of arbitrary recognition that time was passing, as a means of drawing the evening's entertainment to a close. The introduction of antimasque further complicated this problem of form, for in relating the dramatic aspects of antimasque to the main masque Jonson often abandoned the emblem, or symbolic, qualities of the main masque and hence the philosophical motive for the masquers to step off-stage and dance with the audience. These new developments in the masque also disturbed the balance of the relation of music, poetry, and picture to one another, and although composers for several of Jonson's later masques employed declamatory settings these settings seldom convey the philosophical intentions—of heightened and affective eloquence—that lay behind the development of this style of singing. The reason for this can be found in the function the songs now have within the masque.

Jonson's most successful masques in this later period were *Love Freed from Ignorance and Folly*, *The Vision of Delight*, and *Pleasure Reconciled to Virtue*. Each adapts in its own way the conceptual and dramatic aspects of masque, revels, and antimasque to create what must have been a satisfying and complete occasion. In *Oberon*, the masque for Prince Henry two years after *Queens*, Jonson first tackled the problem of unifying masque and antimasque.

I

In *Oberon* Jonson made the fictional stage-world as self-contained as possible. This was achieved largely by the use of a set different in design from those for the earlier masques, a series of painted flats sliding in grooves instead of the machines and pageant cars the sets had used up to this time.[1] By using this set Jonson was able to integrate his antimas-

---

[1] The whole masque is discussed in detail by Orgel, *Jonsonian Masque*, pp. 82–91; Introduction to *Complete Masques*, pp. 17–20; 'To Make the Boards to Speak', pp. 131–5.

Landscape with rocks: design for *Oberon*.

Oberon's palace: design for *Oberon*.

Descent of the daughters of the Morn:
design for *Love Freed from Ignorance and Folly*.

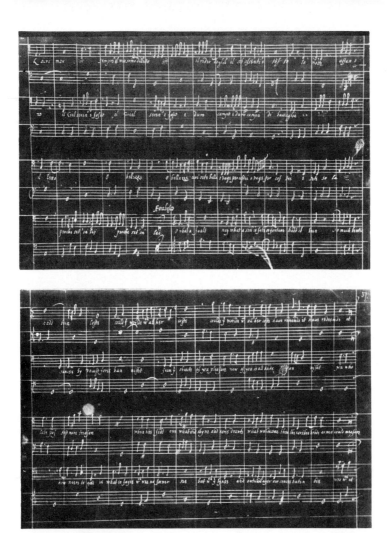
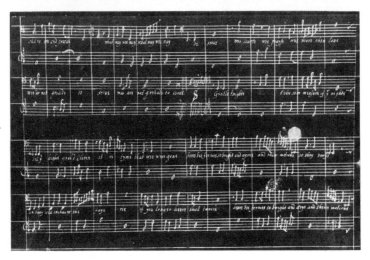

Tenbury MS 1018, folios 36ᵛ–37ᵛ.

que within the masque itself, something which was difficult in *Queens* with its two different types of set: pictorial and emblematic. The integration in *Oberon* was achieved not by 'banishing' the antimasque set but by enlarging it so that the antimasque developed into the masque. The set opened up and revealed more and more, taking the antimasque figures with it until they became the audience for the main masque, the opening of Oberon's palace. The first scene was a rocky landscape at night (see Pl. IV):

The first face of the Scene *appeared all obscure, & nothing perceiu'd but a darke Rocke, with trees beyond it; and all wildnesse, that could be presented* . . .

(ll. 1–3)

The satyrs, the antimasque figures, belonged in this fiction and these now appeared questioning Silenus, *'who is euer the* Præfect *of the* SATYRES', about the promised arrival of Oberon. As the satyrs were speaking of the wonders which Oberon would perform Silenus cried suddenly:

> See, the rocke begins to ope,
> Now you shall enioy your hope;
> 'Tis about the houre, I know.

(ll. 135–7)

The first scene's flats were drawn aside to reveal another set of painted flats behind, this time depicting the outside of Oberon's palace, guarded by two sleeping Sylvanes whom the satyrs tried to awaken by singing 'a charme into their eares'.[2] (See Pl. V.) The second 'scene' ended with an 'antique dance' by the satyrs after which Silenus drew their attention to the fact that day was breaking:

> Stay, the cheerefull *Chanticleere*
> Tells you, that the time is neere:
> See, the gates alreadie spread!
> Euery *Satyre* bow his head.

(ll. 287–90)

At this, we are told,

the whole palace open'd, and the nation of Faies *were discouer'd, some with instruments, some bearing lights; others singing; and within a farre off in perspectiue, the knights masquers sitting in their seuerall sieges: At the further end of all,* OBERON, *in a chariot, which to a lowd triumphant musique began to moue forward, drawne by two white beares* . . .

(ll. 291–6)

The chariot came forward to *'the face of the* scene', and the satyrs, who were watching from the sides of the stage, '[leapt] *and expresse*[d] *their ioy'*.[3]

---

[2] l. 208.
[3] ll. 314–16.

After the speeches by a Sylvane and Silenus Oberon and his knights descended to dance with the courtiers.

Jonson managed the transition from antimasque to masque here by expressing it as an enlargement of the set. This represented a growing awareness on the part of the satyrs. But to some degree the satyrs had replaced the audience itself. At the point where Oberon and his knights stepped off the stage Jonson had to convince his audience that this was not Oberon, a character in a fiction, but Prince Henry; and that Arthur, whom Oberon recognized in the audience, was in fact King James. The awkwardness of the shift from fiction to symbolism here has been pointed out by Stephen Orgel and is expressed by the stiffness of the poetry.[4] Up to now the audience had been required to be merely passive spectators: suddenly they were called upon to become part of the fiction, and to recognize the fiction as an emblem of their own lives.

This lack of a smooth transition from masque to revels was reflected in the very conventional function of the songs sung during the revels: there is a flatness in the way they merely encouraged further dancing and reminded the audience that it was late. Music by Ferrabosco is extant for two of the songs in the main masque.[5] The first was sung between the first and second masque dances:

> Nay, nay,
> You must not stay,
> Nor be weary, yet;
> This 's no time to cast away;
> Or, for *Faies* so to forget
> The vertue of their feet.
> Knottie legs, and plants of clay
> Seeke for ease, or loue delay.
> But with you it still should fare
> As, with the ayre of which you are.
>
> (ll. 396–405)

The second song was sung at the end of the revels:

> Gentle knights,
> Knowe some measure of your nights.
> Tell the high-grac'd OBERON,
> It is time, that we were gone.
> Here be formes, so bright, and aery,
> And their motions so they vary
> As they will enchant the *Faery*,
> If you longer, here, should tarry.

---

[4] Orgel, see references above.

[5] St Michael's College, Tenbury, MS 1018, ff. 36 and 37ᵛ–38. See also Cutts, 'Le Rôle de la musique', pp. 298–300; Sabol, *Songs and Dances*, pp. 43–6. In the Tenbury MS version the words of the last line of 'Nay, nay' have been confused.

EXAMPLE 20. 'Nay nay you must not stay'

Nay nay you must not stay nor bee we - rie

yet this is no tyme to cast a - way or for Faye -

- ries to for - get the ver - tu of their feete

knot - tie logges and plantes of claye seeke for ease or

loue de - lay but with you it [still should fare]

as with ye ayer as with ye ayer.

Alfonso farrabosco.

St Michael's College, Tenbury MS 1018, *f*.36.

Note

17–18: MS gives a bar between these two which has been crossed out, thus:

still should

EXAMPLE 21. 'Gentle knights'

Gent - le knights [gent - le knights] know som

mea - sure of your nights tell ye highe grac'd O - be - ron

it is tyme that wee were gone heere bee formes

_____ so bright and aye-rie and their mo - tions

so they va - rye as they will in - chaunt the

faye - - rie if you long - er

heere shall tar - - rie heere bee

formes so bright and aer - ye and theire mo -

[*f.* 38]

- tions so they var - ye as the[y] will in -

- chaunt   the   fay - - - - rie

if   you long-er   heer should tar - ry   if   you   long- er

heer   shoulde   tar - rie. _____

A Farabosco.

St. Michael's College, Tenbury MS 1018, *ff*. 37ᵛ–38.

There is also a setting, although probably some years later than the
performance of the masque, by Edward Nelham, for the catch which
was sung by the satyrs (ll. 210–17).[6] The function of the song was very
similar to the function of some songs in plays for children: that is, it was
an entertainment or an interlude, without any pretence at promoting
the 'action' or significance of the masque. This song is characteristic of
songs in later antimasques. However, the development of *Oberon* in the
direction of drama is evident not only in the function of this antimasque
song—which is a very simple one—but in the function of those in the
main masque and revels as well.

The extant settings of two of these may indicate the style in which the
others were set. The setting of 'Nay, nay, You must not stay' is far less
declamatory, far more 'tuneful' ayre than the setting of 'Gentle
knights', although the rhetorical qualities of the text of 'Nay, nay' are to
some degree reflected in the music: for instance, the rhythmic pattern of

[6] *Catch that Catch Can* (1667), p. 75.

EXAMPLE 22. 'Buz quoth the Blew Fly' Mr. *Edmund Nelham*

Catch that Catch can: OR THE Musical Companion (London, 1667), p. 75.

bars 1 and 2, the treatment of 'wearie' (bar 4), or the double cadence (bars 10 and 12) which emphasizes the conflict of rhyme and grammatical sense in the text itself. These devices are expressed, however, in a melodic pattern which has musical shape of its own apart from the words. 'Gentle knights' on the other hand is far more declamatory in style, the vocal line constructed of often wide and simple intervals—fifths, thirds, and sixths—and melismatic passages. Part of the reason for the 'flatness' of these songs' function may lie in the text: the songs in the earlier masques summed up more clearly aspects of the masque's emblem, so that, although in some ways the 'tone' of the poetry was difficult to assess, the formal or poetic structure of the song as part of its philosophical statement was given an importance to which the settings drew attention. By contrast, the songs for the main masque and revels of *Oberon* are more simply instructional: their formal poetic qualities appear to be less important than their actual statement. Where the setting is required to project neither 'tone' nor formal aspects simple declamation is the most obvious solution. As regards its relation to the masque as concept, the rhetorical point of the declamatory setting—speech as heightened eloquence—is evident. But in this masque the 'philosophical' significance of these songs must have seemed only nominal, for they cannot have been regarded as complementary to the visual aspects as were the songs in those early masques with emblem sets. By approaching closer to the self-contained fiction of drama and a pictorial set the whole masque would have been more detached from its audience. Now the songs would have appeared merely virtuoso performances to impress a passive audience and to sustain an elaborate but flimsy fiction throughout the duration of the revels. From the point of view of virtuoso performance the second song must have offered more possibilities than the simpler melodic setting of 'Nay, nay, You must not stay'.

Despite the very simple harmonic accompaniment suggested by the shape of the melody and the unfigured bass, the treble and bass form in which these songs are recorded probably does not give us an adequate indication of the way they sounded in performance. The accounts which survive for this masque indicate that Ferrabosco provided ‚'[ten] singers and 6 plaiers on the lute'; the accompaniments for even the solo songs may have been more complex than we imagine.

Music for the antimasque dances of fairies and satyrs survives and is probably by Robert Johnson. There is a set of main-masque dances in the British Library manuscript entitled 'The Princes Masque' and this may belong to the main masque of *Oberon*.[7] As in earlier masques the music for the dance of satyrs and the dance of fairies does not attempt to

---

[7] The music for the satyrs' dance (l. 282) occurs in B.L. MS Add. 10444, ff. 31 and 82ᵛ. There is an arrangement of this in Thomas Simpson's *Taffel-Consort* (Hamburg, 1621), no. XXIV, ascribed to Robert Johnson. See Cutts, 'Robert Johnson and the Court Masque', p. 117; Sabol, *Songs and Dances*, p. 169, note to no. 48. Music for the fairies' dance (l. 382) occurs in B.L. MS Add. 10444, ff. 31ᵛ and 83, entitled 'The Fairey Masque', in B.L. MS Add. 38539, f. 10, entitled 'The fayris Daunce', and in Cambridge University Library MS Nn. 6. 36, f. 24ᵛ, untitled. Sabol discusses the association of the extant music for the fairies' dance with *Oberon* in *Songs and Dances*, pp. 169–70, note to no. 49. B.L. MS Add. 10444 contains music for three main-masque dances entitled 'The Prince's Masque', ff. 16 and 70ᵛ, 'The Princes 2 Masque', ff. 16ᵛ and 71, and 'The Prince's Third Masque', ff. 16ᵛ–17 and 71ᵛ. Cutts assigns these as the masque dances in *Oberon* (ll. 394, 407, 444): 'Jacobean Masque and Stage Music'. This can be only a very tentative ascription; cf. Sabol's caution about some of Cutts's ascriptions, *Songs and Dances*, p. 168, note to no. 39.

In a later article, 'Robert Johnson and the Court Masque', pp. 117–18, Cutts suggests that the two almans by Robert Johnson (B.L. MSS Add. 38539, ff. 16 and 17; Add. 36661, ff. 54ᵛ and 54; the arrangements by Giles Farnaby in the Fitzwilliam Virginal Book, nos. 146 and 145) are more appropriate to *Oberon*. In B.L. MS Add. 36661, the alman on f. 54 is called 'The Princes Almayne By Johnson' and Cutts uses this plus the fact that the dances occur in most sources together (the exception is the second alman which occurs alone in Cambridge University Library MS Dd. 442, f. 10) to support his suggestion that the pieces belong in Jonson's masque. He says, p. 118, n. 15: 'On stylistic grounds the music for the two antimasques and the two Almans is complementary, and obviously one unit.'

The number of masque dances simply called 'The Prince's Masque' in B.L. MS Add. 10444 makes assigning them to specific masques a matter of almost pure speculation. Other dances with this title occur as follows:

be in any way illustrative of the nature of these characters but would have provided a rhythmic basis for the elaborate choreographic patterns. As usual, it is the choreography rather than the music to which Jonson draws attention. The satyrs' dance is described as 'full of gesture, and swift motion'. Like the songs, however, the dances would have lost some of their 'philosophical' point because they would have had little conceptual relationship to the visual set.

II

Oberon was performed on 1 January 1611, in honour of Prince Henry. In February another masque of Jonson's, this time for the Queen, was performed: *Love Freed from Ignorance and Folly*. The closeness in date of these two makes a comparison of them interesting, for the later masque solved some of the awkward aspects of *Oberon* and developed some of its virtues.[8] The link between antimasque and masque was no longer presented as a change in scene but rather as a recognition of the audience so that the audience could become an integral part of the masque proper. This allowed the antimasque to develop by itself as a little drama, for part of its meaning lay precisely in the fact that it *was* separate from the audience, the court and the values for which it stood. When the court had been recognized the antimasque set did not vanish but was transformed by the response of the audience itself.

ff. 45ᵛ–46/95ᵛ	'The First of the Princes Masques'
ff. 46/95ᵛ	'The Second'
ff. 46/95ᵛ–96	'The Third'
ff. 51ᵛ/101	'The first of the Prince his Masque'
ff. 52/101	'The second'
ff. 52/101ᵛ	'The third'
ff. 52ᵛ–53/102	'The Prince his Masq:'
ff. 54/103ᵛ	'The first of the Prince his'
ff. 54/103ᵛ	'The second'

Two of these groups of dances can be assigned with some certainty. The first group (ff. 45ᵛ–46/95ᵛ–96) is preceded by 'The Goates Masque' and therefore possibly belongs to Jonson's reworking of *Pleasure Reconciled to Virtue* as *For the Honour of Wales* (1618). See below, p. 276.

The first dance on ff. 54/103ᵛ occurs in several other sources which identify it as belonging specifically to Chapman's masque of the Middle Temple and Lincoln's Inn for the wedding of the Princess Elisabeth in 1613. In William Brade's *Newe ausserlesene liebliche Branden* (Hamburg, 1617) the piece occurs as no. XXXI entitled 'Der erste Mascharda des Pfaltzgraffen'; in Margaret Board's lute manuscript it occurs twice: f. 28 (no. 92) 'The Princis Masque' and f. 30ᵛ (no. 103) 'The La: Elyza her masque'; in Christ Church MS Mus. 92, f. 10 it is entitled 'Lincolns Inn Mask Gibbons'. Its title in Skene MS, p. 44: 'Prince Henreis Maske', is obviously an error, possibly explained by the association of Henry's death in November 1612 with the postponement of the marriage festivities and by the fact that Chapman was sewer in ordinary to Prince Henry.

[8] It is possible that Jonson worked on these two masques together. *Love Freed* was originally to have been performed during the Christmas festivities of 1610, was put off until 6 January 1611, and further postponed until 3 February. It seems to have been actually performed on 13 February. (H & S x, pp. 527–8.)

EXAMPLE 23. The Satyres Masque

B.L. MS Add. 10444, *ff*. 31, 82ᵛ.

Notes.

1	Bass III: MS = D	22	Bass: Time Signature = 31 This is not given in Treble
15	Bass II: MS = D	32	Bass: No notes given for this bar.
21	Treble I: MS = minim	33	Bass: No time signature given.
		35	Treble I: MS = minim
		45	Bass I: MS = ○
		46	Bass: Time signature not given.
		61	Treble II: MS gives no rest

EXAMPLE 24(a). The Fairey Masque

B.L. MS Add. 10444, *ff*.31^V, 83.

Notes.

7	Treble II: MS = C
27	Treble and Bass: MS = semibreve.
30	Bass III: MS = G
32	Treble: MS gives time signature:
42	Treble: MS gives time signature:
54	Bass I and II: MS = E
55	Bass I: MS = D

EXAMPLE 24(b). the fayris Daunce

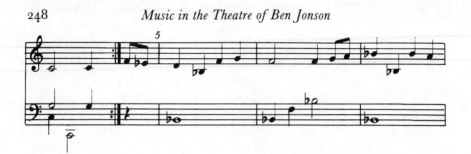

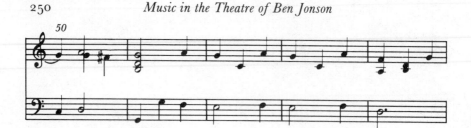

B.L. MS Add. 38539, *f.* 10.

The Prince's Masque   EXAMPLE 25.

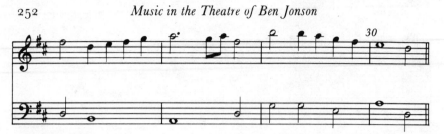

B.L. MS Add. 10444, *ff.* 16 and 70^v

The Princes 2 Masque

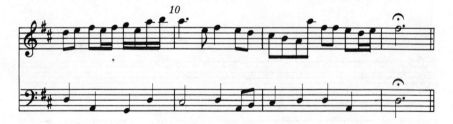

B.L. MS Add. 10444, *ff.* 16^v and 71.

The Princes Third Masque

B.L. MS Add.10444, *ff.* 16^V-17 and 71^V.
Note.
14 Bass: MS = semibreve.

EXAMPLE 26(a).

Allmayne by mʳ Ro: **Johnson**

finis Allmayne by mʳ Ro: Johnson

B.L. MS Add. 38539, *f.* 16.

Notes.

3	Treble IV and V: MS =	♩
4	Bass IV and V: MS =	♪
15	Bass V: MS =	

Allmayne by Mr Robert Johnson

finis Allmayne by Mr Robert Johnson

B.L. MS Add. 38539, *f.* 17.

EXAMPLE 26(b)

Mr Johnsonns Almayne

B.L. MS Add. 36661, *f.* 54ᵛ.   *Finis*

The Princes Almayne By Johnson

Finis The Princes Almayne By Johnson

B.L. MS Add. 36661, *f.* 54.

It is unfortunate that we know very little about the set for this masque: Jonson's text is almost completely literary and non-descriptive. We do know from the accounts that Jones made the designs for the masque however, and so can accept as very plausible Roy Strong's ascription of the Chatsworth design (Simpson and Bell, no. 17) to this masque. (See Pl. VI.) Moreover, the prison in this design has characteristics of Oberon's palace (Simpson and Bell, no. 42) and this suggests that it belonged to a masque close in time to *Oberon*.[9] The accounts also tell us that Ferrabosco 'made' the songs: settings of two of them—'O what a fault' (l. 338) and 'How neere to good' (l. 348) —ascribed to Ferrabosco occur in the same manuscript collection as the extant songs from the main masque of *Oberon*.[10]

Once more Jonson chose the neo-Platonic theme of the praise of goodness and beauty, and here the antimasque of Sphynx helped to define, as an attribute of supreme wisdom, Love and Beauty in the main masque and in the court audience. The antimasque expressed one aspect of love—love bound—as bad poetry. Ignorance, or Sphynx, made Love (her captive at the beginning of the masque) merely into Blind Cupid (ll. 18–19, 39–40); and Cupid, who was to answer Sphynx's riddle in order that the daughters of the Morne might be released from the prison of the night, responded at first with a conventional, bad love-poetry answer. To begin with, the antimasque verse was doggerel which was later to be offset by the more flexible poetry and eloquent song of the masque-proper—after the entry of the Muses' priests. But at the beginning Cupid's protestations of the philosophical

[9] Both Oberon's palace and the prison of night are Elizabethan Gothic castles. Oberon's palace in particular is a curious but very delicate balance of classical forms with the Gothic crenellations and corbelled towers. *Oberon* is the only masque in which Jonson makes explicit use of the late Renaissance cult of medievalism and chivalry, although the Barriers for which he wrote texts quite clearly belong to this tradition. Strong assigns the illustrations for the 'Fallen House of Chivalry' and 'St. George's Portico' (Simpson and Bell, nos. 194 and 195) to Prince Henry's Barriers, a year before *Oberon*, 6 January 1610 (Strong, *Designs*, nos. 19 and 20). These designs also show a fusing of classical and Gothic elements. Strong suggests that the illustrations of costumes (Simpson and Bell, nos. 13, 430, and 433) may be also from these Barriers (*Designs*, nos. 22–4). See also 'A Cave Hung with Impresa Shields' (Simpson and Bell, no. 404), which may be a detailed design for the House of Chivalry (*Designs*, no. 25). Cf. the discussion of Accession Day tilts in Elizabethan England: Yates, 'Elizabethan Chivalry'. The use of a neo-Gothic design for the set of *Love Freed* is interesting because that masque seems to have few of the chivalric and romantic characteristics that *Oberon* has. It is probable that the *Oberon* sets were very much admired and that Jones was simply trying to repeat that success in his next masque (possibly hurriedly adapting a design already prepared). A fusing of classical and Gothic elements is evident in the style of Bolsover Castle, Derbyshire, begun at about the same time as Prince Henry's Barriers, *Oberon*, and *Love Freed*. For a full discussion of this kind of architecture see Girouard, *Robert Smythson*, Chapter 6. Another example is the picture of the *Theatrum Orbi[s]* in Robert Fludd's *History of the Two Worlds* (Oppenheim, 1619), which is discussed at length by Yates, *Theatre of the World*: see especially Chapter 8 and Plate 20.

[10] St Michael's College, Tenbury, MS 1018, ff. 36ᵛ–37ᵛ. See also Sabol, *Songs and Dances*, pp. 44–50.

origins of Love and of his importance as a harmonizing influence in the world were merely comic:

> Cruell SPHYNX, I rather striue
> How to keepe the world aliue,
> And vphold it; without mee,
> All againe would *Chaos* bee.
>
> (ll. 27–30)

However, the figure of Love the audience saw bound at the beginning of the masque was not completely separate from the ideal Platonic Love which was celebrated later in the masque. His tetrameter couplets became more flexible as he related the story of his journey, before he was bound by Ignorance, with the daughters of the Morne to the palace of Phoebus; the verse became expressive both of his urgency and of their dignity. This dual, shifting, and uncertain character of the 'antimasque' Cupid is explained by Jonson's gloss later in the masque text:

This shewes, that *Loues* expositions are not alway serious, till it be diuinely instructed; and that sometimes it may be in the danger of Ignorance and Folly, who are the mother, and issue: for no folly but is borne of ignorance.

(Gloss to l. 250)

Although the backdrop to the opening of the masque presumably depicted the prison of night in which Ignorance had imprisoned the daughters of the Morne, if we take simply the evidence of the text there seems to have been intended no such sharp distinction between the stage set and the audience as there was in *Oberon*. When we are told that at the beginning '*a* Sphynx *came forth dauncing, leading* LOVE *bound*' (ll. 3–4) it is not necessary to define whether this was on a stage or actually among the audience—as in some Tudor interludes, for instance. This lack of clear definition, such as a picture stage might create, between audience and masque is important; for throughout the 'antimasque' Cupid actually addressed the audience when he was not directly replying to the Sphynx. His whole narration of the journey of the daughters of the Morne was made to the audience:

> Know, then, all you *Glories* here.
>
> (l. 65)

This direct address made Love's narration different, for instance, from the narration of Niger at the beginning of *Blackness*. But Cupid's appeals to the audience were clearly (and significantly) without any response—as would be appeals made from a fictional stage set—so he would have appeared to address mere shadows or an empty hall:

> Hath this place
> None will pittie CVPIDS case?
> Some soft eye, (while I can see
> Who it is, that melts for mee)
> Weepe a fit. Are all eyes here
> Made of marble?
>
> (ll. 37–42)

The audience's quite natural lack of response at this point was itself part of the antimasque's meaning. Further, Cupid's dilemma was dramatically heightened by Sphynx's exultation:

> Thinks poore LOVE, can Ladies lookes
> Saue him from the SPHYNXES hookes?
>
> (ll. 56–7)

The image of the prison of night ominously overshadowed the antimasque. It stood as a visual representation of Love's frantic groping towards some communication with the audience he could see but from whom he was cut off by Ignorance. The audience's silence and lack of participation would have heightened the nightmare sense of isolation that ignorance creates. Even Cupid's flippant and conventional answers to the riddle of Sphynx conveyed his desperation at gaining no response. Cupid's growing awareness of the emptiness of his own words, and of Ignorance's, or Sphynx's, tightening grip would have been clear in the following exchange:

> SPHYNX.
> I say, you first must cast about
> To finde a world, the world without.
>
> LOVE.
> I say, that is alreadie done,
> And is the new world i' the Moone.
>
> SPHYNX.
> *Cupid*, you doe cast too farre;
> This world is neerer by a starre.
> So much light Ile giue you to'it.
>
> LOVE.
> Without a Glasse? Well, I shall do't.
> Your world's a Lady, then; each creature
> Humane, is a world in feature,
> Is it not?
>
> SPHYNX.
> Yes, but finde out
> A world you must, the world without.

LOVE.
Why, if her seruant be not here,
She doth a single world appeare
Without her world.

SPHYNX.
Well, you shall runne.

LOVE.
Nay, SPHYNX, thus far is wel begunne.

(ll. 174–99)

However, it must have been obvious that neither Sphynx nor Cupid thought that the answer to the riddle was 'wel begunne': Cupid became more and more entrapped until finally he was hopelessly wrong. He still recognized one thing however: that the chief characteristic of ignorance is her abuse of language and wisdom. He recognized that the riddle of the Sphynx might contain a perfect wisdom and truth though its utterance was 'lame'.

Ignorance
Thinkes she doth her selfe aduance,
If of problemes cleare, shee make
Riddles, and the sense forsake,
Which came gentle from the Muses,
Till her vttring, it abuses.

(ll. 235–40)

Sphynx saw Cupid's recognition of her confusion of language simply as 'rayling' and in glee at her triumph called forth her Follies, *'which were twelue shee-fooles'*, to dance. The dance, for which music occurs in the British Library manuscript collection of masque music, was the culmination of the 'antimasque'. Like the antimasque dances for earlier masques this dance appears to have been characterized by grotesque costume and gesture rather than by any particular features of the music itself.[11] The dance was to represent and illustrate Folly, and thus would not have carried the symbolic significance of the dances in the main masque.

After this dance, before Love was borne away 'to the cliffe' to be torn 'Peece-meale', he made a final appeal to the audience:

Ladies, haue your lookes no power
To helpe LOVE, at such an hower?
Will you loose him thus? adiew,
Thinke, what will become of you,
Who shall praise you, who admire,

[11] B.L. MS Add. 10444, ff. 29ᵛ and 81.

Who shall whisper, by the fire
As you stand, soft tales, who bring you
Prettie newes, in rimes who sing you,
Who shall bathe him in the streames
Of your blood, and send you dreames
Of delight.

(ll. 255–65)

It is a pathetic appeal, but its very pathos, its exaggeration, has a latent comicality which must also have reinforced the 'antimasque' nature of Cupid: *this* audience could not respond to him. But just as he was to be carried off the twelve Priests of the Muses arrived singing and dancing; 'their song, to a measure'. Song and dance were one and this dance was the stately and noble pavane.[12] Their entry re-created Love: as Jonson's gloss expresses it, they 'inspire [Love] with their owne soule'. At their instruction Love could now look directly at the audience especially 'In the brightest face here shining' (l. 280), the face of James, and learn the answer to the riddle. Love's tetrameter couplets now took on a new and positive quality; they were no longer either flippant or pathetic. Love's recognition of the true qualities of his audience, his seeing them as they were in truth, and not simply as conventional 'mistresses' whose beauty was merely a physical attribute, was expressed as a different kind of poetry: wisdom was also eloquent. The development of the masque towards the revels had begun. Sphynx was banished and Love could now, simply by his eloquence, release the daughters of the Morne from the prison of night and darkness. Significantly, it appears from Jones's design, the prison of night did not vanish nor open up: instead the masquers, the Queen and her ladies, descended in a cloud machine which made the prison simply irrelevant. This suggests that their imprisonment was not to be regarded as literal but as allegorical. Their descent from above would have indicated the spiritual qualities for which they stood, qualities which were now represented in the 'action'. As Ignorance and Folly vanished and Love was freed, the Graces (Beauty, Love, and Pleasure), symbolic of the triadic nature of Love, came forward singing to crown Cupid.

The movement of antimasque to masque, and the way Jonson deliberately used the various aspects of masque (its music, poetry, dance, song, and picture) to draw together different modes (allegorical, iconographical, philosophical, and dramatic) within a single meaning was most intricately worked out. For it was Love's *words*, inspired by the song and dance of the Muses' priests, which released the daughters of the Morne: eloquence banished Ignorance and unlocked night's prison to release not merely beautiful masquers, but morning and light.

[12] See above, p. 140.

EXAMPLE 27. The Fooles Masque

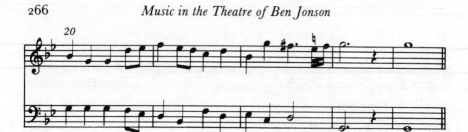

B.L. MS Add. 10444, *ff.* 29^v and 81.

Note.

11	Bass I: not given in MS.
20	Treble I: MS = a
23	Treble and Bass II: editorial rest.
37	Treble IV: no note given in MS.
40	Bass III: MS = o

At this point too, James as Phoebus, the Sun, could be recognized in the audience. This Love, the Love crowned by the Graces, was no longer the ignorant Cupid of the antimasque, and yet he was, philosophically and literally, the same: the same actor played both parts and he did not change in appearance.

In the dialogue song between the Graces and the Chorus which followed the crowning of Love we are told that the masquers, these 'gentle formes' that 'moue/To honour *Loue*', were the 'beames' of the daughters of the Morne, and that 'night is lost, or fled away;/For where such *Beautie* shines, is euer day'.[13] The masquers then danced, and the revels were preceded by a song by one of the Muses' priests, celebrating the solving of the riddle, the release of Beauty, and the freeing of Love. After this the masquers could join with the audience in the revels in recognition that James's court itself signified the triadic Love: Beauty, Love, and Pleasure.

Music survives for two songs in the masque: the song sung after the masque dance and just before the revels and that sung to end the revels, before the last masque dance. The settings which occur in the Tenbury manuscript are by Ferrabosco.[14] The first of these songs is, according to Jonson's text, to be sung by one of the Muses' Priests and a Chorus:

PRIE: O what a fault, nay, what a sinne
           In *Fate*, or *Fortune* had it beene,
           So much beautie to haue lost!
           Could the world with all her cost
           Haue redeem'd it? CHO. No, no, no.
PRIE: How so?
CHO.   It would *Nature* quite vndoe,
           For losing these, you lost her too.

(ll. 338–45)

In the Tenbury manuscript (see Pl. VII) the song ends at 'haue redeemde it' and is directly followed by a song which does not occur in Jonson's masque text:

sences by vniust force bannisht
from ye obiecte of you[r] pleasure
now of you is all ende vannisht
you who late possest more treasure
when eies fedd one what did shyne
and eares dranke what was deuine
then the earthes brode armes could measure.

This, in turn, is followed in the manuscript by the only other song in Jonson's masque text for which a setting survives: 'How neere to good'.

[13] ll. 326–35.
[14] The settings are for voice and unfigured bass and are ascribed.

EXAMPLE 28.

'O what a fault'

O what a fault   nay what a sin in fate

or — for - tune hadd it   been   so ___ much bew - tie

f. 37   10

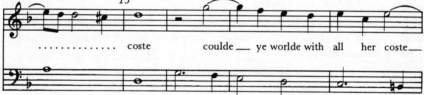

hadd ___ been ___   loste   could   ye   worlde with all   her . .

15

.... coste   coulde ___ ye worlde with all   her coste ___

20

___ haue re - deemde it haue ___   re - deemde it. ___

'sences by vniust force bannisht'

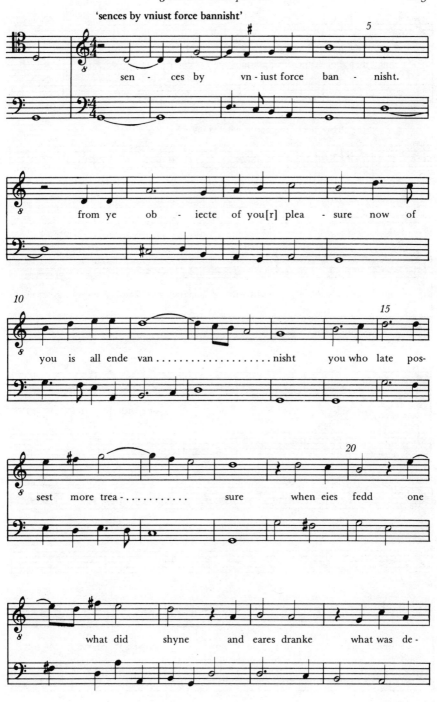

sen - ces by vn - iust force ban - nisht.

from ye ob - iecte of you[r] plea - sure now of

you is all ende van . . . . nisht you who late pos-

sest more trea - . . . . sure when eies fedd one

what did shyne and eares dranke what was de -

'How neere to good is what is fayre'

uine then the earthes brode armes could mea - sure.

How— neere to good is what is fayre which wee no

soon' - er see but with ye lynes and owt - ward ayer

our sen-ces tak - en bee wee wish it still to

see ————— and prooue what way wee may what way . . . . .

wee . . . . may de - serue wee courte wee

prayse . . . . . . wee___ more . . . . then loue wee ar not greude

to serue we are not greeude to serue.___

A. Forobosco

St. Michael's College, Tenbury, MS 1018, *ff.* 36ᵛ–37ᵛ.

The grouping of the songs in the manuscript implies that the middle song was sung either with 'O what a fault' or after the revels with 'How neere to good'; or perhaps as an interlude in the revels themselves. Unfortunately the text of this second song is corrupt: its meaning for the context is not at all obvious, and before assuming it was, indeed, part of *Love Freed*, the authority of the manuscript itself as a source for masque songs would have to be established. A. J. Sabol has suggested that 'sences by vniust force bannisht' is a 'version used in performance and later rejected by Jonson'.[15]

The settings of all three songs, like Ferrabosco's settings of earlier masque songs, use certain declamatory techniques within a basically tuneful form. An example of this is the first eleven bars of 'O what a fault' which set the first three lines of Jonson's text. The rhetorical

[15] See Sabol, *Songs and Dances*, p. 164, note to no. 16. If Jonson omitted this song when he revised the text of the masque for publication he may at that time have also added the final lines of text to 'O what a fault', although it is more likely that these were omitted in the Tenbury manuscript because that represents a version of the song for private, solo use. Knowledge of the origin of this manuscript might throw light also on the practice of collaboration in the writing of masque music. In the accounts which survive for this masque we note that 'mr alfonso Ferabosco' received twenty pounds 'for making the songes' and that 'mr Robert Iohnson' was paid five pounds 'for setting the songes to the lutes'. (See H & S x, p. 529.) This is the only instance which records collaboration in song settings—as opposed to collaboration in the dance music which was common practice. The treble and bass version in the Tenbury manuscript may well represent the outlines of the songs as Ferrabosco wrote them for Robert Johnson to set to the lutes. However, songs in this form of treble and unfigured bass, either for bass viol accompaniment or for realization on another instrument, are very common in early seventeenth-century manuscripts, and there is no evidence except for the peculiarity in the grouping of these three songs to suggest that this collection is different from other private commonplace books.

pattern of the first line of the text is imitated by the sequence at bars 1–4, even in the detail of the syncopation at bar 3, and the intervals in the melody are simple and harmonically basic ones, the third and the fifth. To this degree the setting might be called declamatory here; but declamatory and more lyrical qualities are united in the way the melodic phrase structure pushes the statement of the text in ll. 2 and 3 towards the cadence, decorated with a melisma, at bar 11. Ferrabosco uses a very similar device for representing the statement of the opening lines of the second song: 'sences by vniust force bannisht', although here the musical phrases (the opening sequence and melisma on 'van-nisht') less clearly set out the grammatical sense of the words. Of the three the third song comes closest to a declamatory setting, basing its melody on simple harmonic intervals.

Like Ferrabosco's songs for earlier masques, and certainly more clearly than the extant songs for *Oberon*, these settings both project the expository nature of the verse and at the same time recreate within a fundamentally musical form the essence of the exposition, the conceptual qualities of the masque. In the way the music complements the verses' celebration of Beauty and Love Ferrabosco has recognized the philosophical significance, for this masque, of music as a formal, lyrical pattern and not only as a function of rhetorical exposition. Unlike the extant songs for *Oberon*, the songs for the revels of *Love Freed* can support this philosophical significance; for King James was identified in the masque as Apollo, the leader of the Muses. The court and the masque fiction were one.

III

After *Love Freed* Ferrabosco appears not to have collaborated with Jonson for nearly ten years. He is mentioned, with Lanier, as having composed music for the *Masque of Augurs* (1622) but the only music which survives from this masque is a single song ascribed to Lanier. No settings by Ferrabosco for later masque songs survive. He probably maintained his association with the presentation of masques between 1611 and 1622 however, since he was appointed musician to Prince Charles after the death of Prince Henry, thus retaining his post at court.[16]

[16] Ferrabosco may have quarrelled with Jonson and such a suggestion is supported by the fact that in the 1616 folio text of his works (which included the masques) Jonson cancelled the passage in the quarto edition of *Hymenaei* (1606) in which he mentioned Jones as designer of the masque, Thomas Giles as choreographer, and had special praise for Ferrabosco, who, it appears, performed in the masque as well as composed the songs:

And here, that no mans Deservings complain of iniustice (though I should have done it timelier, I acknowledge) I doe for honours sake, and the pledge of our Friendship, name Ma. ALPHONSO FERRABOSCO, a Man, planted by himselfe, in that divine *Spheare*; & mastring all the spirits of

Very little music for songs in later masques survives, although some of the dance tunes in the British Library manuscript have been ascribed to later Jonsonian masques. The lack of very rich sources for the songs is disappointing, particularly since the changes in musical style were becoming evident in English song from about 1612 on. By this time the lute ayre was becoming old-fashioned: most of the collections had been published before this date and those published later, such as Campion's last two books of ayres, contained music which was probably composed many years earlier. The new, partially declamatory style of ayre, of which Ferrabosco's are among the earliest published and, in many respects, most subtle and complex, was becoming popular. From descriptions of later Jonsonian masques we learn that these new styles of music were particularly popular in the masque. The developments of the use of music in the later Jonsonian masque appear to have been twofold. The innovations in the actual song settings are difficult to assess when surviving songs are so few: but along with these innovations there appears to have been a shift of emphasis in the conceptual function of music in the masque, and this needs to be considered even if the actual music is lost.

The masques which followed *Love Freed* developed in various ways the ideas and techniques Jonson had used up to now. In most of his later masques Jonson kept the relation of antimasque to masque very simple and experimented with different aspects of the form. One of the developments in later masques was the practice of setting most, or even the whole, of the main masque to music. The earliest masque to be performed in this way may have been *The Golden Age Restored* (1615), although there is no specific evidence except the verse form itself.[17] But of the masque *Lovers Made Men* (1617), performed two years later at the house of Lord Hay, we are told that '*the whole Maske was sung (after the Italian manner) Stylo* recitativo, *by Master* Nicholas Lanier'.[18] Presum-

---

Musique: To whose iudiciall Care, and as absolute Performance, were committed all those Difficulties both of *Song*, and otherwise. Wherein, what his Merit made to the *Soule* of our *Invention*, would aske to be exprest in Tunes, no lesse ravishing then his. *Vertuous* friend, take well this abrupt testimonie, and thinke whose it is: It cannot be Flatterie, in me, who never did it to *Great ones*; and lesse then Love, and Truth it is not, where it is done out of *Knowledge*.
The passage is quoted in H & S vii, p. 232.

[17] This is suggested by Orgel: see *Complete Masques*, ed. Orgel, Introduction, p. 26.

[18] *Lovers Made Men*, ll. 26–8. The words 'stylo recitativo' have caused a good deal of speculation on the nature of the music, none of which now exists. However, the passage does not occur in the quarto of the masque (1617) but only in the folio of 1640, and hence it was probably in retrospect that Jonson thought of the masque as sung in recitative, a style not common in England until later than 1617. (See above, p. 44.) The settings were probably declamatory ayres. There is a reconstruction of the masque by Sabol. Lanier (1588–1666) made his début as composer of songs for masques with Campion's Somerset masque of 1614, for which he set 'Bring away this sacred tree'.

ably the point of having Nicholas Lanier, '*who ordered and made both the Scene, and the Musicke*', set the whole masque text was to heighten the masque's affective power and thus to project its philosophical significance. However, *Lovers Made Men* is, far more than any other masque by Jonson, a little drama enclosed by the self-contained fiction of its elaborate perspective set and with no distinct antimasque. The audience was recognized when the Lovers had been transformed from ghosts to men by drinking the waters of Lethe, but they were recognized as if they too were actors within the set, not recognized as themselves or as part of some symbolic fiction. Cupid commanded:

> Goe, take the Ladies forth, and talke,
> And touch, and taste too: Ghosts can walke.
>
> (ll. 175–6)

The fiction of the masque was complete in itself and had no direct philosophical bearing on the audience as a social group. In this masque, then, the music would have been simply decorative: it would have been merely a part of the elaborate fiction the set itself represented and could have had no mythic or symbolic function. The fact that the masque was not written for court performance, not, that is, for Jonson's 'ideal' audience, may be responsible for its unique structure and theme when viewed in relation to the whole of Jonson's masque-writing career.

IV

A month before *Lovers Made Men* was performed, *The Vision of Delight* was presented at court on Twelfth Night, 1617. In this masque the new style of music Lanier was writing was integrated into an intricate and highly sophisticated structure. Besides the music the sets seem to have been elaborate: but now Jonson used the picture stage in an almost satirical way. This masque was followed by *Pleasure Reconciled to Virtue* in January 1618, a masque which has been regarded as Jonson's most successful. These two court masques of 1617 and 1618 may be considered together, for they pushed almost to its utmost limits the possibilities of the masque form as Jonson developed it.

The theme of *The Vision of Delight* was an examination of the nature of pleasure and revels, of 'delight'. The three 'antimasques' presented various kinds of entertainment and revelry, until finally true delight was found not in these shows but in the masque itself, which was also identified as James's court. As Stephen Orgel has pointed out, the visual sets became less and less 'realistic' as the 'action' approached nearer to the Truth, imaged in the mythical set of the main masque, the Bower of Spring.[19] The masque opened with a view of 'A Street in

---

[19] *Complete Masques*, ed. Orgel, Introduction, p. 35.

perspective of faire building' and this realistic setting served for the first antimasque of grotesque figures: '*A she Monster delivered of sixe* Burratines, *that dance with sixe* Pantalones'.[20] This was to represent the realism of daytime and of the actual occasion, Christmas, and the pantomime figures associated with its entertainments. The next entertainment was not 'of the day' but 'of the humorous night'. Night rose in her chariot and called Phant'sie to 'create of ayrie formes, a streame'

> And though it be a waking dreame;
>   Yet let it like an odour rise
>   to all the Sences here,
>   And fall like sleep upon their eies,
>   or musicke in their eare.
>
> (ll. 48–54)

At this the scene changed '*to Cloud*' out of which Phant'sie broke. Her 'vision' was a narration—in the deliberately old-fashioned ballad-royal metre—of grotesque events and sights, a kind of dream sequence. This was concluded by a dance of Phantasmes, and Phant'sie now drew the audience's attention to the changing scene: the 'gold-hair'd Houre' descended, 'And [made] another face of things appeare'.[21] The scene now changed to the Bower of Zephyrus, and Peace sang the opening song. When Wonder expressed surprise, Phant'sie promised even more: the Bower opened and the masquers were discovered. This was the King's own 'entertainment', the King 'Whose presence maketh this perpetuall *Spring*, / The glories of which Spring grow in that Bower, / And are the marks and beauties of his power'.[22] The court itself (and the emblem of the court which the set, the Bower, was) was to be seen as more wonderful than any of Phant'sie's visions.

A good deal of the masque, particularly the part of Delight, was sung, probably in a declamatory style. At the opening we are told that Delight 'spake in song (*stylo recitativo*)'. Delight was the superintendent of this night's entertainment: she represented the spirit of the masque, which, as the audience was to discover, was also the spirit of James's court. So too her singing represented the ideal nature of James's court, something expressible only in heightened eloquence, and thus contrasting with Phant'sie's grotesque comic verse and the antimasque dances. The court was celebrated in the song Peace sang as the Bower of Zephyrus was discovered, as winter turned to spring, as phantasies and revelry gave place to a new 'reality'.

Music survives for only the last song in the masque. After the revels,

[20] ll. 22–3. See also Welsford, *Court Masque*, pp. 200–3, and the passage quoted in H & S x, pp. 570–1.

[21] ll. 122 and 125.

[22] ll. 202–4.

we are told, 'Aurora *appeared* (*the* Night *and* Moone *descended*) *and this* Epilogue *followed*'.[23] The Epilogue is Aurora's song, a single vocal line ascribed to Nicholas Lanier, in the British Library manuscript, Egerton 2013. Although it is ornate in style a musical shape is clear through its ornamentation.[24] Her song was followed by the final song by the whole 'Quire'.

> They yeild to Time, and so must all.
> As Night to sport, Day doth to action call,
> Which they the rather doe obey,
> Because the Morne, with Roses strew's the way.

It may seem that once again Jonson ended the masque arbitrarily with the simple admonition that it was growing late. But here the effect of the ending must have been different from some of those earlier masques. For the masquers were not called back into their Bower—indeed, the Bower now was James's court; and we recognize this transformation as we recognized the transformation of that other court at the end of *The Courtier*. The dancers 'yeild to Time . . . *Because* the Morne, with Roses strew's the way'.

Although *The Vision of Delight* had successfully reconciled concept and reality, in *Pleasure Reconciled to Virtue*, a year later, Jonson again confronted the relation of masque to revels.[25] Here he made clear that the reconciliation of Virtue and Pleasure on this occasion at James's court was single and unique. There was no pretence of a 'lasting Spring'; rather, Jonson stressed the impermanent quality of the reconciliation as something at best achieved only for an evening. More than any other, this masque demonstrated how important a part Jonson believed the audience played in the meaning of the masque and how the comprehension of the possibility of a 'lasting Spring' rested entirely with them. It was, indeed, even more profoundly than was *The Vision of Delight*, a masque about masques.

In the antimasque to *Pleasure Reconciled* disorder was represented as bad speech. The first entry, of Comus and his followers, 'to a wild

---

[23] ll. 233–5.

[24] B.L. MS Egerton 2013, f. 45[v]. The song is discussed and reproduced by Cutts, 'Ben Jonson's Masque, "The Vision of Delight"', and by Emslie, 'Nicholas Lanier's Innovations in English Song'.

[25] The masque has been discussed at length by Orgel, *Jonsonian Masque*, pp. 149–85 and by Furniss, 'Ben Jonson's Masques'. It was the first in which the young Prince Charles had a part. It was reworked and revived on 18 February 1618 as *For the Honour of Wales*, and music for the antimasque of goats in this revival and for the main-masque dances (probably of both versions of the masque) occurs in B.L. MS Add. 10444, ff. 45[v]–46/95–96. The three pieces merely entitled 'The First of the Princes Masques', 'The Second', 'The Third' can be fairly certainly assigned to this masque both by the fact that they follow 'The Goates Masque' directly and by the title of the second Prince's masque in Brade's *Newe ausserlesene liebliche Branden* (no. VIII), 'Des jungen Printzen Intrada'.

EXAMPLE 29. 'I was not wearier where I lay'

I . was not weari - er where I

lay _____ by frozen Ti - tans side to

Night, _____

Then I am will - inge nowe to stay, _____ and be

a part of your de - light

But I am urg - ed by the Daye a -

gainst my will to bid

you _____ come a - way come a - way.

B.L. MS Egerton 2013, *f.* 45^v.

Notes.

After each stave of voice part a blank stave has been left, the first two of these ruled with an extra line, probably for lute tablature. This has not been filled in. There is no ascription.

1. C blotted out, altered to D.

2. First note may also be a semiquaver. The pen-stroke of the second line is very faint at this end.

3. May be semiquavers, but what looks like a second line is probably a flourish.

[ ] = very faint, possibly intended to be deleted?

EXAMPLE 30. The Goates Masque.

B.L. MS Add. 10444, *ff.* 45^{v}, 95.

EXAMPLE 31

The First of the Princes Masques

[f. 46]

B.L. MS Add. 10444, *ff.* 45^{v} - 46,95^{v}.

The Second

B.L. MS Add. 10444, *ff.* 46,95ᵛ.

The Third

B.L. MS Add. 10444, *ff.* 46,95ᵛ–96.

Musique of *Cimbals Flutes*, & *Tabers'*, was followed by a doggerel song which degenerated into merely a list. This was a representation of a Christmas festival, a revelry. Comus is described as 'ye god of *cheere*, or ye *belly*' and his song began with the traditional exhortation of interlude characters for 'Roome, roome'. The song was followed by a long speech, in prose, in praise of Comus and of 'saturnalls', and after this was the first antimasque dance of 'twelve extravagant masquers, one of whom was in a barrel, all but his extremities, his companions being similarly cased in huge wicker flasks . . .'.[26] Hercules now entered fighting with Antaeus whom he slew; he then banished the revellers in verse which by comparison with their doggerel was taut and energetic:

> Burdens, & shames of nature, perish, dye,
> for yet you neuer liv'd; But in ye stye
> of vice haue wallow'd; & in yt Swines Strife
> byn buried vnder the offence of life.

(ll. 101–4)

The grove from which the revellers appeared vanished and musicians were discovered sitting at the foot of the mountain. Pleasure and Virtue were seated above; and now the '*Quire* invyte[d] *Hercules* to rest' with their song. The movement from revelry and bacchanals to the idealized fiction of the masque itself was expressed as a progression from doggerel to poetry and, finally, to song and dance. The importance of song is clear in that when, for instance, the 'Pigmees' who represented deformity, another aspect of Vice, threatened Hercules as he was sleeping, the 'Quire's' song provided protection for him besides being in direct contrast to the doggerel rhymes of the 'Pigmees'.

Now Mercury, the messenger of the gods and hence the Presenter of the main masque, descended from the hill and told Hercules and the audience that

---

[26] The description is given in Busino's account of the masque. See H & S x, p. 582, trans. *A Book of Masques*, p. 233. The description of Hercules' entry, fighting with Antaeus, is also recorded only by Busino and is not in Jonson's text, although we can infer this from Hercules' verse.

ye time's ariv'd, yt *Atlas* told thee of: How
B⟨y⟩'vn-altrd law, & working of the stars,
there should be a cessation of all iars
'twixt Vertue, & hir noted opposite,
Pleasure.

(ll. 187–91)

The mountain opened and Daedalus, the archetypal artist, led the masquers forth singing.

The climax of the masque came, as always, with the masque dances. But in this masque Jonson had Daedalus, the supreme artist, direct the masquers' steps and instruct them in their meaning, by preceding each dance with an explanatory song. Stephen Orgel has pointed out how these dances led the masquers progressively closer to the audience.[27] The first masque dance, he says, was to teach the dancers wisdom and the second to teach them the meaning of Beauty, those '*silent arts*' of '*Designe, & Picture*'. The third would teach Love, and at this lesson the masquers were to learn that dance is a social affair, that the Wisdom and Beauty of the masque dances must lead the dancers out to the audience so the revels could begin. In this masque the point of the revels was different from that in earlier masques. Here the revels did not so much represent the audience's recognition of the Truth of the masque but were, rather, a way of mediating the values of the masque to the real world. And now the court was no longer regarded as the perfect society but as the actual, frail world of flesh and sin. The revels here explicitly recognized the imperfections of the court and its need to be informed by the absolutes of the masque (absolutes known otherwise only by faith or divine revelation). The audience was told that Daedalus who led the masque dances '[gives] *ye law/to all your sport*'; but in the final song Mercury made clear that it *was* only 'sport':

> *you were sent,*
> *and went,*
> *to walke wth Pleasure, not to dwell.*
> *Theis, theis are howres, by Vertue spar'd*
> *hirself, she being hir owne reward.*

(ll. 325–9)

So the masquers had to return to their Hill '*and there aduance/with labour, and inhabit still / that height, and crowne*'.[28] The 'cessation of all iars/'twixt Vertue & her noted opposite' was something that the courtiers could experience for an evening only: the masque could teach wisdom if the

---

[27] *Jonsonian Masque*, pp. 178–82.
[28] ll. 334–6.

'beholder' had 'powre to rise to it',[29] but such 'powre', it is clear, must be continually striven for by a long and conscious effort.

V

In *Pleasure Reconciled to Virtue* Jonson maintained his control over the form by deliberately limiting the masque to a single occasion and addressing his masque only to those who would comprehend it: the masque 'maketh ye beholder wise, / *as* he hath powre to rise to it'. But this was not Jonson's last masque: this was one solution, but by including the audience as itself and not simply as a philosophical concept, an ideal, the masque had become overtly didactic.

The masques which followed did not reach the heights of the masques of 1617 and 1618 again. They could not solve the problem of the audience's actual response to the revels (as opposed to that the masque fiction imposed on them), a problem which *Pleasure Reconciled* exposed; at best they could only avoid it. For instance, the very popular *Gypsies Metamorphosed* (1621) was almost all antimasque; and although it is the masque for which most music survives its structure no longer used music organically. The songs were merely part of the entertainment of the Gypsies' fortune-telling; they are in the style of ballad and popular song.[30]

---

[29] ll. 271–2.

[30] For a full discussion of this masque see Dale Randall, *Jonson's Gypsies Unmasked*. Three songs survive for *The Gypsies Metamorphosed*: Song 1, 'ffrom the famous *Peake of Darby*' (ll. 120–44), in *The Musicall Companion* (London, 1672), pp. 88–9, ascribed to Robert Johnson; Song 3, 'To the old, longe life and treasure' (ll. 301–11), in New York Public Library MS Drexel 4257, no. 177, B.L. MS Add. 31806, f. 134, ascribed 'S. Webbe, 1774'; 'Why, this is a sport' (ll. 707–32), in B.L. MS Add. 29396, ff. 71ᵛ–72ᵛ, ascribed to 'Mr. Chilmeade'. The words only of '*Cock-Lorell* would needes haue the *Diuell* his guest' (ll. 1061–1137) occur in New York Public Library MS Drexel 4257, no. 92. There is a setting of the words to a popular tune which served for many songs in D'Urfey's *Wit and Mirth, or Pills to Purge Melancholy*, Part II (1700), pp. 101–3.

The ascription of 'Why, this is a sport' to Edmund Chilmead in B.L. MS Add. 29396 raises some problems. Chilmead was born in 1610 so is unlikely to have composed a setting for a masque of 1621. Since 'From the famous *Peake of Darby*' is ascribed to Robert Johnson and since Johnson is known to have been paid for music for this masque, J. P. Cutts (*La Musique*, p. 171) assigns the setting to him rather than to Chilmead. In two discussions of this manuscript ('B.L. MS Add. 29396' and 'Drolls, Drolleries') I have argued that the setting is not wrongly ascribed to Chilmead and that it provides evidence for at least the last part of the masque's having been revived for performance on its own during the time the theatres were officially closed (1642–60). I have suggested that the probability of such musical/dramatic performances—performances associated in genre with the drolls Kirkman published—may explain why so many earlier seventeenth-century play (and some masque) songs occur in mid-seventeenth-century manuscripts and Playford publications.

A piece entitled 'The Gypsies Masque' occurs in B.L. MS 10444, ff. 32ᵛ/83ᵛ, and in Christ Church, Oxford, MS Mus. 44, f. 132ᵛ (entitled 'the Gipsies Maske'). These two versions are very similar. A different piece, entitled 'the Gipsies dance', occurs in Margaret Board's MS, f. 38ᵛ and a version of this piece for virginals occurs in Anne Cromwell's Virginal Book, ff. 21ᵛ–22, no. 30 (entitled 'The Duke of Buckeingham's Masque'). If both dances belong to *The Gypsies Metamorphos'd* they represent two of several antimasque dances recorded in Jonson's text.

EXAMPLE 32 'From the famous Peak of *Darby*'

a.2. Voc. (The Gipsies Song) *Rob. Johnson.*

From the fa - mous Peak of *Dar* - by,

and the De - vils Arse that's hard by; where we year -

ly ' make our mus - ters; There the *Gip* - *sies* throng in

clus - ters. Be not fright - ed with our fa - shion,

though we seem a tatter' - d Na - tion: We account our

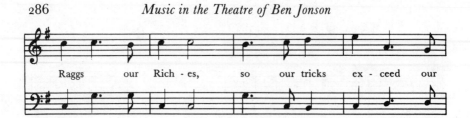

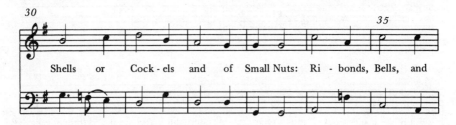

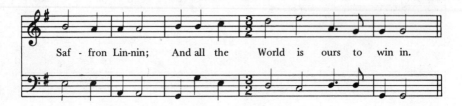

The Musicall Companion (London, 1672), pp. 88-9.

EXAMPLE 33. 'To the old longe life and treasure'

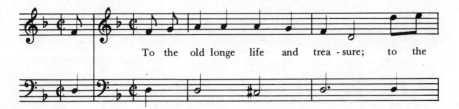

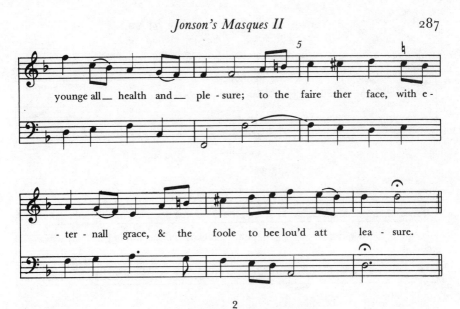

younge all_ health and_ ple - sure; to the faire ther face, with e -

- ter - nall grace, & the foole to bee lou'd att lea - sure.

2

To the wittie all faire merror
To the ffoollish ther darke error
to the louley spritt
a secure delightt
and the jealous his owne falce terror

New York Public Library, Drexel MS 4257, no. 177.

Note.
8 Treble II = 𝅘𝅥𝅭 Bass I = 𝅗𝅥

EXAMPLE 34 'Why this is a sport'

The Gypisies Patrico & Jackman

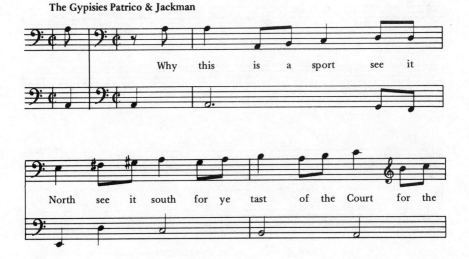

Why this is a sport see it

North see it south for ye tast of the Court for the

Courts owne Mouth   Come Wind – sor ye towne wth ye Mai-or & op -

- pose wee'le put them all   downe   Downe [downe downe] like my Hose

A Gyp-sie in his shape more calls ye be - hold - er   then ye

fel - lowe with ye Ape   Or Ye   Ape   on his shoul-der

Hee's a sight yt will take   an Old   Judge from his wench I and

Keepe him a - wake yes a - wake on ye Bench   And h'as so much

worth tho he sitt i' the stokes He will draw ye Girles forth, I⎯ forth i' their

smockes,   Tut, a mans a man: let ye Clownes wth their slutts come

mend⎯vs if they can If they can for their gutts⎯⎯ Come

Chorus

mend vs come lend vs their showts & their noyse Like

Like

thun - der & won - der at Pto - lo - myes
thun - der & won - der at Pto - lo - myes
boyes, come mend vs come lend vs their shouts & their noyse like
boyes, come mend [vs come lend vs their shouts & their noyse] like
thun - der & won - der at Pto - lo - myes boyes.
thun - der & won - der at Pto - lo - myes boyes.

Mr. Chilmeade.

B.L. MS Add. 29396, ff. 71ᵛ–72ᵛ.

EXAMPLE 35. The Gypsies Masque

[f. 84]

B.L. MS Add. 10444, *ff.* 32^V, 83^V–84.

Note.

23 Bass III–IV: MS gives lower G for both notes.

EXAMPLE 36(a). the Gipsies dance

Board MS *f.* 38ᵛ.

Notes

11 Treble V: MS = ♪
13 Treble I and II: MS = ♩ ♪
14 Treble II and III: MS gives an additional G between II and III.

EXAMPLE 36(b). The Duke of Buckeinghams Masque

Cromwell MS no.30 *ff.* 21ᵛ–22

Notes
4 Bass I: upper note of chord is A not F in MS
24 Bass I-III: MS gives crotchet rest between C and B

From the two songs which survive for Jonson's last masques it appears that a declamatory style continued to be used in setting the songs of the main masques, and from the texts of the masques it is clear that the main masque was often sung throughout. The conceptual quality of song seems to have been the main point, but in effect these main masques must have been simply virtuoso pieces, concerts on a set theme.[31] After *Pleasure Reconciled* the masque gradually became an

[31] One song is from *The Masque of Augurs* (1622), the other from *Neptune's Triumph*, which was prepared for the return of Charles from Spain in 1624 but not performed, and later revised, with virtually the same main masque, for the celebration of his engagement to Henrietta Maria in 1625, as *The Fortunate Isles*: see H & S vii, p. 677. Of *Augurs* we are told that '*The* Musique [was] *compos'd by that excellent paire of Kinsemen, Mr* ALPHONSO FERRABOSCO, *and Mr* NICHOLAS LANIER'. (H & S vii, p. 625.) This note occurs only in the British Library copy, press-mark C. 39. c. 34, Sig. B.4ᵛ. The song which Apollo sang after the revels, '*Doe not expect to heare*' (l. 411), was set by Lanier and survives in B.L. MS Add. 11608, f. 17ᵛ. (See also Sabol, *Songs and Dances*, pp. 74–5; Emslie, 'Three Early Settings of Jonson'.) The song is in two sections, the first making use of the declamatory figure ♩♪♪♪. Because ll. 1–3 and 4–6 are set to the same melody any close imitation in the music of the spoken accentuation is impossible. The break in the melodic line at the end of l.1 (and l. 4), the long tied note at the end of bar 4, and the major-sixth leap at bars 5–6 distort the sense of the words. In the second section the grammatical and poetic sense of the text are more closely followed in the setting. For instance, bars 8–15 press forward to make, in effect, one continuous phrase pointed up by the interrupted cadence at bars 11 ('peace') and 15 ('increase'). The main emphasis of the section—as in the text—comes on the perfect cadence at 'son' (bar 17). If this setting is representative of those of other songs in the main masque they would have provided a clear contrast with the antimasque song, John Urson's ballad (l. 165). A late setting of this ballad occurs in D'Urfey's *Wit and Mirth*, Part ii (1700), pp. 38–9. The piece entitled 'The Beares Dance' in B.L. MS Add. 10444, ff. 19/73 may belong to this masque. It occurs also in Board MS, f. 39ᵛ ('the beares danc[e]') and in National Library of Scotland MS Jean Campbell's Virginal Book, no. 1, f. 3.

Two settings of the song 'Come noble nymphs' from *Neptune's Triumph* (l. 472) and *The Fortunate Isles* (l. 587) survive: see Playford, *Ayres*, (1659, 1669), p. 14, ascribed to William Webb, and Bodleian MS Don. c. 57, no. 97. Sabol, *Songs and Dances*, pp. 76–7, prints Playford's version. For a discussion of the Bodleian manuscript see Cutts, 'A Bodleian Song Book', which suggests 1650 as the upper date for the collection. The Bodleian setting is very simple, and although it uses the ♩♪♪♪ declamatory figure this seems imposed as a device only (see bars 9, 10, 12). Webb, on the other hand, uses the figure to represent the way the sense of the lines pushes through the rhymes—e.g. bars 3 and 15—and expands the figure in a melodic sequence at bars 14 V to 15 I. Webb has followed the sense of the words in shifting the rhythm from ₵ to 3/2 for the question (ll. 3–4) and in using the ♪♩ figure (bars 12–15) to illustrate 'the curious parts'.

Music probably for the '*Antimaske* of Volatees' in *News from the New World* (1620) occurs in B.L. MS Add. 10444, ff. 19ᵛ/73ᵛ, entitled 'The Birds dance'.

elaborate entertainment: the audience remained audience and was no longer required to identify with, or rise to, the wisdom of the masque. The superficial impression is that the masque had gained assurance of its own validity, for both antimasque and main masque were more elaborate and lengthy. Some masques, for instance *Augurs*, *Neptune's Triumph*, and *The Fortunate Isles*, avoided the difficulties of relating antimasque, masque, and revels by setting the antimasque in the court itself and making its 'action' a discussion of the most appropriate masque for this special occasion. The artifice was made clear from the beginning.[32]

The strain expressed in Jonson's last masques, their lack of conviction and their retreat into virtuosity, is obvious in other directions as well. Towards 1630 there was growing tension between Jones and Jonson over the relative functions of each of the arts in masque.[33] Jonson himself had obviously been aware for some time that the masque was becoming something other than an image of a coherent and perfectible society.

But the lesson of the masque is not one of defeat. Jonson's earlier masques had great influence on the Jacobean theatre, and when Jonson himself began writing plays again after a silence of ten years (from *The Devil is an Ass*, 1616 to *The Staple of News*, 1626) his own work in the masque enriched his later plays. The full fruits of his masque experience are apparent in *The New Inn* (1629), almost his last play. Before attempting a reassessment of *The New Inn*—as the culmination of Jonson's experience as both playwright and masque writer—I turn to two plays of Shakespeare written almost twenty years earlier, these also quite clearly influenced by the kinds of problems Jonson himself was struggling with then in the masque. *The Winter's Tale* and *The Tempest* may provide us with a viewpoint from which to assess, finally, the direction and achievements of Jonson's own work.

[32] For a full discussion of *Neptune's Triumph* see Orgel, *Jonsonian Masque*, pp. 91–9. Apart from those songs discussed in note 31 only one piece which can be definitely associated with a later masque survives. This is the country dance 'Half Hannikin' which was incorporated into the last part of *Time Vindicated to Himself and to his Honours* (1623). In the Officebook of the Master of the Revels for 1622–3 there is an account of the masque. It says of the Revels and the ending of the masque: 'The measures, braules, corrantos and galliards being ended, the Masquers with the ladyes did daunce 2 contrey daunces, namely The Soldiers Marche, and Huff Hamukin . . .' (quoted in H & S x, p. 649). The tune and the steps to 'Half Hannikin' occur in Playford's *English Dancing Master* (1651), p. 43, and were included in subsequent editions. A keyboard arrangement with variations by Richard Farnaby occurs in Fitzwilliam Virginal Book, no. 297 entitled 'Hanskin', and a lute arrangement occurs in Board MS, f. 38. The inclusion of a country dance in the masque proper is probably new.

[33] The quarrel between Jonson and Jones has been well documented. See H & S x, pp. 689–97; Gordon, 'Poet and Architect'. See also the three poems 'An expostulacon with Inigo Jones', 'To Inigo Marquess Would be a Corollary', 'To a ffreind an Epigram of him', all in H & S viii, pp. 402–8; and the two Epigrammes, CXV and CXXIX: 'On the Townes Honest Man' and 'To Mime'. H & S's inference of growing coldness from Jonson's lack of reference to Jones in several of the masques (see H & S vii, p. 689) may in fact be unjust. Certainly, in *Love Freed*, Jonson thought of the masque as almost entirely literary.

EXAMPLE 37. 'Doe not expect to heare'

Doe not ex - pect to heare of all
Thus much ye fates would have con - ceal'd

yor good at once least it fore - stall _____ some sweet -
from vs ye gods least beeing re - veal'd _____ our Peares __

_____ nesse would bee New.
_____ would En - vie you.

It is E - nough yor peo - ple

learn the Rev'-rence of their peace, as well as strang - ers

doe dis - cerne the Glor - ies by th'in - crease. &

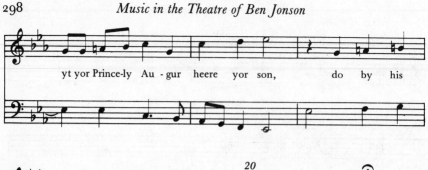

yt yor Prince-ly Au - gur heere yor son, do by his

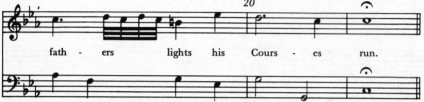

fath - ers lights his Cours - es run.

Mr. Nicholas Laneir.

B.L. MS Add. 11608, *f*. 17ᵛ.

Note

6 Bass, preceding I MS gives crotchet rest.

8 Treble I-II = ♪ (♩) ♩

19 Bass IV, Treble VII: MS gives a mark (crotchet?) on A, Bass gives ⟨C⟩ (crotchet) which suggests a differently harmonized ending from that given.

EXAMPLE 38(a). The Beares Dance

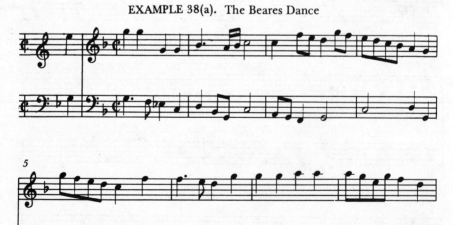

B.L. MS Add. Add. 10444, *ff.* 19 and 73.

EXAMPLE 38(b). the beares danc[e] .

Board MS *f.* 39ᵛ.

Note

7, first chord: MS gives a middle note to this chord but it is smudged and difficult to read.

EXAMPLE 39. 'Come noble Nymphs'

Come come _____ noble Nymphs & do not hide the

joys _____ for which you so pro-vide; If not to _____

ming - le with us men, what make you here? go ___ home a -

gen. Your dress - ings do con-fess by what we see, so cur - ious parts of

Pal-las, and A-rack - nes ___ Arts, that you could mean no less.

Mr. *William Webb.*

II

Why do you were the Silk-worms toyls?
Or glory in the Shel-fish spoils?
Or strive to shew the grains of Ore
That you have gatherered long before?
    Whereof to make a Stock
To graff the greener Emrauld on,
Or any better water'd Stone,
    Or Ruby of the Rock.

III

Why do you smeel of Amber-greece,
Whereof was formed *Neptunes* Neece,
The Queen of Love? unlesse you can
Like Sea-born-*Venus,* love a man?
    Try, put your selves unto't:
Your Looks, and Smiles, and Thoughts that meet;
Ambrosian-hands, and Silver-feet,
    Do promise you will do't.

'At a Masque, to invite the Ladies to Dance' , in
John Playford, *Select Ayres and Dialogues* (1669), p. 14, Sig. E.1ᵛ.

EXAMPLE 40. 'Come noble Nymphs'.

your dress-ings do con - fesse by wt we see so cur - ious

parts of Pal - las and A - rach - nes arts

yt you could meane no Lesse.

Bodleian MS Don. c. 57, no. 97 (p. 102).

Note
15 Treble I—VII: MS =

EXAMPLE 41. The Birds dance.

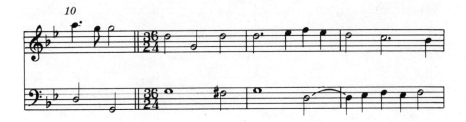

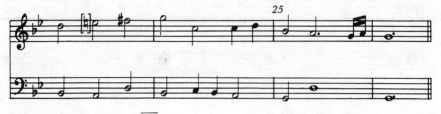

B.L. MS Add. 10444, *ff.* 19ᵛ and 73ᵛ.

Note
17 Treble I: MS gives no note for this beat.

PART THREE

7

Shakespeare: The Winter's Tale *and* The Tempest

THE INFLUENCE of the court masque on both *The Winter's Tale* and *The Tempest* has been long recognized and often discussed. In the case of *The Winter's Tale* evidence of specific influence from Jonson's *Oberon* has been seen, and used to suggest that the play could not have been written before 1 January 1611.[1] Two instances of influence from *Oberon* are usually pointed to in *The Winter's Tale*. The first is the introduction of the bear in Act III, scene iii who chases Antigonus and later eats him. Bears, whether real or simply a man draped in a bear's skin, were very popular in plays at this time; and Oberon's chariot had been drawn by white bears.[2] More decisive evidence for the influence of *Oberon* is found in the satyrs' dance in Act IV, scene iv and the comments which precede it (ll. 337–43). The satyrs' dance by the carters, shepherds, neatherds, and swineherds which is part of the sheep-shearing festival is believed to be a direct imitation of the satyrs' dance in *Oberon*; the servant makes the comment, before the dance is performed in *The Winter's Tale*, that 'three of them, by their own report . . . [have] danced before the king'. This is believed to be a reference not simply to King Polixenes but to James himself, and thus the occasion referred to may be the performance of *Oberon*. If this is so, then it is also likely that the music for a satyrs' dance which occurs in British Library MS Add. 10444 and which is usually attributed to *Oberon* may also have been used in *The Winter's Tale*.[3]

However, the influence on *The Winter's Tale* of masque, and of *Oberon* in particular, is not confined simply to their both sharing in the popularity of bears on-stage, and to the single satyrs' dance. *The Winter's Tale* seems to be quite consciously experimenting with the ideals surrounding the masque as a form, and this is particularly clear in the ending of the play, the statue scene.[4] The staging of this final scene has much in

---

[1] The play is believed to have been written early in 1611, between 1 January, the date of Jonson's *Oberon*, and 15 May, when we know from his own account that Simon Forman saw the play performed at the Globe. The account is reproduced, and the evidence discussed, by Pafford in his Introduction to the Arden edition, pp. xxi–xxiv.

[2] *Oberon*, ll. 294–7.

[3] See Lawrence, 'Notes on a Collection of Masque Music', and Cutts, 'Jacobean Masque and Stage Music'.

[4] Inga-Stina Ewbank, 'The Triumph of Time in *The Winter's Tale*', p. 98, footnote 1, points out that although some critics have regarded the statue scene as an adaptation of a masque device

common with Jonson's staging of antimasque and main masque in *Oberon*, where these were related within a single stage set. In *Oberon* the antimasque figures, the satyrs, did not vanish and the scene did not change completely (as the witches and their 'hell' did in *Queens*). Instead, the acting space opened up, by drawing aside into the wings the flats on which the scenes were painted, and revealed the set behind—also on flats which could, in their turn, be drawn aside. Gradually Oberon's palace was revealed, then opened, and Oberon was seen in his chariot at the end of the vista. All this time the satyrs

---

there is no instance of statues coming to life in masques before *The Winter's Tale* was written and several instances after. The two masques presented at the wedding of Princess Elisabeth and Count Palatine, 14 February 1612/13 (at the celebration of which *The Winter's Tale* was also performed—see Chambers, *Shakespeare*, 11, p. 343), Beaumont's *Masque of the Inner Temple* and Campion's *Lords' Masque*, both used statues which came alive. In Beaumont's masque the statues came alive and danced as part of the first antimasque. In the *Lords' Masque* the device was more integral, and influence from *The Winter's Tale* on the whole design of the masque is evident. The masque began with what appears to have been an antimasque but which, the audience found later, was an enactment of the past time which brought about the present situation. Mania, or madness, had imprisoned Entheus, poetic fury: Orpheus therefore summoned Mania to set Entheus free. It was Jove who ordered this, and he also ordered that Entheus and Orpheus 'create Inventions rare, this night . . .'. Orpheus and Entheus were to create, at Jove's command, the masque that now followed. First of all, however, they called on Prometheus, the power of Love itself. Orpheus said:

> Loe, through that vale I see *Prometheus* stand
> Before those glorious lights which his false hand
> Stole out of heu'n the full earth to enflame
> With the affects of Loue and honor'd Fame.
>
> (*Works*, ed. Vivian, p. 91, ll. 31–4)

Prometheus was revealed and said that he would aid Entheus and Orpheus in the masque. So the masque was created and guided by Poetry, Music, and Love. Now Prometheus' stars were transformed into men (p. 94, ll. 1 f.). When this transformation was complete and the masquers had performed a dance, the wood, the pastoral scene, was '*insensibly changed*' (p. 94, l. 34) and '*in place thereof appeared foure Noble women-statues of siluer, standing in seuerall nices, accompanied with ornaments of Architecture, which filled all the end of the house, and seemed to be all of gold-smithes work*' (p. 94, ll. 34–7). The pastoral setting gave place, then, to a rich *human* art. However, the description goes on to tell us that '*Ouer euery statue was placed a history in gold, which seemed to be of base releaue; the conceits which were figured in them were these. In the first was* Prometheus, *embossing in clay the figure of a woman, in the second he was represented stealing fire from the chariot-wheele of the Sunne; in the third he is exprest putting life with this fire into his figure of clay; and in the fourth square* Iupiter, *enraged, turns these new made women into statues*' (p. 94, ll. 42–3, p. 95, ll. 1–6). In his divine anger Jove had turned life to statues, and now in this masque, which he himself commanded, Love and Music restored the statues to life. The parallels with *The Winter's Tale* are obvious. Jove's rage parallels Leontes'; and it was, in the end, only Jove—as it is only Leontes—who could restore the life of these statues. Prometheus' stars were given human shapes in a pastoral setting and this had to precede the transformation of the women-statues. This appears parallel to the love of Florizel and Perdita within *their* pastoral, love which is one of the conditions of Paulina's revival of Hermione. So too, Orpheus said when the first four ladies were transformed:

> See, *Ioue* is pleas'd; Statues haue life and moue:
> Go, new-borne men, and entertaine with loue
> These new-borne women.
>
> (p. 95, ll. 38–9, p. 96, l. 1)

were seated at the sides of the stage, or acting space, and watched him as he came forward, passed them, and finally, after two masque dances, moved off the stage on to the dance floor among the audience. In this masque, the satyrs, the antimasque characters, 'learnt' with the audience: the sliding flats revealed, one by one, scenes equally new to them as to the audience, they shared with the audience in the gradual discovery of who Oberon was. When Oberon in his chariot *'was come as far forth as the face of the* scene'[5] the satyrs who danced and skipped for joy were warned to 'giue place': Oberon had not come forth solely for them, they must turn their eyes in the direction Oberon looked, and there they would see Arthur, to whom Oberon and his knights had come 'to pay / Their annuall vowes'.[6] When Oberon and his knights descended from the stage after the masque dances, the satyrs were left behind on-stage; they remained part of the fictional world Jones's sets created. Jones's use of the *scena ductilis* (the scenes painted on flats which slid sideways in grooves) illustrated the kind of lesson the masque represented for its audience. In passing from the end of the vista forward to the edge of the set and beyond it, Oberon acknowledged all the stages of the revelation as part of his world; but finally and paradoxically, it was in the audience that the vista ended.

At the end of *The Winter's Tale* all the main characters are on-stage and throughout the scene Hermione's statue is the focus of attention. All watch the statue gradually coming to life, and this is not simply some kind of magic but the final stage in a process of gradual understanding which the play, as it unfolds, requires and creates: requires not only of its main characters but also its audience. As in *Oberon* the 'education' of the characters, their learning and their understanding, is also ours: the gradual revelation is for us as for them. Like Oberon's chariot, Hermione's statue stands at the end of a 'vista' which is gradually revealed to us and, paradoxically, does not recede from our world but ends in our world. When Hermione finally descends she speaks at first not to Leontes but to Perdita; it is Perdita who 'interposes' between Leontes and Hermione. As though Leontes were at 'the face of the scene', he and his experience are closest to us, the audience: he mediates, as it were, between us and the play, and it is his understanding and his 'learning' that bring Hermione to life. But a staging of the play could not literally place Leontes, the central figure, although observer, in the final act, down-stage as the satyrs in the masque were: he must be visible to the audience, up-stage and near the centre. So too, Hermione and Leontes do not, at the end of the play, step off the stage and literally mingle with the audience, as masquers in a masque would

---

[5] *Oberon*, ll. 314–15.
[6] *Oberon*, ll. 327–8.

have done. They go off backstage. The audience of the Globe was not the homogeneous audience of the court masque, nor had it come expecting to act a part.

In *The Winter's Tale* there is no need for the characters literally to step off the stage, for unlike the movement from masque to revels there is no transition from one fiction to another. In this play the fiction and the reality are of a different kind from that asserted by *Oberon*. Paulina makes this clear when she says of Hermione:

> That she is living,
> Were it but told you, should be hooted at
> Like an old tale: but it appears she lives.
>
> (v. iii. 115–17)

We are not simply 'told', we are shown. Her comment in itself may not describe anything essentially different from our response to any good play. The meaning of the actions in a good play are like those in a good story: in Sidney's words, 'Wee seeme not to heare of them, but cleerely to see through them.'[7] Throughout the final act of *The Winter's Tale* both the extremes of unbelief (the romance qualities, the 'old tale') and belief through showing are insisted on, and in Act IV scene i Time made the distinction between the audience and the story clear. Yet in the final scene, where Hermione's statue is revealed to us, no distinction is made between what we know and what the characters on-stage know. The world on-stage—an 'old tale', not, as in the masque, an emblem—gradually comes to life as we watch it and learn with it. And its coming to life—for us as for Leontes—depends as Paulina says on our awakened 'faith'. The play insists on its romance qualities: but the difference between this play's use of old tales and Shakespeare's use of them in earlier plays is important. The difference is clear in the structure of *The Winter's Tale*. The structure of the play is usually regarded from the point of view of other, conventional plays of the period and has thus been the subject of controversy. Yet, when examined from the point of view of the masque—and particularly of the masque as an affective art—the play as a whole demonstrates the serious way in which the Shakespearean theatre may literally have been regarded as a place of learning for life.

I

By contrast with Shakespeare's earlier plays, *The Winter's Tale* breaks into two parts with a lapse of sixteen years between in which events are explained by the figure Time (iv. i). This larger structure is reflected

---

[7] Sidney, *An Apologie for Poetry*, ed. Smith, i, p. 166.

also in the sharp contrasts which gradually, in our response, become merged and inform one another. In the first part of the play where our attention is focused on details—rather than on narrative qualities of motive and action—the contrast is between Hermione and Leontes. The events of these early scenes are shown from Leontes' point of view. In that no motive is given for his jealousy, that he is determined on public justice, and wants to assert his kingly authority, we see Leontes attempting to control time itself. Hermione, on the other hand, like Viola in *Twelfth Night*, has committed herself to time, which, we see, paradoxically means that she is free of time. Our attention is drawn to details: her gracious conversation with Polixenes in which she judges and responds to the tenor of the conversation (I. ii); a mother with her son (II. i); and in the trial scene (III. ii) she appeals to Leontes not as a king but as her husband. It is her last attempt to make Leontes look *at* her, speak *to* her; but in the end we realize that she is reaching out to him over a gaping chasm. It is not by chance that Camillo's words to Archidamus in I. i echo, at this point with bitter irony, in our minds: 'they [Polixenes and Leontes] have seemed to be together, though absent; shook hands, as over a vast; and embraced, as it were, from the ends of opposed winds' (I. i. 28–31). Now Hermione says to Leontes:

> Sir,
> You speak a language that I understand not:
> My life stands in the level of your dreams,
> Which I'll lay down.
>
> (III. ii. 79–81)

However, in consulting the Oracle of Apollo and not relying entirely on his own judgement Leontes still recognizes a dimension of Truth beyond his royal authority. The way Apollo's shrine is spoken of in III. i. reminds us of the values of Hermione herself; and so the consulting of the Oracle is not the *deus ex machina* which saves the play, but a recognition of another view of life which may finally, as a fully human and humane view, prevail. So after Leontes' cursing of the Oracle the consequent deaths of his son and wife are not simply the angry retribution of a jealous god—although this is what Leontes himself believes. In the deaths of Mamillius and Hermione we see Leontes' own 'death': he has killed his wife and his hope and cut himself off from the world promised us in the description of Delphos, III. i. To adapt Hermione's words, his life stands in the level of his own dreams: he becomes the man who 'dwelt by a churchyard' of Mamillius's 'sad tale' (II. i. 30). Paulina's words at the end of the scene, in their mysteriously penetrating quality which leads us beyond simple moralism, point to Leontes' need to recognize his personal responsibility:

What's gone and what's past help
Should be past grief. Do not receive affliction
At my petition; I beseech you, rather
Let me be punish'd, that have minded you
Of what you should forget.

(III. ii. 222–6)

The scene which concludes Act III and the first part of the play may
be summed up in the Shepherd's words to his son: 'thou met'st with
things dying, I with things new-born' (III. iii. 112–13). The scene looks
both back to what has gone and forward to what is to come; and in its
very romance qualities, with its balancing of tragic and comic, it
reflects and refracts the pattern of the earlier scenes. Antigonus's dream
looks back towards the horror of what Leontes created in his kingdom:
together with the storm and the shipwreck he looks towards death. The
last we see of Antigonus, as the storm begins to break, is his hasty 'exit,
pursued by a bear'.[8] But our reaction to this is mixed—of horror as well
as amusement; and even his sympathy with Perdita and his sorrow for
Hermione are transmuted to the Shepherd's comic *other* way of saying:

I would there were no age between ten and three-and-twenty, or that youth
would sleep out the rest; for there is nothing in the between but getting
wenches with child, wronging the ancientry, stealing, fighting . . .

(III. iii. 59–64)

The quality of our response to Antigonus's death can be gauged by the
Clown's narration of the death and the shipwreck. Already the scene
has become a 'tale', already we share with the Shepherd his wonder and
surprise at the narration; and we share too the new hope which the
finding of Perdita creates. The whole event is something not to be
completely and rationally comprehended:

O, the most piteous cry of the poor souls! sometimes to see 'em, and not to see
'em: now the ship boring the moon with her main-mast, and anon swallowed
with yest and froth, as you'd thrust a cork into a hogs-head. And then for the
land-service, to see how the bear tore out his shoulder-bone, how he cried to
me for help and said his name was Antigonus, a nobleman.

(III. iii. 90–6)

This carries us forward to the pastoral of Act IV where we next see the

---

[8] There has been much debate about whether or not Shakespeare intended a live bear here. See
Arden edition of *The Winter's Tale*, note to III. iii. 58, p. 69. Cf. Biggins, '"Exit, pursued by a
Beare"'. For a discussion of the bear as a romance convention see Bryant, '*The Winter's Tale* and
the Pastoral Tradition', pp. 392–3. Bryant suggests that Wilson Knight's claim (*Crown of Life*,
p. 98) that the bear represents 'man's insecurity in the face of untamed nature' is rather extravagant here. For a full discussion of the audience's dual response to the bear in this scene see Pyle,
Commentary, pp. 65–7.

Clown in a comic re-enactment of his 'tale', helping Autolycus, the thief, whose 'shoulder-blade is out' (IV. iii. 72–3).

The qualities of Act III, scene iii, the bridge scene are deepened and sharpened for us in the speech by Time which begins Act IV. Time's speech gathers together the events of the play within a single definition, 'both joy and terror / Of good and bad, that makes and unfolds error' (IV. i. 1–2).[9] Time is personified here as the romance storyteller: '[that] which follows after, / Is th'argument of Time' (IV. i. 28–9); and he claims the prerogative of the storyteller to 'slide / O'er sixteen years' (IV. i. 5–6). But the speech takes us further than this. Time is not merely someone conveniently appearing to fill in the gap between Act III, scene iii and Act IV, scene ii. Time's complex nature, not merely his function 'to make and unfold error', is, we are becoming aware, something with which the play is deeply concerned. Time's address makes clear the important position of the audience itself in relation to the play it is watching. He says:

> I turn my glass, and give my scene such growing
> As you had slept between: Leontes leaving,
> Th'effects of his fond jealousies so grieving
> That he shuts up himself, imagine me,
> Gentle spectators, that I now may be
> In fair Bohemia.
>
> (IV. i. 16–21)

The balancing in the poetry of

> As you had slept between: Leontes leaving,
> Th'effects of his fond jealousies so grieving . . .

deliberately associates *our* knowledge and growing understanding of Time's tale with Leontes'. Leontes' sixteen years' 'grieving' and our sixteen years' 'sleeping' are drawn together as a single response.

The sheep-shearing festival in Act IV, scene iv is both idyll and potentially dramatic. The precarious quality is clear even in Perdita's definition of the season,

> Not yet on summer's death nor on the birth
> Of trembling winter
>
> (IV. iv. 80–1)

and in her uneasiness about her role in the festival.[10] Florizel's courtly and idyllic vision of the festival as pastoral is clear even in his admira-

---

[9] Green's *Pandosto*, the source for *The Winter's Tale*, was subtitled 'The Triumph of Time' and had for its motto *Temporis filia veritas*. This has obviously influenced Shakespeare in his development of his source. For a full discussion see Inga-Stina Ewbank, 'The Triumph of Time in *The Winter's Tale*'.

[10] The uncertain and unpredictable quality of the scene is conveyed especially in Autolycus's role. Armstrong, *Paradise Myth*, pp. 73–4, points out how the ballad which Mopsa and Dorcas sing

tion of Perdita with which the scene opens. But although the idyll is shattered by the revelation of Polixenes and Camillo, and Florizel's response is as of one awakened from a dream, it is as if he had found his dream more, not less, real. He is no longer gazing at an image of Flora but is committed to Perdita. His words to the old Shepherd make this clear:

> Why look you so upon me?
> I am but sorry, not afeard; delay'd,
> But nothing alter'd: what I was, I am;
> More straining on for plucking back; not following
> My leash unwillingly.

> (IV. iv. 463–7)

Even from the beginning of the scene we have seen that the love of Florizel and Perdita reaches beyond the simple, stable world of the old Shepherd, a world dependent on the cycle of the seasons, the continuance of the traditions established by his dead wife (IV. iv. 55–62), and the desire to 'die upon the bed my father died' (IV. iv. 456).

It is, we feel, almost *because* of Florizel's commitment, an attitude which reminds us of Hermione, that we can return in Act V to Leontes' court, before Perdita and Florizel arrive; and it is from Leontes' point of view that the final scenes of the play are shown to us. The early scenes in Act V prepare us for the final scene in which Hermione comes to life. For from the very opening of this last act Leontes speaks of Hermione not as someone who has been dead for sixteen years, someone whom he should now forget, as Cleomenes suggests he should, but as a living presence. His words to Paulina,

> O, that ever I
> Had squar'd me to thy counsel! Then, even now,
> I might have look'd upon my queen's full eyes,
> Have taken treasure from her lips

> (v. i. 50–3)

---

with Autolycus suggests the attraction of a larger, mysterious world beyond the pastoral, and that the sense of mystery is conveyed in the lines Autolycus himself sings: IV. iv. 298–309. Unlike the other songs Autolycus sings in Act I V, which are simple catches or pedlars' songs, this seems to have been composed especially for the play. A setting exists in New York Public Library MSS Drexel 4175. f. 23, and 4041, ff. 127–9. Cutts suggests that Robert Johnson is the composer: see 'An Unpublished Contemporary Setting' and *La musique*, pp. 17–19 and 126–8. Although presumably Mopsa and Dorcas could have picked any ballad from Autolycus's pack, this song seems not to be a mere interpolation. The declamatory style of the setting emphasizes the urgency of the questions in the song and its sense of mystery which reaches out beyond the world of Mopsa and Dorcas, of popular catches and ballads. For a discussion of pedlars' songs see Pafford (ed.), note to IV. iv. 220, p. 103. Autolycus' other five songs occur as follows: 'When daffodils begin to peer', IV. iii. 1; 'But shall I go mourn for that, my dear?' IV. iii. 15; 'Jog on, jog on, the foot-path way', IV. iii. 119; 'Lawn as white as driven snow', IV. iv. 220; 'Will you buy any tape', IV. iv. 316. Music exists for 'Lawn as white as driven snow' in John Wilson, *Cheerfull Ayres* (Oxford, 1659), pp. 64–6. This is reproduced in Cutts, *La Musique*, pp. 20–1. See also Pafford, 'Music and Songs in *The Winter's Tale*'.

are positive beside Cleomenes' sympathetic sentimentality and suggest something quite different from forgetting and forgiving. Cleomenes says:

> Sir, you have done enough, and have perform'd
> A saint-like sorrow: no fault could you make,
> Which you have not redeem'd; indeed, paid down
> More penitence than done trespass: at the last,
> Do as the heavens have done, forget your evil;
> With them, forgive yourself.
>
> (v. i. 1–6)

Leontes' attitude, by contrast, shows that simple penitence, as simple 'repayment' over a specified period of time, is not sufficient.

After his discussion with Paulina about Hermione Leontes says very little in this scene, although it contains all the important events which will lead to the dénouement and Leontes is the central figure in this. He watches what happens, as we do, he questions but he does not judge. Leontes' blessing of Florizel and Perdita (v. i. 167–77) reminds us of his words earlier in the scene, about Hermione: he shows a directness which he has not shown in the earlier scenes of the play. And when he promises to speak for Florizel and Perdita to Polixenes, and Paulina rebukes him for being attracted to Perdita when he should think only of Hermione, he says that Perdita reminds him of Hermione and it is for her sake that he intercedes:

> *Paul.*   Sir, my liege,
> Your eye hath too much youth in't; not a month
> 'Fore your queen died, she was more worth such gazes
> Than what you look on now.
> *Leon.*   I thought of her,
> Even as these looks I made.
>
> (v. i. 223–7)

II

The reconciliation in the final scene of the play recognizes the dependability of the natural cycle. The fulfilment of the Oracle and the continuation of the kingdom through finding an heir are stressed for us as part of a seasonal cycle, as is the interdependence of youth and maturity, of spring and winter which Polixenes recognized even in the early part of the play. There he spoke of his young son, Florizel, as one who

> with his varying childness cures in me
> Thoughts that would thick my blood.
>
> (i. ii. 170–1)

The ending asserts the harmony of nature and the essential nobility of courtly life which is the pattern of many of Shakespeare's comedies, as it is too the final assertion of the masque. But this play does not merely assert the dependability of inherited wisdom, of the seasonal cycle, of old tales; its wisdom is more personal. The strong narrative power of the play—reflected in its structure, with the long sixteen years' break between the first and second parts and the emphasis on its being Time's 'tale'—makes clear the play's romance quality. But the method by which the romance elements are made significant for the audience owes something to the ideals and method of the masque. The tale, we were told, was Time's; but we too have been implicated, we are more than passive listeners. We recognize too that in many respects the whole final act is created in, and seen through, Leontes' own growing awareness and perception. The 'tale' is Time's; but it is created only by a personal faith. Only in this way, Leontes learns—as Hermione and Paulina have already learnt—can he control time. He becomes as it were the author of, and chief character in, Time's tale.

The statue of Hermione, like the masque, represents the perfect art which expresses the essence of nature. The courtiers who discuss it speak of it as a marvel: 'now newly performed by that rare Italian master, Julio Romano, who, had he himself eternity and could put breath into his work, would beguile Nature of her custom, so perfectly he is her ape: he so near to Hermione hath done Hermione, that they say one could speak to her and stand in hope of answer.' That, of course, describes simple wonder in the conventional terms of Renaissance art criticism—the phrases *signa spirantes*, statues which appear to breathe and *vox sola deest*, only the voice is lacking.[11] When we are taken to Paulina's chapel we understand that this perfection of art is intimately related to a perfection of life and cannot be separated from it. Paulina says:

> As she liv'd peerless,
> So her dead likeness, I do well believe,
> Excels whatever yet you look'd upon,
> Or hand of man hath done; therefore I keep it
> Lonely, apart. But here it is: prepare

---

[11] The discussion of Hermione's statue is in v. ii. 93–103. A comparison of this with the response of Leontes and Perdita to the statue in v. iii makes clear by contrast the conventional quality of the earlier comments. Compare the Third Gentleman's words with the following comment by Petrarch on a stucco relief of St. Ambrose which he greatly admired. The passage is quoted by Baxandall, *Giotto and the Orators*, p. 51. Baxandall's point is the conventional hyperbole of the passage: '. . . it almost lives and breathes in the stone, and I often look up at it with reverence. It is no small reward for my coming here. I cannot say how much power there is in its expression, how much grandeur in the brow, serenity in the eyes; only the lack of a voice prevents one seeing the living Ambrose.'

> To see the life as lively mock'd as ever
> Still sleep mock'd death: behold, and say 'tis well.
>
> (v. iii. 14–20)

The cryptic and paradoxical quality of the last two lines points to a complex and intimate relationship between life and death, sleep and art, art and life, while sleep, Hermione's 'sleep', not only *imitates* death but *mocks at* death. There is no absolute antithesis between life and death where art and life and time are in harmony— the art of the statue, the art of Hermione's courtliness. Paulina has shown this wisdom when she has said to Leontes:

> Care not for issue:
> The crown will find an heir

and it is her wisdom now which mediates between life and death. The statue is Hermione's 'dead likeness' in that she remains a 'statue' until Leontes' faith has prepared him to see her living: although Hermione is in fact alive she has no more significance than a statue, something only to be contemplated, until Leontes himself is prepared for the transformation. We watch the statue come to life within Leontes' consciousness—and also within our own for we know no more of Hermione's being alive than Leontes does.

So at first Leontes is moved simply by the beauty of the statue, although he is upset that it is not the young Hermione he looks at. Paulina reminds him of the great artist's understanding of life: she says,

> So much the more our carver's excellence,
> Which lets go by some sixteen years and makes her
> As she liv'd now.
>
> (v. iii. 30–2)

Leontes then affirms that he could gaze on the statue for twenty years and believe he had spent only a minute. The ecstasy to which the statue moves him is the timeless moment expressed also by the masque emblem. But as does the masque, so Paulina promises more. She will make the statue 'move indeed' if the onlookers will 'awake [their] faith'.

In making the statue move, Paulina calls for music: Hermione 'awakes' to music. The music, played by Paulina's household musicians, is part of the art which the statue is, and completes it. It signifies the harmony and understanding of the universe within Leontes' mind which allows him to understand the pattern of spring renewal within the seasonal cycle—not merely in the simple, traditional way of the old shepherd, but as a force drawing the natural and civilized worlds together. The music is not simply 'mood' music; it is also different in meaning from the traditional association of music and the supernatural common in drama from the middle ages. This, like Ficino's hymns to

Apollo, brings about the understanding in Leontes' mind. As in the masque, music, the 'spherical motion' as Ficino had called it, gives life to the picture as the dancers move off the stage to mingle with the audience, so here it gives life to the statue and complements the 'art' of the carver which has already shown Hermione as subject to time. And in the way that at this point in the masque the truth of the masque emblem is recognized by its audience, so too in the play the statue is recognized by the spectators on-stage as exemplifying a truth which had always been part of their world although until now not comprehended.

But by the manner in which it has been shown us Leontes' 'tale' has also become ours, imperceptibly.[12] What is missing in the relation of art and life which the masque revels create is precisely this element of showing, of acquiescence. And, paradoxically, *The Winter's Tale* shows us that this element belongs to the world of art, the drama, and not to reality itself. The music gives life to the ideal visual form; music which imitates a timeless perfection also imitates and affects our world. When Hermione steps down from her pedestal she is wooed not merely to the timeless ideal of Love but to Life and Time. But at the end of the play we are left not with what we must acknowledge to be another fiction—as in the masque, we recognize, the revels were—but with a living version of the masque's ideal which the revels celebrated: living, because it remains, paradoxically, within the art of the play and does not attempt to include reality literally. At the end the emphasis is placed firmly on life and trust in life, not on magic or even the coincidence common to romance. Hermione herself says, to Perdita:

> for thou shalt hear that I,
> Knowing by Paulina that the Oracle
> Gave hope thou wast in being, have preserv'd
> Myself to see the issue.
>
> (v. iii. 125–8)

In the way in which the end of the masque attempted to reach beyond its emblem set so too the ending of this play reaches out beyond the form of the play itself: but here the music of the dance is not after all the music of one night's entertainment, but the music of our life and our time.

III

The Tempest too examines the relation of art to its audience and this play seems to develop directly from *The Winter's Tale*. The specific influence

---

[12] Pyle points out (*Commentary*, p .119) how confident Shakespeare is of holding his audience in the whole scene, of creating in us a reverence and expectation akin to that of the spectators on-stage.

of masque on *The Tempest* has been well documented: the betrothal masque for Miranda and Ferdinand is perhaps the most significant single instance.[13] The discussion which follows is concerned not so much with individual examples of masque influence, nor with the influence of masque scenery and machinery on *The Tempest*, but rather with the influence of ideas and ideals of the early Jacobean masque, especially as we have seen them in Jonson's masques. In particular, it seems to me that the play examines the possibilities for drama of what, for the masque, is an ideal relation of the mythic and the dramatic: the personal realm of the mind in contemplation and the temporal realm of action. This ideal is characterized particularly by the philosophical function of music in the masque—as an image of the divine nature of the universe and an affective medium for expressing this divinity. Similarly, in *The Tempest* music, like that to which Hermione's statue moves, has not merely an illustrative significance: it does not merely depict the 'baseless fabric' of the Island. Rather, it defines for us the status of the Island. Music is here specifically related to a non-dramatic time sequence: in some respects the play may be regarded (like *The Winter's Tale*) as an examination of the meaning of time.

From this point of view, Prospero's long and detailed description of Antonio's treachery in Act I, scene ii is central in many respects. Antonio has destroyed two kinds of order or Degree by his expulsion of Prospero—the order of the state and the order of the family. Yet Prospero's own relation to the ideal order is not completely straightforward. Prospero's state was 'at that time / Through all the signories . . . the first' and he himself reputed to be the first 'in dignity'. This 'dignity' contains within its definition his also being 'for the liberal Arts/Without a parallel' (I. ii. 70–4). Antonio's idea of state rule is described as the understanding of a formula only: he has learnt the 'rules' of courtly life and courtly power but has no more than a superficial understanding of their significance. They were simply rules which could, at best, be manipulated for his own purposes. This is described by Prospero as actual musical composition, and it is not too far-fetched, I think, to see here an implied relation between the management of state, indeed the actual state itself as a whole, and the creation of a work of art: Antonio has learnt only the 'rules for setting'. Obviously a simple extension of the metaphorical uses of 'harmony' is intended here:

---

[13] The best discussion of the play from this point of view is that by Miss Welsford, *Court Masque*, pp. 336–49. The play was performed at court in 1611 and again in 1612/13 when it formed part of the celebrations for the marriage of Princess Elisabeth. See Chambers, *Shakespeare*, II, p. 342, and Kermode's Introduction to the Arden edition, pp. xxi–xxiv.

                    new created
       The creatures that were mine, I say, or chang'd 'em,
       Or else new form'd 'em; having both the key
       Of officer and office, set all hearts i' th' state
       To what tune pleas'd his ear.

                                                    (I. ii. 81–5)

Prospero, on the other hand, has grown a 'stranger' to his state and
become 'transported and rapt in secret studies'. But Prospero clearly
understands the state he is leaving and the brother to whom he is
leaving it. In his comment—

                    of temporal royalties
              He thinks me now incapable

                                                    (I. ii. 110–11)

we can see the implication of Prospero's 'neglect' of state. He is perfectly aware that for Antonio temporal royalties are all; and at the same
time he is not denying that temporal royalties are important. For
Antonio, the opposition between temporal and spiritual royalties is
complete and absolute, but for Prospero the two exist together. At the
same time, the language in which Prospero described Antonio's view of
statecraft, of 'temporal royalties', does suggest the distinction between
his and Antonio's definition of 'temporal', and the way in which, for
Prospero, 'temporal royalties' are a part of the 'transported and rapt'
state. Antonio knows the rules but not the essence. Although Prospero
has dedicated himself for the meantime to an ideal of purely personal
perfection and hence has put himself outside human or social time— he
is 'transported and rapt in secret studies'—his neglect of his social
duties is a conscious part of this perfection which will in the end include
the temporal. The whole passage (I. ii. 66–116) not only makes clear
the direction in which the play moves but is important for its suggestion
of a potentially fruitful interrelation of two concepts of time which must
be made to exist as one whole. The idea is explicitly stated in respect of
the ideal state— the courtly world and observance of the rules of courtly
behaviour. It is the extremely complex relation of time and knowledge
and, ultimately, of life and a continuation of life itself which is examined
on the Island; and this involves an examination of the very bases of the
courtly and artistic ideal. It is in this complex relationship that the
significance of Prospero's Art lies too.

                              IV

We cannot, of course, say that Prospero 'stands for' or 'symbolizes' the
artist and that he hence manipulates, as though they were part of some
fantastic story, the spirits of the Island and the shipwrecked people

themselves; although in a very general sense, this is true. The significance of Prospero's art is examined far more carefully and subtly than simply as a form of magic.

First of all, then, it is important that Prospero himself defines time very carefully; and he is the only one to mention clock time until the ending of the play when Alonso says that Ferdinand's 'eld'st acquaintance' with Miranda 'cannot be three hours' (v. i. 186). Prospero's imposition of clock time—he mentions it explicitly twice (i. ii. 239–41 and v. i. 2–6)—on the 'rapt' and dream-like time pattern which exists on the Island is important. By drawing our attention to the seeming discrepancy between literal and personal time, Prospero is preparing for the gathering of these together towards the end into one relationship in human terms—that is as clock time. This is the time lived also by the play's audience. But there is a further complexity, for we notice that within the play the characters who plot evil—Sebastian and Antonio, Stephano and Trinculo—exist only in the world of clock time.

The storm of the opening scene lies between the two time 'schemes' of the play. It is, apparently, completely dramatic; and it is only in the non-dramatic second scene that we realize that the storm too is part of Prospero's design, part of the dream of the Island, and hence that it exists in both temporal worlds at once. The story does not, in fact, begin with the storm—it has already begun with Claribel's marriage in Tunis. The first mention of this is by Ariel:

> and for the rest o' th' fleet,
> Which I dispers'd, they all have met again,
> And are upon the Mediterranean flote,
> Bound sadly home for Naples;
> Supposing that they saw the King's ship wrack'd,
> And his great person perish;
>
> (i. ii. 232–7)

and it is discussed several times among Gonzalo, Alonso, Sebastian, and Antonio. The significance of Claribel's wedding pervades the whole play, although the play's real relation to this is not pointed out until almost the very end when a human time sequence, enriched by recognition of the 'dream' sequence of the Island, is regained. It is Gonzalo who points this out, the only one who has stood throughout half-way between dream and waking. Because we never meet Claribel, nor take part in her marriage, nor move from the Island to Tunis, but feel only the pervasive influence of that initial voyage, the bounds of Prospero's Art seem marvellously widened and inclusive. It is, we notice, only Sebastian and Antonio who agree that Tunis is 'ten leagues beyond man's life' (ii. i. 241–2).

Only in the scenes in which Antonio and Sebastian plot Alonso's destruction (and again in the Caliban, Stephano, Trinculo plot to destroy Prospero) does one feel that the time sequence is a straightforward and dramatic one: it is also shown as a limited and limiting one. The supposed distance of Naples from Tunis to Antonio's perception is one example. At the same time, Antonio and Sebastian are unable to hear Ariel's music and do not sleep when Alonso, Gonzalo, and the others do: their concept of sleep is limited to cessation of visible action. Thus Antonio sees no difference between sleep and death, and this is explicitly related, too, to the physical distance which he again emphasizes between Claribel and Naples. He describes this as

> A space whose ev'ry cubit
> Seems to cry out, 'How shall that Claribel
> Measure us back to Naples? Keep in Tunis,
> And let Sebastian wake.' Say, this were death
> That now hath seiz'd them; why, they were no worse
> Than now they are.

(II. i. 252–7)

Even without the lesson of *The Winter's Tale* of the complex relation of sleep and death, the limitations of this world of Antonio's are quite explicit: it is a world in which intelligence and reason are used solely for destruction, a world which is bounded by cynicism and hence finally destroys itself. Sebastian's arguments which follow (ll. 265 f.), then, have not only no meaning for Antonio to whom conscience is merely 'a kibe', but are empty, and hence unjustifiable, words for Sebastian too. This was the reality of court life at Naples when they left it; and it is clearly of this that Gonzalo thinks when he is planning his ideal state (II. i. 139–64). Gonzalo's state, without labour or evil, may be seen in this context not as Utopia but as denying the moral basis of life. For the whole significance of the play, and the 'dream' of the Island, is the painfulness of experience, which brings with it the capacity to distinguish (as Miranda also learns) between good and evil. In the early scenes Gonzalo's goodness (and his kindness to Prospero too) are to some extent only theoretical, only a repetition of learnt courtly formulae. For at the end he includes himself among those who have found themselves 'when no man was his own' (v. i. 213).

V

The scenes in which Prospero is involved take place in a time sequence which, we are continually reminded, is three hours in duration, yet in essence has no specific boundary. These scenes are controlled by him and the kind of control he gives is interesting. The first hint of this is in

his narration to Miranda of their expulsion, years ago, from the court of
Milan. Speaking of Antonio's 'treacherous army' Prospero says:

> they hurried us aboard a bark,
> Bore us some leagues to sea; where they prepared
> A rotten carcass of a butt, not rigg'd,
> Nor tackle, sail, nor mast; the very rats
> Instinctively have quit it: there they hoist us,
> To cry to th' sea that roar'd to us; to sigh
> To th' winds, whose pity, sighing back again,
> Did us but loving wrong.
>
> (I. ii. 144–51)

Prospero's tale is here not a simple narration of events: it has become
like a fabulous tale. Frank Kermode has pointed out how the passage
'turns into what is almost a parody of Elizabethan conceited writing'.[14]
The significance of this is clear. The human evil of the past has, in
Prospero's mind, suffered a 'sea-change' and become immortal-
ized—like the eyes that become pearls—as something durable, and
endurable, because now different and no longer 'real'. This in itself
marks the beginning of a return. The direction is given in the very
conceits—particularly the personification—which Prospero employs.
The constant references to the sea in the play, the pervasive feeling of
not only its implacability but also its benevolence, as here, point to the
basis of Prospero's command of life which is, fundamentally, an understanding of life. Prospero's complete sympathy with, and knowledge of,
the elements allows him to direct the return to a properly and consciously ordered *human* life.[15]

In order that we may understand the inclusiveness of Prospero's
vision, it is necessary that we are reminded of the almost phase-by-
phase parallel between Prospero's arrival on the Island and Sycorax's;
and Caliban must also be included (I. ii. 263–93). Although Caliban

---

[14] Kermode, note to I. ii. 149, p. 18.

[15] It is interesting to compare this passage with Francisco's reference to a personified nature in
II. i. 109–19. Attempting to console Alonso and suggest that Ferdinand may not be dead,
Francisco says—

> Sir he may live;
> I saw him beat the surges under him,
> And ride upon their backs; he trod the water,
> Whose enmity he flung aside, and breasted
> The surge most swoln that met him; his bold head
> 'Bove the contentious waves he kept, and oared
> Himself with his good arms in lusty stroke
> To th'shore, that o'er his wave-worn basis bowed,
> As stooping to relieve him: I not doubt
> He came alive to land.

Alonso's response is complete despair—'No, no, he's gone.'

has been taught to speak, his only profit is that he knows how to curse.
Language is the basis of civilization; and Caliban had not even known
his own meaning. His knowledge of the Island is useless to him because
it is unordered, and this is later emphasized when we see that he alone is
unafraid of Ariel's music.

> Be not afeard; the isle is full of noises,
> Sounds and sweet airs, that give delight, and hurt not.
> Sometimes a thousand twangling instruments
> Will hum about mine ears; and sometime voices,
> That, if I then had wak'd after long sleep,
> Will make me sleep again: and then, in dreaming,
> The clouds methought would open, and show riches
> Ready to drop upon me; that, when I wak'd,
> I cried to dream again.
>
> (III. ii. 133–41)

It has been pointed out that Caliban's account here is a complete
confusion of verb-tenses.[16] The effect of a suspension in time which this
creates stresses Caliban's own lack of understanding of the significance
of the music. It is understanding, communicable through words and
seen here as an understanding of time, which creates of life a complete
pattern. What is most important, then, is the fact that comprehension
of life and self is expressed as a function of speech.

VI

Prospero's understanding and wisdom enable him to control, through
Ariel, the 'dream' sequence of the Island. Ariel's music is particularly
important in a discussion of the nature of this 'dream'. Ariel's songs
must be regarded within the Renaissance tradition of music—as conceptual as well as affective—and they may be considered as expressing
the essence of the kind of knowledge Prospero owns. The music is
complementary to the poetry: its role is to make the listener more
receptive to the poem. Music adds to the poem the quality which
Puttenham called 'enargia', the quality which enables the essential
form of the poem to shine forth.[17] The songs are not merely supernatural music: the songs Ariel sings to Ferdinand express the
completeness of Prospero's artistic vision. They may be regarded as
microcosms of the larger structure of the play. The words of both 'Come
unto these yellow sands' and 'Full fathom five' suggest a fusion of the
civilized and courtly world with the natural world.

[16] Robert Graves, *The White Goddess*, 3rd edn. (London, 1952), p. 147.
[17] Puttenham, *Arte of English Poesie*, ed. Smith, II, p. 148.

Come unto these yellow sands,
    And then take hands:
Courtsied when you have and kiss'd
    The wild waves whist:
Foot it featly here and there,
    And sweet sprites bear
The burthen. Hark, hark.
Burthen dispersedly. *Bow-wow.*
The watch dogs bark:
[Burthen dispersedly.] *Bow-wow.*
Hark, hark! I hear
The strain of strutting chanticleer
Cry—[Burthen dispersedly]. *Cock a diddle dow.*

(i. ii. 377–89)

Full fadom five thy father lies;
    Of his bones are coral made;
Those are pearls that were his eyes:
    Nothing of him that doth fade,
But doth suffer a sea-change
Into something rich and strange.
Sea-nymphs hourly ring his knell:
        Burthen: *Ding-dong.*
Hark! now I hear them,—Ding-dong, bell.

(i. ii. 399–407)

The poems suggest a reconciliation and order which is not an idea removed from a context in life, not a fantasy, but one in which an ideal of life—and of art, for the dance and the sea-change are both creative and ordered—includes the whole order of creation. Ariel's songs point to the significance of the 'brave new world' to which the courtiers will return in Milan. Ariel's first song is both of 'th'air' and of 'th'earth' and it is concluded by 'the strain of strutting Chanticleer', the herald of approaching day. There is no music extant for 'Come unto these yellow sands', but music for 'Full fathom five' occurs in John Wilson's *Cheerfull Ayres* (1659), pp. 6–7. The music is ascribed to Robert Johnson, a musician in the King's Men company at the time *The Tempest* was written, and it is possible that this setting was composed for the play's first performance.[18] The setting is simple and follows the spoken accentuation of the words and the verbal phrase-lengths; it is not declamatory but controls the words within a musical form. The setting points both to a narrative significance in the words and to the poetry as a formal whole, in this way emphasizing its conceptual significance—as a microcosm of the meaning of the Island. The 'dream' of the Island which is expressed by this combination of words and music may be seen

[18] See also Cutts, *La Musique*, pp. 24 and 131–2.

thus as a 'lyric' time sequence compared with which the narrative (or dramatic) time sequence, which is all that Sebastian and Antonio acknowledge, expresses treachery. It seems that Shakespeare has used here the normal condition of a play (a dramatic time sequence) to illustrate both the power and the impotence of treachery. At the end of the play we see that Sebastian and Antonio cannot properly control or understand clock time without an understanding also of the 'dream' time which finally subsumes it.

Ferdinand is the first to hear the music and it has an immediate effect on him. He is, perhaps, the most innocent of those shipwrecked on the Island and thus most easily able to learn the significance of the courtly 'rules' he has been taught. He is described by Ariel (I. ii. 221–4) in a gently ironic way: he has taken up the posture of grief, and it is the insufficiency of this to which Ariel points. Through his contact with Miranda and Prospero's imposed tasks Ferdinand learns the meaning of the code of life he has been taught. This is something he learns gradually and something which permeates and enriches his romantic vision of life. Even in the very expression of his love for Miranda he speaks in conventional terms: it is only in his love for her that he learns the real meaning of these words (III. i. 33–6 and 39–48).

In contrast to Ariel's songs are the drunken songs of Stephano, Trinculo, and Caliban which Ariel mocks on crude instruments—their kind of instruments, the tabor and pipe. Indeed, there is a direct relationship between the people Ariel sings to and the music he sings. Stephano, hearing that the isle is 'full of noises', immediately says:

> This will prove a brave kingdom for me, where I
> Shall have my music for nothing.
>
> (III. ii. 142–3)

He sees the music surrounding the court life simply as a trapping of royalty, something that he will have to pay for if he is king. He can never be capable of understanding music's courtly function as an expression of the highest form of wisdom.

VII

Ariel's other music, in Act III, scene iii, develops from the function of his songs to Ferdinand. At the beginning of the scene Alonso has reached the depths of despair. He is wearied and his spirits are 'dulled'; and here he speaks of hope as a flatterer, that is, in the terms of the only kind of court life he has known. Having plotted treachery himself he is unable to conceive of power as anything other than deceit and corruption. The search for Ferdinand, 'whom thus we stray to find', he says, and whom he now fully believes to be drowned, is 'frustrate' and aimless; and it seems that both the sea and the earth together mock his loss. This is the lowest point of despair, the kind of despair which breeds the 'valour' Ariel speaks of later in the same scene (III. iii. 59–60). Alonso feels he is completely alone in a world in which even the sea mocks him and in which, after all, he will let his son go. He has reached a point at which the outward forms with which he had surrounded and protected himself in his position as King have been stripped away from him, and in which nothing has even seeming value any more. It is now that Ariel's music and disguising can have some effect on him. The whole scene, from line 17 to line 83, has the form of a dream, and indeed we are not certain exactly how Alonso, Gonzalo, and the rest actually hear Ariel's speech as a harpy. The dance of the 'several strange shapes' which precedes Ariel's speech is, like the songs which he sings to Ferdinand, a celebration in a stylized way of the ideal courtly life—and, significantly, Alonso recognizes it as such:

> I cannot too much muse
> Such shapes, such gesture, and such sound, expressing—
> Although they want the use of tongue—a kind
> Of excellent dumb discourse.
>
> (III. iii. 36–9)

In his recognition of the relation between this 'dance' and 'discourse' he is prepared for Ariel's following speech and finally for the restoration of his kingship and his humanity.

In his lengthy discussion of the play, Derek Traversi has commented in detail on Ariel's speech: he speaks of its 'weighted simplicity'.[19] Ariel's speech is part of the 'masque' of shapes and is included within the two dances which the shapes perform. This, considered with the fact that the verse is at once direct and prophetic, gives the whole scene complexity and richness. While it is in some ways a statement of 'what *The Tempest* is about',[20] we do not forget that it is part of a pageant which is—as Gonzalo points out in the final speech of the scene—also an imitation of conscience. The 'show' is an image of the mind itself: it represents a way of making tangible and expressible what is internal and fundamentally inexpressible. This is clear by the very personal interpretation each of Ariel's audience gives the show. It is as if Ariel spoke separately to each one of them. The whole episode, the speech preceded and followed by dance, shows that the decrees of Destiny and Fate are inextricably bound up in a social and human order, for the 'show' is both statement and concept. Alonso, Antonio, and Sebastian have violated the order and harmony of society and therefore are

---

[19] *Last Phase*, pp. 248 f.
[20] Ibid.

unable—and forbidden—to partake of the celebration, the banquet. Alonso is completely distracted; and what he has heard is the *speaking* and the *singing* of the elements themselves:

> Methought the billows spoke, and told me of it;
> The winds did sing it to me; and the thunder,
> That deep and dreadful organ-pipe, pronounc'd
> The name of Prosper: it did bass my trespass.
>
> (III. iii. 96–9)

After Ariel's pageant Prospero's masque of Ceres for the betrothal of Ferdinand and Miranda demonstrates finally the necessity of a perfect union of art and nature. The 'vision' is to be considered as the supreme art, and is, hence, like Jonson's masques, theoretically durable. But there is a flaw in this masque, the flaw of the masque form itself. Ferdinand says, gazing at it in wonder:

> Let me live here ever;
> So rare a wonder'd father and a wise
> Makes this place Paradise;
>
> (IV. I. 122–4)

and we recall that both Leontes and Perdita, gazing on Hermione's statue, vowed that they could 'stand by, a looker on' for twenty years. The statue, like Jonson's masques, and like Prospero's masque, creates a stasis. Paulina promised her audience more than simply to 'stand by, a looker on', but it is they themselves who must give the stasis life. So too, Ferdinand has yet to learn of something more than the conventional and static 'Paradise' of his rhyming couplet.[21] And it is at this point that the vision is shattered, that Prospero remembers Caliban and the necessity of coming to terms with him which human time includes. At the point where Prospero 'starts suddenly and speaks' and the Reapers 'heavily vanish' the meaning of life and 'immortality', seen here in terms of its expression as a pastoral ideal, is questioned. 'Spirit: we must prepare to meet with Caliban', Prospero says to Ariel. And it is after this 'meeting' that Prospero acknowledges his kinship with Alonso and the others (v. i. 11–30).

VIII

Ariel's last song is pure lyric and pure joy. The more profound aspects of his art have been performed at Prospero's instruction. His final song is of blossom and of summer and reflects in part the new birth which has been brought about by love; by the love of Ferdinand and Miranda and

---

[21] See the note in the Arden edition for these lines. Kermode's suggestion that 'wise' be replaced by 'wife', which would avoid the couplet, unusual for this play, and would support the 'Adam-like situation', seems to destroy the larger significance of Ferdinand's response.

by the forgiveness Prospero shows for his usurpers.[22] At the same time the song demonstrates the difference which must now exist between Ariel's world and Prospero's.

Now with his 'abjuring' of his 'rough magic' Prospero shows a more permanent and more complete relation between art and nature, between the 'dream' time and reality. Prospero's final demonstration of his Art is the revelation of Ferdinand and Miranda playing at chess (v. i. 172). This marks the fusion of two realms of experience—the actual and the 'dream'—and the actual has been performed and transmuted by the ideals of perfect art. Prospero's last wonder is performed without the aid of Ariel, and the 'characters' who take part this time are human and not spirits. They are 'discovered' too, in what might be thought of as a 'literary' attitude, in a situation which, as Frank Kermode has pointed out, traditionally suggests 'high-born and romantic love'.[23] The whole episode marks the transition between the 'dream' world and the real world, and points to their complete interdependence. And so to Alonso's

> Is she the goddess that hath sever'd us,
> And brought us thus together?
>
> (v. i. 187–8)

Ferdinand replies

> Sir she is mortal;
> But by immortal Providence she's mine.
>
> (v. i. 188–9)

Both are, in a sense, right; but the directness of Ferdinand's words points to where the real value lies: Miranda is not a goddess.

The return is to a world which has itself been re-created: it is, indeed, Miranda's 'Brave new world'. Prospero's resolution of the tension between art and reality proves their interdependence, and proves too that the only time sequence which has meaning is one which is personally valuable, that the 'new world' has meaning and value personally rather than externally. The vision of Miranda and Ferdinand playing at chess makes clear the interdependence and gives, too, a further dimension to Gonzalo's 'summing up' of the voyage:

> in one voyage
> Did Claribel her husband find at Tunis,
> And Ferdinand, her brother, found a wife
> Where he himself was lost.
>
> (v. i. 208–11)

---

[22] This is shown particularly in the manner in which Prospero gives 'assurance that a living Prince/Does now speak' to Alonso, v. i. 108–9.

[23] Note to v. i. 171, p. 122.

This perfection, which is both a literary and a real one, is, like the perfection at the end of *The Courtier*, one which is brought about and crowned by Love. We can see now the significance of the action, guided by 'immortal Providence' and by Destiny, which is contained within the celebration of two marriages and which links not only Naples and Milan, but, in including Tunis, encompasses a far wider space. However, Shakespeare does not leave us merely with the promise of a golden world, of Miranda's 'Brave new world' which Prospero himself qualified with '''Tis new to thee' (v. i. 184). In the return to Naples and to Milan Antonio and Sebastian are not left behind as a later, eighteenth-century version, by Waldron, left them, thus simplifying and stultifying the moral significance of the ending.[24] Trinculo, Stephano, and Caliban are not happily regenerate at the end either. Prospero makes this clear when he says to Alonso,

> Two of these fellows you
> Must know and own; this thing of darkness I
> Acknowledge mine.

> (v. i. 274–6)

The return to Milan and to Naples—to the human world—is a return effected not by magic but by human wisdom, and its meaning can be maintained only by self-discipline and understanding. It is a world which is particularly conscious of its temporal meaning: Prospero's 'every third thought' will be of his grave.

XII

While one might point to various instances in this play of influence from the techniques of the Jacobean masque, the relation of the play as a whole to the early seventeenth-century masque seems deeper and more important than a discussion of technical matters alone can indicate. *The Tempest* shows the validity of the masque's conceptual basis within a dramatic form; and formally it presents an answer which the masque cannot give, partly because the masque attempted to mingle concept and reality literally—in the relation of masque and revels. The treatment of time in *The Tempest* includes the time pattern which the masque makes use of. Further, the insistence on the three hours' duration, in this play, may be seen as parallel to one of the functions of the revels in a masque: for this is the time the audience spends at the theatre and is hence one way of including them. *The Tempest* examines the ways in which the courtly ideal of art can become, properly, part of life itself; but the play impinges on our experience neither simply, as idea, nor literally, as a masque would do. Just as the Island and Tunis must be taken into account by the Dukedoms of Milan and Naples, so must *The*

[24] F. G. Waldron, *The Virgin Queen* (London, 1797).

Tempest be contained within, and expressive of, the everyday world of its audience.

By examining these ideas within the form of the drama Shakespeare can express the more complex relation of time patterns and thus go further than the simple twofold relationship of masque and revels. The masque moved towards its full meaning in the revels, and this was accomplished by simple means, the literal inclusion of life. While acknowledging the importance of the ideal which the masque form implies, Shakespeare avoids the masque's formal problems by moving back towards a dramatic imitation of life. Not until the end of the play do Naples and Milan become in any real sense part of a dramatic world, a world in imitation of our own. Yet this is the end of the *play*. However, throughout we have been continually reminded that the time of the 'dream' of the Island is also the time of our visit to the theatre. And now, in the Epilogue, Prospero comes forward and speaks to us directly—not as the actor, breaking out of the convention of the play, but as Prospero himself, including us as much as the other characters in his 'Please you, draw near' (v. i. 318). It is *our* power which will send him to his dukedom, Milan, or confine him on the 'bare island':

> *Gentle breath of yours my sails*
> *Must fill, or else my project fails.*

Prospero cannot make us applaud by magic:

> *Now I want*
> *Spirits to enforce, Art to enchant.*

The commitment of the audience is, itself, the meaning of the play. In the Epilogue we are shown that the return to life in the play—to Milan and to Naples—can be achieved, that the play can become a 'play', only if we, the audience, make it so by acknowledging its 'dream', its myth, as our own. Although at the end of the play Prospero's Art is 'overthrown' (he 'buries' his staff and 'drowns' his book) the lesson of the Epilogue is that no longer are these actions of any great importance. The play itself remains for us if we will admit it, for the 'overthrow' of Prospero's art has shown us the value of a life which is enriched by this very art. The vision of Miranda and Ferdinand playing chess which turns out to be real and not a 'vision of the Island' has defined, beautifully and precisely, the concepts which are basic to the Renaissance Platonic ideal of life and art.

In *The Winter's Tale* we watched the 'old tale' take on the validity of experience. At the end of *The Tempest* we do not watch art become reality: we are required to acknowledge the art itself, and in doing so to acknowledge the interdependence of art and reality.

8

The New Inn *and* The Sad Shepherd

JONSON'S MASQUES and Shakespeare's *Winter's Tale* and *Tempest* fully justify Jonson's claim that the poet is the 'interpreter and arbiter of nature, a teacher of things diuine no less then humane'.[1] These works show us the close relationship between the meaning of the masque or play and the audience's capacity—either to make a higher life of which art is a necessary part or to accept life and the surface forms of art at the level of a Trinculo, Stephano, and Antonio.

Jonson's return to the public theatre in 1626 shows this continuing preoccupation. In none of the plays is the relation between audience and play so explicit as in *The Staple of News*, but the springs of that play are close to despair. *The Staple of News* is a bitter satire on a society sickened by its insatiable desire for novelty without regard for wisdom or for traditional values in language and manners. Specifically, in this play Jonson expresses his fear that one of the most important functions of plays and the theatre is threatened.[2] With the publication of the first regular newspapers in 1622 the playhouse was in danger of losing its role as the 'mirror of nature'. Three years after *The Staple of News* Jonson wrote *The New Inn* (1629), in which he again voiced his concern with the decline of the theatre. Although the mode of *The New Inn* is quite different from that of *The Staple of News* certain aspects of the earlier play are taken up and recast in *The New Inn*. One aspect in particular which these two plays share is Jonson's emphasis on the importance of the audience's response, the role the audience must take if the play is to be successful. In *The Staple of News* Jonson is critical of the typical London audience. The function of the Chorus of Gossips who sit on the stage and pass comments on the action of the play may be partly that of a traditional Chorus, interpreting the action; but it is mainly that of satire on an audience. Their comments are a mixture of shrewd observation and complete gullibility.

In the opening lines of the Epilogue to *The New Inn* Jonson made explicit the importance of the audience's response:

> *Playes in themselues haue neither hopes, nor feares,*
> *Their fate is only in their hearers eares.*

[1] *Volpone*, Dedication, ll. 27–9.
[2] For a full discussion see McKenzie, '*The Staple of News* and the Late Plays'.

His awareness of the importance of a play's relation to its audience must have been sharpened by twenty years' experience in providing masques for court. In the masques, we have seen, the 'powre' of the audience to 'rise' to the wisdom of the masque was at least as important as the affective powers of the masque itself.[3] The problem of relating fiction and audience, a problem particularly inherent in the masque form, is one for which Jonson in *The New Inn*, appears to be seeking a solution within a dramatic context. Both in its structure and in its thematic material the play appears to have grown out of the masques. In its barest outline the structure can be seen from a summary of the play's plot.

The plot of *The New Inn* rests on a series of outrageously improbable disguises. The Host of the inn turns out to be the lost Lord Frampul and the old one-eyed beggar, who has been living at the inn as Nurse to the Host's adopted son, turns out to be his wife. Furthermore, we discover that Frank, the adopted son is, in fact, the daughter of Lord Frampul the Host, a daughter Laetitia who was believed lost as a child. During the play, Lady Frances Frampul (the elder daughter of the Host but not acknowledged or revealed to the audience as such until the end of the play) comes to the inn with a party of followers including Lord Latimer, Lord Beaufort, Colonel Sir Glorious Tipto, and Prudence her chambermaid. Lovel, a melancholy guest at the inn, takes fright when he hears of Lady Frampul's arrival, for he is hopelessly in love with her: but he is persuaded to stay and to take part in the 'sports' which Lady Frampul organizes at the inn to entertain her followers and amuse herself. For these 'sports' she borrows the Host's son, Frank, dresses him up as a girl, and gives him the name of Laetitia, after her own lost sister. The elaborate disguises in the play form a double plot structure:[4] it has been recognized that the play is fairly self-contained up to Act V, scene v when the Nurse, on hearing that Frank/Laetitia has been married to Lord Beaufort, breaks into the Host's merriment with the revelation of her own and Frank's identities.[5] This in turn leads to the Host's revelation of his own identity as Lord Frampul and to the marriages and reconciliations with which the play ends.

In some respects this double ending may be regarded as parallel to the relation of masque to revels. *The Staple of News* too had borrowed from the masque—by including a kind of mock masque at its climax. In Act IV the Princess Pecunia is taken to lunch at the Apollo room of the Devil Tavern, and there Madrigal the poet composes verses in her

---

[3] See Daedalus' claims for dance in *Pleasure Reconciled*, ll. 269–72, H & S vii, p. 489.

[4] The structure of the play has been discussed in some detail by Thayer, *Ben Jonson*; Partridge, *Broken Compass*; Duncan, 'Guide to *The New Inn*'.

[5] Duncan, 'Guide', makes this point very clearly.

honour which are then set to music. The performances of Madrigal's
song in praise of Pecunia and of the dance which follows it take the play
into the mode of the court masque. But this is a parody of a masque and
its significance, for this, central, scene expresses and praises only the
'universal harmony' that sack and Pecunia provide.

In one important respect—in its thematic material—*The New Inn*
has developed directly from the masques. And here too Jonson has
taken up and turned in a positive way an image which overshadows the
satire of the whole of *The Staple of News*. The spirit of that play is
summed up in the Induction where the Gossips talk to the actor who is
about to speak the Prologue. Mirth, one of the Gossips, who has been
backstage, describes Jonson, the poet, like this:

Yonder he is within . . . rowling himselfe vp and downe like a tun, i' the midst of 'hem, and
spurges, neuer did vessel of wort, or wine worke so! . . . He doth sit like an vnbrac'd Drum
with one of his heads beaten out: For, that you must note, a Poet *hath two heads, as a Drum*
has, one for making, the other repeating, and his repeating head is all to pieces . . . ; for he
hath torne the booke in a Poeticall *fury, and put himselfe to silence in dead* Sacke, *which,*
were there no other vexation, were sufficient to make him the most miserable Embleme *of*
patience.

(Induction, ll. 61–74)

The poet is described here in melancholic posture: and in the Prologue
itself Jonson expressed his melancholy in his distrust of the audience's
judgement.

In *The New Inn* Jonson makes a last, but this time positive, stand for
the social value of the theatre. To reverse the image of the melancholic
poet he turned to the fundamentally optimistic masque ethic. However,
his claims are not for the social ideals of the aristocratic entertainment
alone but for the public theatre. The elaborations of the plot of *The New*
Inn are not an end in themselves but provide a basis for emphasizing the
more formal qualities—which recreate the play's 'invention'—patterning of scenes, grouping of characters, colours of costumes.[6] Such an
emphasis does not imply that Jonson has now succumbed to a popular
demand for 'shewes' rather than 'more remou'd *mysteries*'; rather, as in
the early masques, the 'shewe' itself reveals the 'more remou'd *mys-*
teries'. In this play it seems that Jonson is making a final claim for the
comic theatre itself—as a kind of talisman, a *figura mundi*.

I

In *The New Inn* Jonson has taken his emblem of the melancholic poet in

[6] Duncan, 'Guide', p. 325 speaks of the revelations of identity at the end of the play as
burlesquing conventional romantic revelations. He says that the ending represents Jonson's 'wry
recognition that the theatre in a declining age was bound to have more in common with a
puppet-show than a philosophical feast'. Duncan has misjudged the tone of the whole play: I
hope to show that there is certainly nothing wry or burlesque about its ending.

The Staple of News and shown us the other side of the playwright's humour. Apart from the unfinished *Sad Shepherd*, this play is Jonson's only non-satiric comedy, and by contrast with the satiric sharpness of *The Staple of News* its genial quality is most apparent. Jonson has carried through the theme of melancholy and the theatre in the character of Lovel, the melancholy man in *The New Inn*; but Lovel's melancholy is 'cured' by the action of the play and his humour is balanced by that of the other main character—the Host of the New Inn.

The Host is the central figure in the play and yet stands apart from its action, at least until the very last scene when he reveals his true identity. So, although Jonson has provided a synopsis of the play's argument so that his reader knows the Host's strange story of his having abandoned his wife and the consequent misunderstanding between them, the audience at a performance of the play would have no knowledge that the Host is Lord Frampul until the very end. In the Host's conversations with Lovel early in the play we are given some indication that the Host of the Light Heart has been bred to a different station in life and that he has some special reason for retiring from the world: we learn that he is a 'scholar' and that Frank, his 'son', has been educated by him. But the early scenes do not so much emphasize the fact that the Host is deliberately disguising himself or deliberately escaping from society, but rather draw attention to a detached quality which appears to be essential to the function of the Host of the Light Heart. The Host describes his position in the inn as similar to that of a spectator in the theatre: he talks of observing the 'comedy' of life without becoming involved in it. Here, he says, he can

> imagine all the world's a Play;
> The state, and mens affaires, all passages
> Of life, to spring new *scenes*, come in, goe out,
> And shift, and vanish; and if I haue got
> A seat, to sit at ease here, i' mine Inne,
> To see the *Comedy*; and laugh, and chuck
> At the variety, and throng of humors,
> And dispositions, that come iustling in,
> And out still, as they one droue hence another:
> Why, will you enuy me my happinesse?
>
> (I. iii. 128–37)

That the inn is to be likened to the comic theatre is further suggested by Lovel's speaking of the Host's inn as 'your round roofe', an epithet which reminds us of the traditional physical shape of the theatre and its traditional function (as the name Globe, for instance, suggests) as an image of the world.[7] The Host himself, we have seen, has spoken of the

---

[7] Cf. Yates's discussion of the Globe theatre in *Theatre of the World*.

inn as the comic theatre of life.[8] Like the theatre, the inn has a central
place in society: but it can also be compared to the Banqueting Hall, the
setting for masques and court festivities, for it is a place for feasting and
revelry. The comic spirit of the inn and of its Host is made clear in that
the Host several times refers to himself, the guests, and the place as
'jovial'. When at the beginning of the play the Host is explaining the
inn-sign to Ferret, Lovel's servant, he insists on its point as an emblem
of the inn's spirit:

> A heart weigh'd with a fether, and out-weigh'd too:
> A brayne-child o' mine owne! and I am proud on't!
> And if his worship thinke, here, to be melancholy,
> In spight of me or my wit, he is deceiu'd;
> I will maintayne the *Rebus* 'gainst all humors,
> And all complexions i' the body of Man,
> That's my word, or i' the Isle of Britaine!
>
> (i. i. 5–11)

A little further on he insists:

> I must ha' iouiall guests to driue my ploughs,
> And whistling boyes to bring my haruest home,
> Or I shall heare no Flayles thwack.
>
> (i. i. 22–4)

When Lovel himself enters and says that he and Ferret intend to stay,
the Host affirms:

> Sir set your heart at rest, you shall not doe it:
> Vnlesse you can be iouiall. Brayne o'man,
> Be iouiall first, and drinke, and dance, and drinke.
>
> (i. ii. 12–14)

As the 'jovial' Host of the inn, his position and character remind us of
Iophiel, the 'aery spirit' in *The Fortunate Isles* who presents both masque
and antimasque to the king. On the other hand, the Host is in some
ways in a position similar to that of the monarch watching a masque or
revels or misrule, in that he provides the setting for the festivities and
also provides a continuity between the holiday world of festival and
disguise and the everyday world. He is, of course, unlike the monarch in
that the sports at the inn are not addressed to him—as a masque is
addressed to the monarch. Still, the analogy, which the play stresses,
with the theatre and the comic spirit makes clear the Host's role as both
presenter and audience, as representative of the jovial spirit of misrule.
He presides over the inn and yet does not interfere with the free-will of
his guests who may take part in, and interpret, the sports as they will.

---

[8] I would stress the conventional and traditional image of the theatre here. The play itself was
not acted at the Globe but at Blackfrairs theatre, a rectangular building.

The tradition of revelry associated with the inn is already contained in Fly, who, the Host says, was part of the inheritance of the Light Heart and to whom the Host refers at the end of the play as 'my fellow *Gipsey*'. The Host says:

> I had him when I came to take the Inne, here,
> Assign'd me ouer, in the Inuentory,
> As an old implement, a peice of house-hold stuffe,
> And so he doth remaine.
>
> (ii. iv. 16–19)

But the Host bequeaths the inn to Fly at the end of the play when he and all the other characters prepare to leave it; and we recognize then that the revelry of Fly's inn can only be represented by the mundane kind of drunken stupor we have seen in the scenes below-stairs. Only while the Host presides is a truly jovial spirit maintained at the inn.

The Host lives at the inn with his 'son' Frank, whose name suggests the bounteous spirit of the inn. And the Host is pleased to let Frank join in the sports of the Lady Frances Frampul because her behaviour, like her name, signifies the spirit of his inn, the Light Heart. The Host approves of the fact that she 'consumes' her inheritance with 'cloathes, and feasting,/And the authoriz'd meanes of riot'.[9] However, the 'rightness' of Lady Frampul's sports is questionable. When we first learn of her arrival, Lovel and the Host discuss her strange family history. At this point in the play we are given no hint that the Host is actually her father; but we do learn that her father, Lord Frampul, who has not been heard of for a long time, is 'the mad Lord *Frampul*'; and we are told it is he 'of whom the tale went, to turne Puppet-mr . . . And lie, and liue with the *Gipsies* halfe a yeare/Together, from his wife'.[10] We are also told that Frances was not the only daughter:

> There were two of 'hem *Frances* and *Laetitia*;
> But *Laetice* was lost yong; and, as the rumor
> Flew then, the mother vpon it lost her selfe.
>
> (i. v. 67–9)

Thus, although Lady Frances Frampul's desire for pleasure sorts well with the Light Heart's freedom from restraints, nevertheless her sports and feastings lack her sister, Laetitia or joy. In fact, Laetitia is present—in the person of Frank, the Host's adopted 'son'—but her presence cannot be discovered until the revelations at the end of the play dispel all melancholy.

However, Lady Frampul recognizes the fact that her sports lack

---

[9] I. v. 79–80.
[10] I. v. 61–4.

something and so she borrows Frank, dresses him up as a girl, and pretends he is her sister, Laetitia. As Prudence later points out, this deceit is only a 'counterfeit mirth'.[11] Lady Frampul's entertainment without true joy points up a distinction central to the play between good and bad disguises—the healthful comedy of misrule which can restore sanity and cure melancholy and the gloom of deceit, of 'counterfeit mirth'.

I I

Into the revelry of the Light Heart Lovel and his servant Ferret have come. The Host questions Lovel's reasons for coming and guesses them fairly accurately:

> 'Tis more,
> And iustlier, Sir, my wonder, why you tooke
> My house vp, *Fidlers* Hall, the Seate of noyse,
> And mirth, an Inne here, to be drousie in,
> And lodge you lethargie in the Light Heart,
> As if some cloud from Court had been your Harbinger,
> Or Cheape-side debt-Bookes, or some Mistresse charge,
> Seeing your loue grow corpulent, gi' it a dyet,
> By absence, some such mouldy passion!
>
> *Lovel*   'Tis guess'd vnhappily.
>
> (I. iii. 141–50)

The Host suggests that Lovel is using the inn merely as a place of escape from his troubles and he points out that his melancholy is a bad advertisement for the inn. Indeed, Lovel does not even eat and drink as the spirit of the Light Heart demands. Lovel's character is quite contrary to the jovial nature of the Host and the frank, open, liberal character of the inn. Lovel himself points to this opposition when he describes himself as '*Saturnine*'.[12]

Lovel is the melancholy scholar, and one aspect of his scholar's melancholy is referred to by the Host when he complains of the way Lovel and Ferret have spent the past fortnight:

> Here, your master.
> And you ha' beene this for ⟨t⟩ night, drawing fleas
> Out of my mattes, and pounding 'hem in cages
> Cut out of cards, & those rop'd round with pack-thred,
> Drawne thorow birdlime! a fine subtilty!
> Or poring through a multiplying glasse,
> Vpon a captiu'd crab-louse, or a cheese-mite

[11] v. iv. 48.
[12] I. ii. 40.

To be dissected, as the sports of nature,
With a neat Spanish needle! Speculations
That doe become the age, I doe confesse!

(I. i. 24–33)

The Host regards Lovel's saturnine interest in what he can only see as ludicrous pursuits as harmful and undesirable. However, that Lovel regards himself differently and that we too may do so is indicated by the assurance he has of his right to lodge in the Light Heart, and obviously he regards his pursuits at the inn as inspired melancholy, the melancholy of the philosopher. Even early in the play Lovel is assured about his place in the Host's Light Heart. When the Host complains of his activities Lovel replies firmly:

We ha' set our rest vp here, Sir, i'your Heart;

(I. ii. 11)

and later his reply to the Host's bustling is forthright:

> *Lovel*   Humerous Host.
> *Host* I care not if I be. *Lov.* But airy also,
> Not to defraud you of your rights, or trench
> Vpo' your priviledges, or great charter,
> (For those are euery hostlers language now)
> Say, you were borne beneath those smiling starres,
> Haue made you Lord, and owner of the Heart,
> Of the Light Heart in *Barnet*; suffer vs
> Who are more *Saturnine*, t'enioy the shade
> Of your round roofe yet.

(I. ii. 32–41)

Jonson makes use of the ambiguity of Saturn's influence in Renaissance astrology to create for us this ambiguous view of Lovel which the action of the play will finally resolve.[13]

But Lovel's melancholy has another facet. When he is left alone he expands on his real reason for being at the inn, a hint of which the Host has already elicited from him. In Act I, scene iv Lovel breaks out into a melodramatic and passionate soliloquy:

---

[13] Two traditions linked studiousness with melancholy. The first is the Aristotelian notion that the melancholic man was also the philosopher, and the Renaissance included in this definition Plato's idea of divine *furor*. The other tradition regarded the relation between studiousness and melancholy as undesirable, as wasting the vital spirits which linked body and soul. For a discussion of the latter see Lyons, *Voices of Melancholy*, pp. 3, 11, 26. For the Renaissance views see Klibansky *et al.*, *Saturn and Melancholy*, pp. 251–4. Ficino states the Renaissance view in the following paradox: '[the black bile] obliges thought to penetrate and explore the centre of its objects, because the black bile is itself akin to the centre of the earth. Likewise it raises thought to the comprehension of the highest, because it corresponds to the highest of the planets.' (Quoted in Klibansky *et al.*, p. 259.)

> O loue, what passion art thou!
> So tyrannous! and trecherous! first t'en-slaue,
> And then betray, all that in truth do serue thee!
> That not the wisest, nor the wariest creature,
> Can more dissemble thee, then he can beare
> Hot burning coales, in his bare palme, or bosome!
> And lesse, conceale, or hide thee, then a flash
> Of enflam'd powder, whose whole light doth lay it
> Open, to all discouery, euen of those,
> Who haue but halfe an eye, and lesse of nose!
>
> (i. iv. 1–10)

Lovel takes himself so seriously here that his staginess, the typical melancholic posing or role-playing, becomes amusing.[14] The potential comedy of the saturnine Lovel's love-sickness is developed in the later scene where Pru holds her Court of Love.[15] It is Lady Frampul herself with whom Lovel is in love, and when Ferret announces her arrival at the inn Lovel's first reaction is to settle his account with the Host as quickly as possible and take himself off. But almost immediately after his first response Lady Frampul's arrival establishes a bond between Lovel and his Host—as though the Host affords Lovel some protection. So when Ferret returns to say that the horses are ready and the bill discharged Lovel replies:

> Charge it again, good *Ferret*.
> And make vnready the horses: Thou knowst how.
> Chalke, and renew the rondels. I am, now,
> Resolu'd to stay.
>
> (i. vi. 3–6)

Lovel's presence at the inn is already known to Lady Frampul and she sends her chambermaid, Pru, to request him to join in her intended sports. At first Lovel refuses; his excuse is gracious but firm:

> But for me to thinke,
> I can be any rag, or particle
> O'your Ladyes care, more then to fill her list,
> She being the Lady, that professeth still
> To loue no soule, or body, but for endes;

---

[14] Shakespeare made serious use of the love-melancholic's escaping from himself in 'acting' or adopting roles in Hamlet and satirized it in Jaques in *As You Like it*. For a discussion of Hamlet and melancholy see Lyons, *Voices of Melancholy*, Chapter IV, and especially pp. 82–5.

[15] The astrological conjunction of Saturn and Venus had been used in a comic situation before this. The audience might well recall Prince Hal's wry comment on Falstaff's amorousness in *2 Henry IV*, ii. iv. 286: 'Saturn and Venus this year in conjunction! What says th'almanac to that?'. The danger of the simultaneous influence of Saturn and Venus was well known. See Ficino, *De Vita Triplici*, ii. 16, *Opera*, p. 523. The reference is given in Klibansky *et al.*, *Saturn and Melancholy*, footnote 101, pp. 271–2. Klibansky points out that 'the greatest contrast exists between Saturn and Venus'.

Which are her sports: And is not nice to speake this,
But doth proclame it, in all companies:
Her Ladiship must pardon my weak counsels,
And weaker will, if it decline t'obay her.

(I. vi. 51–9)

Lovel is persuaded to take part in the sports in which Pru is 'sovereign'
of misrule when Pru points out to him that Lady Frampul's behaviour
in the sports she has planned cannot be judged by Lovel's standards of
responsible behaviour. Pru makes clear the nature of the sports, their
special quality of misrule. Further, the acting which will take place in
these sports at the inn may be turned, like all good comedy, to a positive
end. Pru says:

Yet, if her Ladyships
Slighting, or disesteeme, Sir, of your seruice,
Hath formerly begot any distaste,
Which I not know of: here, I vow vnto you,
Vpon a Chambermaids simplicity,
Reseruing, still, the honour of my Lady,
I will be bold to hold the glasse vp to her,
To shew her Ladyship where she hath err'd,
And how to tender satisfaction:
So you vouchsafe to proue, but the dayes venter.

(I. vi. 70–9)

However, we realize that the part Lovel will play in the sports is still
uncertain when, in reply to the Host's question whether his name is
Loue-ill or *Loue-well*, we find that he is unsure even of his real identity.
He replies: 'I doe not know't my selfe.'[16]

III

In her role as 'sovereign' of the day's sports Pru's speech has a tautness,
almost a tartness, which directs our attention to the nice balance in the
central scenes between the ludicrous and the serious. Even from the
beginning of Pru's 'reign' this quality is clear.[17] Pru goes further and
takes more licence than Lady Frampul had thought she would, and the
directness of her command that Lady Frampul immediately kiss Lovel
shows us, in their embarrassment, the real feeling each had for the
other—although neither is fully aware of its true nature. Lady Frampul's awkward

Doe not you
Triumph on my obedience, seeing it forc't thus.
There 'tis—

(II. vi. 112–14)

[16] I. vi. 95–6.
[17] II. vi. 90 ff.

is received by Lovel almost in silence: his emotional response breaks out only in an 'aside', to himself, and as the most exaggeratedly eloquent poetry, even ending in a rhyming couplet. This is indeed the *furor poeticus* of the love melancholic!

> Was there euer kisse
> That relish'd thus! or had a sting like this,
> Of so much *Nectar*, but, with *Aloes* mixt.
> . . .
> It had, me thinks, a *quintessence* of either,
> But that which was the better, drown'd the bitter.
> How soone it pass'd away! how vnrecouered!
> The distillation of another soule
> Was not so sweet! and till I meet againe,
> That kisse, those lips, like relish, and this taste,
> Let me turne all, consumption, and here waste.
>
> (II. vi. 114–24)

This scene prepares us for the two sessions of the Court of Love which follow, one hour after dinner, another after supper. Lovel is to discourse on Love for one hour and on 'gentle courtship' for the other.

Although the Court of Love in *The New Inn* may have been intended as a satire on the practices of Henrietta Maria's court, its point seems far broader than this and its comedy has none of the sharpness of satire.[18] It has been suggested that the comedy of the scene depends solely on the extravagance of Lovel's speech.[19] But Lovel's speeches are not, in themselves, extravagant: they are comic because they are 'set' speeches and because of their context.

Lovel's definition of Love is a straightforward statement of the Platonic philosophy.[20] He defines Love like this:

> . . . I make
> The efficient cause, what's beautifull, and faire.
> The formall cause, the appetite of vnion.
> The finall cause, the vnion it selfe.
> But larger, if you'l haue it, by description,

---

[18] Cf. Thayer, *Ben Jonson*, p. 217. Thayer suggests satire.

[19] Partridge first made the suggestion that Lovel's speeches should be regarded as satire. See *Broken Compass*, pp. 194–5.

[20] The speech is discussed in H & S x, pp. 318–19 in the notes on the play. The main source is Plato's *Symposium* and Ficino's *Commentary* on it. The division into 'causes' is Aristotelian. Compare *Blackness*, ll. 141–2 where Niger calls the Sun 'the best iudge, and most formall cause / Of all dames beauties'. But Gordon, '*Blacknesse* and *Beautie*', pp. 129–30, says: 'The terminology—'most formall cause of all dames beauties' (ll. 141–2)—is Platonic and takes us straight to Pico's *Commentary*, to the passage in which he is explaining the modes of being of Sensible Beauty. He has just defined 'amore volgare' as being the desire of Sensible Beauty which comes through the sense of sight, 'appetito di bellezza sensibile per il senso del viso'. Sensible Beauty has three modes of being: Causal, Essential or Formal, and Participated. Sensible Beauty, the beauty that can be perceived through the sense of sight finds its Formal or Essential cause in the colours given by the light of the sun . . .'

> It is a flame, and ardor of the minde,
> Dead, in the proper corps, quick in anothers:
> Trans-ferres the Louer into the Loued.
>
> . . .
>
> Loue is a spirituall coupling of two soules,
> So much more excellent, as it least relates
> Vnto the body; circular, eternall.

(III. ii. 91–8, 105–7)

Lovel's definition of Love as '[transferring] the Louer into the Loued' and as 'circular, eternall' points to the quality of Love which the Platonists imaged in the three Graces.[21] (See Pl. III.) In representations of them in Renaissance art they are depicted dancing in a circle: Amor (Love), the receiving Grace, in the middle of the trio, turns slightly from the giving Grace, Pulchritudo (Beauty), and looks towards Voluptas (Pleasure), who returns to Beauty—in the onlooker's eye. In Botticelli's most famous representation of the Graces, in the *Primavera*, their dance is presided over by Venus who draws together, as it were in one figure, the triadic nature of Love represented by the Graces and their dance.[22]

However, the point of Lovel's speeches is not simply that they outline the Platonic doctrine of Love. They may remind us of Bembo's long discourse on Love in the Fourth Book of *The Courtier*, not only by their subject-matter but for the inspired eloquence with which Lovel delivers them.[23] The melancholy Lovel speaks here with a passion comparable to Bembo's *furor poeticus*. The difference—and this is the point of the scene—lies in the contexts, and in Lovel's case the context has been quite clearly set by sovereign Pru. All who take part in Pru's sports are supposed to be acting; and yet in the case of both Lovel and Lady Frampul we are not sure. In Lovel's case there is a double twist, because in some respects here, as in his earlier speeches about Love, Lovel's over-seriousness appears in itself to be a kind of self-dramatization. Here, as earlier, we observe a literary-ness in his eloquence. On the other hand it appears that Lovel takes the 'role' Pru has assigned him very seriously: he is completely identified with his part in the sports. Lovel's self-seriousness is pointed up by Lady Frampul's enthusiastic response to his eloquence. Pru is convinced that Lady Frampul is acting—and acting very well. In response to her ecstatic

> O speake, and speake for euer! let min⟨e⟩ eare
> Be feasted still, and filled with this banquet . . .

(III. ii 201f.)

---

[21] See above, Chapter IV.

[22] See the very full discussion of the representation of the Graces in the visual arts, and especially in Botticelli's *Primavera*, by Wind, *Pagan Mysteries*, pp. 26–127.

[23] Duncan, 'Guide', p. 320, also compares Lovel's speeches to Bembo's discourse.

Pru exclaims,

> Excellent actor! how she hits this passion!
>
> (III. ii. 210)

Lord Latimer, who has remained an onlooker and is more critically cautious, asks Pru,

> But doe you thinke she playes?
>
> (III. ii. 214)

But Pru is certain Lady Frampul is acting, as she herself—as sovereign of the sports—is. Our uncertainty of response is heightened by the extravagance of Lady Frampul's speeches which continually parallel, and appear to be attempting to outdo, Lovel's. At the end of the hour, when both Lovel and Lady Frampul are upset that Pru has ended the session so peremptorily, Lovel now complains that Lady Frampul is not, as Pru saw her, acting well, nor, as Lord Latimer saw her, in deadly earnest, but that she is personating, dissembling, counterfeiting. In reply to the Host's attempts to cheer him up he bursts out:

> Tut, she dissembles! All is personated,
> And counterfeit comes from her! If it were not,
> The *Spanish* Monarchy, with both the *Indies*,
> Could not buy off the treasure of this kisse,
> Or halfe giue balance for my happinesse.
>
> (III. ii. 259–63)

Pru's sports have failed, they have become a kind of false comedy, because she is the only actor who is clearly acting. In both Lovel and Lady Frampul where identity and role are not distinguished the 'session' points up only the negative theatrical forms—dissembling, personating, and self-dramatizing. What Lord Beaufort calls this '*philosophicall* feast'[24] is in itself a mock image of the triadic Love of which Lovel has spoken.

It has been argued that the image of the three Graces, who represent for the Renaissance Platonists the triadic Love discussed in this session, was regarded as a talisman against melancholy. If we consider the staging of this scene bearing this in mind the failure of Pru's comedy becomes clear.[25] Lovel's eloquent Platonic sentiments are undercut as statements of Love by the fact that in this scenario, this 'dance', the 'giving' Grace, Beauty, is Lady Frances Frampul, beautiful to Lovel's eyes but here—attended by her two other suitors—frank and liberal in

---

[24] III. ii. 125.

[25] Yates, *Bruno*, p. 77. Miss Yates regards Botticelli's work as 'an image of the world to attract the favourable planets and to avoid Saturn'. Pico possessed a medal depicting the Graces. Miss Yates believes this, too, was made as a talisman against melancholy: *Bruno*, p. 90. See also Wind, Chapter III.

a sense quite other than the chaste Pulchritudo of, for example, Botticelli's image. Nor does Love—represented by Lovel himself—lead to Pleasure here, but to an agony of torment, frustration, and shame. The third Grace in this dance, the image of Pleasure, is Laetitia, with whom Beaufort dallies throughout. Apart from the incongruity of the two kinds of love which Lovel and Beaufort show, Beaufort's comments, aside, deflate, but do not argue with, Lovel's eloquent sentiments and in this way emphasize the static quality of the scene. Furthermore, we know that Laetitia is really Frank dressed up, that she is 'counterfeit' Pleasure. So the circle of Love is broken, the dance frozen; and although the Host tries to suggest that the sports have at least roused Lovel from his silent melancholy we are painfully aware how inappropriate is his description of Lovel's part in the scene:

> Why, as it is yet, it glads my light Heart
> To see you rouz'd thus from a sleepy humor,
> Of drouzy, accidentall melancholy;
> And all those braue parts of your soule awake,
> That did before seem drown'd, and buried in you!
> That you expresse your selfe, as you had back'd
> The *Muses* Horse! or got *Bellerophons* armes!
>
> (III. ii. 264–70)

That this comedy of misrule cannot dispel melancholy is emphasized by the fact that at this very moment Fly bursts in with

> Newes, of a newer Lady,
> A finer, fresher, brauer, bonnier beauty,
> A very *bona-Roba*, and a Bouncer.
> In yeallow, glistering, golden Satten.
>
> (III. ii. 271–4)

Pinnacia Stuffe, with her tailor husband disguised as her footman, has arrived decked out in the gown Pru was to have worn in the sports. Pinnacia believes herself to look like a countess; as we gradually realize that this is the gown intended for 'sovereign' Pru we realize too the astringency of Fly's announcement. The dissembling, personating, and counterfeiting of this comedy become full-blown in Pinnacia Stuffe, a monstrous parody not only of the spirit of misrule but of Lady Frampul herself.

I V

From the beginning Pru made the distinction clear between 'play' clothes and clothes which indicate actual status: Lady Frampul did not. The point is made in the earlier scene (II. i) where we see Pru's uneasiness at dressing for the 'sports' in a gown of Lady Frampul's because her own has not arrived, and in her shocked reply to Lady Frampul's remark that although the dress she has lent Pru does not fit very well, Pru can sell it to the players when the day's sports are over.

> *Lady F.* 'Tis rich enough! But 'tis not what I meant thee!
> I would ha' had thee brauer then my selfe,
> And brighter farre. 'Twill fit the *Players* yet,
> When thou hast done with it, and yeeld thee somwhat.
> *Pru.* That were illiberall, madam, and mere sordid
> In me, to let a sute of yours come there.
> *Lady F.* Tut, all are *Players*, and but serue the *Scene*.
>
> (II. i. 33–9)

Pru keeps clear the distinction between real life and playing. In the Court of Love, we saw she was the only one to do so. Here she sees the dresses as expressing not only status but the decorum that belongs with status. Lady Frampul's dress does not fit Pru, and this may project the uneasiness and incongruity Pru feels in it. But her embarrassment is not at its bad fit but at Lady Frampul's failure to distinguish between misrule and reality. This failure is made to appear comic in Lady Frampul's reaction to Lovel's addresses in the Court of Love.

Pru's dress, we learn from Fly, is of 'yeallow, glistering, golden Satten', which heightens the comedy of Pinnacia's affectation in wearing it now. The colour of the dress is suitable to Pru's function as 'sovereign' of the revels for yellow was a colour worn in revels. The colour was very popular at this time and its symbolic significance of 'improvident gaiety' makes it appropriate for feasting.[26] Gold is also the colour of Sol whose influence is a protection against melancholy, the evil influence of Saturn. It is the colour which Pru should have worn in the Court of Love to avert its ending in gloom and recrimination. So when Pinnacia arrives in Pru's dress there is some humour in the fact that Lady Frampul for a time believes that she is indeed a countess.

A yellow satin dress is most appropriate to 'sovereign' Pru, for it makes clear that her part in the 'sports' at the inn is in direct opposition to her position as Lady Frampul's chambermaid. As chambermaid she must be dressed in grey, the colour of ordinary coarse homespun wool and symbolically appropriate to the virtue of Prudence. The dress she actually wears for the 'sports', Lady Frampul's dress, is a quiet colour. We have seen that Lady Frampul would have liked her to be 'brauer then [herself] And brighter farre'. The colours most commonly affected

---

[26] Jonson may also have intended a comment on the court here, for it was a colour especially popular with the Queen, Henrietta Maria. Van Dyck's portrait of the Queen dating from about this time (several copies of which are extant) shows her in a yellow silk dress. See Piper, *National Portrait Gallery*, no. 227, p. 161.

by the aristocracy were brown or dark blue, and these symbolized respectively solidity and serenity.[27]

The episode involving the Stuffes and Pru's dress is both the dramatic and the symbolic centre of the play. We first see the Stuffes below-stairs where the company under the direction of Colonel Tipto is drinking and feasting. The scenes in which Pinnacia is stripped also deflate Tipto's boasts of valour, and this episode is the last of the scenes which show us the feasting below-stairs as in some respects parallel to, and a commentary on, Pru's misrule above. It is ironic that Tipto is the only character below-stairs to treat the Stuffes with any deference or respect. He, like Lady Frampul whom he follows, is deceived by Pinnacia. As Pinnacia and her husband approach, both Burst and Huffle hail her derisively, Huffle with the refrain of a popular song:

> *Bur.* Slid heer's a Lady! *Huf.* And a Lady gay!
> . . .
> *Huf.* A Lady gay, gay.
> For she is a Lady gay, gay, gay. For she's a Lady gay.
> (IV. ii. 53, 65–6)[28]

While Pinnacia is quarrelling with her husband over his calling her 'wife' in company, the drunken disorder below-stairs has dissolved in the courtyard into confusion as Tipto challenges Hodge Huffle for his jeering at Pinnacia.

Before Pinnacia appears again, this time to the company above, we are given an account by Latimer and Beaufort of the riot in the courtyard and learn of Lovel's 'heroic' intervention. The irony of the 'battle' is heightened both by the fact that it is over Pinnacia Stuffe and by the comparison between the accounts of Tipto's cowardice and Lovel's 'valour'. Latimer says of Tipto:

> But what a *glorious* beast our *Tipto* shew'd!
> He would not discompose himselfe, the Don!
> (IV. iii. 4–5)

And Lady Frampul says of Lovel:

> I nere saw
> A lightning shoot so, as my seruant did,
> His rapier was a *Meteor*, and he wau'd it
> Ouer 'hem, like a *Comet!* as they fled him!
> I mark'd his manhood! euery stoope he made
> Was like an Eagles, at a flight of Cranes!
> (As I haue read somewhere).
> (IV. iii. 11–17)

[27] Linthicum, *Costume in the Drama*, pp. 24 and 49. For a full discussion of the relation between Pinnacia and her husband see Thayer, *Ben Jonson*, pp. 208–9. I am indebted to Mrs Dorothy Cooper for detailed information on Caroline costume.

[28] 'Lady lady' is the refrain of an old ballad imitated in many songs and referred to frequently. There is a note on the refrain in the notes to *The Magnetic Lady*, H & S x, p. 358, note to IV. viii. 72.

The martial Colonel Sir Glorious Tipto, one of Lady Frampul's train, provides a comic contrast with the saturnine Lovel. He must be removed from the central position he usurped in the merry-making below-stairs before a resolution of the 'sports' above can be reached. Latimer's comment on the battle clearly takes the measure of Tipto and he has very little further part in the play. Conversely, Lady Frampul's infatuation with Lovel's 'valour' prepares us for the second session of Pru's court and the outcome of the day's sports. But the second session of the Court of Love will not be merely a repetition of the first, for the events have changed Lovel and Lady Frampul. The turmoil of these scenes is itself a kind of allegory of the change in both; and the commotion at the centre of the play and the absurd rhetoric which described it (and the description, it seems, is all) became inflated to match the grotesqueness and the bombast of Pinnacia's own 'acting'. Now, with the 'pillaging' of the 'Pinnace', the serious direction of the play's comedy becomes clear and the action begins to unwind.[29]

V

After the Stuffes have departed Lovel enters (IV. iv) reading his 'meditation/Or rather a vision . . . Of Beauty'. Immediately, we are aware of a new direction: certainly the lack of any self-conscious attitudes and the lucid simplicity and control in the lyric itself sets it apart as something quite different from, although it has grown out of, the first session of the Court of Love:

> It was a beauty that I saw
> So pure, so perfect, as the frame
> Of all the universe was lame,
> To that one figure, could I draw,
> Or giue least line of it a law!
>
> A skeine of silke without a knot!
> A faire march made without a halt!
> A curious forme without a fault!
> A printed booke without a blot.
> All beauty, and without a spot.
>
> (IV. iv. 4–15)

Lovel says his page is practising the song in order that it may be sung after the second session of the Court, which Lady Frampul, still infatuated with Lovel's heroic behaviour, has now requested might be of 'Valour' and not 'Gentle courtship' as previously decreed. The 'Vision', and Lady Frampul's reaction to it, direct and qualify our understanding of the second session of the Court. Lady Frampul's immediate response is ours:

[29] IV. iii. 90.

> They are gentle words, and would deserue a note,
> Set to 'hem, as gentle;
>
> (IV. iv. 14–15)

and although her following words take on again much of her former extravagance we respond uneasily now as we recognize how close their tone is, in fact, to our own reaction to Lovel's reading of his song:

> In what calme he speakes,
> After this noise, and tumult, so vnmou'd,
> With that serenity of countenance,
> As if his thoughts did acquiesce in that
> Which is the obiect of the second houre,
> And nothing else.
>
> (IV. iv. 18–23)

We are uneasy because Lady Frampul has once more distanced Lovel, has made him into a stereotype that she may concentrate on her own, false, emotion; and although Pru's brusque 'Well then summon the Court' almost re-establishes the comic tone of the first session, nevertheless we realize that now our attention is being focused in a different way. The complete cessation of temporal trivialities which Lovel's reading of his poem has created, the groping half-awareness of this in Lady Frampul, and the shift of emphasis away from the dalliance of Beaufort with Frank-Laetitia, place the emphasis in this second session of the Court on the awakening self-awareness of Lady Frampul and Lovel. Now there can be no doubt about the meaning of Lady Frampul's 'asides'. Latimer says to Pru: 'I feare she meanes it, *Pru*, in too good earnest.'[30]

Pru will not allow Lovel's song to be sung at the end of the second session: perhaps Lovel is still too 'saturnine' for music—for 'Saturn [has] only voices and no music,' Ficino has said.[31] The Court is dismissed abruptly and Lady Frampul and Lovel are both left disconsolate and upset, believing they have made fools of themselves. The discomfort of each now is depicted more sensitively, with strokes more delicate than the broad comic strokes of the earlier, corresponding scene. There is now a poise between humour and sympathy which demands a resolution outside the day's sports and revelry, a resolution not contained within the Host's own, farcical resolution: his suggestion that Beaufort marry Frank-Laetitia.[32]

VI

The significance of Lovel's 'Vision', the meaning of our response to it in its earlier context, and the reason why Pru dismisses the court before it

---

[30] IV. iv. 146.
[31] *Op. Omn.*, p. 563. Quoted in Walker, *Spiritual and Demonic Magic*, p. 17.
[32] IV. iv. 237–8.

can be sung are made clear to us in the outcome. The singing of the song at the end gathers together the play's underlying seriousness and value. If we pause at this point to draw a parallel between the structure of *The New Inn* and that of *The Vision of Delight* and *Pleasure Reconciled to Virtue* we can illuminate the significance of the play's ending. In *The Vision of Delight*, Delight presented to the audience 'visions' which, beginning with a street-scene, became progressively more and more 'fantastic', less and less realistic, until the core of the masque, the Bower of Spring—a mythical and completely unrealistic set—was also recognized as the court of James, and the masquers stepped down from their Bower to dance with the audience. Here, reality and Truth were found not in the realism of the opening scene but in the Platonic myth of the Bower. But there remained yet another 'scene', one which this masque did not reveal but about which many of Jonson's masques seem uneasy: this was the real world, the world *outside* the Banqueting Hall, the world beyond the night's revels. No masque approached this problem more explicitly than *Pleasure Reconciled to Virtue*; and the answer that masque gave was that there was no resolution. *The New Inn* exposes this problem once again. If we over-simplify the 'structure' of this play we can observe a 'progression' similar to that of the revelations of Delight in the masque. In the opening scenes of the play the inn is an image of a real inn, although the Host, we see, regards it metaphorically as a theatre as well. As the guests arrive in the train of Lady Frampul the metaphorical description of the inn as a 'theatre of life' shifts and the inn becomes indeed a banqueting hall, a place for acting and for revels. In the end the Host participates in these revels—by urging the marriage of Frank-Laetitia to Beaufort; and the absurdity of this as any resolution to what has actually taken place in the 'sports' is clear in that it is Fly who gives Laetitia in marriage and in the new stable. But the duping of Beaufort, by encouraging him to marry a boy, is not the end of the play, although it is the end of the sports for the day. Furthermore, the sports have not been simple revelry: the parts of both Lovel and Lady Frampul, and their ending in depression and gloom do not allow us to regard the Host's ending to the sports as an ending to the play. We ask, what do these sports mean? And why, just before Beaufort returns with his 'bride', does Pru reappear—when the sports are over—dressed in her sovereign's gown of 'yeallow satten', rescued from Pinnacia? Now, as the Host—hoping to conclude the day's revelry in laughter—announces that Beaufort has married a boy, the Nurse rushes in (v. iv. 51). The revelations and unmaskings of the final scene (v. v), which purport to show us reality now, do not take us into a realistic world but, paradoxically, retreat from realism into what appears to be the world of the conventional reconciliations and marriages of comedy.

The inn has indeed become the theatre. But the play has come full circle; for just as we, the audience, will leave the theatre now the play is over so the Host will now leave the inn, bequeathing it to Fly, and rejoin with a new and more positive spirit the society he has escaped for so long. Furthermore, to give a double twist to this end we feel that the inn, Fly's inn now, becomes mundane, for its essence has been represented merely by the drunken stupor below-stairs. The day's revels have restored the true Laetitia, joy and happiness, in revealing identities and in its lesson in self-knowledge for all the characters—although Lord Beaufort is at first reluctant to exchange the illusion for the reality.[33] Lovel has learnt that his name means not *Loue-ill* but *Loue-well*.

And what of Pru in her new gown? As Pru arrives in her yellow gown the 'revels' can really begin. The significance of this is recognized by at least one character within the play: Lord Latimer offers to marry her—without a dowry. Until now, Lord Latimer has stood largely apart from the sports, watching them and commenting on them from a position similar to that of the audience. It is Latimer who recognizes Pru's worth. So the role of Prudence, in this final scene as throughout, directs us firmly towards the lesson of the play.

The Host had said that 'all the cheat be of myself in keeping this light-heart'; and indeed the Host himself would have completed the day's entertainment with a simple trick played on Beaufort. The 'cheat' of his 'theatre' is the cheat which only the audience which refuses to look beyond the mere superficial amusement and entertainment of the play will sustain. It is a harsh judgement and a trenchant one, but it is a judgement which also takes us back to the meaning of the final 'scene' of *The Vision of Delight*. Now, when Lovel appears in the midst of the revelations, he asks, as we might have asked of the masque scene:

> Is this a dreame now, after my first sleepe?
> Or are these phant'sies made i' the light Heart?
> And sold i' the new Inne?
>
> (v. v. 120–2)

The final, and most significant, recognition of Laetitia's presence is Lovel's. For just as the melancholy Lovel has to discover joy in the sports at the inn (and, we know, Laetitia was there throughout although unrecognized), so too the audience who comes to see a comedy as a cure for its 'melancholy' has a responsibility. The audience must 'rise' (as Daedalus in *Pleasure Reconciled* instructed his dancers) to the joy which a good comedy contains. The play's ending thus makes a double—and a rather sharp—point. The comic theatre, like the inn which is its image, may provide all the benign influences of a talisman

---

[33] v. v. 38–46.

against melancholy.[34] But for such a talisman to be effective the audience is also required not only to be sufficiently perceptive that they may discriminate between good and bad comedy, but also to have faith in the conventions of the theatre. At the beginning of the play the Host suggested that Lovel had come to his inn to escape from reality and Lovel himself admitted it. Now we learn that the theatre is not a means of escape but rather that its illusion and its conventions, properly understood, enable its audience to rejoin the real world with a new understanding after the play is done. At the end of this play it is Lovel who has the 'vision'. As all the characters are about to go off he checks them:

> Stay, let my Mrs
> But heare my vision sung, my dreame of beauty,
> Which I haue brought, prepar'd, to bid vs ioy,
> And light vs all to bed, 'twill be instead
> Of ayring of the sheets with a sweet odour.
>
> (v. v. 148–52)

This is the true vision of delight, the recognition that the meaning of the day's sports is not mainly to be found within the sports themselves. The final stage direction is '*They goe out, with a* Song'. The song, for which no music—unfortunately—now exists, could not be sung before, for earlier in the play it could not be given its true meaning, it had no context. Now the singing of the song recognizes the difference between the '*Loue-ill*' of the sports and the '*Loue-well*' of Jonson's play.

The final stage direction also draws the play firmly into comedy. Reality and the play-world come together through the play itself. Like *The Tempest*—and in a way that the literal character of the masque's ending does not—*The New Inn* assumes the audience into its 'wisdom'—but on terms which the play itself prescribed: those of the traditional literature of the comic theatre. Like Bembo's speech on Love in Book I V of *The Courtier* the play can, by its benign influence, lift its audience above temporal exigencies into the realm of Lovel's 'Vision'. In this Jonson trusts in the 'wisdom' of his audience: he does not need, as in *Pleasure Reconciled to Virtue*, to assert its importance.

VII

After *The New Inn* Jonson finished only one more play: *The Magnetic Lady* (1632). In 1633 he reshaped what was probably an early play, *A Tale of*

---

[34] Ficino pointed out that Jupiter and the Sun are the best mediators between Saturn and Venus, *Op. Omn.*, p. 523. 'Optima vero disciplina est, perquaedam Phoebi Iovisque, qui inter Saturnum Veneremque sunt medii, studia similiaque remedia homines ad alterutrum declinantes ad medium revocare.' This is quoted in Klibansky *et al.*, *Saturn and Melancholy*, footnote 101, pp. 271–2. (See also note 15 above.)

a Tub. [35] There remain two uncompleted plays, a fragment of a history play, *Mortimer his Fall*, and two-and-a-half acts of *The Sad Shepherd*. [36] It is with a consideration of this last, unfinished, play that I conclude my study. *The Sad Shepherd* is important in that it represents Jonson's last word for a theatre which he already recognized he had outlived; [37] and yet, like *The New Inn*, *The Sad Shepherd* seems not to be a signing off, a falling away from the old traditions and ideas, but a reshaping of the ideas which Jonson had used both in his masques and in his earlier plays, and a reaffirmation of their importance.

The New Inn, we saw, turned away from direct social satire and drew on the ideas and the structure of the masque. Here Jonson affirmed the validity of the play itself as a means of demonstrating the value of the masque's ethic—for the masque itself had seemed always to fall short of complete conviction. Like *The Tempest*, *The New Inn* asserted the interdependence of art and life—as the masque had attempted to assert it.

Like *The New Inn*, *The Sad Shepherd* turns away from social satire. It moves into the mythic world of pastoral, and in this it deliberately moves away from drama and back towards masque. But *The Sad Shepherd* is not just another masque: it revitalizes the over-stylized rhetoric of the Caroline masque; and it remains self-contained in a way the masque—which must finally acknowledge dependence on ideas and correspondences outside its own form—could not. In a study of this play we can see Jonson gathering together the fruits of forty years' experience as poet, playwright, and masque writer: the play was not simply to end but to crown a lifetime's work.

I have suggested that *The Sad Shepherd* relates to masque in its use of the pastoral setting as myth, and in making such a claim the set which Jonson describes for the play—a set which, of course, was never realized—seems very important. It owes much to the sets of the masques from *Oberon* on. The play was to be acted within a single, unchanging set, one which—like the sets for masques—was not to be realistic. It would embody in picture the essence of the play itself. Jonson describes it like this:

> The SCENE is *Sher-wood*.
> Consisting of a Landt-shape of Forrest, Hils, Vallies,
> Cottages, A Castle, A River, Pastures, Heards, Flocks, all
> full of Countrey simplicity. *Robin-hoods* Bower, his Well,
> The Witches *Dimble*, the Swine'ards *Oake*, The Hermits *Cell*.
> (ll. 26–30)

[35] H & S ix, p. 268 suggest that the play in its original form was written in 1596 or 1597.

[36] Various endings have been suggested. See, for instance, the endings of the play devised by Francis Waldron in the eighteenth century and Alan Porter in the twentieth. Thayer's very full and sympathetic discussion of this play (*Ben Jonson*, pp. 251 ff.) also suggests an ending for it.

[37] See the Ode: 'Come leaue the lothed stage' (H & S vi, p. 492) written after the bad reception of *The New Inn*.

The single set, an unchanging backdrop to the play's action, includes all the scenes of the play. In this it would constantly remind the audience that all aspects of the setting are present in any single scene or place. Thus, Robin-hood's Bower includes the Witches Dimble and the Oak. The play's pastoral world is not the fantasy, escape world of, for instance, Fletcher's pastoral tragi-comedies; rather, as in the masque, its allegorical set is an extension of the poetry of the play. Again unlike Fletcher's pastoral settings, the set for *The Sad Shepherd* establishes, as all allegory must, the interdependence of audience and play, and is thus not simply ornamental backdrop to dialogue and action. But the masque finally extended its allegorical world into the reality of the court; and in doing so it partially destroyed the shape and significance of its allegory. By contrast, *The Sad Shepherd* would have remained self-contained. The play's sub-title is 'A Tale of *Robin-hood*'; and the pastoral of the play is not the rarefied pastoral of court drama but the pastoral of folk-play. The countryside of Jonson's allegory is not a fantasy paradise, but is fully realized in verse which takes us back to the directness and sanity of Jonson's praise of country life in 'To Penshurst', for instance. The play is itself an image of the kind of amalgamation of life and art which belongs with mummings and disguises, with seasonal festivities. We have seen that Jonson has approached this already by the way in which he drew on the characters and the lore of mummings in several of his antimasques. Now we may say that in some respects *The Sad Shepherd*, had it been completed, might have contained a perfect resolution of masque and antimasque qualities within the single and self-contained form of the play.

The other single characteristic which relates *The Sad Shepherd* to masque and also confirms the positive direction in which *The New Inn* looks is the function of the one song in the play. Song had traditionally been part of pastoral drama: witness, for instance, the large number of songs in Lyly's plays written in the 1580s for Paul's Boys. However, in Lyly's plays song is used mainly as interlude (as it commonly was in children's plays), and this function for song in pastoral seems to have been developed later by Fletcher in his pastoral tragi-comedies. The songs in Fletcher's plays help to establish a deliberately a-moral world set apart from its audience, a virtuoso world requiring to be looked at rather than imaginatively participated in. Jonson's masques for the Caroline court also used song more as performance for its own sake than as part of the concept of the masque. This is part of a general hardening, an over-sophistication of Renaissance ideas which can be seen in Caroline poetry and music generally—an element of show and virtuosity which demands applause and which does not require penetration beneath a rigid rhetorical surface.[38] This is also a general tendency of the theatrical literature, a tendency against which *The New Inn* turned. The function of the song in *The Sad Shepherd* also turns against this tendency and reasserts the Renaissance concepts of pastoral. In its doing so we are reminded of the function of the songs in the first and last acts of *Cynthia's Revels*.

Lovel's song, his 'Vision', contains the essence of *The New Inn*. His elaborate professions of love become real and believable through their very simple expression in his song, and the play ends with the singing of this song as 'incense' to the 'Sacrifice of *loue*'. The song embodies, in miniature, the lesson of the play: the relation of idea to art and of this art to the London of its audience. It may also be claimed that the song in *The Sad Shepherd* characterizes the fragment which remains of the play. This can be shown through a consideration of this surviving fragment.

VIII

Aeglamour is the Sad Shepherd who has lost his beloved Earine. Maudlin, the witch, or Envy (as Jonson's gloss of the *dramatis personae* tells us) has stolen her and imprisoned her in a tree as a wife for her own son Lorel, and she has made Aeglamour believe that Earine has been drowned in the River Trent. Aeglamour's grief and his desire for revenge form the central subject of the 'action' of the play, and his grief, Clarion says, 'hath given allay,/Both to the Mirth and Musicke of this day'.[39] The occasion of the play is a feast given by Robin-hood and Marian. We recall that the Inn too was a place for feasting; and that in *Neptune's Triumph* the poet must yield one antimasque to the cook in recognition that the Banqueting House belongs to the cook as well as to the poet, that feasting is a celebration of the values the poet points to and not necessarily (as the 'sowrer sort of Shepherds' to whom Clarion refers—I. iv. 18–19—would say) in opposition to them.

The festive character of the gathering and the idyllic love of Marian and Robin-hood are darkened by Aeglamour's loss, through Envy; and also by Maudlin's disguising herself as Marian to deceive Robin-hood. In this respect Jonson has developed the characters of Marian and Maudlin complexly. He retains the traditional ambiguity of Marian in the old folk-tale, both her role as 'Lady of Mis-rule' in Christmas festivities and her association with Mary Magdalene.[40] It appears from Jonson's synopsis that in later, unwritten scenes, Puck-hairy was to have an important role,[41] and it is possible that Jonson intended to

---

[38] Cf. Mellers, *Harmonious Meeting*, pp. 108 and 114–15; also more generally the whole chapter on 'Henry Lawes and the Caroline Lyric'.

[39] I. iv. 59–60.

[40] Cf. Thayer's discussion of this, *Ben Jonson*, p. 257.

[41] See Jonson's synopsis of Act III: H & S vii, pp. 42–3.

develop the traditional associations between Robin-hood and Puck (who was also known as Robin Goodfellow).[42] So the characters of both Marian and Robin-hood symbolize two, opposing, aspects of life; and the fact that Jonson regards this as positive is reflected in the way they speak. So too the feast becomes assumed into a larger context, which is represented by the set itself; and we have seen that the set includes both Robin-hood's Bower and the Witches Dimble—idyll as well as the destructive forces of evil. In the relation of Robin-hood to Marian and of Aeglamour to the lost Earine, the play examines the relation of Love to Life, the vulnerability of innocent love to envy and evil, and the ways in which the idyll of the pastoral can ultimately be safely assumed into the world of time as something 'Richer than *Time*, and as *Time's* vertue, rare'.[43] As his name suggests, Aeglamour belongs in the rarefied world of the literary pastoral. His love is idealized and he expresses his grief with an extravagance which reminds us of Lovel's early expression of his love, although the context is quite different. Certainly, by comparison with Robin-hood's and Marian's, Aeglamour's expression of his love is 'literary'. When Robin-hood asks him to leave his grief and join in 'all the profer'd solace of the Spring', he says:

> A Spring, now she is dead: of what, of thornes?
> Briars, and Brambles? Thistles? Burs, and Docks?
> Cold Hemlock? Yewgh? the Mandrake, or the Boxe?
> These may grow still; but what can spring beside?
> Did not the whole Earth sicken, when she died?
> As if there since did fall one drop of dew,
> But what was wept for her! or any stalke
> Did beare a Flower! or any branch a bloome;
> After her wreath was made: In faith, in faith
> You doe not faire, to put these things upon me,
> Which can in no sort be: *Earine*,
> Who had her very being, and her name,
> With the first knots, or buddings of the Spring,
> Borne with the Primrose, and the Violet,
> Or earliest Roses blowne . . .
>
> (IV. 33–47)

Aeglamour is so engrossed in his grief that when he later sees Maudlin's daughter, Douce, disguised as Earine and speaking to Karolin (III. ii) he shows no concern nor surprise at having seen what he thinks is Earine's ghost but merely takes the occasion to philosophize on how Earine's soul

[42] See Thayer, *Ben Jonson*, pp. 257–8.
[43] Jonson, 'Epode', l. 60, from *Love's Martyr*. Also printed in *The Forrest*, H & S VIII, p. 111.

> doth haste
> To get up to the *Moone*, and *Mercury*;
> And whisper *Venus* in her *Orbe*; then spring
> Up to old *Saturne*, and come downe by *Mars*,
> Consulting *Jupiter*; and seate her selfe
> Just in the midst with *Phoebus*; tempring all
> The jarring Spheeres, and giving to the World
> Againe, his first and tunefull planetting.
>
> (III. ii. 25-32)

Aeglamour's expression of his love is fragile and vulnerable by comparison with the firmness of Robin-hood's and Marian's greetings to one another:

Rob. My *Marian*, and my Mistris! *Mar.* My lov'd *Robin*!
   . . .
Mar. How hath this morning paid me, for my rising!
     First, with my sports; but most with meeting you!
     I did not halfe so well reward my hounds,
     As she hath me to day: although I gave them
     All the sweet morsels, Calle, Tongue, Eares, and Dowcets!
Rob. What? and the inch-pin? *Mar.* Yes. *Rob.* Your sports then pleas'd you?
Mar. You are a wanton. *Rob.* One I doe confesse
     I wanted till you came, but now I have you,
     Ile growe to your embraces, till two soules
     Distilled into kisses, through our lips
     Doe make one spirit of love.
(I. vi. 1-13)

It is the robust sensitivity of their relationship which permits Robin-hood to recognize the 'false Marian' as Maudlin, and not to be deceived by Envy as Aeglamour has been. We see a similar quality of perception in the sage, Alkin's description to the Hunters of the Witches Dimble.[44] It is a description which does not belittle the horrors of the vision of Hell which the Dimble presents but one which also directs a positive response to, and a revulsion from, this as evil.

If we consider now the significance of the only song in the play we shall see how it mirrors and distils the subtle and complex possibilities of the pastoral. The singing of the song would, properly, belong to Aeglamour—as the forsaken lover and the most 'literary-pastoral' of the characters. But Aeglamour does not sing the song: he merely looks at a copy of it while Karolin sings it to him. Furthermore, the song is to be a consolation for Aeglamour, to be a means of allaying his grief. Clarion says to Karolin:

> Good *Karolin* sing,
> Helpe to divert this Phant'sie.
(I. v. 63-4)

[44] II. viii. 15-34.

And the song that Karolin sings is this:

> *Though I am young, and cannot tell,*
> *   Either what Death, or Love is well,*
> *Yet I have heard, they both beare darts,*
> *   And both doe ayme at humane hearts:*
> *And then againe, I have beene told*
> *   Love wounds with heat, as Death with cold;*
> *So that I feare, they doe but bring*
> *   Extreames to touch, and meane one thing.*
>
> *As in a ruine, we it call*
> *   One thing to be blowne up, or fall;*
> *Or to our end, like way may have,*
> *   By a flash of lightning, or a wave:*
> *So Loves inflamed shaft, or brand,*
> *   May kill as soone as Deaths cold hand;*
> *Except Loves fires the vertue have*
> *   To fright the frost out of the grave.*

The song comments on Aeglamour's plight and at the same time the 'I' of the song is Aeglamour himself. In a sense the song is conventional lyric, a song about Love and Death based on the images of heat and cold, and such a lament is appropriate to Aeglamour's conscious 'literary-ness'. But the song is important precisely because it is at once 'conventional' and also something more. The second stanza turns the conventional paradoxes of the first into images direct and striking; it turns its simpleness into simplicity and its final four lines comment on the quality of love which we will have examined for us within the play. The 'vertue' of 'loves fires' which will 'fright the frost out of the grave' and could restore Earine to Aeglamour is not something magical which exists in the removed enclosed pastoral of Aeglamour's vapid lamentation: the 'vertue' is, rather, the positive quality, a quality of Love itself, which we see expressed in the verse of Marian and Robin-hood, a positive response to life which can be observed also in the verse of Alkin.

Two different settings of the song exist, one by Nicholas Lanier, and the other by John Wilson, both writers of music for the Jacobean and Caroline stage.[45] Although neither setting can have been composed for a performance of the play, Lanier's setting seems to take account of the function of the song in the play and to complement the simple stanzaic quality of the words in a way that Wilson's virtuoso setting, for two voices, does not. Lanier's setting seems closer to recognizing the song's

[45] The song-text was also published as a separate poem with the title 'A Sonnet' in quarto and duodecimo editions of Jonson's poems, 1640. A list of musical sources is given in Duckles, 'Music for the Lyrics . . . Bibliography', p. 146. Duckles does not refer to the version of Wilson's setting in Folger MS 1.8, f. 9. This is discussed in Cutts's article on the Bodleian MS, Mus. b. 1. 'Seventeenth-Century Lyrics: Oxford Bodleian MS Mus. b. 1', p. 196.

EXAMPLE 42. 'Though I am yong, & cannot tell'

heat,   love   wounds with heat,   &   death   with____   cold.

heat,   love   wounds with heat,   &   death   with   cold.

heat,   love wounds with   heat,   &   death   with   cold.

Mr. *Nicholas Lanneare.*

Yet I have heard they both beare darts,
And both doe aime at humane hearts;
So that I feare they doe but bring
Extreams to touch, and meane one thing.

John Playford, *Select Musical Ayres and Dialogues* (1652), Part II, p.24. (The words in the second and third parts may be Playford's addition.)
Note.
7 Bass II: Playford gives G.

EXAMPLE 43 'Thoug I am yong, & cannot tell'.

[Voice I]   John Wilson.

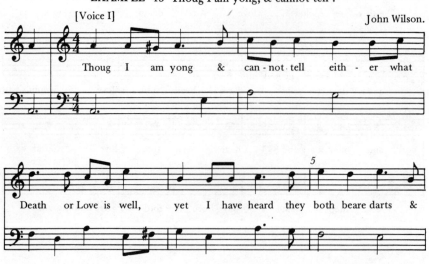

Thoug   I   am yong   &   can - not · tell   eith - er   what

Death   or Love is   well,   yet   I   have heard   they   both   beare darts   &

fires ___ ye ver - tue ___ have to fright a ___ frost

fires ye ver - tue have to fright a ___ frost

from out ye Grave. Vn - les his fires the ver-tue

from out ye Grave. Vn - les his fires the ver -

have to fright a ___ frost from ___ out the grave.

- tue have to fright a frost from ___ out the grave.

Bodleian MS Mus. B. 1. *ff.* 137ᵛ–138.

Note
13 second voice III: MS = quaver.

dramatic context, while Wilson has treated the lyric simply as 'words-for-music'.

A comparison of the treatment of the words by each composer may help to clarify our response to Karolin's performance at this point in the play. The settings may both date from approximately the same period. Lanier's setting occurs as a three-part song in Playford's *Select Musical Ayres and Dialogues* (1652), Part II, p. 24. It is possible that the two lower parts are Playford's addition, perhaps an arrangement of an instrumental accompaniment. In any case, the upper part is clearly the predominant part in a largely homophonic arrangement. Only the first stanza of Jonson's text is given for Lanier's setting, and the stanza is divided into two four-line 'stanzas' each to be sung to the same music so that the same melody would be sung four times were both Jonson's stanzas to be sung. By breaking Jonson's eight-line stanzas into four four-line stanzas Lanier's setting would dissipate the contrasting yet complementary character of Jonson's stanzas. Yet the setting as it stands reflects the essential qualities of the song in its dramatic context. The melodic line is very simple and follows the natural accentuation of the words both in rhythm and in the placing of the cadences. This simple musical form would draw the personal reference of the poem as describing Aeglamour's plight into the larger allegorical context and at the same time would complement the more formal or conventional nature of the poem's imagery and expression.

John Wilson's setting which occurs in Bodleian MS Mus. b. 1, ff. 137^v–138 makes something quite different of Jonson's verse and seems to remove any thought of a dramatic context for the song. Wilson has made the song into a little drama itself, a dialogue-song for two voices and three-part chorus. Unless Wilson's setting was intended for some special occasion it is difficult to understand why his setting takes so little account of the actual text. For not only is the verse not really suitable as a dialogue, the vocal line completely distorts the rhythmic and poetic sense of the words without giving their meaning any obviously significant pointing. Even the point of the stanzaic form is lost, not so much because of Wilson's through-composed setting as by the fact that the Chorus sings the last two lines of the first stanza but the last four of the second, destroying the balance and symmetry of the text. Wilson's setting may have been intended to be performed with a very ornate vocal line. If this were the case the curious rhythmic accentuation of unimportant words would be less obvious and attention would be drawn to the virtuoso qualities of the performer and away from the poetic qualities of the text, which in any case is treated like prose. In the respect that the setting turns the song into a showy and theatrical piece Wilson's setting would be inappropriate to the song's context in the play. For Jonson's song-text is not so much a statement as an image which subsumes all the subtly woven strands of our response to the play; and hence a setting which, like Lanier's, takes notice of the formal qualities of the song seems to be required.

IX

The Sad Shepherd has been considered by some to be an early play which was abandoned, not a play left unfinished at Jonson's death. I believe that the play must have been the last piece Jonson wrote: for it seems to draw together a lifetime's preoccupation with the essential qualities of Elizabethan drama. *The Sad Shepherd* takes us back to the pastoral drama whose conventions lie behind scenes in the first and last acts of *Cynthia's Revels*, and it takes us back to the robust, positive qualities of *Volpone* asserted there within the lasting truths of traditional fable. But it also carries us forward through the idealism of the masque world, its attempts to vindicate an artistic theory which will unite all art forms as a single Truth; and beyond, to *The New Inn* where the fleeting images of the masque are to be preserved within the theatre itself as a centre of community life. So although *The New Inn* was badly received and although the Caroline public now looked for something more sensational, no longer believing that a play's 'teaching' could also 'delight', the inadequacies of such an audience are now of no real significance. The lessons of this play belonged in the more stable world of the Jacobean period and had found their expression almost twenty years before in Shakespeare's last plays. *The Sad Shepherd* would have restated the values of *The New Inn*, but in a form which, centred on its elaborate picture set, would have relied more heavily on the popular qualities of the masque—while making no concession to popularity. Music in other plays for the late Jacobean and the Caroline theatre developed more sensational and virtuoso characteristics. This concentration on surface brilliance is a characteristic which we observe Jonson avoiding anew in each of his later works.

The New Inn* and *The Sad Shepherd* suggest an answer to the possibilities and problems raised by the masque in its attempt to create an ideal union of the arts. They also suggest an answer to the problem of how to resolve within its audience the image which the masque presented. In working out these problems Jonson exposed to scrutiny the very nature of his art.

Bibliography

PART I. CONTEMPORARY MANUSCRIPT AND PRINTED SOURCES OF MUSIC FOR JONSON'S PLAYS AND MASQUES

I. MANUSCRIPTS

Bodleian Library

Don. c. 57. Songs, mainly treble and bass, probably entered between 1630 and 1660.

    J. P. Cutts, 'A Bodleian Song-Book'.

    G. A. Thewlis, 'Some Notes on a Bodleian Manuscript'.

no. 97: 'Come noble Nymphs.' *Neptune's Triumph* and *The Fortunate Isles*.

Mus. b. 1. Songs, mainly treble and bass, by John Wilson, *c.*1656.

    M. Crum, 'A Manuscript of John Wilson's Songs'.

    J. P. Cutts, 'Seventeenth-Century Lyrics'.

ff. 137ᵛ–138: 'Though I am young & cannot tell.' *The Sad Shepherd*.

British Library

Additional 10444. A collection mainly of masque dances, treble and bass in separate books now bound as one volume, the treble part in the hand of Sir Nicholas Le Strange. The pieces were probably entered *c.* 1624–6.

    J. P. Cutts, 'Jacobean Masque and Stage Music'.

    J. Knowlton, 'Dating the Masque Dances in British Museum Add. MS 10444'.

    W. J. Lawrence, 'Notes on a Collection of Masque Music'.

    A. J. Sabol, *Songs and Dances for the Stuart Masque*.

    P. J. Willetts, 'Sir Nicholas Le Strange's Collection of Masque Music'.

ff. 42/92; 42ᵛ–43/92–92ᵛ: Antimasque and three main-masque dances for *Hymenaei*.

ff. 21–21ᵛ/74ᵛ–75: The first and second witches' dances from *Queens*.

ff. 31/82ᵛ: Satyrs' masque; ff. 31ᵛ/83: Fairies' masque from *Oberon*.

ff. 16/70ᵛ–71; 16ᵛ/71; 16ᵛ–17/71ᵛ: A group of three main-masque dances entitled 'The Prince's Masque' which *may* belong to *Oberon*.

ff. 29ᵛ/81: Fools' dance: antimasque dance for *Love Freed*.

ff. 45ᵛ/95: The Goats' Masque; ff. 45ᵛ–46/95ᵛ–96: antimasque and main-masque dances from *Pleasure Reconciled* and *For the Honour of Wales*.

ff. 19ᵛ/73ᵛ: Birds' Dance: antimasque dance for *News From the New World*.

ff. 32ᵛ/83ᵛ–84: Gypsies' masque from *The Gypsies Metamorphosed*.

ff. 19/73 Bears' dance: antimasque dance for *Augurs*.

Additional 11608. Songs, treble and bass, mostly entered in the hand of John Hilton but with ornaments and embellishments in one or, possibly, two other hands. *c.* 1642–59.

    M. Chan, 'British Library MS Add. 11, 608'.

f. 80ᵛ: 'Beauties have you seen a toy.' *Haddington Masque*.

f. 81: 'Beauties, have yee seene a Toy.' *Haddington Masque* (three-part setting).

f. 17ᵛ: 'Doe not expect to heare.' *Augurs*.

Additional 15117. Songs and instrumental pieces with tablature. The manuscript is in several hands and may have belonged to an acting company.

M. Joiner, 'British Museum MS Add. 15117.'

f. 20ᵛ: 'Come my Celia,' *Volpone*.

f. 17ᵛ: 'Haue you seene but a whyte lillie grow.' *The Devil is an Ass*.

Additional 17786–91. Part-songs mostly from late sixteenth and early seventeenth centuries. Compiled early seventeenth century.

f. 5: 'The wyche': first witches' dance for the antimasque of *Queens*.

Additional 24665. Songs, treble and bass. The book belonged to Giles Earle and is early seventeenth century.

ff. 59ᵛ–60: 'Yf I freely may discouer.'

Additional 29396. Songs, treble and bass, in the hand of Edward Lowe. *c.*1636–80.

M. Chan, 'British Library MS Add. 29, 396: the case for re-dating'.

M. Chan, 'Drolls, Drolleries and mid-seventeenth-century dramatic music'.

ff. 71ᵛ–72ᵛ: 'Why this is a sport.' *The Gypsies Metamorphosed*.

Additional 29481. Songs, treble and bass. Early seventeenth century.

f. 21 'Haue you seene the white lillie flower.' *The Devil is an Ass*.

Additional 36661. Virginal music. Early seventeenth century.

ff. 54ᵛ & 54 Two almans by Robert Johnson which *may* belong to the main masque of *Oberon*.

Additional 38539. A collection of lute music in tablature possibly compiled by John Sturt. Early seventeenth century.

f. 4: First witches' dance for the antimasque of *Queens*.

f. 10: Fairies' dance for the antimasque of *Oberon*.

ff. 16 & 17: Two almans by Robert Johnson which may belong to the main masque of *Oberon*.

Additional 53723. Henry Lawes autograph song-book. Compiled *c.*1634–50.

P. J. Willetts, *The Henry Lawes Manuscript*.

f. 5: 'O yt Joye soe soone should waste.' *Cynthia's Revels*.

f. 7: 'If I freely may discouer.' *Poetaster*.

f. 36ᵛ: 'Beautyes haue yee seene a Toye.' *Haddington Masque*.

Egerton 2013. Songs, mostly treble and bass, some with tablature. Mid-seventeenth century.

f. 45ᵛ: 'I was not wearier.' *Vision of Delight*.

Christ Church Library, Oxford

Mus. 44. Music in treble and bass, mid-seventeenth century.

f. 132ᵛ 'The Gipsies Maske'. *The Gypsies Metamorphosed*

Mus. 87. Songs, treble and bass. The book belonged to 'Mrs. Elizabeth Davenant' in 1624.

J. P. Cutts, '"Mʳⁱˢ Elizabeth Davenant 1624" Christ Church MS Mus 87'.

ff. 4ᵛ–5: 'Haue you seene the white lilly grow,' *The Devil is an Ass.*

Mus. 92. Virginal music. Early seventeenth century.

ff. 15–15ᵛ: The second witches' dance for the antimasque of *Queens.*

Mus. 439. Songs, treble and bass, from the late sixteenth and early seventeenth centuries.

    M. Chan, '*Cynthia's Revels* and Music for a Choir School'.

pp. 38–9: 'O the joyes.' *Cynthia's Revels.*

p. 31: 'Come away.' *Blackness.*

p. 93: 'If all these cupides.' *Beauty.*

p. 94: 'It was no pollicie of court.' *Beauty.*

p. 96: 'Yes weare the loues.' *Beauty.*

pp. 60–1: 'Why stayes the bridgrome.' *Haddington Masque.*

p. 95: 'If all the ages of the earth.' *Queens.*

New York Public Library

Drexel 4041. Songs, treble and bass. *c.*1630–50.

    J. P. Cutts, 'Drexel MS 4041'.

f. 45ᵛ: 'Still to be neat.' *Epicoene.*

Drexel 4175. Songs in treble and bass, some with tablature accompaniments. Belonged to Ann Twice. Compiled probably before 1630.

    J. P. Cutts, '"Songs unto the Violl and Lute"—Drexel MS 4175'.

no. xlix: 'Haue yu seene ye.' *The Devil is an Ass.* (A version with lute accompaniment is mentioned in the table of contents as no. xxxix but is no longer extant.)

Drexel 4257. Songs, treble and bass. Belonged to John Gamble. Compiled probably *c.*1630–59.

    V. Duckles, 'The Gamble MS as a Source of *Continuo* Song in England'.

    V. Duckles, 'John Gamble's Commonplace Book'.

    C. W. Hughes, 'John Gamble's Commonplace Book'.

no. 25: 'If I freely may discover.' *Poetaster.*

no. 179: 'Still to be neat.' *Epicoene.*

no. 2: 'See the chariot at hand.' *The Devil is an Ass.* (This is the only extant version which sets the first stanza.)

no. 37: 'Beauties, have you seen a toy.' *Haddington Masque.*

no. 177: 'To the old long life and treasure.' *The Gypsies Metamorphosed.*

no. 92: 'Cock lorell would needs have the devil his guest.' *The Gypsies Metamorphosed.*

St Michael's College, Tenbury

1018/1019. Songs, English and Italian, mainly treble and bass. Before 1625.

    J. P. Cutts, 'Early Seventeenth-Century Lyrics at St. Michael's College'.

f. 36: 'Nay nay you must not stay. *Oberon.*

ff. 37ᵛ–38: 'Gentle Knights.' *Oberon.*

f. 36ᵛ: 'O what a fault.' *Love Freed.*

f. 37: 'Sences by vniust force bannisht.'? *Love Freed.*

f. 37–37ᵛ: 'How neere to good is what is fayre.' *Love Freed.*

Cambridge, Fitzwilliam Museum

Fitzwilliam Virginal Book. Virginal music. Belonged to Francis Tregian. Early seventeenth century.

nos. 146 & 145: Two almans by Robert Johnson arranged by Richard Farnaby which *may* belong to the main masque of *Oberon*.

Trinity College, Dublin

D. 1. 21. Lute music in tablature. Belonged to William Ballet. Early seventeenth century.

p. 65: Music for the first witches' dance in the antimasque of *Queens*.

F. 5. 13. The quintus part-book of Thomas Wode's Psalter, with treble part of songs. Early seventeenth century.

no. 201: 'Have you seen but a white lily grow'. *The Devil is an Ass*.

Edinburgh University Library

La. III. 483. The tenor and bass part-books of Thomas Wode's Psalter. Early seventeenth century.

no. 201: 'Have you seen but a white lily grow'. *The Devil is an Ass*.

Cromwell Museum, Huntingdon

MS on loan from The London Museum, Kensington Palace, 46.78/748. Anne Cromwell's Virginal Book, dated 1638.

no. 30 (ff. 21ᵛ–22) 'The Duke of Buckeingham's Masque'. *The Gypsies Metamorphosed*.

In the private collection of Robert Spencer
Margaret Board Manuscript.

f. 26: 'The witches Daunce.' The first dance for the antimasque of *Queens*.

f. 41: Third masque dance for *Queens*.

f. 38ᵛ: 'The Gipsies dance.' *The Gypsies Metamorphosed*.

f. 39ᵛ: 'The beares danc.' *Augurs*.

2. PRINTED SOURCES

Brade, William, *Newe ausserlesene liebliche Branden . . .* (Hamburg, 1617).

no. VIII: 'Des jungen Printzen Intrada', *Pleasure Reconciled* and *For the Honour of Wales*.

no. XLIX: 'Der Hexen Tanz', first witches' dance for *Queens*.

Dowland, Robert, *Varietie of Lute-Lessons* (London, 1610).

Sig. P.1ᵛ–P.2ᵛ: Music for the three main-masque dances and the first witches' dance in *Queens*.

D'Urfey, Thomas, *Wit and Mirth: or Pills to Purge Melancholy* (London, 1700).

Part II, pp. 101–3: A setting to a popular tune of 'Cock-Lorell would needs have the Devil his guest' from *The Gypsies Metamorphosed*.

Ferrabosco, Alfonso, *Ayres* (London, 1609).

no. 3: 'Come away', *Blackness*.

no. 6: 'Come my Celia', *Volpone*.

no. 11: 'Why stays the Bridegroom', *Haddington Masque*.
nos. 18–20: 'If all these Cupids'
　　　　'It was no policy of Court'
　　　　'Yes, were the Loves'
no. 21: 'So Beauty on the waters stood'
no. 22: 'Had those that dwell in error foul', *Beauty*.
no. 23: 'When all the ages of the earth', *Queens*.
Lawes, Henry, *The Second Book of Ayres and Dialogues* (London, 1655).
　Sig. L.3 (p. 41): 'Beauties, have you seen a Toy' (3 parts), *Haddington Masque*.
The Musical Companion (London, 1667).
　Sig. L.2 (p. 75): 'Buz quoth the blue fly', *Oberon*.
The Musical Companion (London, 1672, 1673).
　pp. 88–9: 'From the famous Peak of Derby', *The Gypsies Metamorphosed*.
Playford, John, *Select Musical Ayres and Dialogues* (London, 1652).
　p. 24: 'Though I am young', *The Sad Shepherd*.
—— *Select Ayres and Dialogues* (London, 1659). (Reprinted as Part I of *The Treasury of Music*, 1669).
　p. 14: 'Come noble nymphs', *Neptune's Triumph, The Fortunate Isles*.
—— *Select Ayres and Dialogues*, Second Book (London, 1669).
　(Book II of *The Treasury of Music*, 1669.)
　p. 51: 'Beauties, have you seen a toy', *Haddington Masque*.
　p. 75: 'Still to be neat', *Epicoene*.
Simpson, William, *Taffel-Consort* (Hamburg, 1621).
　no. XXIV: Satyrs' dance from *Oberon*.
Youll, Henry, *Canzonets to Three Voices* (London, 1608).
　Song 8: 'Slow, slow fresh fount', *Cynthia's Revels*.

PART II. WORKS CONSULTED IN THE STUDY OF EARLY SEVENTEENTH-CENTURY MUSIC AND LITERATURE

A Book of Masques, In Honour of Allardyce Nicoll (Cambridge, 1967).
Adams, J. C., *The Globe Playhouse: Its Design and Equipment* (London, 1961).
Adams, J. Q., 'The Sources of Ben Jonson's *Volpone*', *Modern Philology*, ii (1904), p. 289.
Akrigg, G. P. V., '*Twelfth Night* at the Middle Temple', *Shakespeare Quarterly*, ix (1958), p. 422.
Aldrich, Putnam, 'An Approach to the Analysis of Renaissance Music', *The Music Review*, xxx (1969), p. 1.
Alpers, Paul J., 'Narrative and Rhetoric in *The Faerie Queene*', *Elizabethan Poetry: Modern Essays in Criticism*, ed. P. J. Alpers (London, 1969), p. 380.
—— *The Poetry of 'The Faerie Queene'* (Princeton, 1967).
Arkwright, G. E. P., 'Elizabethan Choirboy Plays and their Music', *Proc. Royal Musical Association*, 40th session (1913/14), p. 117.
Armstrong, John, *The Paradise Myth* (London, 1969).

ARMSTRONG, WILLIAM A., 'The English Private Theatres: Facts and Problems', The Society for Theatre Research Pamphlet Series, no. 6 (1957–8). (London, 1958).

ARTHOS, JOHN, '*Pericles, Prince of Tyre*: A Study in the Dramatic Use of Romantic Narrative', *Shakespeare Quarterly*, IV (1953), p. 257.

ASCHAM, ROGER, *Works*, ed. J. A. Giles, 3 Vols. (London, 1864).

BALDWIN, C. S., *Renaissance Literary Theory and Practice: Classicism in the Rhetoric and Poetic of Italy, France and England, 1400–1600* (New York, 1939; reprint, Gloucester, Mass., 1959).

BAMBOROUGH, J. B., *Ben Jonson* (London, 1970).

BARISH, JONAS A., 'The Double Plot in *Volpone*', *Modern Philology*, LI (1953), p. 83.

—— *Ben Jonson and the Language of Prose Comedy* (Cambridge, Mass., 1960).

BARKER, W. L., 'Three English Pantalones: A Study in Relations between the *Commedia dell' Arte* and Elizabethan Drama', Ph. D. dissertation, University of Connecticut, 1966.

BASKERVILL, C. R., *The Sources of Jonson's 'Masque of Christmas' and 'Love's Welcome at Welbeck'*, reprinted from *Modern Philology*, Vol. VI (Chicago, 1908).

—— *The Elizabethan Jig and Related Song Drama* (Chicago, 1929).

BAXANDALL, MICHAEL, *Giotto and the Orators: Humanist Observers of Painting in Italy and the Discovery of Pictorial Composition, 1350–1450* (Oxford, 1971).

BEAUMONT, F. and FLETCHER, J., *Works*, ed. Arnold Glover and A. R. Waller, 10 Vols. (Cambridge, 1905–12).

BEAUMONT, F. and FLETCHER, J., *The Dramatic Works of Beaumont and Fletcher and the Fletcher Canon*, ed. F. Bowers, Vols. I and II only (Cambridge, 1966).

BECK, SIDNEY, 'The Case of "O Mistress Mine"', *Renaissance News*, VI (1953), p. 19.

BECK (ed.) s.v. MORLEY

BELL s.v. SIMPSON.

BENTLEY, GERALD EADES, *The Jacobean and Caroline Stage*, 5 Vols. (Oxford, 1941–56).

BERGERON, DAVID M., 'The Emblematic Nature of English Civic Pageantry', *Renaissance Drama*, New Series, I, ed. S. Schoenbaum (Evanston, 1968).

—— *English Civic Pageantry, 1558–1642* (London, 1971).

BEST, M. R., 'A Note on the Songs in Lyly's Plays', *Notes and Queries*, n.s. XII (1965), p. 93.

BETHEL, S. L., '*The Winter's Tale*': A Study (London, n.d.: ? 1945/8).

BIGGINS, DENIS, '"Exit, pursued by a Beare": A Problem in *The Winter's Tale*', *Shakespeare Quarterly*, XIII (1962), p. 3.

BOARD, MARGARET, *The Board Lute Book*. With an introductory study by Robert Spencer. Boethius Press Reproductions of Early Music IV (Leeds, 1976).

BOCCACCIO, GIOVANNI, *Decameron* (In *Decameron, Filocolo, Ameto, Fiammetta*), A cura di Enrico Bianchi (Milan, 1952).

—— *Decameron*, translated anon, 1620. Edited with an introduction by Edward Hutton. Tudor Translations, Vols. XLI–XLIV (A.M.S. reprint, New York, 1967).

BONTOUX, GERMAINE, *La Chanson en Angleterre au temps d'Elisabeth* (London, 1936).

BOUGHNER, DANIEL C., *The Devil's Disciple* (New York, 1968).

—— 'Jonsonian Structure in *The Tempest*', *Shakespeare Quarterly*, XXI (1970), p. 3.

BOUGHTON, RUTLAND, 'Shakespeare's Ariel: A Study of Musical Character', *Musical Quarterly*, II (1916), p. 538.

BOWDEN, WILLIAM R., *The English Dramatic Lyric* (New Haven, 1951).

BOYD, M. C., *Elizabethan Music and Musical Criticism* (Philadelphia, 1940).

BRADBROOK, M. C., *Themes and Conventions of Elizabethan Tragedy* (Cambridge, 1935).

—— *Shakespeare and Elizabethan Poetry* (London, 1951).

—— *The Growth and Structure of Elizabethan Comedy* (London, 1955).

—— *Shakespeare the Craftsman*, The Clark Lectures, 1968 (London, 1969).

—— 'Social Change and the Evolution of Ben Jonson's Court Masques', *Studies in the Literary Imagination*, VI (1973), p. 101.

BRADNER, LEICESTER, *The Life and Poems of Richard Edwards*, Yale Studies in English (New Haven, 1927).

BRENNECKE, ERNEST, 'Shakespeare's Musical Collaboration with Morley', *Publications of the Modern Language Association*, LIV (1939), p. 139.

—— 'Shakespeare's "Singing Man of Windsor"', *Publications of the Modern Language Association*, LXVI (1951), p. 1188.

—— 'A Singing Man of Windsor', *Music and Letters*, XXXIX (1958), p. 33.

BRETT, PHILIP, 'The English Consort Song, 1570–1625', *Proc. Royal Musical Association*, 88th session (1961/62), p. 73.

—— 'The Songs of William Byrd', Ph.D. thesis, Cambridge, 1965.

—— (ed.), *Consort Songs*, Musica Britannica, XXII (London, 1967).

BRIDGE, J. F., *Shakespearean Music in the Plays and Early Operas* (London, 1923).

BROTANEK, R., *Die englischen Maskenspiele*, Schipper's Wiener Beiträge . . . , 15 (Vienna and Leipzig, 1902).

BROWN, DAVID, *Thomas Weelkes. A biographical and critical study* (London, 1969).

BRYANT, JERRY H., '*The Winter's Tale* and the Pastoral Tradition', *Shakespeare Quarterly*, XIV (1963), p. 387.

BUSH, DOUGLAS, *Mythology and the Renaissance Tradition in English Poetry* (Minneapolis and London, 1932).

BUSH, GEOFFREY, *Shakespeare and the Natural Condition* (Cambridge, Mass., 1956).

BUXTON, JOHN, *Sir Philip Sidney and the English Renaissance* (London, 1954).

BYRD, WILLIAM, *The Collected Works of William Byrd*, ed. E. H. Fellowes, 20 Vols. London, 1937–50).

CAMDEN, WILLIAM, *Annales rerum Anglicarum et Hibernicarum, Regnante Elizabetha, ad Annum salutis. MDLXXXIX* (London, 1615).

CAMPBELL, LILY B., *Scenes and Machines on the English Stage During the Renaissance* (Cambridge, 1923).

CAMPION, THOMAS, *The Works of Thomas Campion*, ed. Percival Vivian (Oxford, 1909, 1966).

CARAPETYAN, ARMEN, 'The Concept of *Imitazione della Natura* in the Sixteenth Century', *Journal of Renaissance and Baroque Music*, I (1946), p. 47.

CARPENTER, NAN COOKE, 'The Word "Simbolisme" in "The Praise of Music" by John Case (1586)', *Notes and Queries*, n.s. III (1956). p. 416.

CARROLL, WILLIAM MEREDITH, *Animal Conventions in English Renaissance Non-religious Prose (1550–1600)* (New York, 1954).

CASTIGLIONE, B., *Il libro del cortegiano* (Florence, 1528).

——*The Book of the Courtier*. Done into English by Sir Thomas Hoby, anno 1561. Edited with an introduction by Walter Raleigh (London, 1900).

CAXTON, WILLIAM, *The History of Renard the Fox*, edited from the edition of 1481 with an introduction and notes by D. B. Sands (Cambridge, Mass., 1960).

CHAMBERS, E. K., *The Elizabethan Stage*, 4 Vols. (Oxford, 1923).

CHAMPION, LARRY S., *Ben Jonson's 'Dotages': A Reconsideration of the Late Plays* (Lexington, 1967).

CHAN. s.v. STERNFELD.

CHAN, MARY, '*Cynthia's Revels* and Music for a Choir School: Christ Church MS Mus 439', *Studies in the Renaissance*, XVIII (1971), p. 134.

——'British Library Manuscript Additional 29,396: the case for re-dating', *Music and Letters*, LIX (1978), p. 440.

——'Drolls, Drolleries and mid-seventeenth-century dramatic music', Royal Musical Association *Research Chronicle* XV (1979), p. 117.

——'British Library Manuscript Additional 11,608: John Hilton's Manuscript', *Music and Letters* (forthcoming).

CHAPMAN, G., *The Plays and Poems of George Chapman*, edited with introduction and notes by T. M. Parrott. Library of Scholarship and Letters, 2 Vols. only (London, 1910–14).

CHAPPELL, WILLIAM, *The Ballad Literature and Popular Music of the Olden Time*, 2 Vols. (London, 1855–9). Edited with introduction and notes by F. W. Sternfeld, 2 Vols. (New York, 1965).

CHUTE, MARCHETTE, *Ben Jonson of Westminster* (London, 1954).

CLEMEN, WOLFGANG, *English Tragedy Before Shakespeare*, trans. T. S. Dorsch (London, 1961).

COATES. s.v. DART.

COPE, JACKSON, I., *The Theater and the Dream: from Metaphor to Form in Renaissance Drama* (Baltimore and London, 1973).

COVELL, R., 'Music for *The Tempest*', *Studies in Music*, II (1968), p. 43.

COWLING, G. H., *Music on the Shakespearean Stage* (Cambridge, 1913).

CRAIK, T. W., *The Tudor Interlude: Stage, Costume and Acting* (Leicester, 1958).

CRANE, WILLIAM G., *Wit and Rhetoric in the Renaissance: the Formal Basis of Elizabethan Prose Style* (New York, 1937).

CROMWELL, ANNE, *Anne Cromwell's Virginal Book 1638*. Transcribed and edited by Howard Ferguson. (London, 1974).

CRUM, MARGARET, 'A Manuscript of John Wilson's Songs', *The Library*, 5th ser. x (1955), p. 55.

CUNLIFFE, J. W. (ed), *Early English Classical Tragedies* (Oxford, 1912).

CUTTS, J. P., 'Two Jacobean Theatre Songs', *Music and Letters*, XXXIII (1952), p. 333.

——'British Museum Manuscript Additional 31432: William Lawes' writing for the theatre and the court', *The Library*, 5th ser. VII (1952), p. 225.

——'A Bodleian Song-Book: Don. c.57', *Music and Letters*, XXXIV (1953), p. 192.

——'Jacobean Masque and Stage Music', *Music and Letters*, XXXV (1954), p. 185.

——'Original Music to Browne's Inner Temple Masque and Other Jacobean Masque Music', *Notes and Queries*, n.s. I (1954), p. 194.

——'Robert Johnson: King's Musician in His Majesty's Public Entertainment', *Music and Letters*, XXXVI (1955), p. 110.

——'Some Jacobean and Caroline Dramatic Lyrics', *Notes and Queries*, n.s. II (1955), p. 106.

——'Thomas Goffe's "The Courageous Turke"', *Notes and Queries*, n.s. II (1955), p. 333.

——'An Unpublished Contemporary Setting of a Shakespeare Song', *Shakespeare Survey*, IX (1956), p. 86.

——'Ben Jonson's Masque, "The Vision of Delight"', *Notes and Queries*, n.s. III (1956), p. 64.

——'Early Seventeenth-Century Lyrics at St. Michael's College', *Music and Letters*, XXXVII (1956), p. 221.

——'Le Rôle de la musique dans les masques de Ben Jonson et notamment dans *Obéron* (1610–11)', *Les Fêtes de la Renaissance*, 2 Vols. Éditions du centre national de la recherche scientifique (Paris, 1956), I, p. 285.

——'Seventeenth-Century Lyrics: Oxford Bodleian MS Mus. b. 1', *Musica Disciplina*, x (1956), p. 142.

——'The Original Music of a Song in *2 Henry IV*', *Shakespeare Quarterly*, VII (1956), p. 385.

——'The Original Music to Middleton's *The Witch*', *Shakespeare Quarterly*, VII (1956), p. 203.

——'Music and the Supernatural in *The Tempest*: A Study in Interpretation', *Music and Letters*, XXXIX (1958), p. 347.

——'Peele's *Hunting of Cupid*', *Studies in the Renaissance*, V (1958), p. 121.

——'Who Wrote the Hecate Scene?', *Shakespeare Jahrbuch*, XCIV (1958), p. 200.

——*La Musique de la troupe de Shakespeare: The King's Men sous la règne de Jacques Ier*. Édition critique par J. P. Cutts; Préface par Allardyce Nicoll. Éditions du centre national de la recherche scientifique (Paris, 1959).

——'Seventeenth-Century Songs and Lyrics in Edinburgh University Library, Music MS Dc. 1. 69', *Musica Disciplina*, XIII (1959), p. 169.

——'"M^ris Elizabeth Davenant 1624" Christ Church MS Mus 87', *Review of English Studies*, x (1959), p. 26.

——'Falstaff's "Heauenlie Iewel", Incidental Music for *The Merry Wives of Windsor*', *Shakespeare Quarterly*, XI (1960), p. 89.

—— 'Pericles' "Most Heauenly Musicke"', *Notes and Queries*, n.s. VII (1960), p. 172.

—— 'Robert Johnson and the Court Masque', *Music and Letters*, XLI (1960), p. 111.

—— '"Speak-demand-we'll answer": Hecate and "the *other* Three Witches"', *Shakespeare Jahrbuch*, XCVI (1960), p. 173.

—— 'Music and *The Mad Lover*', *Studies in the Renaissance*, VIII (1961), p. 236.

—— '"Songs unto the Violl and Lute"—Drexel MS 4175', *Musica Disciplina*, XVI (1962), p. 73.

—— 'The Strange Fortunes of Two Excellent Princes and *The Arbor of Amorous Devises*', *Renaissance News*, XV (1962), p. 2.

—— 'Shakespeare's Song and Masque Hand in *Henry VIII*', *Shakespeare Jahrbuch*, XCIX (1963), p. 184.

—— 'Drexel MS 4041', *Musica Disciplina*, XVIII (1964), p. 152.

DANBY, JOHN, *Poets on Fortune's Hill* (London, 1952).

—— *Shakespeare's Doctrine of Nature* (London, 1961).

DANIEL, SAMUEL, *A Defence of Ryme*. In Smith (ed.), q.v., II, p. 356.

DART, THURSTON, 'Morley's *Consort Lessons* of 1599', *Proc. Royal Musical Association*, 74th session (1947/48), p. 1.

—— 'Jacobean Consort Music', *Proc. Royal Musical Association*, 81st session (1954/55), p. 63.

—— 'Origines et sources de la musique de chambre en Angleterre (1500–1530)', *La Musique instrumentale de la Renaissance*, Éditions du centre national de la recherche scientifique (Paris, 1955), p. 77.

—— 'A Hand-list of English Instrumental Music Printed Before 1681', *Galpin Society Journal*, VIII (1955), p. 13.

—— 'Ornament Signs in Jacobean Music for Lute and Viol', *Galpin Society Journal*, XIV (1961), p. 30.

—— and COATES, WILLIAM (ed.), *Jacobean Consort Music*, Musica Britannica, IX. 2nd rev. edn. (London, 1966).

DAVIS, HERBERT (ed.), *Elizabethan and Jacobean Studies Presented to Frank Percy Wilson* (Oxford, 1959).

DAY, CYRUS L. and MURRIE, ELEANORE B., *English Song Books, 1651–1702* (London, 1940).

DEACON, RICHARD, *John Dee: Scientist, Geographer, Astrologer and Secret Agent to Elizabeth I* (London, 1968).

DENT, E. J., 'The Musical Interpretation of Shakespeare on the Modern Stage', *Musical Quarterly*, II (1916), p. 523.

—— *Foundations of English Opera* (Cambridge, 1928; reprint, New York, 1965).

—— 'The Musical Form of the Madrigal', *Music and Letters*, XI (1930), p. 230.

—— 'Shakespeare and Music', in *Companion to Shakespeare Studies*, ed. H. Granville-Barker and G. B. Harrison (Cambridge, 1934).

DODDS, M. H., 'Songs in Lyly's Plays', *Times Literary Supplement* (28 June 1941), p. 311.

DONALDSON, IAN, 'Jonson's Tortoise', *Review of English Studies*, n.s. XIX (1968), p. 162.

—— *The World Upside-Down: Comedy from Jonson to Fielding* (Oxford, 1970).

—— 'Volpone: Quick and Dead', *Essays in Criticism*, XXI (1971), p. 121.

DONINGTON, ROBERT, 'On Interpreting Early Music', *Music and Letters*, XXVIII (1947), p. 223.

—— *The Instruments of Music* (London, 1949).

—— *The Interpretation of Early Music* (London, 1963).

DORAN, MADELEINE, *Endeavours of Art: A Study of Form in Elizabethan Drama* (Madison, 1954).

DOUGHTIE, EDWARD, 'Ferrabosco and Jonson's "The Houre-glasse"', *Renaissance Quarterly*, XXII (1969), p. 148.

DRYDEN, JOHN, *Essays of John Dryden*. Selected and edited by W. P. Ker, 2 Vols. (New York, 1961; reprint of edn. of 1899).

DUCHARTRE, PIERRE LOUIS, *The Italian Comedy*, trans. R. T. Weaver (London, 1929; reprint New York, 1966).

DUCKLES, VINCENT, 'The Gamble MS as a Source of *Continuo* Song in England', *Journal of the American Musicological Society*, I (1948), p. 23.

—— 'Jacobean Theatre Songs', *Music and Letters*, XXXIV (1953), p. 88.

—— 'John Gamble's Commonplace Book: A Critical Edition of New York Public Library MS Drexel 4257', Ph.D. dissertation, University of California, 1953.

—— 'New Light on "O Mistress Mine"', *Renaissance News*, VII (1954), p. 98.

—— 'The "Curious" Art of John Wilson (1595–1674): An Introduction to his Songs and Lute Music', *Journal of the American Musicological Society*, VII (1954), p. 93.

—— 'The Music for the Lyrics in Early Seventeenth-Century English Drama: A Bibliography of Primary Sources', in *Music in English Renaissance Drama*, ed. John H. Long (Lexington, 1968), p. 117.

DUHAMEL, P. A., 'The Function of Rhetoric as Effective Expression', *Journal of the History of Ideas*, X (1949), p. 344.

DUNCAN, DOUGLAS, 'A Guide to *The New Inn*', *Essays in Criticism*, XX (1970), p. 311.

DUNN, CATHERINE M., 'The Function of Music in Shakespeare's Romances', *Shakespeare Quarterly*, XX (1969), p. 391.

ECCLES, MARK, 'Martin Peerson and the Blackfriars', *Shakespeare Survey*, XI (1958), p. 100.

EDWARDS, RICHARD, *The Excellent Comedie of . . . Damon and Pithias* (London, 1571). Malone Society Reprint, ed. Arthur Brown and F. P. Wilson (Oxford, 1957).

—— *The Paradise of Dainty Devices*, ed. H. E. Rollins (Cambridge, Mass., 1927).

EGGAR, KATHERINE E., 'The Blackfriars Plays and their Music: 1576–1610', *Proc. Royal Musical Association*, 87th session (1960/61), p. 57.

EINSTEIN, ALFRED, 'The Elizabethan Madrigal and "Musica Transalpina"', *Music and Letters*, XXV (1944), p. 66.

EINSTEIN, LEWIS, *The Italian Renaissance in England* (New York, 1902).

ELLIOTT, K. and SHIRE, H. (ed.), *Music of Scotland 1500–1700*, Musica Britannica, XV. 2nd rev. edn. (London, 1964).

ELLIS-FERMOR, UNA, 'Some Functions of Verbal Music in Drama', *Shakespeare Jahrbuch*, XC (1954), p. 37.

ELYOT, SIR THOMAS, *The Book named the Governor*, ed. S. E. Lehmberg. Everyman's Library (London, 1907, 1962).

EMPSON, WILLIAM, *Some Versions of Pastoral* (London, 1935).

—— '*Volpone*', *The Hudson Review*, XXI (1968), p. 651.

EMSLIE, MACDONALD, 'Three Early Settings of Jonson', *Notes and Queries*, CXCVIII (1953), p. 466.

—— 'Dowland, Ornithoparcus, and Musica Mundana', *Notes and Queries*, n.s. I (1954), p. 372.

—— 'Words and Music in English Song 1622–1700', Ph.D. thesis, Cambridge, 1957.

—— 'Nicholas Lanier's Innovations in English Song', *Music and Letters*, XLI (1960), p. 13.

ENRIGHT, D. J., 'Poetic Satire and Satire in Verse: A Consideration of Jonson and Massinger', *Scrutiny*, XVIII (1951/52), p. 211.

ERASMUS, D., *The Praise of Folie*, trans. Sir Thomas Chaloner (1549). Ed. Clarence H. Miller, Early English Text Society (London, 1965).

EVANS, WILLA McCLUNG, *Ben Jonson and Elizabethan Music* (Lancaster, Pennsylvania, 1929).

EWBANK, INGA-STINA, 'The Triumph of Time in *The Winter's Tale*', *Review of English Literature*, V (1964), p. 83.

FELLOWES, E. H. (ed.), *The English Madrigal School*, 36 Vols. (London, 1913–24).

—— (ed.), *The English School of Lutenist Song Writers*, 1st. ser., 16 Vols. (London, 1920–32); 2nd ser., 8 Vols. (London, 1925–6).

—— (ed.), *Songs and Lyrics from the Plays of Beaumont and Fletcher* (London, 1928).

—— 'The Songs of Dowland', *Proc. Royal Musical Association*, 56th session (1929/1930), p. 1.

—— *The Catalogue of Manuscripts in the Library of St. Michael's College Tenbury*, Éditions de l'oiseau-lyre (Paris, 1934).

FELLOWES (ed.) s.v. Byrd.

FELVER, CHARLES S., 'Robert Armin's Fragment of a Bawdy Ballad of "Mary Ambree"', *Notes and Queries*, n.s. VII (1960), p. 14.

FESTUGIÈRE, JEAN, *La Philosophie de l'amour de Marsile Ficin, et son influence sur la littérature française au XVIe siècle*, Études de philosophie médiévale, XXXI (Paris, 1941).

FESTUGIÈRE, A. J., *Hermétisme et mystique païenne* (Paris, 1967).

FICINO, MARSILIO, *Opera* (Basle, 1576).

—— *Commentary on the 'Symposium' of Plato on the Subject of Love*. Text, a translation and introduction by S. R. Jayne, University of Missouri Studies, Vol. XIX, no. 1 (Columbia, 1944).

—— *Five Questions Concerning the Mind*. Trans. Josephine L. Burroughs, in *The Renaissance Philosophy of Man*, ed. Ernst Cassirer, Paul Oscar Kristeller, John Herman Randall, Jr. (Chicago and London, 1948, 1956), p. 185.

FINKELPEARL, PHILIP J., *John Marston of the Middle Temple* (Cambridge, Mass., 1969).

FINNEY, GRETCHEN L., 'Ecstasy and Music in Seventeenth-Century England', *Journal of the History of Ideas*, VIII (1947), p. 153, p. 273.

——'World of Instruments', *English Literary History* (1953), p. 87.

——*Musical Backgrounds for English Literature, 1580–1650* (New Brunswick, N.J., 1962).

FITZGIBBON, H. MACAULAY, 'The Lute Books of Ballet and Dallis', *Music and Letters*, XI (1930), p. 71.

——'Instruments and their music in the Elizabethan Drama', *Musical Quarterly*, XVII (1931), p. 319.

Fitzwilliam Virginal Book, The. Edited from the original MS with an introduction and notes by J. A. Fuller Maitland and W. Barclay Squire. Republication of the work published by Breitkopf and Hartel in 1899. Dover Publications, 2 vol. (New York, 1963).

FLATTER, RICHARD, 'Who Wrote the Hecate Scene?', *Shakespeare Jahrbuch*, XCIII (1957), p. 196.

——'Hecate, "The Other Three Witches", and their Songs', *Shakespeare Jahrbuch*, XCV (1959), p. 225.

FLINN, JOHN, *Le Roman de Renart dans la littérature française et dans les littératures étrangères au moyen âge* (Toronto, 1963).

FLOOD, W. H. GRATTAN, 'The Beginnings of the Chapel Royal', *Music and Letters*, V (1924), p. 85.

——'John Dowland', *The Musical Times* (1927), p. 504.

FRENCH, PETER J., *John Dee: the World of an Elizabethan Magus* (London, 1972).

FRYE, NORTHROP, 'The Argument of Comedy', *English Institute Essays* (New York, 1949).

FULLER, DAVID, 'The Jonsonian Masque and its Music', *Music and Letters*, LIV (1973), p. 440.

——'Ben Jonson's Plays and their Contemporary Music', *Music and Letters*, LVIII (1977), p. 60.

FURNISS, W. TODD, 'Jonson's Antimasques', *Renaissance News*, VII (1954), p. 21.

——'The Annotation of Ben Jonson's *Masque of Queenes*', *Review of English Studies*, n.s. V (1954), p. 344.

——'Ben Jonson's Masques', in *Three Studies in the Renaissance*, Yale Studies in English, Vol. 138 (New Haven, 1958), p. 89.

GALLOWAY, DAVID (ed.), *The Elizabethan Theatre*. Papers given at an International Conference on the Elizabethan Theatre, Vol. I, 1968; Vol. II, 1969 (London, 1969, 1970).

GALPIN, F. W., *Old English Instruments of Music* (London, 1910). 4th edn. revised with supplementary notes by Thurston Dart (London, 1965).

GESNER, CAROL, '*The Tempest* as Pastoral Romance', *Shakespeare Quarterly*, X (1959), p. 531.

GIANAKARIS, C. J., 'Identifying Ethical Values in *Volpone*', *Huntingdon Library Quarterly*, XXXII (1968), p. 45.

GILBERT, ALLAN H., 'The Function of the Masques in *Cynthia's Revels*', *Philological Quarterly*, XXII (1943), p. 211.
——*The Symbolic Persons in the Masques of Ben Jonson* (Durham, North Carolina, 1948).
GIROUARD, MARK, *Robert Smythson and the Architecture of the Elizabethan Era* (London, 1966).
GOMBOSI, OTTO, 'Some Musical Aspects of the English Court Masque', *Journal of the American Musicological Society*, I (1948), p. 3.
GOMBRICH, E. H., '*Icones Symbolicae*: The Visual Image in Neo-Platonic Thought', *Journal of the Warburg and Courtauld Institutes*, XI (1948), p. 163.
GORDON, D. J., 'The Imagery in Ben Jonson's *Masque of Blacknesse* and *Masque of Beautie*', *Journal of the Warburg and Courtauld Institutes*. VI (1943), p. 122.
——'*Hymenaei*: Ben Jonson's Masque of Union', *Journal of the Warburg and Courtauld Institutes*, VIII (1945), p. 107.
——'Ben Jonson's Haddington Masque': The Story and the Fable', *Modern Language Review*, XLII (1947), p. 180.
——'Poet and Architect: The Intellectual Setting of the Quarrel Between Ben Jonson and Inigo Jones', *Journal of the Warburg and Courtauld Institutes*, XII (1949), p. 152.
GORDON, PHILIP, 'The Morley–Shakespeare Myth', *Music and Letters*, XXVIII (1947), p. 121.
GORGES, ARTHUR, *The Poems of Sir Arthur Gorges*, ed. Helen Easterbrook Sandison (Oxford, 1953).
GOSSON, STEPHEN, *Playes confuted in fiue actions* (London, 1582).
——*The Schoole of Abuse . . . 1579*, with an introduction by [J. P. Collier]. Shakespeare Society Publications, no. 2 (London, 1841).
GREEN, A. W., *The Inns of Court and Early English Drama* (New Haven, 1931; reprint New York, 1965).
GREENLAW, EDWIN, 'Shakespeare's Pastorals', *Studies in Philology*, XIII (1916), p. 122.
GREER, DAVID, '"What if a day"—an examination of the words and music', *Music and Letters*, XLIII (1962), p. 304.
GREG, W. W., 'The Authorship of the Songs in Lyly's Plays', *Modern Language Review*, I (1905), p. 43.
——*Pastoral Poetry and Pastoral Drama* (London, 1906).
GURR, ANDREW, *The Shakespearean 1574–1642* (Cambridge, 1970).

HALE, J. R., *England and the Italian Renaissance* (London, 1954; rev. edn. London, 1963).
HARBAGE, A., *Shakespeare's Audience* (New York, 1941).
——*Shakespeare and the Rival Traditions* (New York, 1952).
——and SCHOENBAUM, S., *Annals of English Drama, 975–1700*. Revised S. Schoenbaum (London, 1964).
HARDISON, O. B., Jr., *English Literary Criticism: The Renaissance* (New York, 1963).
HARTNOLL, PHYLLIS (ed.), *Shakespeare in Music* (London, 1964).

HARWOOD, IAN, 'Rosseter's *Lessons for Consort* of 1609', *Lute Society Journal*, VII (1965), p. 15.

HAWKINS, HARRIETT, 'Folly, Incurable Disease, and *Volpone*', *Studies in English Literature*, VIII (1968), p. 335.

HEARTZ, DANIEL, 'Les Styles instrumentaux dans la musique de la Renaissance', *La Musique instrumentale de la Renaissance*. Éditions du centre national de la recherche scientifique (Paris, 1955), p. 61.

HENSLOWE, P., *Henslowe's Diary*, ed. with supplementary material, introduction, and notes by R. A. Foakes and R. T. Rickert (Cambridge, 1961).

HESELTINE, PHILIP, 'Two Unpublished Poems by Thomas Campion?', *London Mercury* (1926), p. 413.

HIBBARD, G. R., 'The Country House Poem of the Seventeenth Century', *Journal of the Warburg and Courtauld Institutes*, XIX (1956), p. 159.

HILLEBRAND, H. N., *The Child Actors*, University of Illinois Studies in Language and Literature, Vol. XI, no. 1 (Feb. 1926).

HOENIGER, F. D., 'Prospero's Storm and Miracle', *Shakespeare Quarterly*, VII (1956), p. 33.

HOLLANDER, JOHN, *The Untuning of the Sky: Ideas of Music in English Poetry 1500–1700* (Princeton, N.J., 1961).

HOLMAN, PETER, 'The Jonsonian Masque', *Music and Letters*, LV (1974), p. 250.

HOOKER, RICHARD, *Of the Laws of Ecclesiastical Polity*, Books I–IV. Everyman's Library, 2 Vols. (London, 1907).

HOSLEY, RICHARD, 'Was there a music-room in Shakespeare's Globe?', *Shakespeare Survey*, XIII (1960), p. 113.

HOTSON, LESLIE, *The First Night of 'Twelfth Night'* (London, 1954).

HUGHES, CHARLES W., 'John Gamble's Commonplace Book', *Music and Letters*, XXVI (1945), p. 215.

HUGHES-HUGHES, A., *Catalogue of the Manuscript Music in the British Museum*, 3 Vols. (London, 1906–9).

HUIZINGA, JOHAN, *Homo Ludens* (London, 1949; Paladin Books, Bungay, Suffolk, 1970).

HUNTER, G. K., *John Lyly: The Humanist as Courtier* (London, 1962).

HUTH, HENRY, *Ancient Ballads and Broadsides published in England in the sixteenth century, chiefly in the earlier years of the reign of Elizabeth*. Reprinted from the unique original copies, mostly in the black-letter, preserved in the library of Henry Huth, Esq. (London, 1867).

HUTTON, JAMES, 'Some English Poems in Praise of Music', *English Miscellany: A Symposium of History, Literature and the Arts*, ed. Mario Praz, 2 Vols. (Rome, 1951), Vol. 2, p. 1.

ING, CATHERINE, *Elizabethan Lyrics* (London, 1951).

INGRAM, R. W., 'Dramatic Use of Music in English Drama, 1603–1642', Ph.D. thesis, London, 1955.

—— 'The Use of Music in the Plays of Marston', *Music and Letters*, XXXVII (1956), p. 154.

—— 'Operatic Tendencies in Stuart Drama', *Musical Quarterly*, XLIV (1958), p. 489.

—— 'Words and Music', in *Elizabethan Poetry*, Stratford-upon-Avon Studies, II (London, 1960), p. 131.

Jacobean Consort Music, Musica Britannica, IX, ed. Thurston Dart and William Coates (London, 1955).

JAMES I and VI, *The Basilicon Doron of King James VI*, ed. with introduction, notes, appendices, and glossary by James Craigie. Scottish Text Society, 2 Vols. (Edinburgh and London, 1944).

JAMES, D. G., *The Dream of Prospero* (Oxford, 1967).

JAYNE, S. R., *John Colet and Marsilio Ficino* (London, 1963).

JAYNE. s.v. FICINO.

JEFFERY, BRIAN, 'The Lute Music of Anthony Holborne', *Proc. Royal Musical Association*, 93rd session (1966/67), p. 25.

—— 'The Lute Music of Robert Johnson', *Early Music*, II (1974), p. 105.

JESI, FURIO, 'John Dee e il suo sapere', *Comunita*, 166 (1972), p. 272.

JOHNSON, ROBERT, *Complete Works for Solo Lute*, ed. Albert Sundermann (London, 1972).

JOINER, MARY, 'Another Campion Song?', *Music and Letters*, XLVIII (1967), p. 138.

—— 'A Song in *Damon and Pithias*', *Music and Letters*, XLIX (1968), Correspondence, p. 98.

—— 'British Museum MS Add. 15117: A Commentary, Index and Bibliography', Royal Musical Association *Research Chronicle*, no. 7 (1969), p. 51.

JONES-DAVIES, M. T., *Inigo Jones, Ben Jonson et le masque* (Paris, 1967).

JONSON, BEN, *Ben Jonson: The Complete Masques*, ed. Stephen Orgel. The Yale Ben Jonson (New Haven and London, 1969).

—— *The New Inn or The Light Heart*, ed. with introduction, notes, and glossary by George Bremner Tennant. Yale Studies in English, XXXIV (New York, 1908).

—— *The Works of Ben Jonson*, ed. C. H. Herford and P. and E. M. Simpson, 11 Vols. (Oxford, 1925–52).

KASTENDIECK, M. M., *England's Musical Poet Thomas Campion* (New York and London, 1938).

KERMAN, JOSEPH, 'Elizabethan Anthologies of Italian Madrigals', *Journal of the American Musicological Society*, IV (1951), p. 122.

—— 'Morley and "The Triumphs of Oriana"', *Music and Letters*, XXXIV (1953), p. 185.

—— *The Elizabethan Madrigal*, American Musicological Society Studies and Documents, no. 4 (New York, 1962).

KERNODLE, GEORGE R., *From Art to Theatre: Form and Convention in the Renaissance* (Chicago, 1944).

KIDSON, FRANK, 'John Playford, and Seventeenth-Century Music Publishing', *Musical Quarterly*, IV (1918), p. 516.

KIEFER, CHRISTIAN, 'Music and Marston's *The Malcontent*', *Studies in Philology*, LI (1954), p. 163.

KLIBANSKY, R., SAXL, F. and PANOFSKY, E., *Saturn and Melancholy* (London, 1964).

KNIGHT, GEORGE WILSON, 'Lyly', *Review of English Studies*, XV (1939), p. 146.

—— *The Crown of Life* (London, 1947; new edn. University Paperbacks, London, 1965).

KNIGHTS, L. C., *Drama and Society in the Age of Jonson* (London, 1937; Peregrine Books, Harmondsworth, 1962).

—— 'On the social background of Metaphysical Poetry', *Scrutiny*, XIII (1945–6), p. 37.

KNOLL, ROBERT E., *Ben Jonson's Plays: An Introduction* (Lincoln (U.S.A.), 1964).

KNOWLTON, JEAN, 'Dating the Masque Dances in British Museum Additional Manuscript 10444', *British Museum Quarterly*, XXXII (1967–8), p. 99.

KRISTELLER, PAUL OSCAR, *The Philosophy of Marsilio Ficino*, trans. Virginia Conant (New York, 1943; reprint Gloucester, Mass., 1964).

—— 'Music and Learning in the Early Italian Renaissance', *Journal of Renaissance and Baroque Music*, I (1947), p. 255.

LASSERRE, FRANÇOIS, *Plutarque de la musique*. Texte, traduction, commentaire, précédés d'une étude sur l'éducation musicale dans la Grèce antique (Olten and Lausanne, 1954).

LAWRENCE, W. J., *The Elizabethan Playhouse and other Studies*, 2 Vols. (Stratford-upon-Avon, 1912).

—— 'The English Theatre Orchestra: Its Rise and Early Characteristics', *Musical Quarterly*, III (1917), p. 9.

—— 'Music in the Elizabethan Theatre', *Musical Quarterly*, VI (1920), p. 192.

—— 'Notes on a Collection of Masque Music', *Music and Letters*, III (1922), p. 49.

—— 'The Problem of Lyly's Songs', *Times Literary Supplement* (20 Dec. 1923), p. 894.

—— 'Thomas Ravenscroft's Theatrical Associations', *Modern Language Review*, XIX (1924), p. 418.

LEA, K. M., *Italian Popular Comedy. A Study in the commedia dell'arte 1560–1620, with special reference to the English Stage* (New York, 1962; reprint of edn. of 1934).

LEBÈGUE, RAYMOND, 'Ronsard et la musique', *Musique et poésie au XVIe siècle*. Éditions du centre national de la recherche scientifique (Paris, 1954), p. 105.

LEFKOWITZ, MURRAY, *William Lawes* (London, 1960).

LEMON, ROBERT, *Catalogue of a Collection of Printed Broadsides in the possession of the Society of Antiquaries of London* (London, 1866).

LEONARDO DA VINCI, *The Literary Works of Leonardo da Vinci*. Compiled and edited from the original MSS by Jean Paul Richter, 2 Vols., 2nd edn. (London, 1938).

LEVIN, HARRY, 'Jonson's Metempsychosis', *Philological Quarterly*, XX (1943), p. 231.

LEVIN, RICHARD, 'The *New Inn* and the Proliferation of Good Bad Drama', *Essays in Criticism*, XXII (1972), p. 41.

LINKLATER, ERIC, *Ben Jonson and King James* (London, 1931).

LINTHICUM, M. CHANNING, *Costume in the Drama of Shakespeare and his Contemporaries* (New York, 1963; reprint of 1936 edn.).

LONG, J. H., 'Beck's "The Case of 'O Mistress Mine'"', *Renaissance News*, VII (1954), p. 15.

—— *Shakespeare's Use of Music* (Gainesville, Florida, 1955).

—— 'Laying the Ghosts in *Pericles*', *Shakespeare Quarterly*, VII (1956), p. 39.

LOWINSKY, E. E., 'The Concept of Physical and Musical Space in the Renaissance', Papers of the American Musicological Society Annual Meeting, 2nd session (1941), p. 57.

—— *Tonality and Atonality in Sixteenth-Century Music* (Los Angeles, 1961).

LYONS, B. G., *Voices of Melancholy: Studies in Literary Treatments of Melancholy in Renaissance England* (New York, 1971).

McCULLEN, J. T., 'The Functions of Songs Aroused by Madness in Elizabethan Drama', in *A Tribute to George Coffin Taylor*, ed. Arnold Williams (Chapel Hill, 1952), p. 185.

McCULLOCH, FLORENCE, *Medieval Latin and French Bestiaries*, University of North Carolina Studies in the Romance Languages and Literatures, no. 33 (Chapel Hill, 1962).

MacDONAGH, THOMAS, *Thomas Campion and the Art of English Poetry* (Dublin, 1913).

McGOWAN, MARGARET M., *L'Art du ballet de cour en France 1581–1643*, Éditions du centre national de la recherche scientifique (Paris, 1963).

McKENZIE, D. F., '*The Staple of News* and the Late Plays', in *A Celebration of Ben Jonson* (Toronto, 1974), p. 83.

MACKERNESS, E. D., *A Social History of Music* (London, 1964).

MACLEAN, HUGH, 'Ben Jonson's Poems: Notes on the Ordered Society', in *Essays in English Literature from the Renaissance to the Victorian Age*, ed. Millar Maclure and F. W. Watt, presented to A. S. P. Woodhouse (Toronto, 1964), p. 43.

MADAN, F. and CRASTER, H. H. E. (ed.), *Summary Catalogue of Western MSS in the Bodleian Library* (Oxford, 1922–4).

MAJOR, JOHN M., '*Comus* and *The Tempest*', *Shakespeare Quarterly*, X (1959), p. 176.

MANIFOLD, J. S., *The Music in English Drama from Shakespeare to Purcell* (London, 1956).

MANNING, ROSEMARY J., 'Lachrimae: A Study of Dowland', *Music and Letters*, XXV (1944), p. 45.

MARCEL, RAYMOND, *Marsile Ficin (1433–1499)*, Société d'édition 'Les belles lettres' (Paris, 1958).

MARK, JEFFREY, 'The Jonsonian Masque', *Music and Letters*, III (1922), p. 358.

MARSTON, JOHN, *Plays*, ed. with introduction and notes by H. H. Wood, 3 Vols. (Edinburgh, 1934–9).

MASON, H. A., *Humanism and Poetry in the Early Tudor Period* (London, 1959).

MAZE, NANCY, 'Tenbury MS 1018: A Key to Caccini's Art of Embellishment', *Journal of the Americal Musicological Society*, IX (1956), p. 61.

MAZZEO, J. A., *Renaissance and Revolution* (London, 1969).

MEAGHER, JOHN C., *Method and Meaning in Jonson's Masques* (Indiana, 1966).

MEHL, DIETER, *The Elizabethan Dumb Show* (London, 1965).

MELLERS, WILFRID, 'La Mélancholie au début du XVIIe siècle et le madrigal anglais', *Musique et poésie au XVIe siècle*, Éditions du centre national de la recherche scientifique (Paris, 1954), p. 153.

—— *Harmonious Meeting* (London, 1965).

MEYER, ERNST H., *English Chamber Music* (London, 1946).

MIDDLETON, T., *Works*. ed. A. H. Bullen, 8 Vols. (London, 1885).

MIES, OTTO HEINRICH, 'Elizabethan Music Prints in an East-Prussian Castle', *Musica Disciplina*, III (1949), p. 171.

—— 'Dowland's Lachrimae Tune', *Musica Disciplina*, IV (1950), p. 59.

MOORE, J. R., 'The Function of the Songs in Shakespeare's Plays', *Shakespeare Studies* (Madison, Wisconsin, 1916), p. 78.

—— 'The Songs in Lyly's Plays', *Publications of the Modern Language Association*, XLII (1927), p. 623.

—— 'The Songs in the Public Theatre in the Time of Shakespeare', *Journal of English and Germanic Philology*, XXVIII (1929), p. 166.

MOORE, ROBERT E., 'The Music to *Macbeth*', *Musical Quarterly*, XLVII (1961), p. 22.

MORLEY, THOMAS, *A Plain and Easy Introduction to Practical Music*, ed. from the edition of 1598 by Alec Harman, with a foreword by Thurston Dart (London, 1952, 1963).

—— *The First Book of Consort Lessons* (1599 and 1611), ed. with an introduction by Sidney Beck (New York, 1959).

MOWAT, BARBARA ADAMS, 'A Tale of Sprights and Goblins', *Shakespeare Quarterly*, XX (1969), p. 37.

Musique et poésie au XVIe siècle, Éditions du centre national de la recherche scientifique (Paris, 1954).

NAYLOR, E. W., *Shakespeare and Music* (London, 1896, 1931).

NELSON, JOHN CHARLES, *Renaissance Theory of Love: The Context of Giordano Bruno's 'Eroici furori'* (New York, 1958).

NICHOLS, JOHN, *Progresses and Public Processions of Queen Elizabeth*, 3 Vols. (London, 1823).

—— *Progresses, Processions and Magnificent Festivities of King James I*, 4 Vols. (London, 1828).

NICOLL, ALLARDYCE, *Masks, Mimes and Miracles: Studies in the Popular Theatre* (London, 1931).

—— *Stuart Masques and the Renaissance Stage* (London, 1937).

—— 'Shakespeare and the Court Masque', *Shakespeare Jahrbuch*, XCIV (1958), p. 51.

—— *The World of Harlequin: A Critical Study of the Commedia dell' Arte* (Cambridge, 1963).

NOBLE, RICHMOND, *Shakespeare's Use of Song* (London, 1923).

NOSWORTHY, J. M., 'Music and its Function in the Romances of Shakespeare', *Shakespeare Survey*, XI (1958), p. 60.

NOYES, R. G., *Ben Jonson on the English Stage 1660–1776*, Harvard Studies in English, Vol. XVII (Cambridge, Mass., 1935; reprint New York, 1966).

NUTTALL, A. D., *Two Concepts of Allegory: A Study of Shakespeare's 'The Tempest' and the Logic of Allegorical Expression* (London, 1967).

OBOUSSIER, PHILIPPE, 'Turpyn's Book of Lute-Songs', *Music and Letters*, XXXIV (1953), p. 145.

O'CONNOR, DANIEL, 'Jonson's "A Hymne to God the Father"', *Notes and Queries*, n.s. XII (1965), p. 379.

OREGLIA, GIACOMO, *The Commedia dell'Arte*, trans. L. F. Edwards (London, 1968, 1970).

ORGEL, STEPHEN, *The Jonsonian Masque* (Cambridge, Mass., 1965).

—— 'To Make the Boards to Speak: Inigo Jones's Stage and the Jonsonian Masque', in *Renaissance Drama*, n.s. I, ed. S. Schoenbaum (Evanston, 1968), p. 121.

ORGEL (ed.). s.v. JONSON.

ORNSTEIN, ROBERT, '*Volpone* and Renaissance Psychology', *Notes and Queries*, n.s. III (1956), p. 471.

PAFFORD, J. H. P., 'Music and Songs in *The Winter's Tale*', *Shakespeare Quarterly*, X (1959), p. 161.

PANOFSKY. s.v. KLIBANSKY.

PARTRIDGE, EDWARD B., *The Broken Compass: A Study of the Major Comedies of Ben Jonson* (London, 1958).

PATTISON, BRUCE, 'Sir Philip Sidney and Music', *Music and Letters*, XV (1934), p. 75.

—— *Music and Poetry of the English Renaissance* (London, 1948, 1970).

PHILLIPS, JAMES E., '*The Tempest* and the Renaissance Idea of Man', *Shakespeare Quarterly*, XV (1964), p. 147.

PICO DELLA MIRANDOLA, GIOVANNI, *Oration on the Dignity of Man*. Trans. Elizabeth Livermore Forbes, in *The Renaissance Philosophy of Man*, ed. Ernst Cassirer, Paul Oscar Kristeller, John Herman Randall, Jr. (Chicago and London, 1948, 1956), p. 223.

PIETZSCH, GERHARD, *Die Klassifikation der Musik von Boetius bis Ugolino von Orviato*, Studien zur Geschichte der Musiktheorie im Mittelalter (I. Halle, 1929).

PIPER, DAVID, *Catalogue of the Seventeenth-Century Portraits in the National Portrait Gallery, 1625–1714* (Cambridge, 1963).

POLLARD, A. W. and REDGRAVE, G. R., *A Short-title Catalogue of Books Printed in England, Scotland and Ireland . . . 1475–1640* (London, 1925).

POULTON, DIANA, *John Dowland* (London, 1971).

PRAZ, MARIO, *Machiavelli and the Elizabethans*, Annual Italian Lecture; Proceedings of the British Academy, 21 Mar. 1928 (London, 1928).

PRENDERGAST, ARTHUR H. D., 'The Masque of the Seventeenth Century, its Origins and Development', *Proc. Royal Musical Association*, 23rd session (1896/97), p. 113.

PRUNIÈRES, HENRY, *Le Ballet de cour en France avant Benserate et Lully* . . . (Paris, 1913).

PUTTENHAM, GEORGE, *The Arte of English Poesie* (1589), ed. G. D. Willcock and A. Walker (Cambridge, 1936).

PYLE, FITZROY, *'The Winter's Tale'; A Commentary on the Structure.* (London, 1969).

RACKIN, PHYLLIS, 'Poetry without Paradox: Jonson's "Hymne" to Cynthia', *Criticism*, IV (1962), p. 186.

RADCLIFFE, PHILIP, 'The Relation of Rhythm and Tonality in the Sixteenth Century', *Proc. Royal Music Association*, 57th session (1930/31), p. 73.

RANDALL, DALE B. J., *Jonson's Gypsies Unmasked: Background and Theme of 'The Gypsies Metamorphos'd'* (Durham, North Carolina, 1975).

RAVENSCROFT, THOMAS. *Deuteromelia* . . . London, 1609.

——*Pammelia* . . . (London, 1609).

——*Melismata* . . . (London, 1611).

——*A Briefe Discourse* . . . (London, 1614).

——*Pammelia, Deutromelia, Melismata*, ed. MacEdward Leach with introduction by Matthias A. Shaaber. Facsimile reprint of the first edns., 1609, 1611. Publications of the American Folklore Society, Vol. XII (New York, 1961).

REDLICH, HANS F., 'The Italian Madrigal: A Bibliographical Contribution', *Music and Letters*, XXXII (1951), p. 154.

REED, ROBERT R. (Jr.), 'The Probable Origin of Ariel', *Shakespeare Quarterly*, XI (1960), p. 61.

Renaissance Drama, ed. S. Schoenbaum, n.s. I (Evanston, 1968).

REYHER, PAUL, *Les Masques anglais* (Paris, 1909).

RICE, EUGENE F., *The Renaissance Idea of Wisdom* (Cambridge, Mass., 1958).

ROBINSON, CLEMENT, *A Handefull of pleasant delites* . . . (London, 1584).

ROEDER, RALPH, *The Man of the Renaissance: Four Lawgivers: Savonarola, Machiavelli, Castiglione, Aretino* (London, 1934).

ROFFE, ALRED, *The Handbook of Shakespearean Music* (London, 1878).

ROLLINS, HYDER E., *'King Lear* and the Ballad of "John Careless"', *Modern Language Review*, XV (1920), p. 87.

ROPER, E. S., 'Music at the English Chapels Royal', *Proc. of the Royal Musical Association*, 54th session (1927/28), p. 19.

ROSSETER, PHILIP, *Lessons for Consort* (London, 1609).

ROUSSET, JEAN, 'L'Eau et les tritons dans les fêtes et ballets de cour 1580–1640', *Fêtes de la Renaissance*, I. Éditions du centre national de la recherche scientifique (Paris, 1956), p. 235.

SABOL, A. J., 'A Newly Discovered Contemporary Song Setting for Jonson's *Cynthia's Revels'*, *Notes and Queries*, n.s. V (1958), p. 384.

——'Two Songs with Accompaniment for an Elizabethan Choirboy Play', *Studies in the Renaissance*, v (1958), p. 145.

——'Ravenscroft's *Melismata* and the Children of Paul's', *Renaissance News*, xii (1959), p. 3.

——*Songs and Dances for the Stuart Masque*, ed. with introductory essay by A. J. Sabol (Providence, Rhode Island, 1959).

——'Two Unpublished Stage Songs for the "Aery of Children"', *Renaissance News*, xiii (1960), p. 222.

——*A Score for 'Lovers Made Men'* (Providence, Rhode Island, 1963).

SACKTON, ALEXANDER H., *Rhetoric as a Dramatic Language in Ben Jonson* (New York, 1948).

SALERNO, HENRY F., *Scenarios of the 'Commedia dell'arte'. Flamineo Scala's 'Il teatro delle favole rappresentative'*, trans. H. F. Salerno (New York and London, 1967).

SARGEAUNT, JOHN, *Annals of Westminster School* (London, 1898).

SAXL. S.V. KLIBANSKY.

SCALA, Flamineo. *Il Teatro delle favole rappresentative* (Venice, 1611).

SCHANZER, ERNEST, 'The Structural Pattern of *The Winter's Tale*', *Review of English Literature*, v (1964), p. 72.

SCHÈVE, D. A., 'Jonson's *Volpone* and Traditional Fox Lore', *Review of English Studies*, n.s. 1 (1950), p. 242.

SCHOENBAUM. S.V. HARBAGE.

SEIGEL, JERROLD E., *Rhetoric and Philosophy in Renaissance Humanism* (Princeton, N.J., 1968).

SENG, PETER J., 'An Early Tune for the Fool's Song in *King Lear*', *Shakespeare Quarterly*, ix (1958), p. 583.

SEZNEC, JEAN, *The Survival of the Pagan Gods: The Mythological Tradition and its place in Renaissance Humanism and Art*, trans. Barbara Sessions. Harper Torchbooks (New York, 1953).

SHAKESPEARE, WILLIAM, *Complete Works*, ed. Peter Alexander. Collins Tudor Shakespeare (London, 1951).

——*The Tempest*, ed. Frank Kermode. The Arden Shakespeare (London, 6th edn. 1962).

——*The Tempest*, ed. Anne Righter. New Penguin Shakespeare (Harmondsworth, 1968).

——*The Winter's Tale*, ed. J. H. P. Pafford. The Arden Shakespeare (London, 1963).

——*The Winter's Tale*, ed. Ernest Schanzer. New Penguin Shakespeare (Harmondsworth, 1969).

SHIRE, S.V. ELLIOTT.

SHORT, R. W., 'The Metrical Theory and Practice of Thomas Campion', *Publications of the Modern Language Association*, lxix (1944), p. 1003.

SIDNEY, PHILIP, *An Apologie for Poetrie*, in Smith (ed.), q.v., 1, p. 148.

SIMPSON, CLAUDE M., *The British Broadside Ballad and its Music* (New Brunswick, N.J., 1966).

SIMPSON, P. and BELL, C. F., *Designs by Inigo Jones for Masques and Plays at Court*, Walpole Society, xii (Oxford, 1923–4).

SMALL, ROSCOE ADDISON, *The Stage-Quarrel Between Ben Jonson and the so-called Poetasters* (Breslau, 1899).

SMALLMAN, BASIL, 'Endor Revisited: English Biblical Dialogues of the Seventeenth Century', *Music and Letters*, XLVI (1965), p. 137.

SMITH, G. G. (ed.), *Elizabethan Critical Essays*, 2 Vols. (London, 1904).

SMITH, IRWIN, *Shakespeare's Blackfriars Playhouse: Its History and its Designs* (London, 1966).

SMITH, WINIFRED, *The Commedia dell 'Arte* (New York, 1964; reprint of edn. of 1912).

SNUGGS, HENRY L., 'The Source of Jonson's Definition of Comedy', *Modern Language Notes*, LXV (1950), p. 543.

SORELL, WALTER, 'Shakespeare and the Dance', *Shakespeare Quarterly*, VIII (1957), p. 367.

SPINK, IAN, *English Song: Dowland to Purcell* (London, 1974).

SPITZER, LEO, 'Classical and Christian Ideas of World Harmony', *Traditio*, II (1944), p. 409; III (1945), p. 307.

STAINER, J. R. F., 'Shakespeare and Orlando Lassus', *The Musical Times*, XLIII, (1902), p. 100.

STEELE, ROBERT, *The Earliest English Music Printing* (London, 1903).

STERNFELD, F. W. 'Le Symbolism musical dans quelques pièces de Shakespeare, presentées à la cour d'Angleterre', in *Les Fêtes de la Renaissance*, 2 Vols. Éditions du centre national de la recherche scientifique (Paris, 1956), I, p. 319.

——'A Song from Campion's Lord's Masque', *Journal of the Warburg and Courtauld Institutes*, XX (1957), p. 373.

——'Lasso's Music for Shakespeare's "Samingo"', *Shakespeare Quarterly*, IX (1958), p. 105.

——'Shakespeare's Use of Popular Song', in *Elizabethan and Jacobean Studies Presented to F. P. Wilson*, ed. H. Davis (Oxford, 1959), p. 150.

——'Song in Jonson's Comedy: A Gloss on *Volpone*', in *Studies in English Renaissance Drama*, ed. Josephine W. Bennett, Oscar Cargill, Vernon Hall, Jr. (London, 1959, 1961), p. 310.

——'The Use of Song in Shakespeare's Tragedies', *Proc. Royal Musical Association*, 86th session (1959/60), p. 45.

——*Music in Shakespearean Tragedy* (London, 1963).

——'La Musique dans les tragédies élisabéthaines inspirées de Sénèque', in *Les tragédies de Sénèque et le théâtre de la Renaissance*. Éditions du centre national de la recherche scientifique (Paris, 1964), p. 139.

——and CHAN, MARY JOINER, '"Come live with me And be my love"', *Comparative Literature*, XXII (1970), p. 173.

STEVENS, DENIS (ed.), *The Mulliner Book*, Musica Britannica, I. 2nd rev. edn. (London, 1954).

——*The Mulliner Book: A Commentary* (London, 1952).

STEVENS, JOHN, *Music and Poetry in the Early Tudor Court* (London, 1961).

——'Shakespeare and the Music of the Elizabethan Stage: An Introductory Essay', in Hartnoll (ed.), q.v., p. 3.

STOKES, E., 'Lists of the King's Musicians from the Audit Office Declared

Accounts', *Musical Antiquary*, I (1909–10), pp. 56, 119, 182, 249; II
(1910–11), pp. 51, 114, 174, 235; III (1911–12), pp. 54, 110, 171, 229; IV
(1912–13), pp. 55, 178.

STRONG, ROY, 'The Popular Celebration of the Accession Day of Queen
Elizabethan I', *Journal of the Warburg and Courtauld Institutes*, XXI (1958),
p. 86.

——*Festival Designs by Inigo Jones* (London, 1967–8).

STRUNK, OLIVER, *Source Readings in Music History* (London, 1952).

SUMMERSON, JOHN, *Inigo Jones* (Harmondsworth, 1966).

TALBERT, E. W., 'The Classical Mythology and the Structure of *Cynthia's
Revels*', *Philological Quarterly*, XXII (1943), p. 193.

——'The Purpose and Technique of Jonson's *Poetaster*', *Studies in Philology*, XLII
(1945), p. 225.

——'The Interpretation of Jonson's Courtly Spectacles', *Publications of the
Modern Language Association*, LXI (1946), p. 454.

TAYLER, E. W., *Nature and Art in Renaissance Literature* (New York and London,
1964).

THAYER, C. G., *Ben Jonson: Studies in the Plays* (Norman, Oklahoma, 1963).

THEWLIS, GEORGE A., 'Some Notes on a Bodleian Manuscript', *Music and
Letters*, XXII (1941), p. 32.

TILLYARD, E. M. W., *The Elizabethan World Picture* (London, 1943).

TOURNEUR, C., *Works*, ed. A. Nicoll (London, 1930).

TRAVERSI, DEREK A., *Shakespeare: The Last Phase* (Stanford, 1954).

TRIMPI, WESLEY, *Ben Jonson's Poems: A Study of the Plain Style* (Stanford, 1962).

TUVE, ROSAMOND, *Elizabethan and Metaphysical Imagery* (Chicago and London,
1947; Phoenix Books, Chicago, 1961).

VARTY, KENNETH, *Reynard the Fox: A Study of the Fox in Medieval English Art*
(Leicester, 1967).

VEEVERS, E. E., 'Sources of Inigo Jones' Masquing Designs', *Journal of the
Warburg and Courtauld Institues*, XXII (1959), p. 373.

VERDENIUS, W. J., *Mimesis: Plato's Doctrine of Artistic Imitation and its Meaning to
Us* (Leyden, 1949).

WAITH, EUGENE M., 'The Poet's Morals in Jonson's *Poetaster*', *Modern Language Quarterly*, XII (1951), p. 13.

——'Things as They Are and the World of Absolutes in Jonson's Plays and
Masques', *The Elizabethan Theatre*, IV, ed. G. R. Hibbard (London, 1975).

WALKER, D. P., 'Musical Humanism in the Sixteenth and Early Seventeenth
Centuries', *Music Review*, II (1941), pp. 1, 111, 220, 288; III (1942), p. 55.

——'The Aims of Baïf's Académie de poésie et de musique', *Journal of Renaissance and Baroque Music*, I (1946), p. 91.

——'Ficino's *Spiritus* and Music', *Annales Musicologiques* (Moyen-âge et Renaissance). Société de musique d'autrefois (Paris, 1953), Vol. I, p. 131.

——'Orpheus the Theologian and Renaissance Platonists', *Journal of the Warburg and Courtauld Institutes*, XVI (1953), p. 100.

——'Le Chant orphique de Marsile Ficin', in *Musique et poésie au XVIe siècle*, Éditions du centre national de la recherche scientifique (Paris, 1954), p. 17.

——*Spiritual and Demonic Magic from Ficino to Campanella*, Warburg Institute Studies, XXII (London, 1958).

WALLACE, C. W., *The Children of the Chapel at Blackfriars, 1597–1603* (London, 1908).

WARD, JOHN, 'Music for *A Handefull of Pleasant Delites*', *Journal of the American Musicological Society*, X (1957), p. 151.

WARLOCK, PETER (ed.), *Elizabethan Songs, that were originally composed for one voice to sing and four stringed instruments to accompany*, 3 Vols. (London, 1926).

WEBSTER, JOHN, *Works*, ed. F. L. Lucas (London, 1927).

WEISS, ROBERTO, *The Renaissance Discovery of Classical Antiquity* (Oxford, 1969).

WELCH, R. D., 'Shakespeare—Musician', *Musical Quarterly*, VIII (1922), p. 510.

WELLS, STANLEY, 'Tom O'Bedlam's Song in *King Lear*', *Shakespeare Quarterly*, XII (1961), p. 311.

WELSFORD, ENID, 'Italian Influence on the English Court Masque', *Modern Language Review*, XVIII (1923), p. 394.

——*The Court Masque* (Cambridge, 1927).

——*The Fool: His Social and Literary History* (London, 1935).

WHEELER, C. F., *Classical Mythology in the Plays, Masques and Poems of Ben Jonson* (Princeton, N.J., 1938).

WHITE, T. H., *The Book of Beasts* (London, 1954).

WICKHAM, GLYNNE, 'Contribution de Ben Jonson et de Dekker aux fêtes du couronnement de Jacques Ier', in *Les Fêtes de la Renaissance*, 2 Vols. Éditions du centre national de la recherche scientifique (Paris, 1956), I, p. 279.

WILLEFORD, WILLIAM, *The Fool and his Sceptre* (London, 1969).

WILLETTS, P. J., 'Sir Nicholas Le Strange and John Jenkins', *Music and Letters*, XLII (1961), p. 30.

——'Sir Nicholas Le Strange's Collection of Masque Music', *The British Museum Quarterly*, XXIX (1965), p. 79.

——*The Henry Lawes Manuscript* (London, 1969).

WILSON, CHRISTOPHER, *Shakespeare and Music* (London, 1922).

WIND, EDGAR, *Pagan Mysteries in the Renaissance* (London, 1958; enlarged and rev. edn. Peregrine Books, Harmondsworth, 1967).

WING, DONALD, *A Short-title Catalogue of Books Printed in England Scotland Ireland and Wales . . . 1641–1700*, 3 Vols. (New York, 1945).

WOODFILL, WALTER L., *Musicians in English Society from Elizabeth to Charles I* (Princeton, N.J., 1953).

YATES, FRANCES, *The French Academies of the Sixteenth Century* (London, 1947).

——'Elizabethan Chivalry: The Romance of the Accession Day Tilts', *Journal of the Warburg and Courtauld Institutes*, XX (1957), p. 4.

——'Boissard's Costume-Book and Two Portraits', *Journal of the Warburg and*

Courtauld Institutes, XXII (1959), p. 365.
——*Giordano Bruno and the Hermetic Tradition* (London, 1964).
——*Theatre of the World* (London, 1969).
——*Shakespeare's Last Plays: A new Approach* (London, 1975).
YOULL, HENRY, *Canzonets to Three Voices* (1608), ed. E. H. Fellowes, English
Madrigal School, 36 Vols. (London, 1913–24), Vol. 28.

ZANDVOORT, REINARD WILLIAM, *Sidney's Arcadia: A Comparison Between the
Two Versions* (Amsterdam, 1929).
ZARLINO, GIOSEFFO, *Le institutioni harmoniche* (Venice, 1573).
ZIMBARDO, ROSE A., 'Form and Disorder in *The Tempest*', *Shakespeare Quarterly*,
XIV (1963), p. 49.
ZITNER, S. P., 'Gosson, Ovid and the Elizabethan Audience', *Shakespeare
Quarterly*, IX (1958), p. 206.
ZUBOV, V. P., *Leonardo da Vinci*, trans. David H. Kraus (Cambridge, Mass.,
1968).

Index

WITHDRAWN